STO

止 ま

THIS IS THE BACK OF THE BOOK!

This manga collection is translated into English, but arranged in right-to-left reading format to maintain the artwork's visual orientation as originally drawn and published in Japan. If you've never read comics this way before, take a look at the diagram below to give yourself an idea of how to go about it. Basically, you'll be starting in the upper-right-hand corner, and will read each word balloon and panel moving right to left. It may take a little getting used to, but you should get the hang of it very quickly. Have fun! If this is the millionth manga you've read this way, never mind.

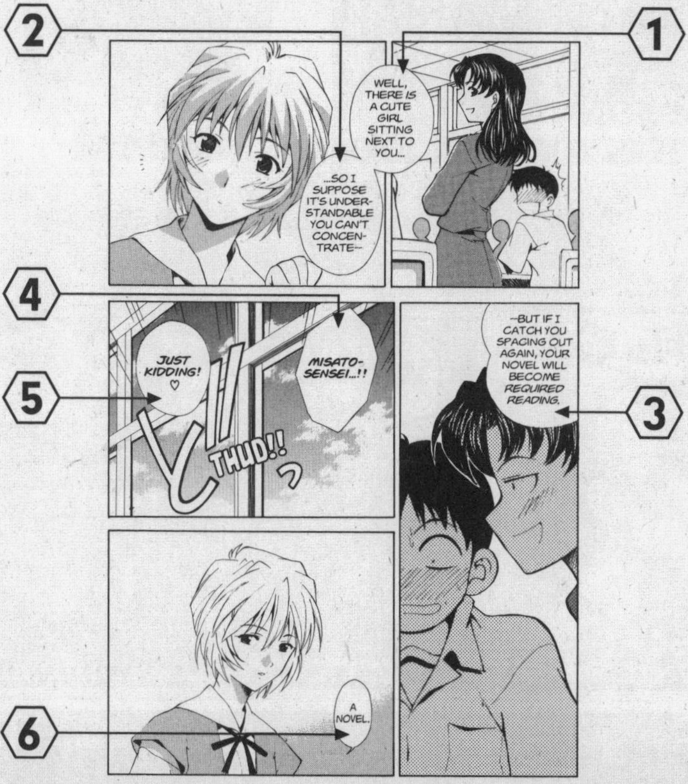
1
WELL, THERE IS A CUTE GIRL SITTING NEXT TO YOU...
2
...SO I SUPPOSE IT'S UNDERSTANDABLE YOU CAN'T CONCENTRATE--
3
--BUT IF I CATCH YOU SPACING OUT AGAIN, YOUR NOVEL WILL BECOME REQUIRED READING.
4
MISATO-SENSEI...!!
5
JUST KIDDING! ♡
THUD!!
6
A NOVEL.

Kosuke Fujishima's *Oh My Goddess!*

Can't wait on the Goddesses? Change directions!

Just gotten into the new unflopped editions of *Oh My Goddess!*, and found you can't wait to see what happens next? Have no fear! The first **20 volumes** of *Oh My Goddess!* are available **right now** in Western-style editions! Released between 1994 and 2005, our *OMG!* Western-style volumes feature premium paper, and pages 40% larger than those of the unflopped editions! If you've already got some of the unflopped volumes and want to know which Western-style ones to get to catch up, check out http://www.darkhorse.com/Zones/Manga for a complete breakdown of how the editions compare!

AVAILABLE AT YOUR LOCAL COMICS SHOP OR BOOKSTORE
*To find a comics shop in your area, call 1-888-266-4226

For more information or to order direct:
• On the web: darkhorse.com
• E-mail: mailorder@darkhorse.com
• Phone: 1-800-862-0052 Mon.-Fri. 9 A.M. to 5 P.M. Pacific Time.

CLOVER

The long-out-of-print classic from Japan's shojo artist supergroup CLAMP!

Clover has never before
been available in English
in its original unflopped,
right-to-left reading
format—until now! Dark
Horse collects all four
volumes of *Clover* in one
bargain omnibus format,
including 17 pages of
bonus art in color!

"Edgy and genre-bending . . . *Clover* certainly challenges
people's perception of what shojo manga should be."
—*Manga: The Complete Guide*

Asuka and Rei call Gendo and Yui "Uncle" and "Auntie" not because that's their actual relation, but because in Japan (as in some other more traditional societies) family terms are often used to describe unrelated people one is close to or whom fit that age category. A recent well-known example of this in Gainax's *Gurren Lagann* is Simon calling Kamina *aniki*, one way to say "big brother," as he acts like a big brother to him.

When Misato insisted on knowing classified details because she's Rei's teacher, the translator commented to me, "Only in Japan!"—meaning that teachers are still regarded with more respect in Japan than they are in the United States. Note that Yui tends to call her "Katsuragi-sensei," using her last name, whereas Shinji and Asuka tend to call her "Misato-sensei," using her first name.

By the way, I'm not, you know, *absolutely* sure who that was on page 148, panel 2, but I *think* it was supposed to be Rei. On the other hand, she laughed, rather than disclaimed responsibility, so it isn't a case of she who denied it, supplied it. On the other hand once again, she *is* a vegetarian. Come to think of it, the very fact we're having this discussion about Rei Ayanami shows we're heading into *terra incognita* here. You know how creators are always trying to do a story twist by having a beloved character die. Well, I say, the shock of having a scene where a beloved character died is nothing compared to a scene where a beloved character farted.

As Takahashi-sensei so aptly put it, see you in vol. 2!

—Carl

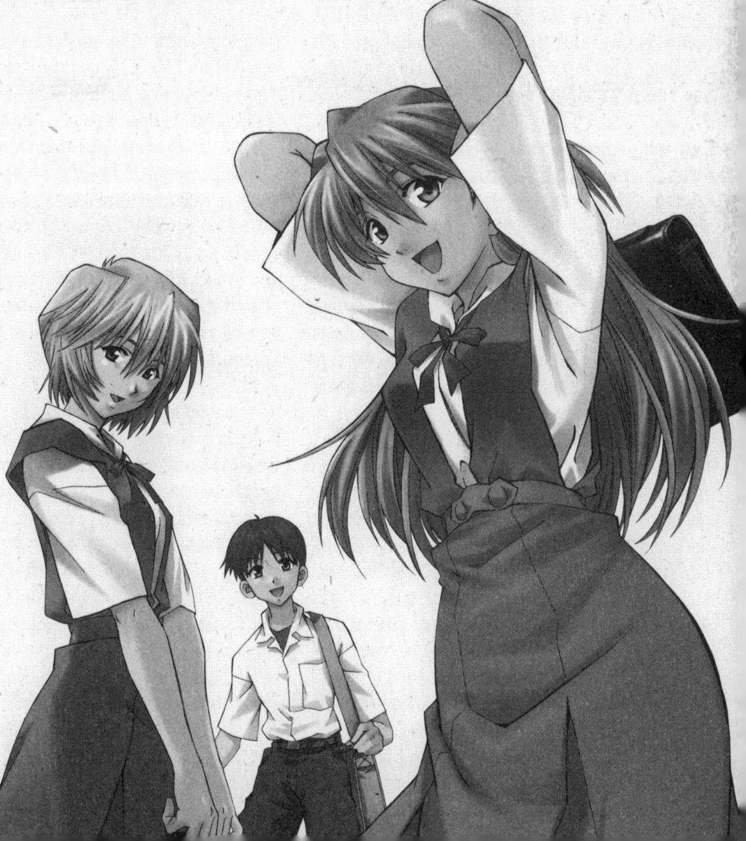

I'll be very interested to see the outcome of his own return to the story. Can *Evangelion* feel as revolutionary in its new incarnation? That depends on what Anno intends to do over this four-film series, whose second part, *Evangelion 2.0: You Can (Not) Advance*, should be coming out in Japan in late June—just about when this manga hits here.

But again, the word *relief* is what comes to mind when I read *The Shinji Ikari Raising Project*—that the characters we know aren't so, you know, *doomed*, and are allowed a little fun, love, and happiness (Watching *Evangelion 1.0*, I wanted to ask Gendo, "Couldn't you at least *fake* liking your son? A few insincere words of encouragement and praise? He'll want to believe you really mean it, and it'll probably make things easier for you, too . . ."). The idea things could take a different, better route, was one of the points of the Instrumentality, after all; apocalyptic change doesn't have much to offer if all it shows you is a series of bad and worse options.

And just when you think you've got this manga figured out as a love comedy, though, Takahashi starts to throw you a few curves, as vol. 1 contains scenes based on those that actually occurred in episodes 1 and 5 of the original anime series. As poor Test Type–san (AKA Unit-01) and Zeruel-san point out in the bonus comic, where exactly *are* the Angels and Evangelions in all this? It becomes more mysterious since we've still got the element of the plug suit, and something that seems like a contact experiment.

Did you notice also, by the way, that although Kensuke mentions SEELE on page 12, a very important name—like, uh, "NERV"—never comes up once in vol. 1? Instead, the facility Shinji's parents work at is called the "Artificial Evolution Lab," which, as hardcore *Eva* fans know, was one of the precursor organizations to NERV. And although many of the character changes from the original story at first seem obvious (such as Yui Ikari being around!), others are more complex than they seemed at first glance (Misato is Shinji's teacher now, but it looks as if her father was involved in this research years ago, just as

in the original series). It's like Osamu Takahashi has taken the same cards from *Neon Genesis Evangelion*, but reshuffled the deck. We'll have to see how things play out . . .

A few notes about the translation. Toji Suzuhara (or Toji Su...zu...ha...ra, as Hikari would say—the evenly weighted syllables of Japanese make it an ideal language for class reps to convey drawn-out exasperation) speaks with an Osaka flavor here, as he did in the original series. Toji's accent here is thick as *takoyaki* sauce, but then, this is what people often expect from Osakans—full value for stereotype. Gainax itself formed in the early 1980s around students who met at the Osaka University of Arts; several of its founding members are Osaka born and raised, and, as related in *The Notenki Memoirs*, can lay on the old brogue when they feel like it.

Now, there are different theories about how to suggest an Osaka accent in American English. When ADV Films dubbed *Azumanga Daioh*, the legendary Ayumu Kasuga—better known as "Osaka" from her city of origin (she's technically from Wakayama, but the distinction is of no interest to her classmates)—was played by voice actress Kira Vincent-Davis, who spoke in a manner described by the translator's notes as "a Southern accent from around the Houston area, which shares the business-oriented attitude with Osaka as well as the country image that colors both the Southern and Osakan accents."

In a coincidence that still mystifies scholars, ADV Films is a southern business located around the Houston area, but the results were, as Hannibal Lecter would say, *chaaaaming*. Nevertheless, I agree with those who say a kind of Brooklyn accent better conveys Osaka in American English (not that you can ever say a certain English accent is an *equivalent* of a certain Japanese accent, in the same way that the English words *raising project* are equivalent to the Japanese words *ikusei keikaku*—I say "conveys," because it's more about giving a suggestion). In fact, as you may know, ADV's manga version of *Azumanga Daioh* did in fact give Osaka a Brooklyn accent; it was the anime dub that took a different approach.

Some things still seem to float, though. The black NERV mug in the background is actually fan made, a *doujinshi*, as it were. We tend to think of *doujinshi* as being self-published manga—and indeed, this is the most common form they take—but the term *doujinshi* can embrace fan-made anything: lapel pins, software, plush dolls, stationery, and, of course, coffee mugs. This particular one I've been drinking from almost every day of my life for over twelve years; a chalice that sustains me like that old knight in *Indiana Jones and the Last Crusade* ("but in Japanese, *Evangelion* is spelled with a 'We'...").

The mug was made by Scott Rider, one of the founders of Anime Central, known as oldcrow back when the, like, thirteen anime fans then existing in the English-speaking world (I'm ex-aggerating very slightly) used to communicate, SEELE-like, on IRC. Even a teenage Daryl Surat, now of today's greatest podcast, animeworl-dorder.com, could be found there. Anyway, Scott brought these mugs to sell at the glorious and ever-memorable Anime Expo '96, a con that will probably never be surpassed for the sheer com-bined talent of its ten Japanese guests—only two of whom were Mamoru Oshii (the year after *Ghost in the Shell*) and Hideaki Anno (the year before the increasingly inaccurately named *The End of Evangelion*).

Anyway, in the best General Products rock-slangin' tradition (if you don't know about Gainax's early days, check out their brutally idealistic *Otaku no video*, available on DVD from animeigo.com, or the book *The Notenki Memoirs*, from ADV—why look, there's a copy on my desk), Scott was sell-ing these fresh-made mugs out of a cardboard box about twenty feet from where Hideaki Anno was signing autographs, although, to be fair, he gave a free one to Anno. You know, for the effort.

I bought two: one for me, one for Trish Ledoux, my *sempai* at *Animerica* magazine, where I had first written about *Evangelion* in February 1995. It was Trish who later asked me if I would be interested in editing the original *Evangelion* manga by Yoshiyuki Sadamoto—my very first assignment as a manga editor. And so I'm here now, all these years later, on a new *Evangelion* manga, in a time when new *Evangelion* movies are being made for the next generation.

Somethingawful.com once wrote that *Evangelion* was about "some unlikable kid who whines about how badly his life sucks while insanely hot female cartoon ladies dance around him." I like to think that this manga, *The Shinji Ikari Raising Project*, is designed to address that criticism. ^_^ But as someone so startled by *The End of Evangelion* back in 1997 that I kept my mouth shut for its last thirty minutes (an amazing achievement), I actual-ly feel a sense of tremendous *relief* to read Osamu Takahashi's alternate take on characters whose other, tragic fates I know very well.

It's odd being a *Neon Genesis Evangelion* fan, because we can switch from taking the series seriously to lightly with tremendous ease. You see this in one of the most sincere expressions of *Eva* fandom (because we're the ones who buy all of it): its merchandise, going as strong as ever, four-teen years after the series' first premiere. Have you ever noticed how little of the things that make *Evangelion* so notorious—its tragedy, its psycho-drama, its cryptic architecture—are reflected in the stuff you find in dealers' rooms? I mean, it's not like you're going to find them selling a Super High Grade Bleeding Bardiel ("*Now your desktop or bookshelf becomes the 1/128 scale blood-slick streets of Tokyo-3!*) No, it's going to be, like, Asuka: The School Crossing Guard! *Kawaii!*

On the other hand, I was lucky enough to see the Japanese version of *Evangelion 1.0: You Are (Not) Alone* last year when Gainax came to Fanime Con (as they always do—if you want to meet them, it's your best chance!), and it's as intense as ever. It basically retells the events of the first six episodes of the TV show, with all-new animation, but in a way that seems even darker and more dramatic than the original (not to men-tion spectacular—the restaged battle against the Angel Ramiel is really something).

I happen to agree with Hideaki Anno that the an-ime industry still hasn't picked up the challenge that *Evangelion* laid down back in 1995–97, and obviously, that it's *Evangelion*-related, and second, that it makes an impression—it could be moody, funny, offbeat, or totally out there, as long as it's something cool. For the three pieces of fan art we like best, we'll send each person one of these—*Evangelion* folding fans, with art by character designer Yoshiyuki Sadamoto. These were only available as a special giveaway to readers of the manga in Japan, but we saved some for you!

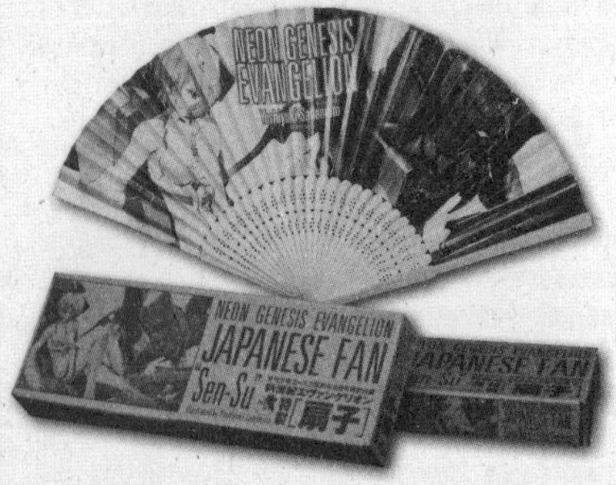
NEON GENESIS EVANGELION
NEON GENESIS EVANGELION
JAPANESE FAN
"Sen-Su"
扇子
JAPANESE FAN

Please note that due to the fact each volume of this manga has to go to the printer's some time before it shows up in your bookstore, we need to receive your submissions for vol. 2 quickly. Volume 1's on-sale date is July 1! You can send them by e-mail or through regular mail, whichever you prefer (the contact info is at the top of page 182). If your art is digital, please make sure the image size is at least as big as one of these manga pages (i.e., about 5" x 7") and that the quality is at least 300 dpi. Because this is going to be a regular feature, if you can't get your stuff in that quickly, it can still be considered for vol. 3—however, there will be a *different* prize given away for vol. 3 (to be revealed in vol. 2! ^_^)

By the way, you don't have to send in just art and photos. Feel free to send your comments and letters on *Evangelion*, too! Speaking of which, I have some of my own.

The stuff you see below isn't being given away, although it would certainly make my desk neater, for this is the stuff upon it. If you want to find something there—say, a vital invoice, or an urgent printout—you need to think in three-dimensional terms, like a geologist. As you dig down through the piled papers, you dig backwards through time; the ratio's about one inch per month.

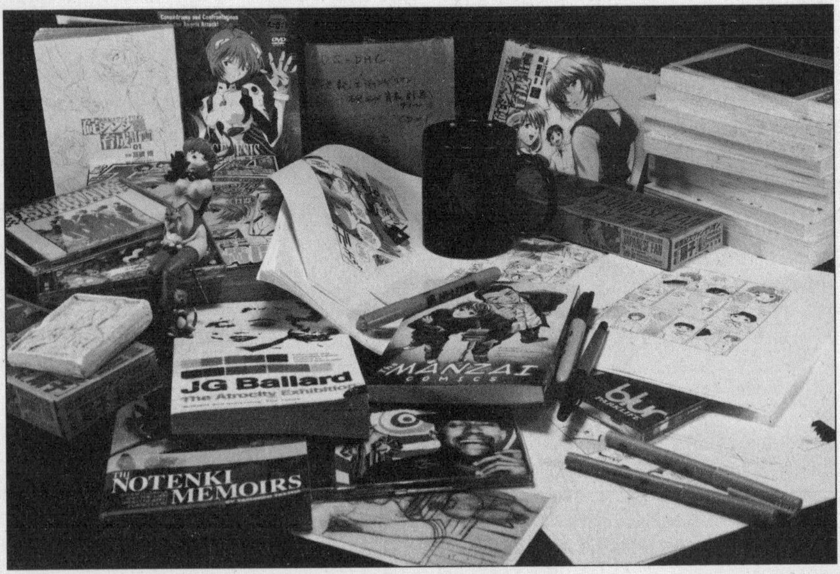
JG Ballard
The Atrocity Exhibition
MANZAI
COMICS
blur
THE
NOTENKI
MEMOIRS
JAPANESE FAN

illustrator—which she did, drawing for *Puck*, the leading U.S. humor magazine of the day (it was so famous in the late nineteenth century that a Japanese imitation of it sprang up, *The Tokyo Puck*, which Frederik Schodt talks about in his much-recommended book *Manga! Manga!*).

You can imagine what it was like for a sixteen-year-old girl in 1890s America to not only dream of becoming a successful cartoonist, but actually achieve that dream, and her life would itself make a great manga—it sometimes *was* very manga-like, as when she moved to New York City she lived at the Convent of St. Regis, where the nuns would insist on accompanying her whenever she went to magazine offices to try to sell her illustrations!

O'Neill was a glamorous and wealthy artist in her time, and the Kewpies became her biggest hit, used in advertisements and spun off into merchandise of all sorts, most notably the Kewpie Dolls, a sales phenomenon in the early twentieth century (they were considered so important to American pop culture that a Kewpie Doll was among the artifacts of our civilization sealed in the time capsule buried at the famous 1939 New York World's Fair—it's supposed to be opened five thousand years from now!). Ironically, they're largely forgotten in America today—but never in Japan, where in 1926, they were first licensed to introduce mayonnaise to the Japanese market by a company today known as Kewpie Kabushiki Kaisha (kewpie.co.jp), one of Japan's largest food corporations. And now you know!

Now, what about you? We'd like to see *your* fan art for vol. 2 of *The Shinji Ikari Raising Project*. Just like the pieces you've seen here, it could be a drawing, a graphic, or a photo of some project. There are two things we're hoping for: first,

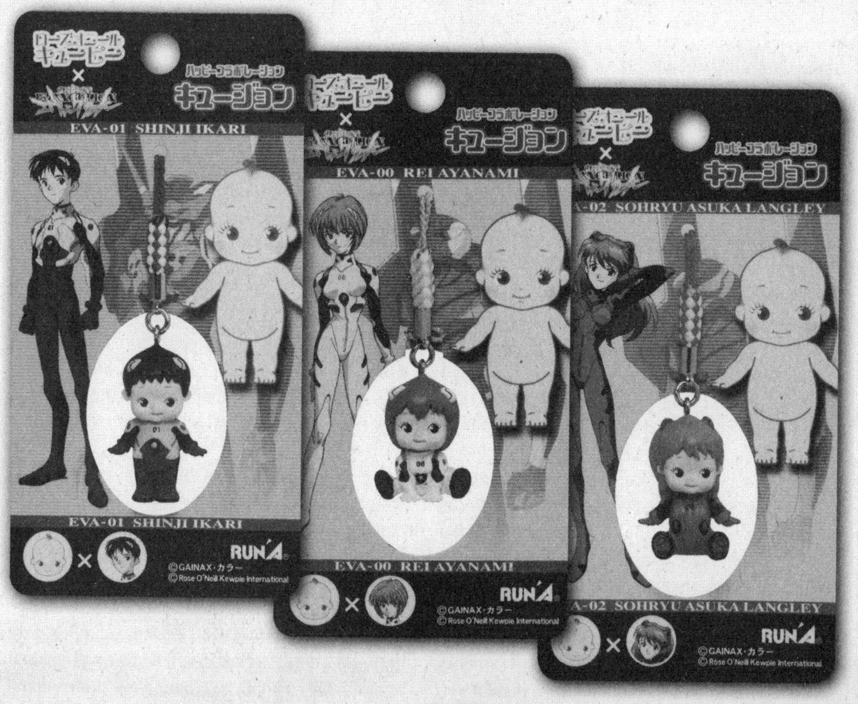

ハッピーコラボレーション
キュージョン
EVA-01 SHINJI IKARI
EVA-01 SHINJI IKARI
RUN'A
©GAINAX·カラー
© Rose O'Neill Kewpie International
ハッピーコラボレーション
キュージョン
EVA-00 REI AYANAMI
EVA-00 REI AYANAMI
RUN'A
©GAINAX·カラー
© Rose O'Neill Kewpie International
ハッピーコラボレーション
キュージョン
SOHRYU ASUKA LANGLEY
SOHRYU ASUKA LANGLEY
RUN'A
©GAINAX·カラー
© Rose O'Neill Kewpie International

the body, trimmed white cheese for the head, and a cherry tomato for the core), Nicholas Walstrom, *décorateur de gâteau*, has here created a confection for the Apocalypse.

Mr. Walstrom's cake is festooned with SEELE monoliths of Hershey's Special Dark. A marshmallow Lilith, gumdrop-masked and Twizzler-lanced, is nailed to a cross of Rice Krispies treats stained with red icing. Blue icing—appropriately, the color of Rei—likewise delineates the graffiti from the Artificial Evolution Laboratory, while green hard candies, melted down like our human forms will be in the Instrumentality, are then reshaped to rise as cruciform souls. As for the orbs of the Sephiroth, however, these were just red Trix; Mr. Walstrom avers that the Systema Sephiroticum itself was printed by Albertsons.

Finally, from Rosa Ramirez (also a fan of Gainax's *Gunbuster 2*) a quiet portrait of three people you may know; Rosa says, "although Kaworu won't show up until vol. 2, I had to include him." Well, as everyone's aware, Shinji has a very complicated personal life. I *think* it's Rei's hand he's choosing to touch there . . .

As a thank you to Carly, Nicholas, and Rosa, we sent them one of the more interesting bits of *Evangelion* merchandise we've come across— these Asuka, Rei, and Shinji key chains (photo on next page).

What's so interesting about these key chains is that they combine *two* different licensed characters: one Japanese, one American. The Japanese part is, of course, *Evangelion*, but the American part is the Kewpie Doll, created by a cartoonist who died half a century before *Evangelion*'s premiere: Rose O'Neill (1874–1944). O'Neill won her first drawing contest at fourteen, and at age sixteen went to New York City to become a professional

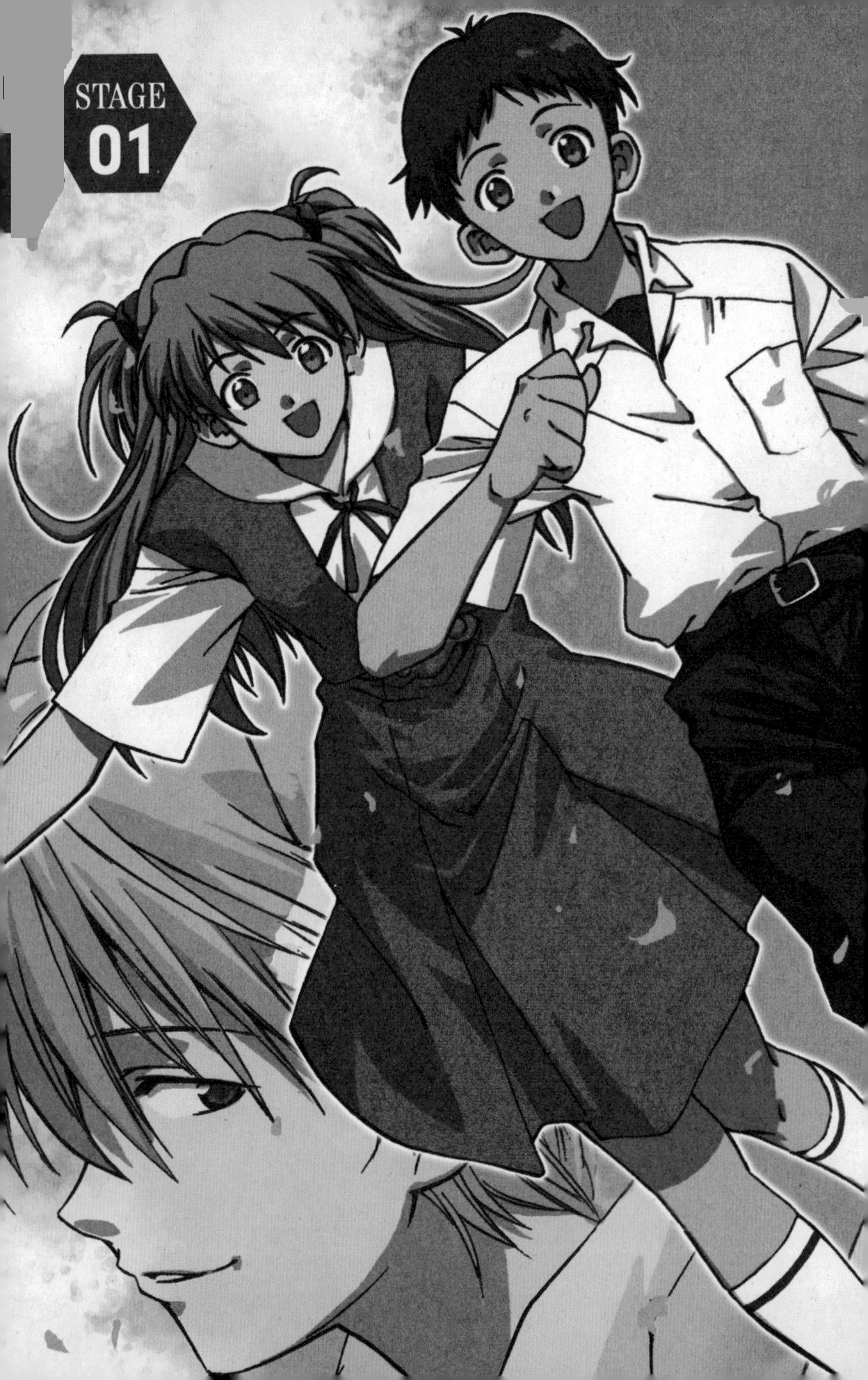
STAGE
01

ON GENESIS EVANGELION

HE SHINJI IKARI AISING PROJECT

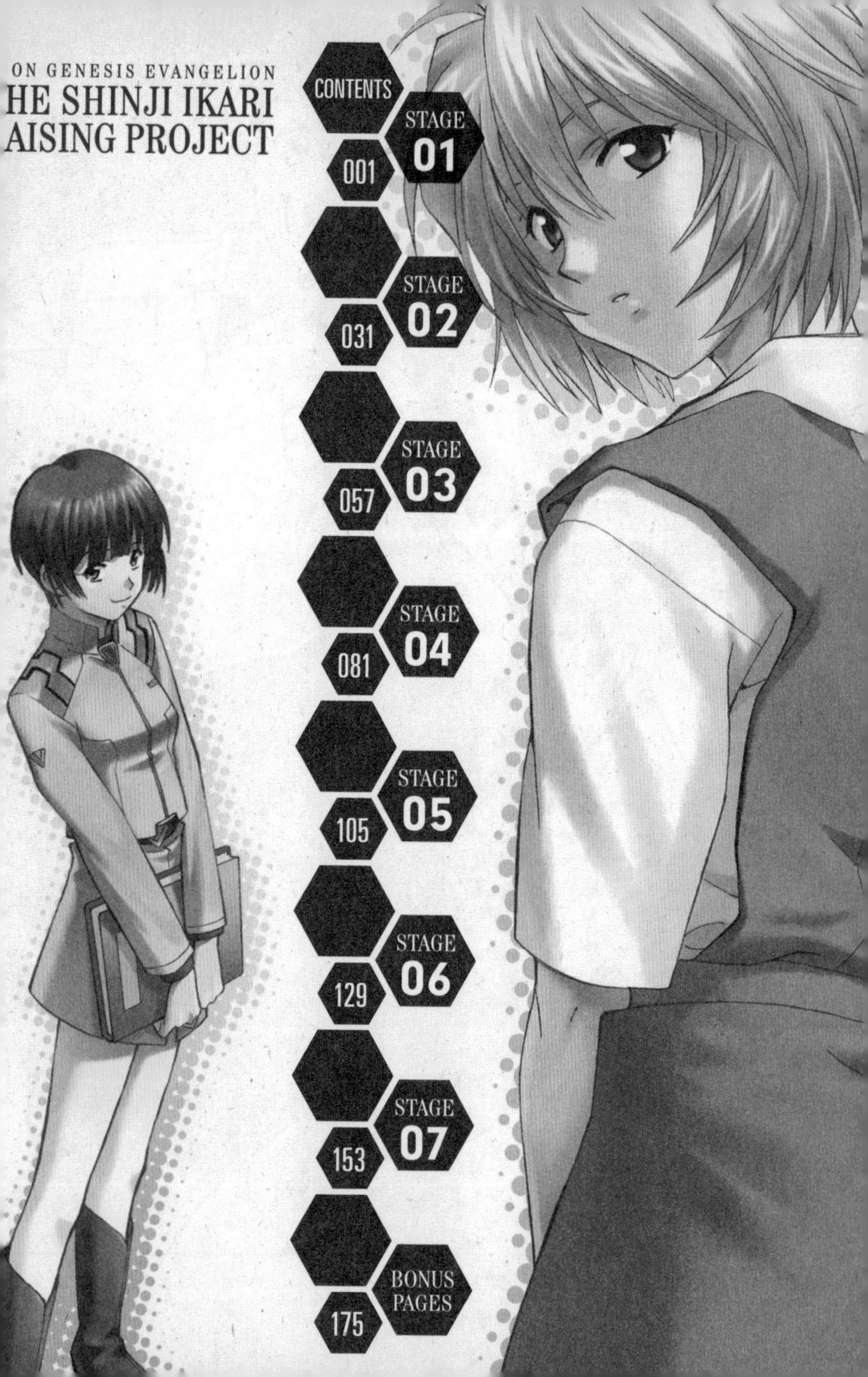

CONTENTS

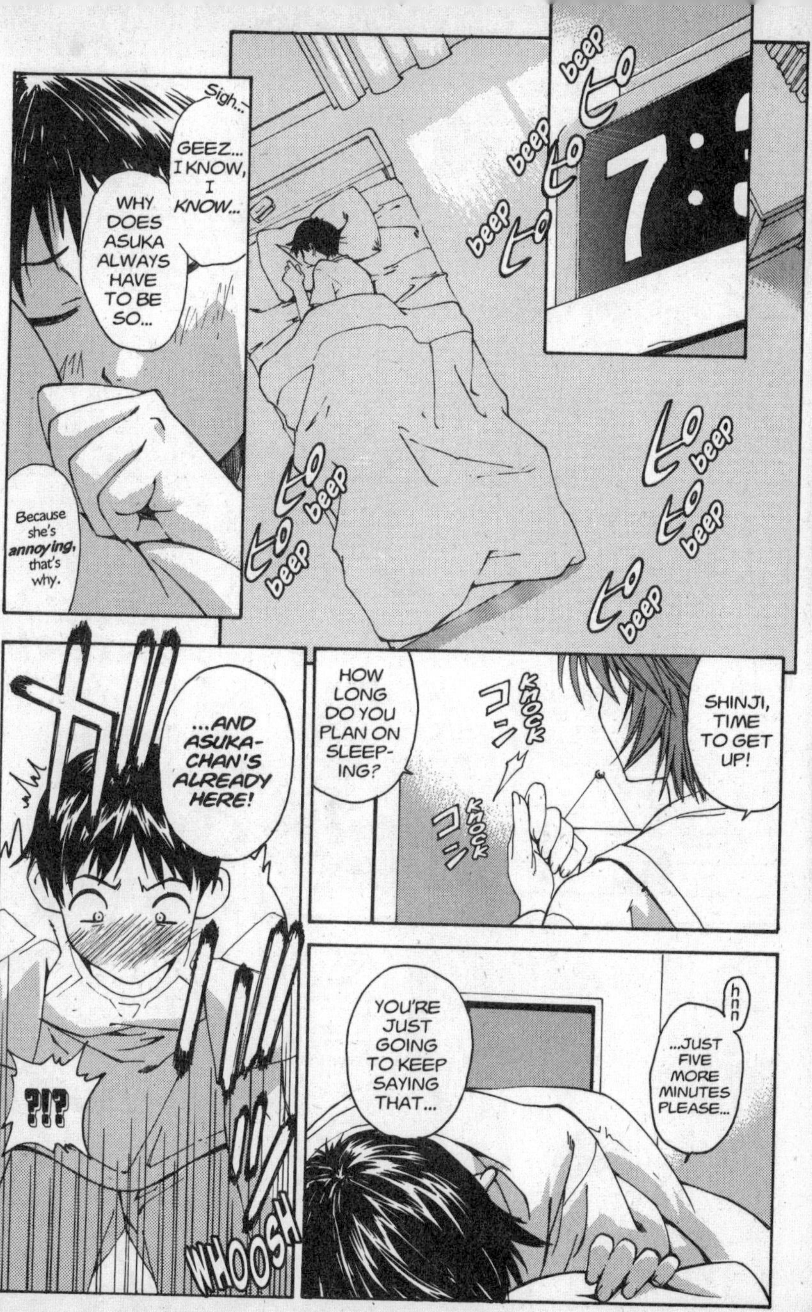
beep
beep
beep
beep
beep
beep
beep
beep
beep
Sigh...
GEEZ... I KNOW, I KNOW...
WHY DOES ASUKA ALWAYS HAVE TO BE SO...
Because she's ***annoying,*** that's why.
SHINJI, TIME TO GET UP!
KNOCK
KNOCK
HOW LONG DO YOU PLAN ON SLEEP-ING?
hnn
...JUST FIVE MORE MINUTES PLEASE...
YOU'RE JUST GOING TO KEEP SAYING THAT...
...AND ASUKA-CHAN'S ALREADY HERE!
?!?
WHOOSH

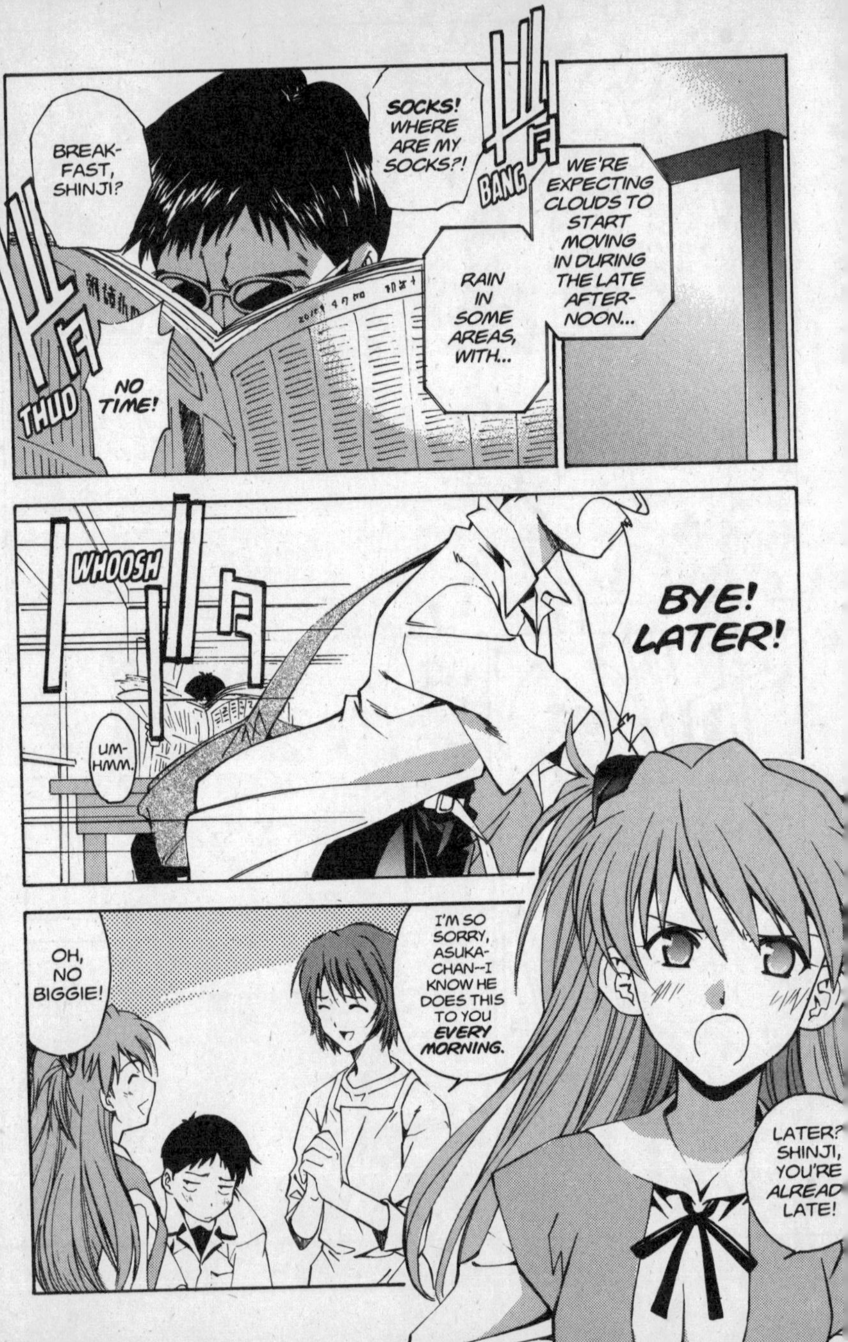

WE'RE EXPECTING CLOUDS TO START MOVING IN DURING THE LATE AFTER-NOON...
BANG
SOCKS! WHERE ARE MY SOCKS?!
RAIN IN SOME AREAS, WITH...
BREAK-FAST, SHINJI?
NO TIME!
THUD
BYE! LATER!
WHOOSH
UM-HMM.
LATER? SHINJI, YOU'RE ALREAD LATE!
I'M SO SORRY, ASUKA-CHAN--I KNOW HE DOES THIS TO YOU EVERY MORNING.
OH, NO BIGGIE!

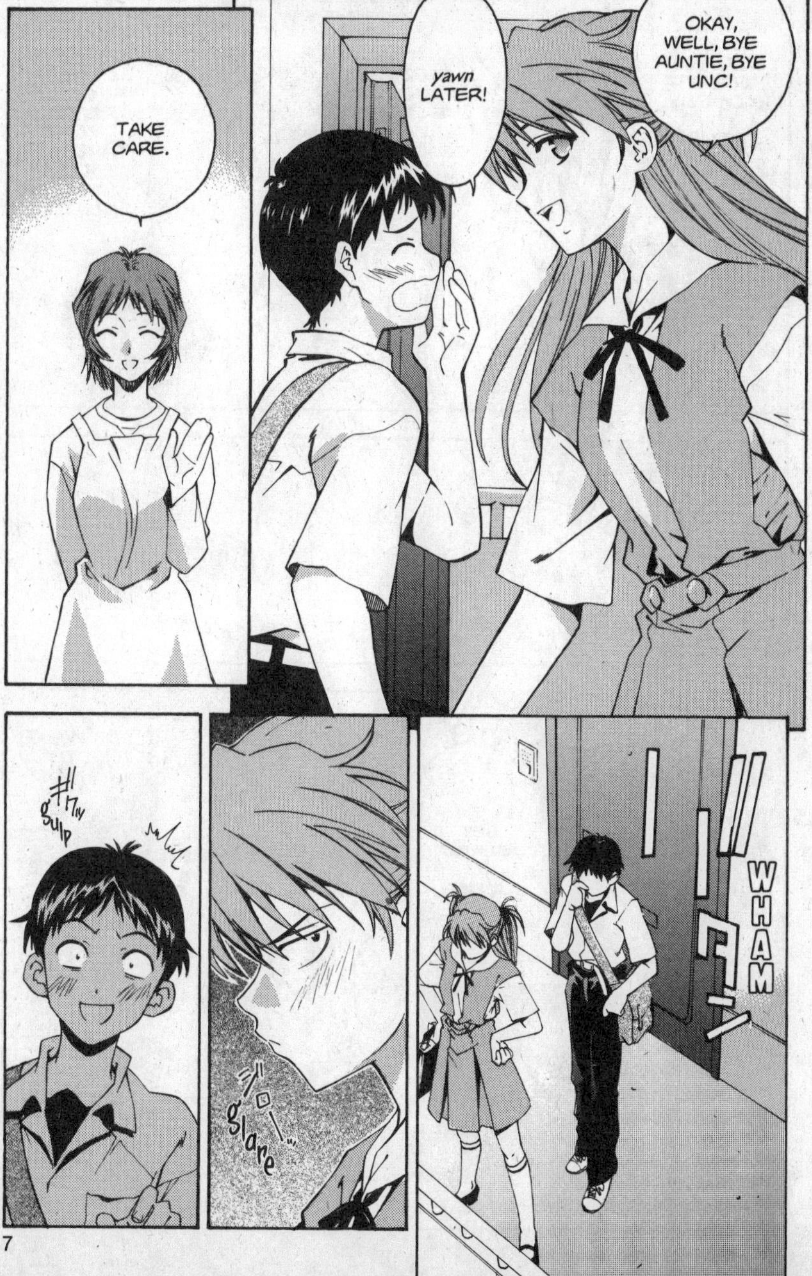
OKAY, WELL, BYE AUNTIE, BYE UNC!
yawn LATER!
TAKE CARE.
WHAM
glare
gulp

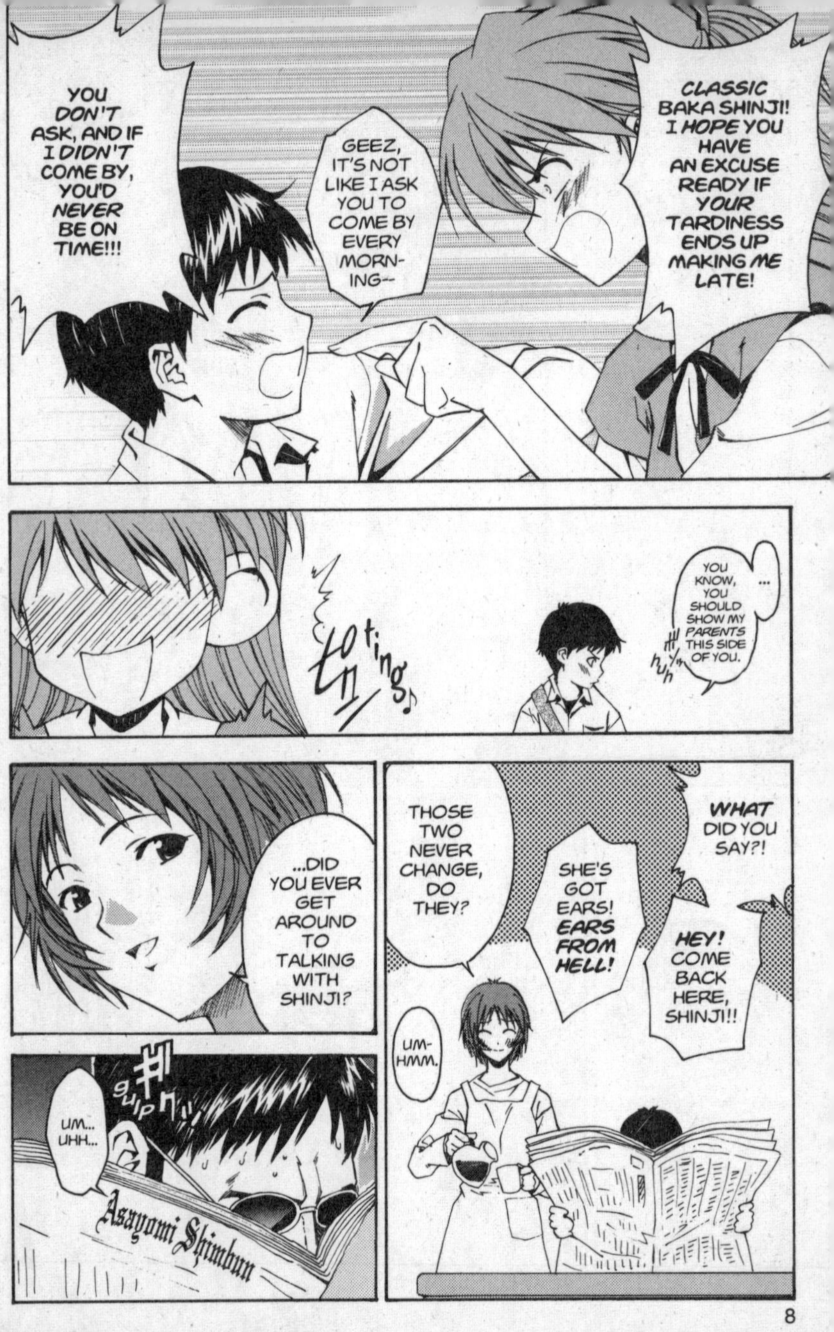
CLASSIC BAKA SHINJI! I HOPE YOU HAVE AN EXCUSE READY IF YOUR TARDINESS ENDS UP MAKING ME LATE!
GEEZ, IT'S NOT LIKE I ASK YOU TO COME BY EVERY MORN-ING--
YOU DON'T ASK, AND IF I DIDN'T COME BY, YOU'D NEVER BE ON TIME!!!
...
YOU KNOW, YOU SHOULD SHOW MY PARENTS THIS SIDE OF YOU.
huh
ting ting♪
WHAT DID YOU SAY?!
HEY! COME BACK HERE, SHINJI!!!
SHE'S GOT EARS! EARS FROM HELL!
THOSE TWO NEVER CHANGE, DO THEY?
UM-HMM.
...DID YOU EVER GET AROUND TO TALKING WITH SHINJI?
gulp
UM... UHH...
Asayomi Shimbun

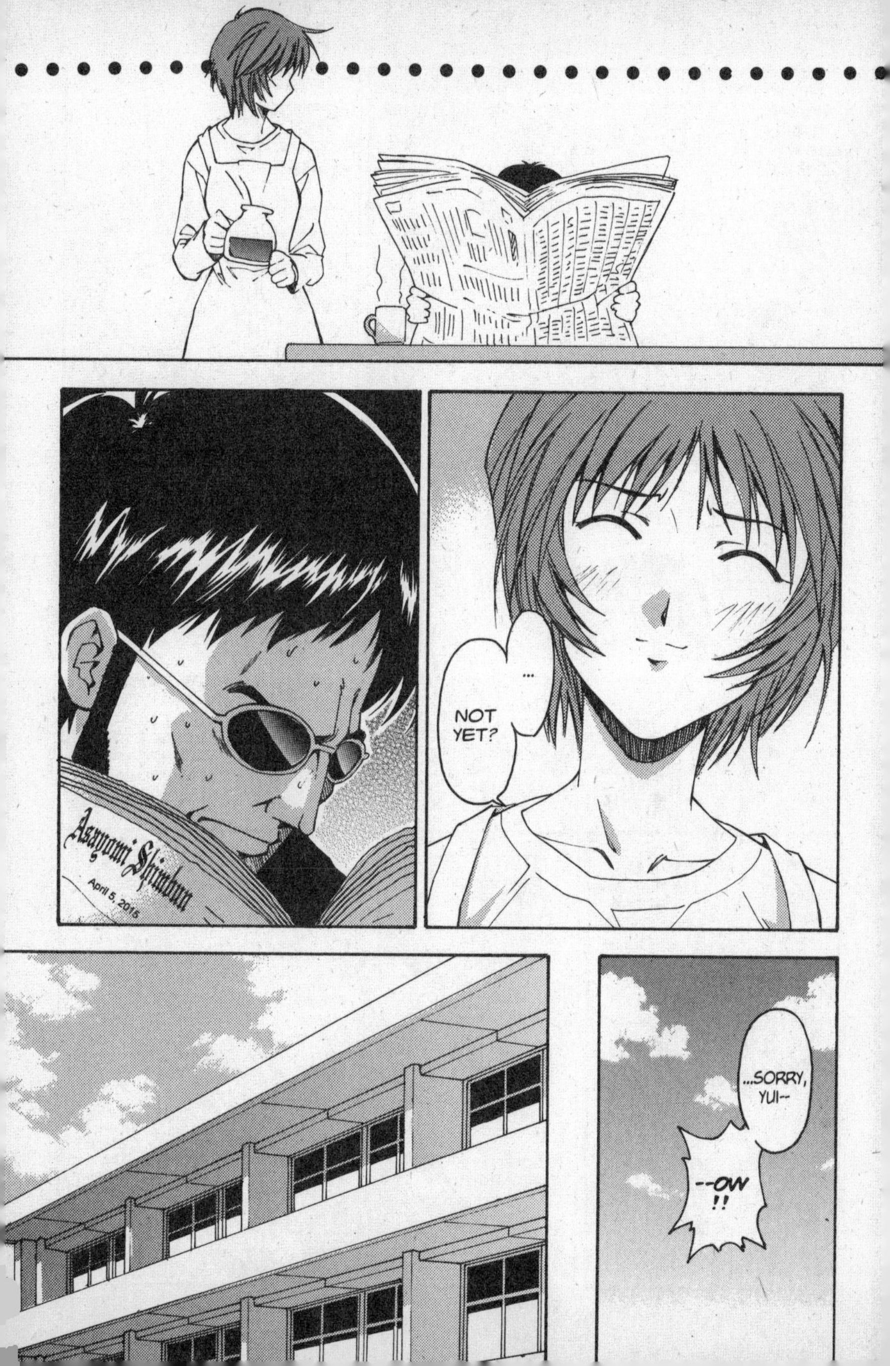
...
NOT YET?
Asayomi Shimbun
April 5, 2015
...SORRY, YUI--
--OW !!

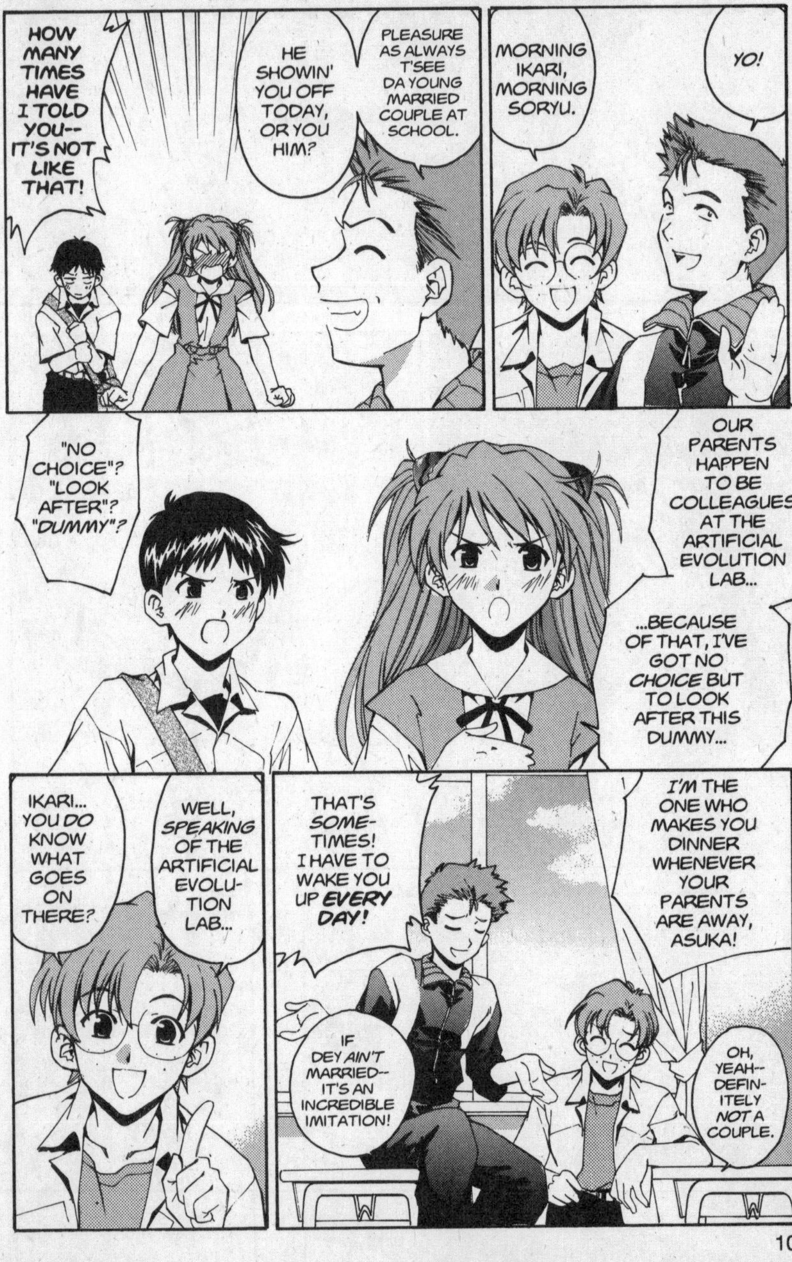
YO!
MORNING IKARI, MORNING SORYU.
PLEASURE AS ALWAYS T'SEE DA YOUNG MARRIED COUPLE AT SCHOOL.
HE SHOWIN' YOU OFF TODAY, OR YOU HIM?
HOW MANY TIMES HAVE I TOLD YOU-- IT'S NOT LIKE THAT!
OUR PARENTS HAPPEN TO BE COLLEAGUES AT THE ARTIFICIAL EVOLUTION LAB...
...BECAUSE OF THAT, I'VE GOT NO CHOICE BUT TO LOOK AFTER THIS DUMMY...
"NO CHOICE"? "LOOK AFTER"? "DUMMY"?
I'M THE ONE WHO MAKES YOU DINNER WHENEVER YOUR PARENTS ARE AWAY, ASUKA!
THAT'S SOME-TIMES! I HAVE TO WAKE YOU UP EVERY DAY!
OH, YEAH-- DEFIN-ITELY NOT A COUPLE.
IF DEY AIN'T MARRIED-- IT'S AN INCREDIBLE IMITATION!
WELL, SPEAKING OF THE ARTIFICIAL EVOLU-TION LAB...
IKARI... YOU DO KNOW WHAT GOES ON THERE?

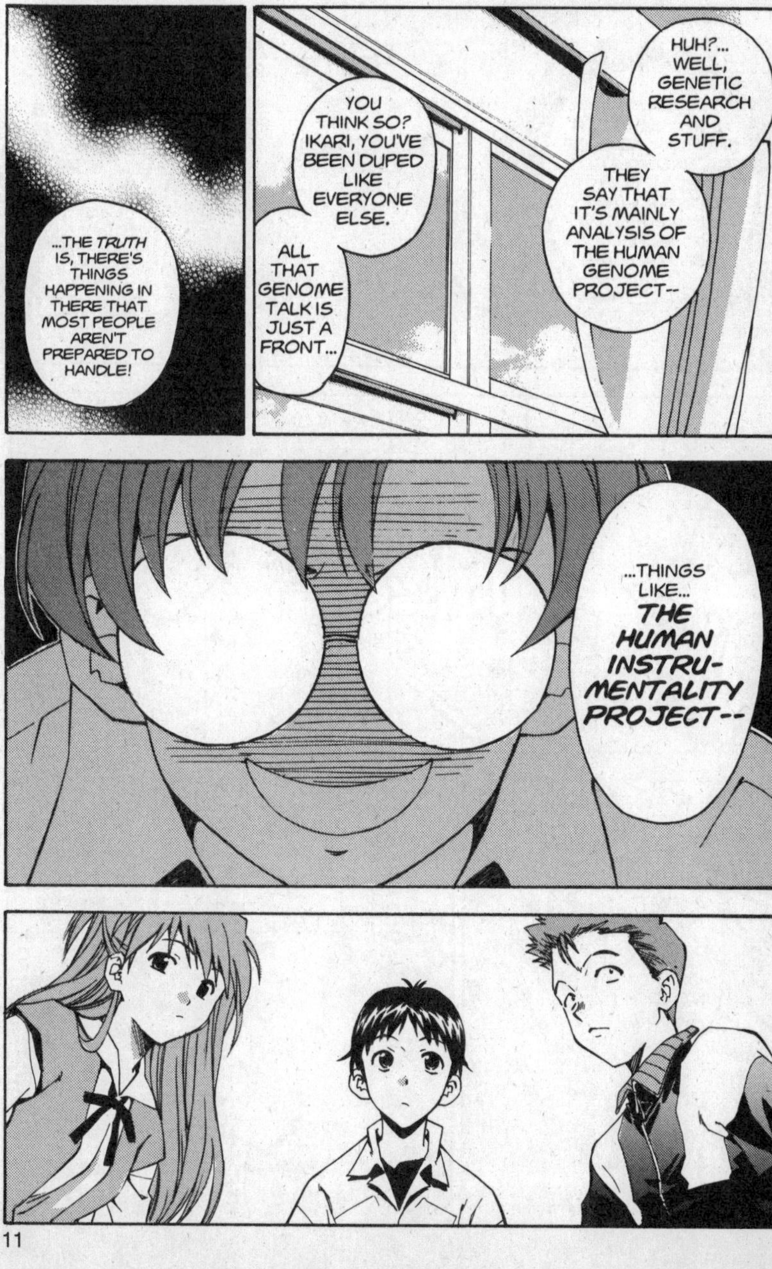
HUH?... WELL, GENETIC RESEARCH AND STUFF.
THEY SAY THAT IT'S MAINLY ANALYSIS OF THE HUMAN GENOME PROJECT--
YOU THINK SO? IKARI, YOU'VE BEEN DUPED LIKE EVERYONE ELSE.
ALL THAT GENOME TALK IS JUST A FRONT...
...THE *TRUTH* IS, THERE'S THINGS HAPPENING IN THERE THAT MOST PEOPLE AREN'T PREPARED TO HANDLE!
...THINGS LIKE... ***THE HUMAN INSTRUMENTALITY PROJECT--***

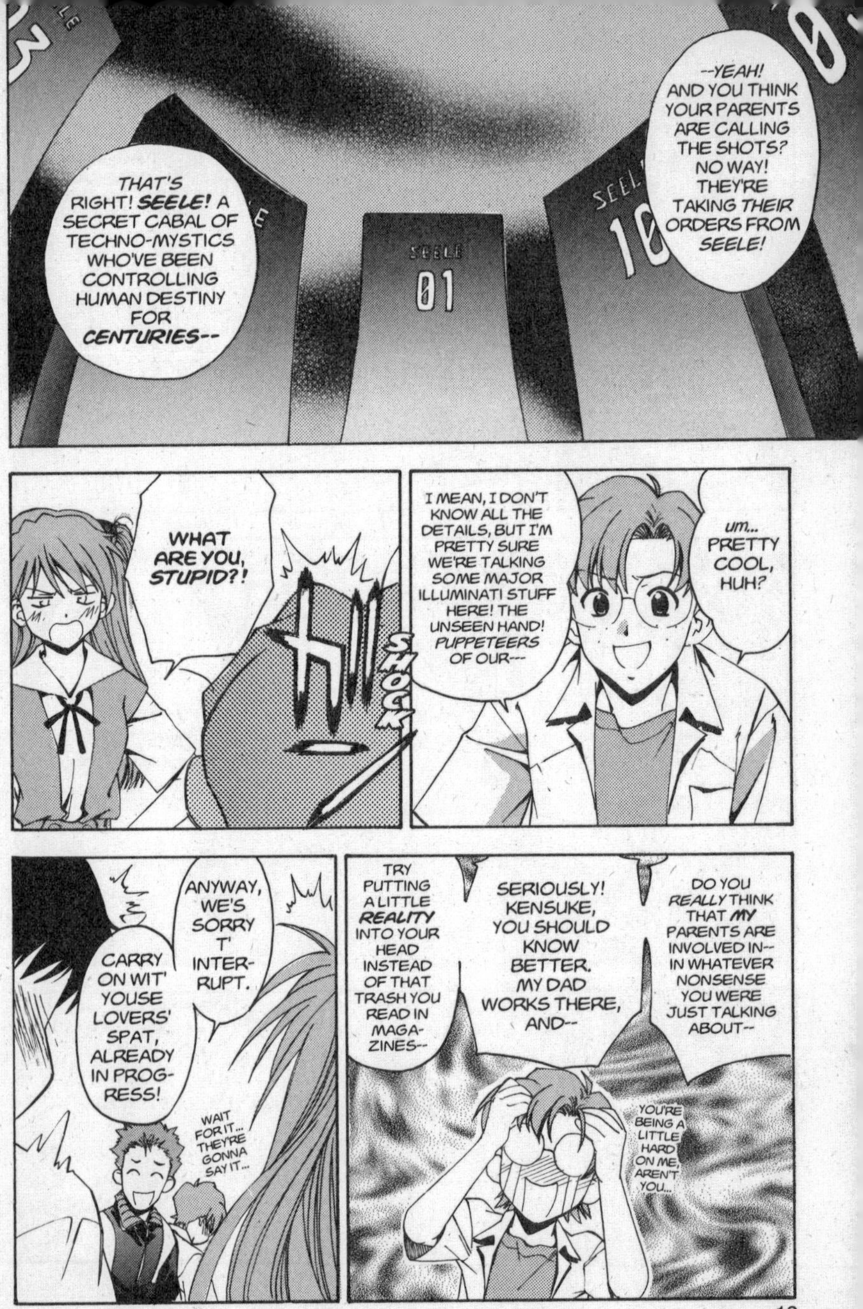
--YEAH! AND YOU THINK YOUR PARENTS ARE CALLING THE SHOTS? NO WAY! THEY'RE TAKING *THEIR* ORDERS FROM *SEELE!*
SEELE 10
SEELE 01
THAT'S RIGHT! **SEELE!** A SECRET CABAL OF TECHNO-MYSTICS WHO'VE BEEN CONTROLLING HUMAN DESTINY FOR **CENTURIES--**
um... PRETTY COOL, HUH?
I MEAN, I DON'T KNOW ALL THE DETAILS, BUT I'M PRETTY SURE WE'RE TALKING SOME MAJOR ILLUMINATI STUFF HERE! THE UNSEEN HAND! *PUPPETEERS* OF OUR---
SHOCK
WHAT ARE YOU, **STUPID?!**
DO YOU *REALLY* THINK THAT ***MY*** PARENTS ARE INVOLVED IN-- IN WHATEVER NONSENSE YOU WERE JUST TALKING ABOUT--
SERIOUSLY! KENSUKE, YOU SHOULD KNOW BETTER. MY DAD WORKS THERE, AND--
TRY PUTTING A LITTLE ***REALITY*** INTO YOUR HEAD INSTEAD OF THAT TRASH YOU READ IN MAGA-ZINES--
YOU'RE BEING A LITTLE HARD ON ME, AREN'T YOU...
ANYWAY, WE'S SORRY T' INTER-RUPT.
CARRY ON WIT' YOUSE LOVERS' SPAT, ALREADY IN PROG-RESS!
WAIT FOR IT... THEY'RE GONNA SAY IT...

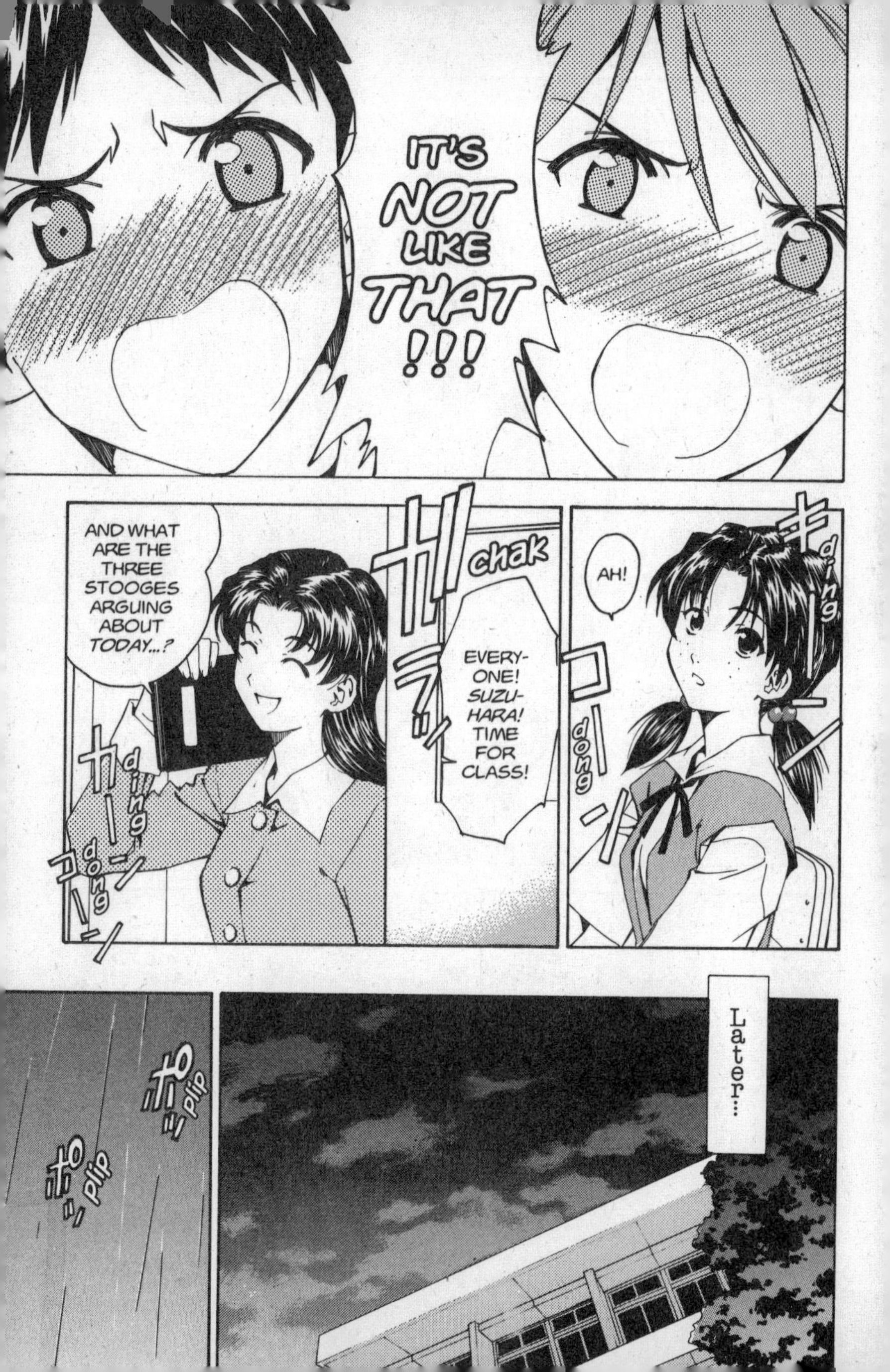
IT'S NOT LIKE THAT!!!
ding
AH!
dong
chak
EVERY-ONE! SUZU-HARA! TIME FOR CLASS!
AND WHAT ARE THE THREE STOOGES ARGUING ABOUT TODAY...?
ding
dong
Later...
plip
plip

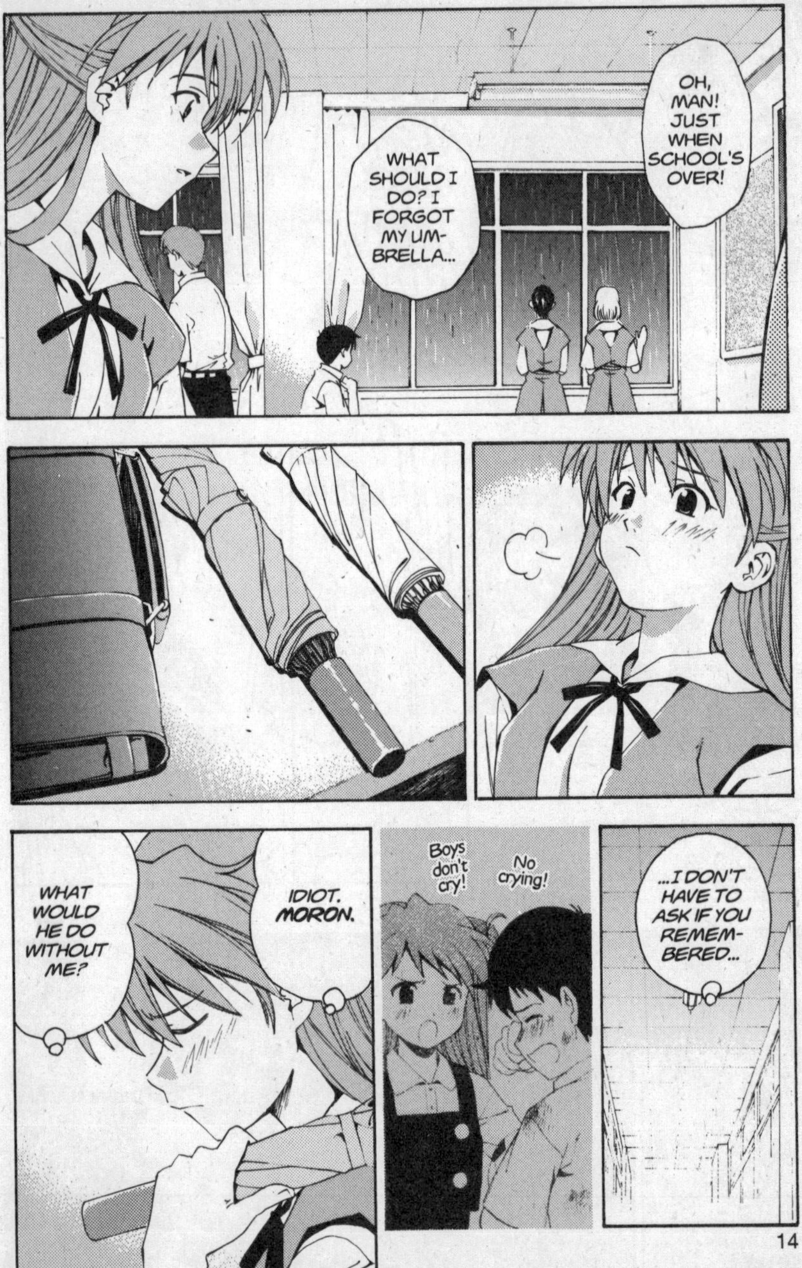
OH, MAN! JUST WHEN SCHOOL'S OVER!
WHAT SHOULD I DO? I FORGOT MY UM-BRELLA...
...I DON'T HAVE TO ASK IF YOU REMEM-BERED...
No crying!
Boys don't cry!
IDIOT. MORON.
WHAT WOULD HE DO WITHOUT ME?

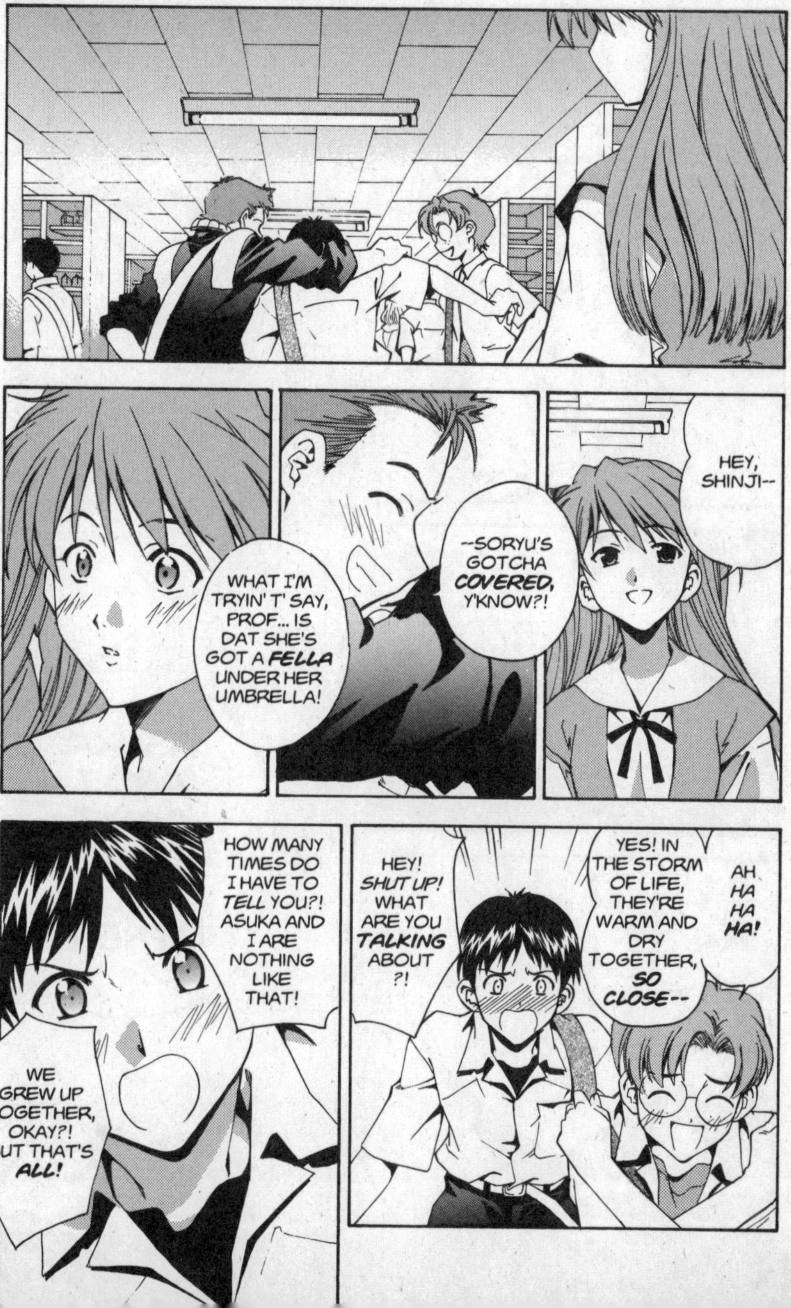
HEY, SHINJI--
--SORYU'S GOTCHA COVERED, Y'KNOW?!
WHAT I'M TRYIN' T' SAY, PROF... IS DAT SHE'S GOT A FELLA UNDER HER UMBRELLA!
AH HA HA HA!
YES! IN THE STORM OF LIFE, THEY'RE WARM AND DRY TOGETHER, SO CLOSE--
HEY! SHUT UP! WHAT ARE YOU TALKING ABOUT?!
HOW MANY TIMES DO I HAVE TO TELL YOU?! ASUKA AND I ARE NOTHING LIKE THAT!
WE GREW UP TOGETHER, OKAY?! BUT THAT'S ALL!

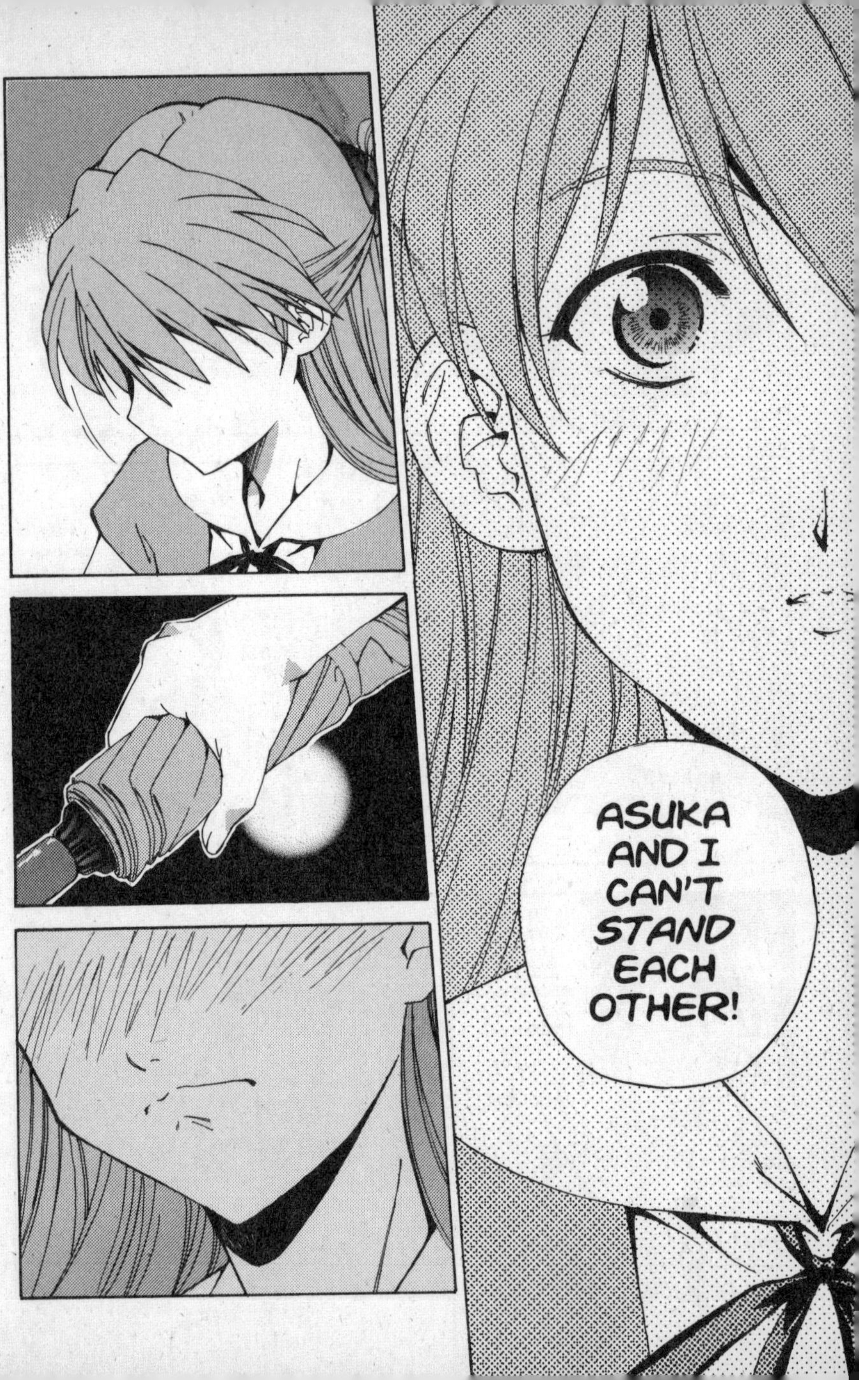
ASUKA AND I CAN'T STAND EACH OTHER!

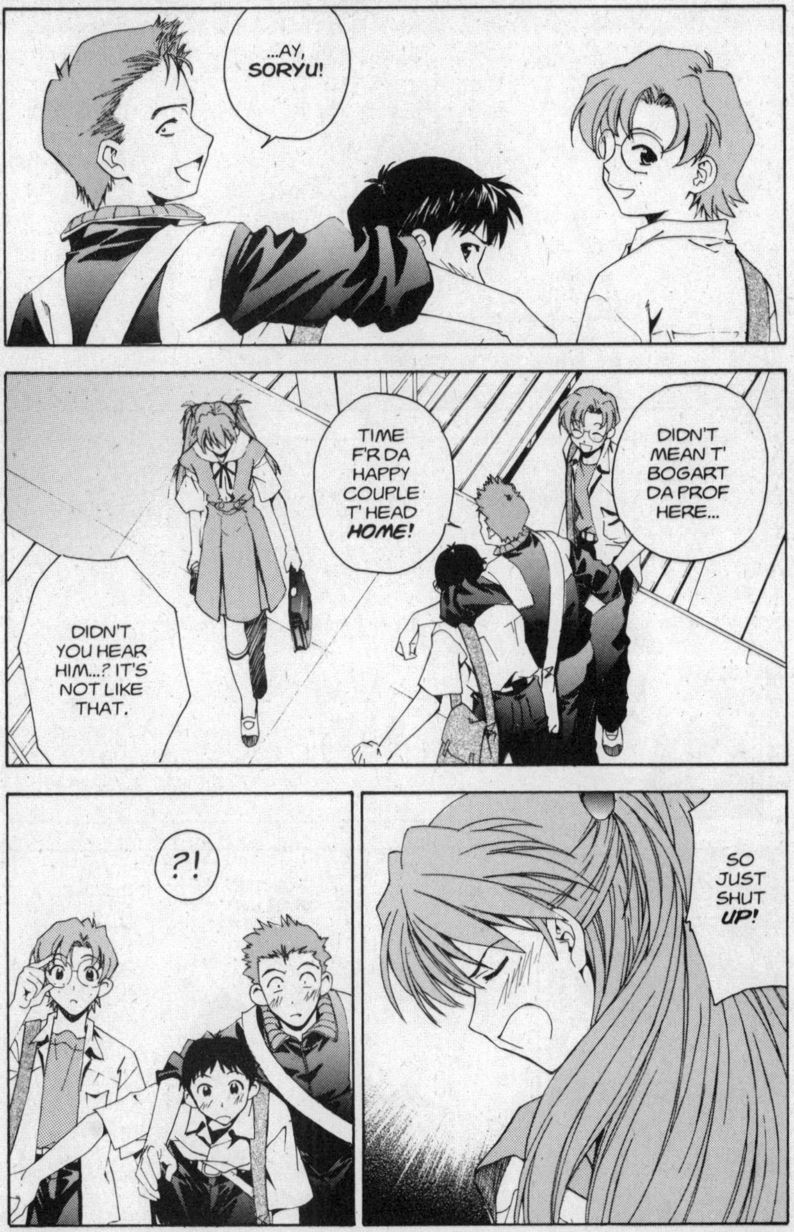

...AY, SORYU!
DIDN'T MEAN T' BOGART DA PROF HERE...
TIME F'R DA HAPPY COUPLE T' HEAD HOME!
DIDN'T YOU HEAR HIM...? IT'S NOT LIKE THAT.
SO JUST SHUT UP!
?!

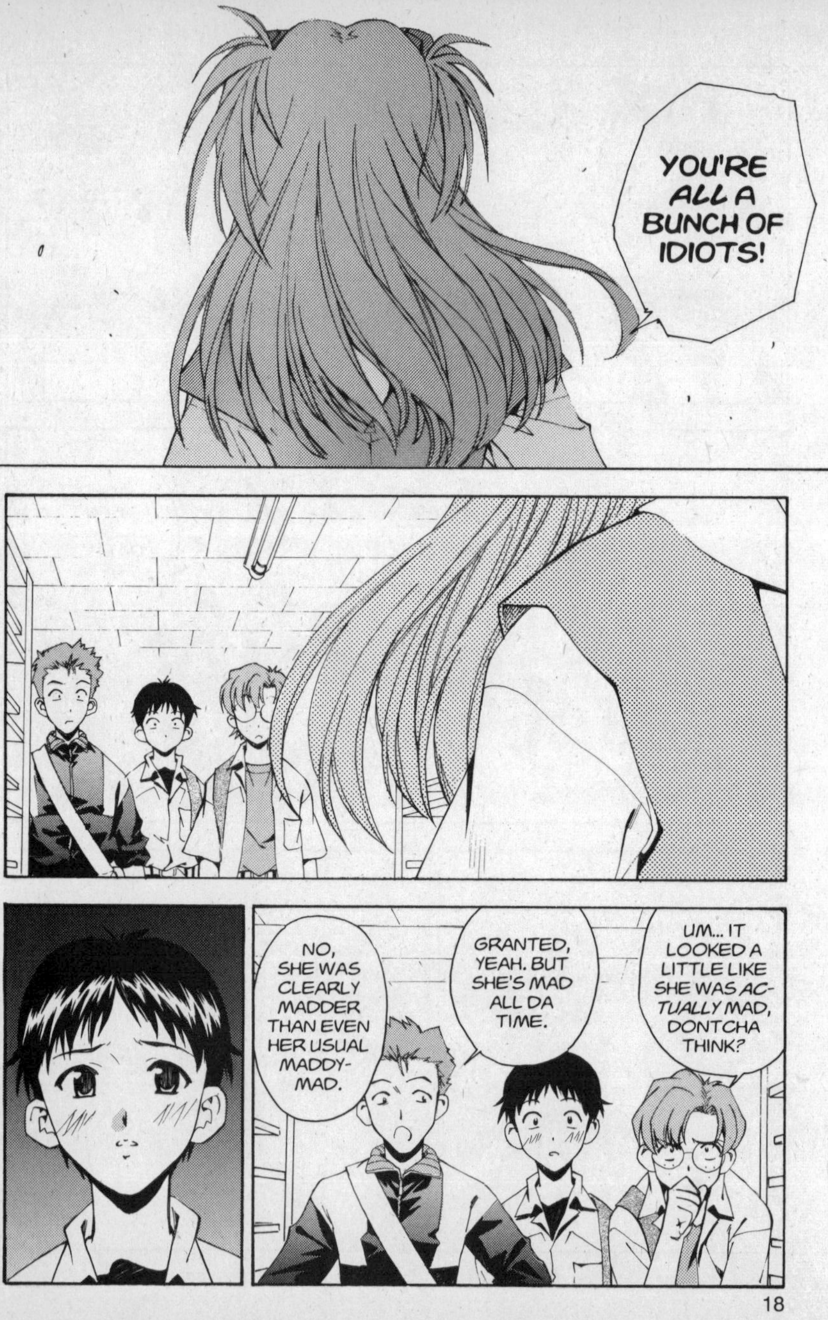
YOU'RE ALL A BUNCH OF IDIOTS!
UM... IT LOOKED A LITTLE LIKE SHE WAS ACTUALLY MAD, DONTCHA THINK?
GRANTED, YEAH. BUT SHE'S MAD ALL DA TIME.
NO, SHE WAS CLEARLY MADDER THAN EVEN HER USUAL MADDY-MAD.

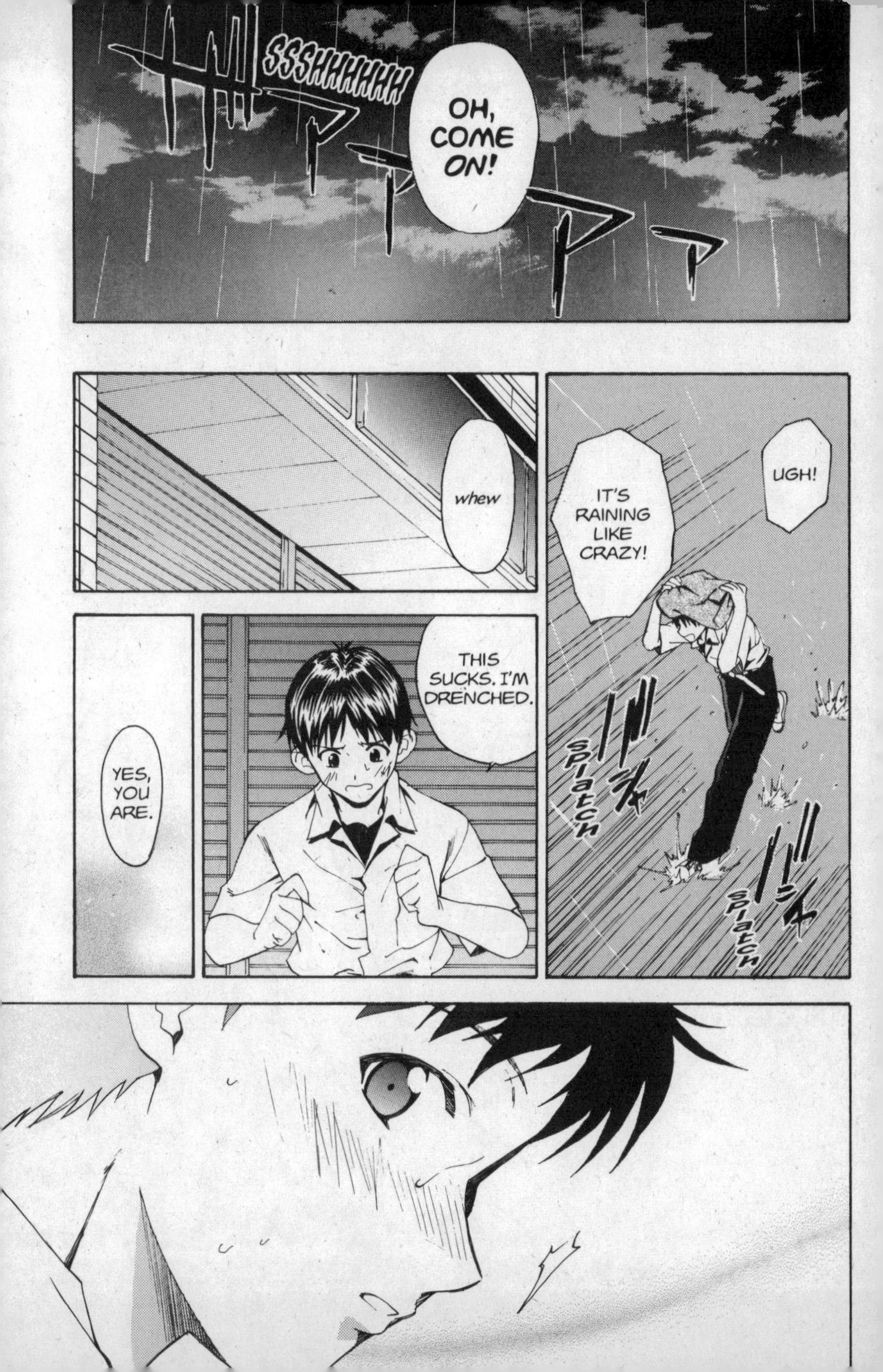
SSSHHHHHH
OH, COME ON!
UGH!
IT'S RAINING LIKE CRAZY!
splatch
splatch
whew
THIS SUCKS. I'M DRENCHED.
YES, YOU ARE.

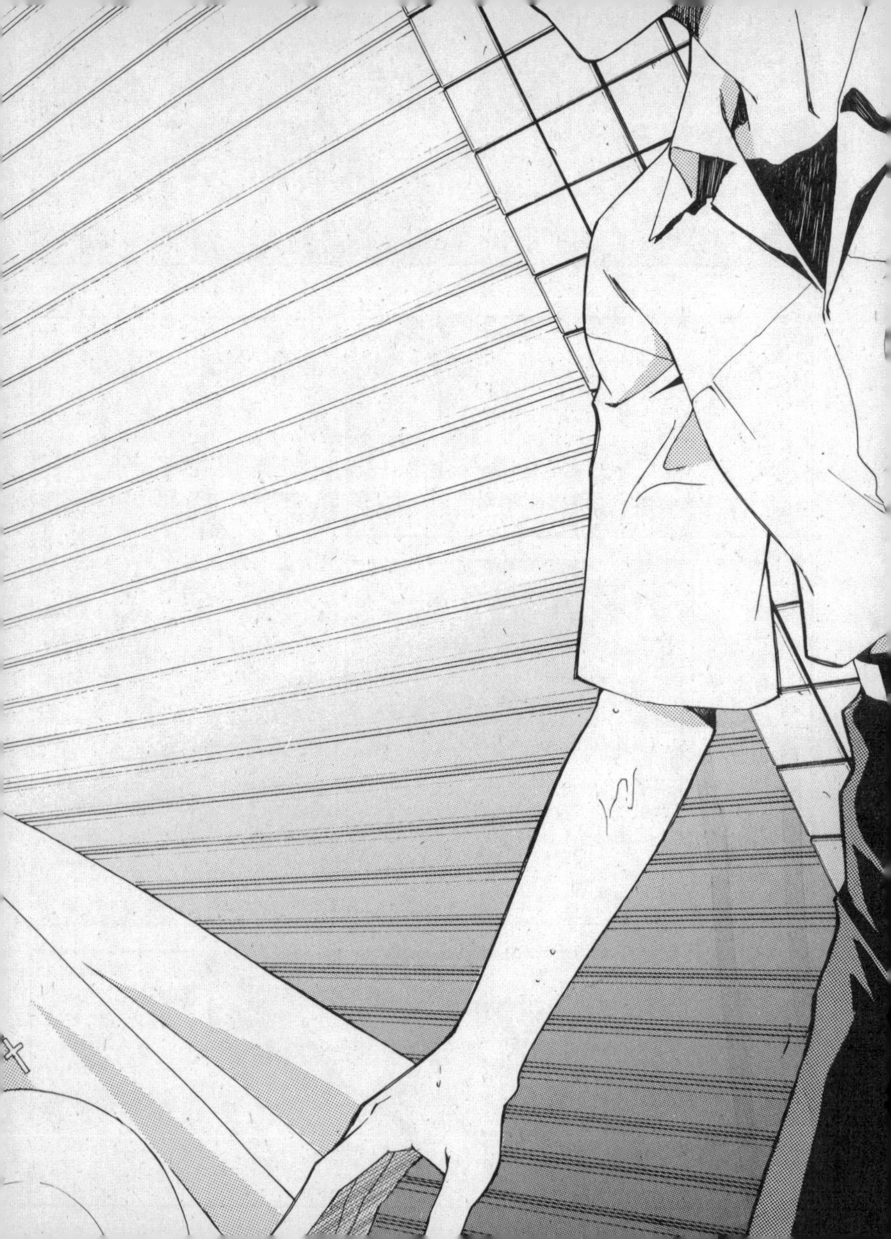

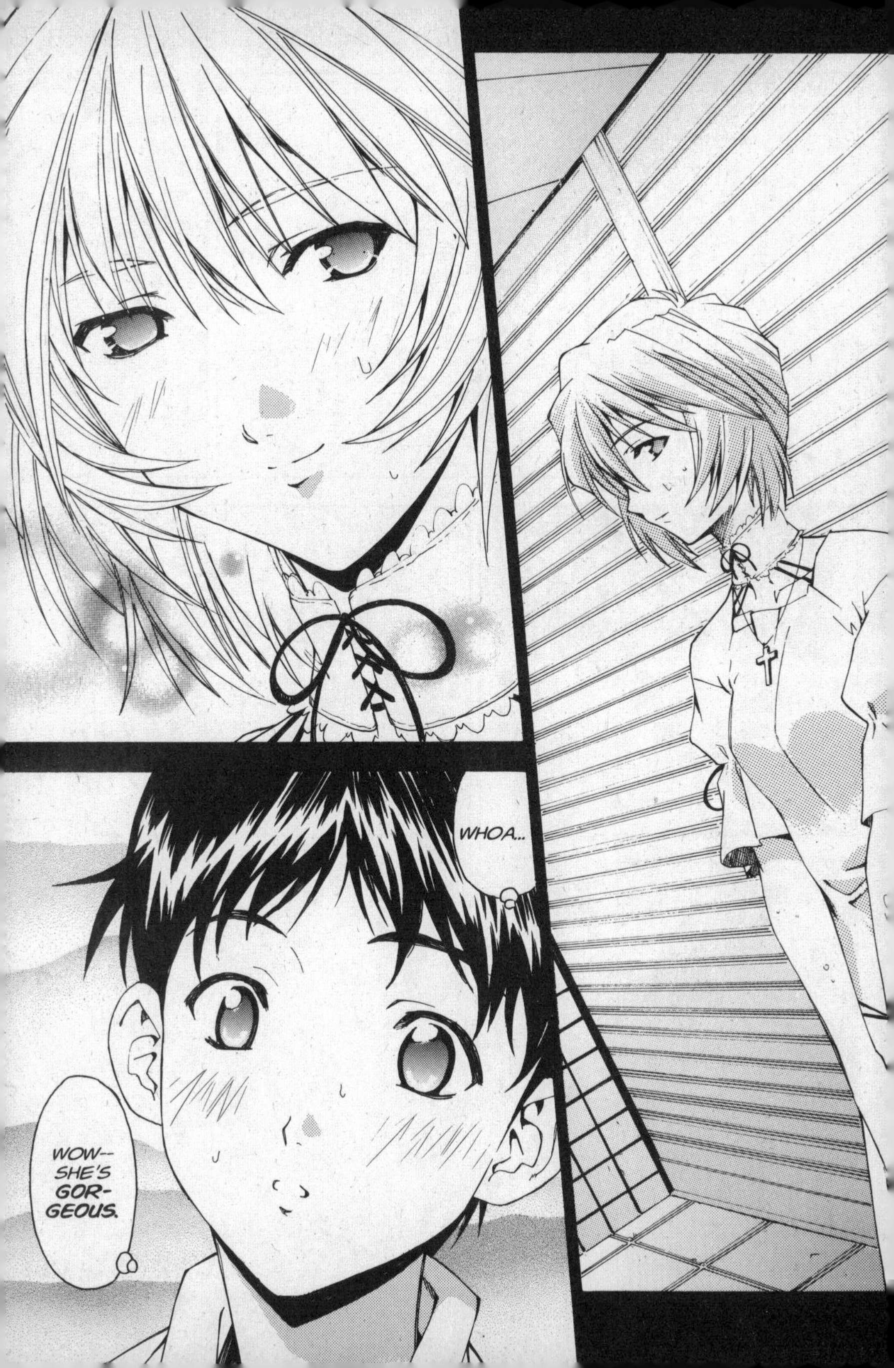
WHOA...
WOW--SHE'S GORGEOUS.

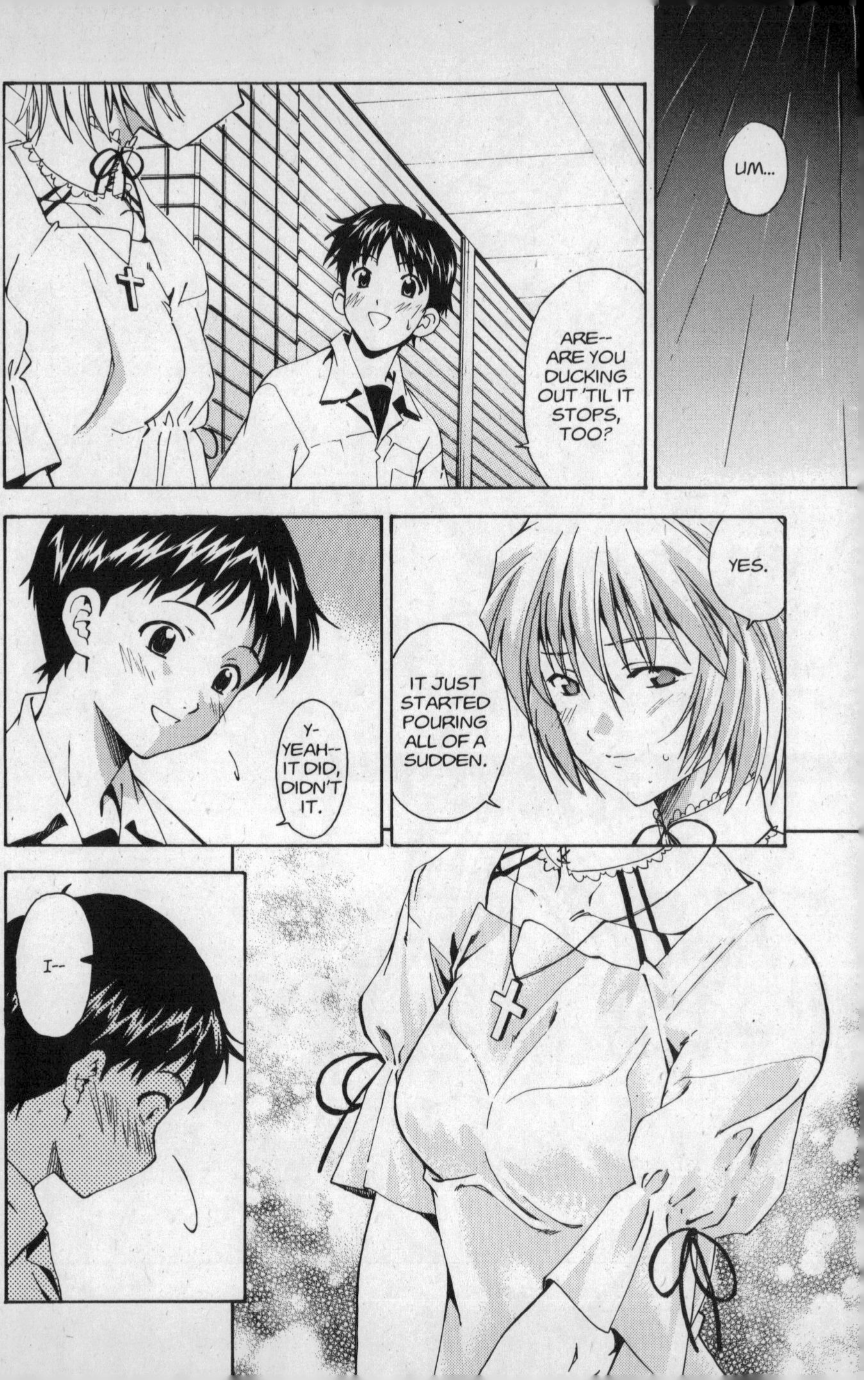
UM...
ARE-- ARE YOU DUCKING OUT 'TIL IT STOPS, TOO?
YES.
IT JUST STARTED POURING ALL OF A SUDDEN.
Y-YEAH-- IT DID, DIDN'T IT.
I--

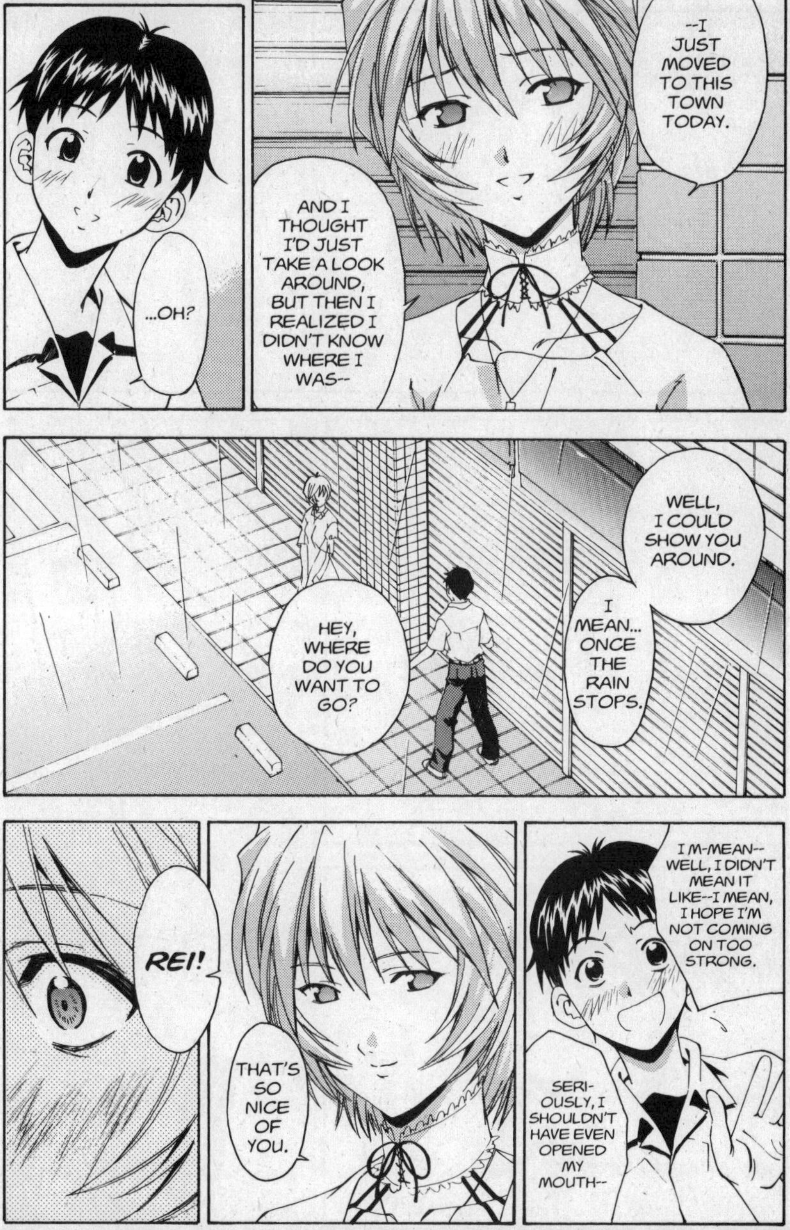
--I JUST MOVED TO THIS TOWN TODAY.
AND I THOUGHT I'D JUST TAKE A LOOK AROUND, BUT THEN I REALIZED I DIDN'T KNOW WHERE I WAS--
...OH?
WELL, I COULD SHOW YOU AROUND.
I MEAN... ONCE THE RAIN STOPS.
HEY, WHERE DO YOU WANT TO GO?
I M-MEAN-- WELL, I DIDN'T MEAN IT LIKE--I MEAN, I HOPE I'M NOT COMING ON TOO STRONG.
SERI-OUSLY, I SHOULDN'T HAVE EVEN OPENED MY MOUTH--
THAT'S SO NICE OF YOU.
REI!

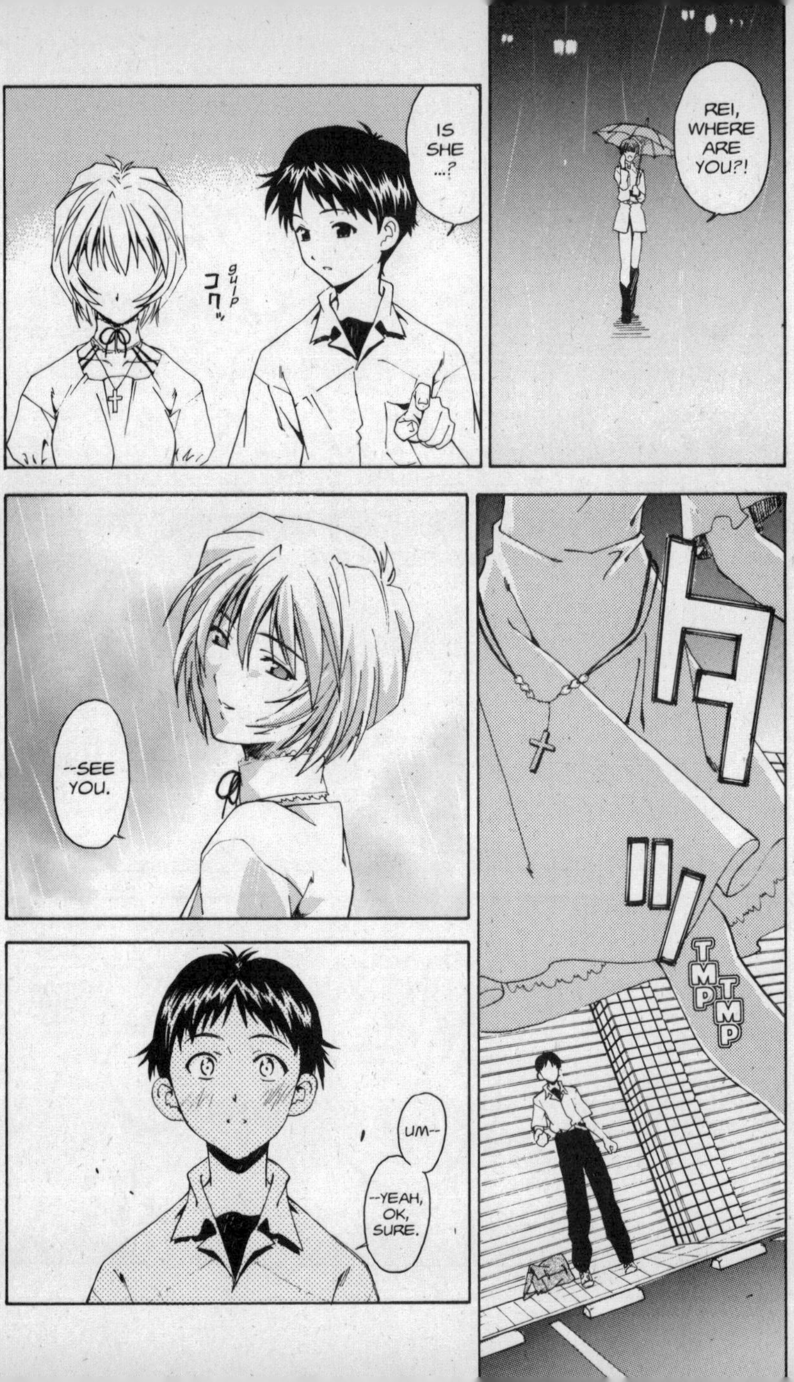
REI, WHERE ARE YOU?!
IS SHE ...?
gulp
TMP TMP
--SEE YOU.
UM--
--YEAH, OK, SURE.

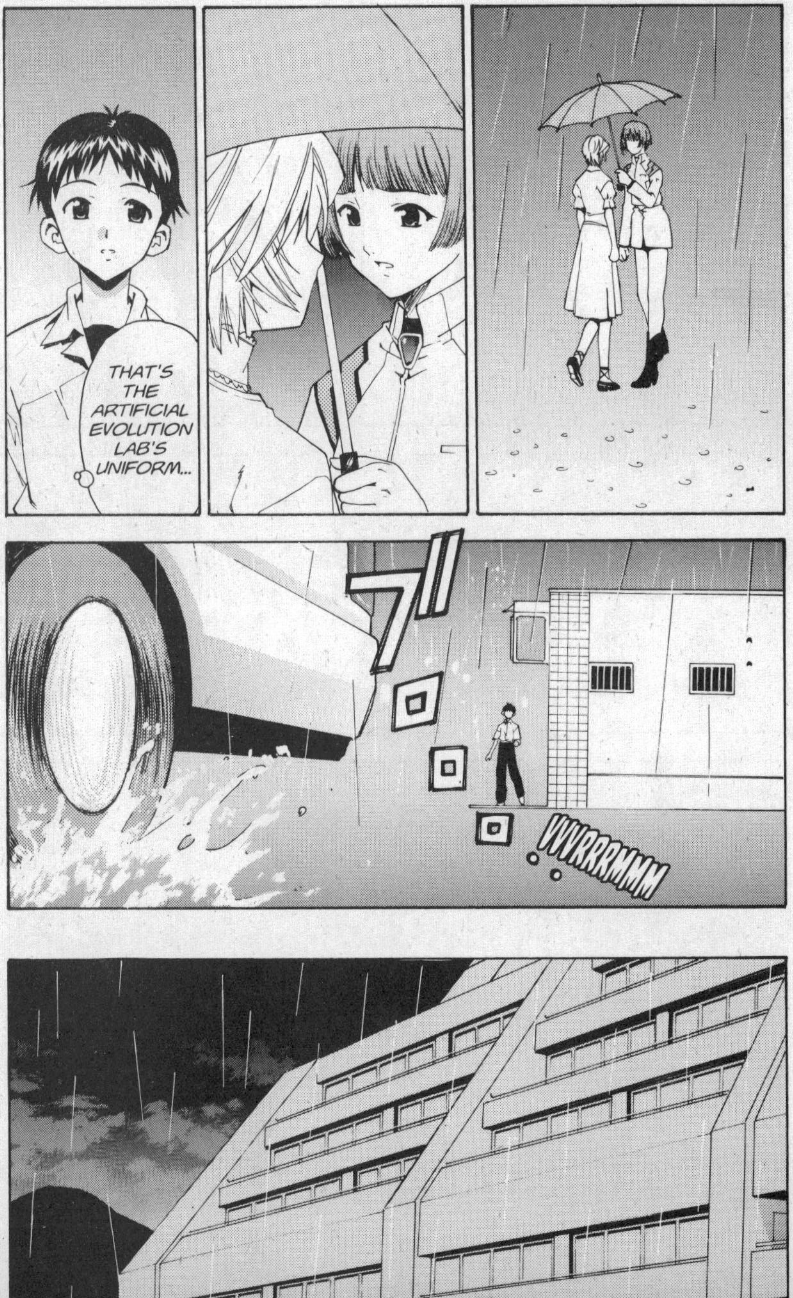
THAT'S THE ARTIFICIAL EVOLUTION LAB'S UNIFORM...
ブロロロ
VVVRRRMMM

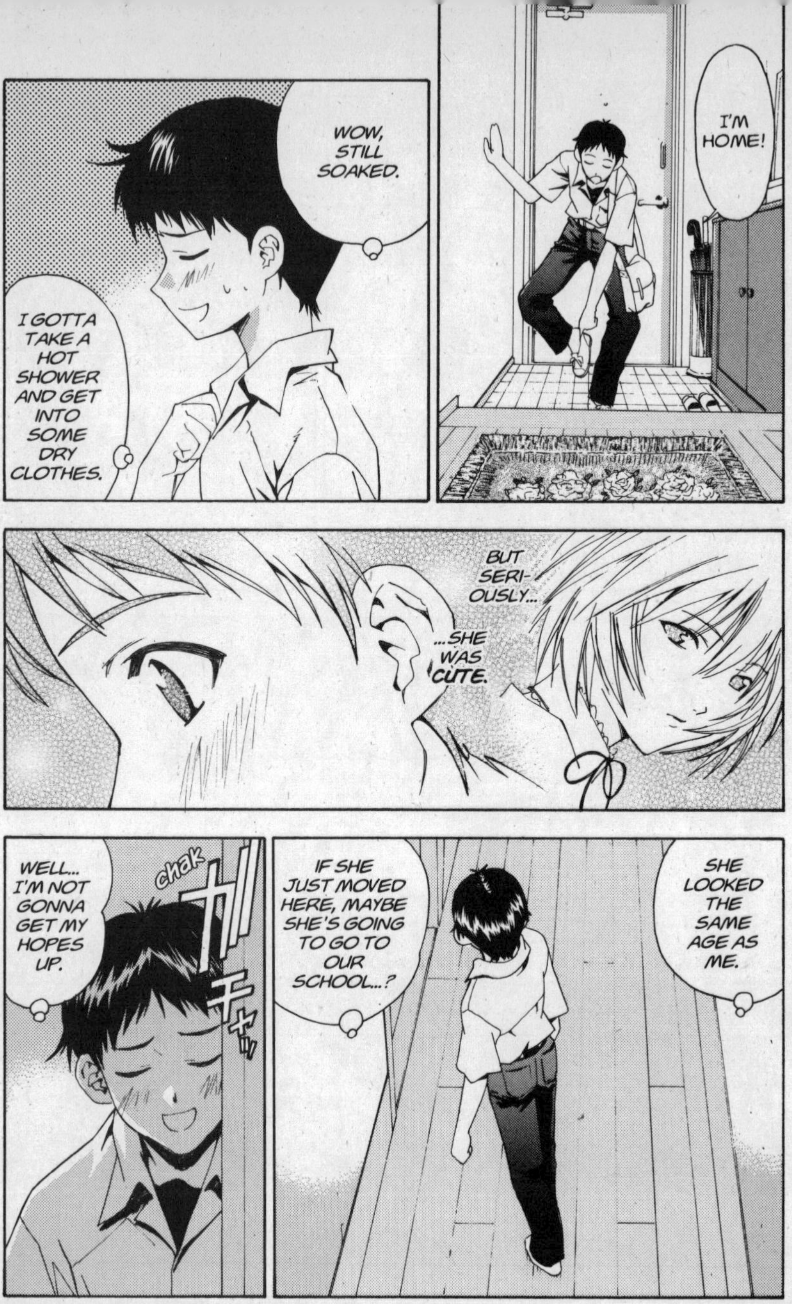
I'M HOME!
WOW, STILL SOAKED.
I GOTTA TAKE A HOT SHOWER AND GET INTO SOME DRY CLOTHES.
BUT SERI-OUSLY...
...SHE WAS CUTE.
SHE LOOKED THE SAME AGE AS ME.
IF SHE JUST MOVED HERE, MAYBE SHE'S GOING TO GO TO OUR SCHOOL...?
WELL... I'M NOT GONNA GET MY HOPES UP.
chak

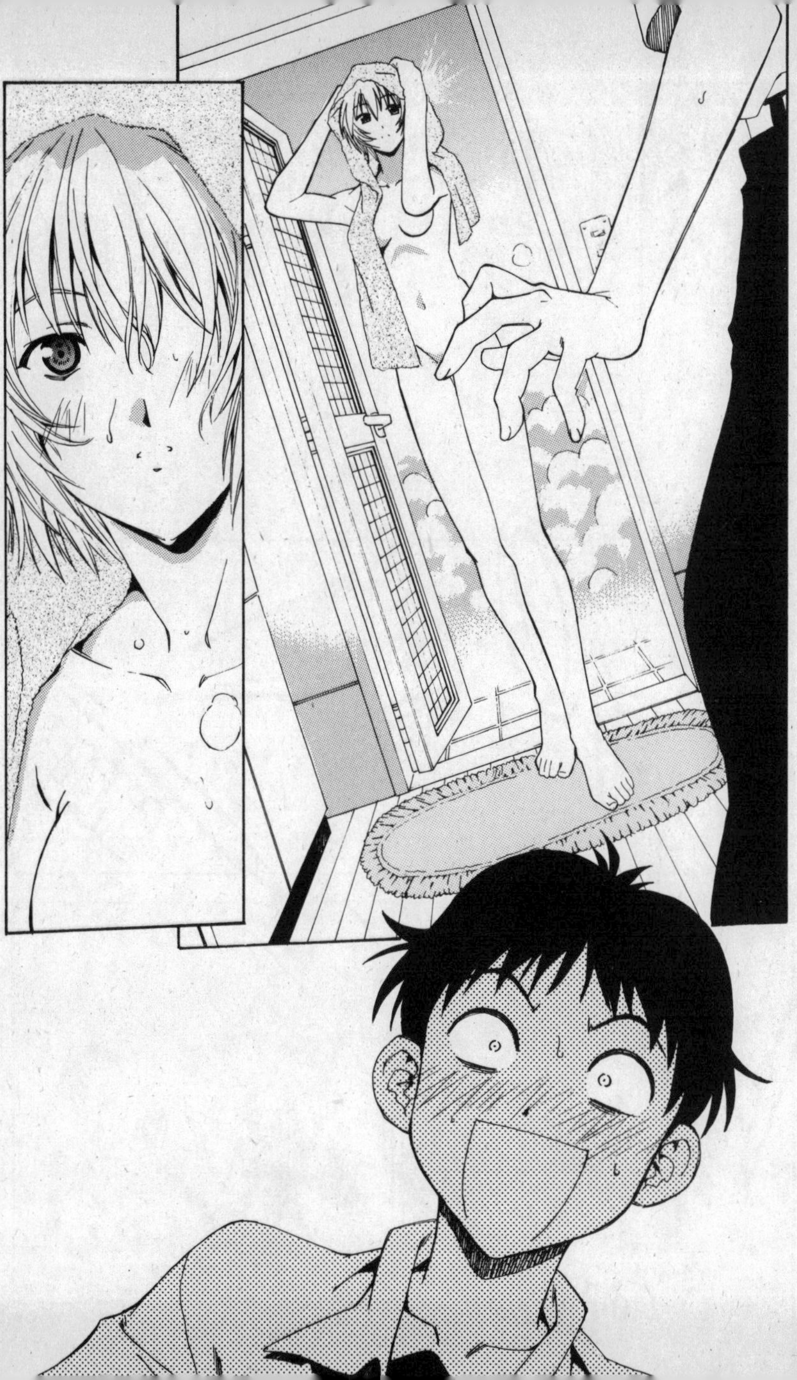

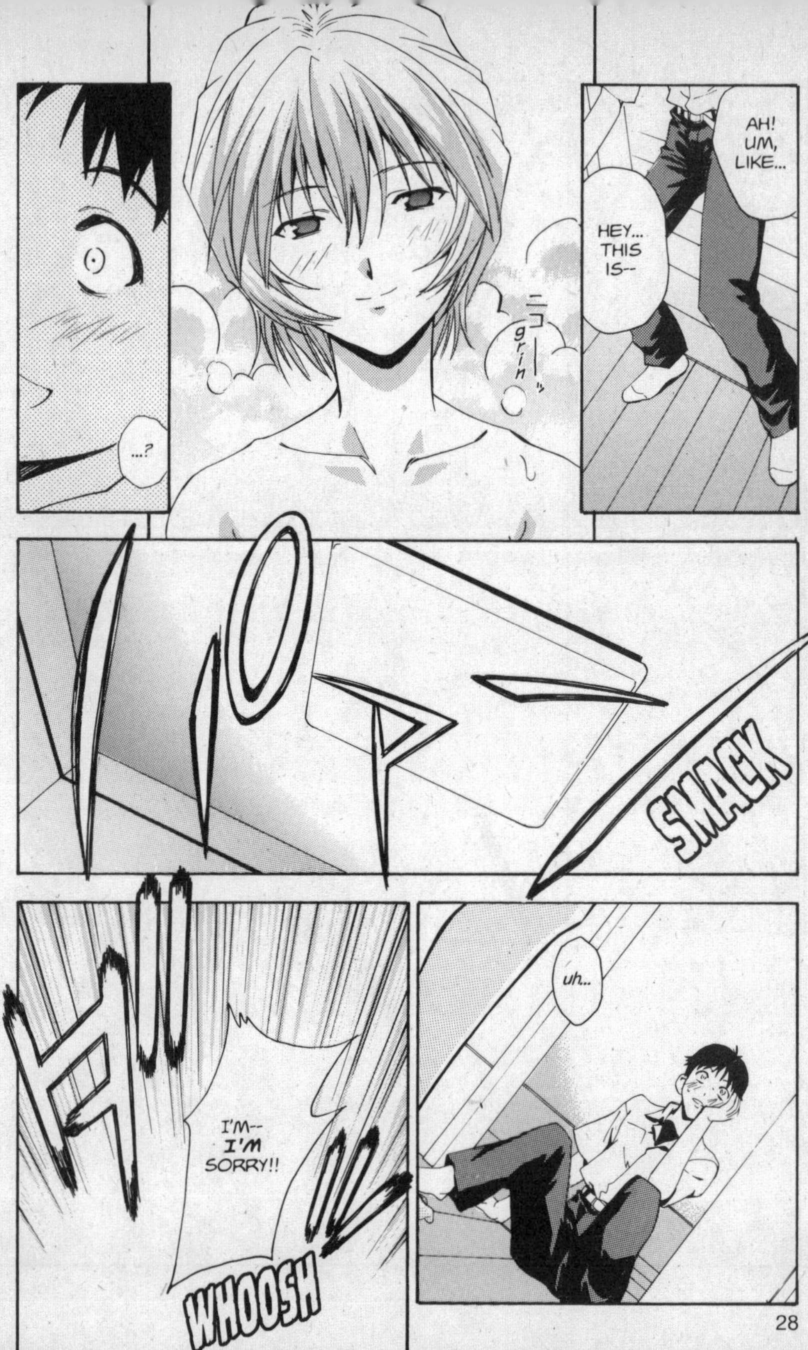
AH! UM, LIKE...
HEY... THIS IS--
grin
...?
SMACK
uh...
I'M-- I'M SORRY!!
WHOOSH

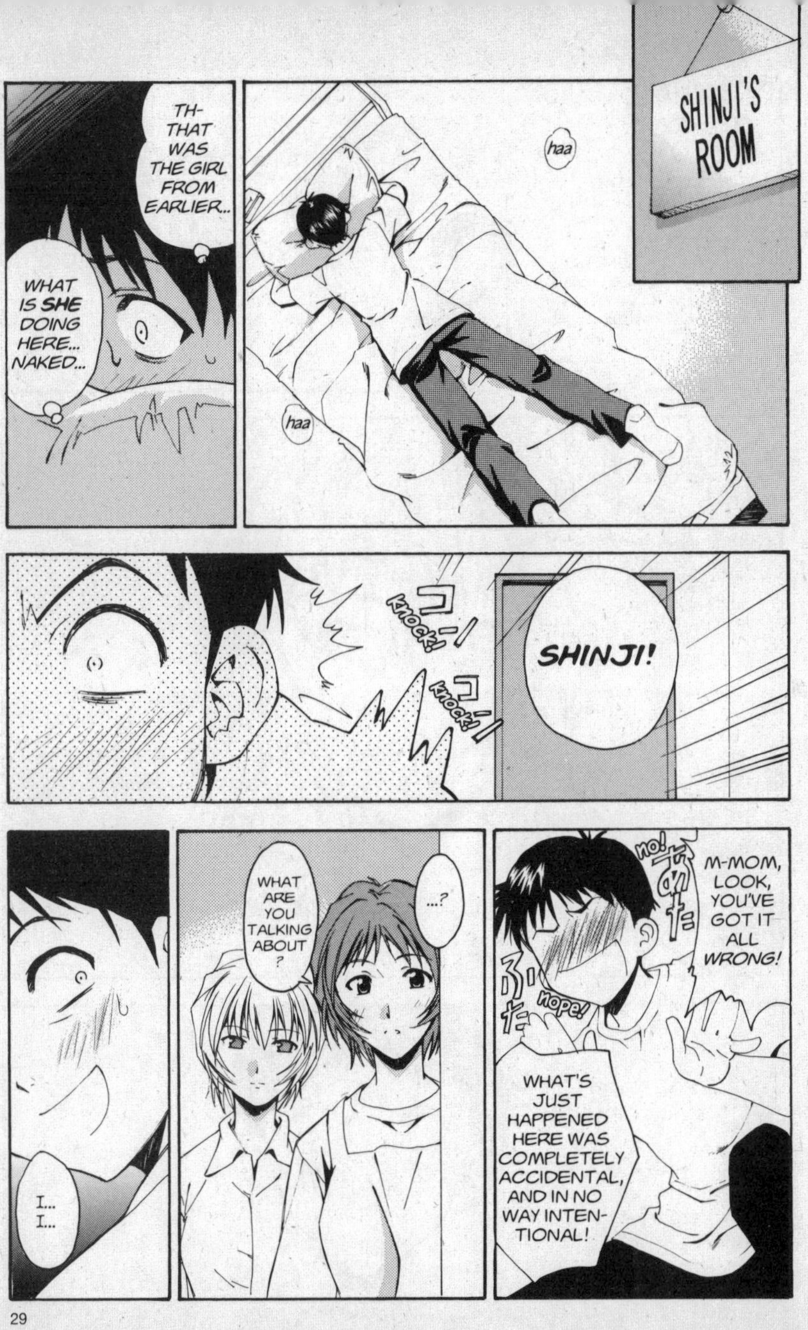
SHINJI'S ROOM
haa
haa
TH-THAT WAS THE GIRL FROM EARLIER...
WHAT IS SHE DOING HERE... NAKED...
SHINJI!
knock!
knock!
no!
M-MOM, LOOK, YOU'VE GOT IT ALL WRONG!
nope!
WHAT'S JUST HAPPENED HERE WAS COMPLETELY ACCIDENTAL, AND IN NO WAY INTEN-TIONAL!
...?
WHAT ARE YOU TALKING ABOUT ?
I... I...

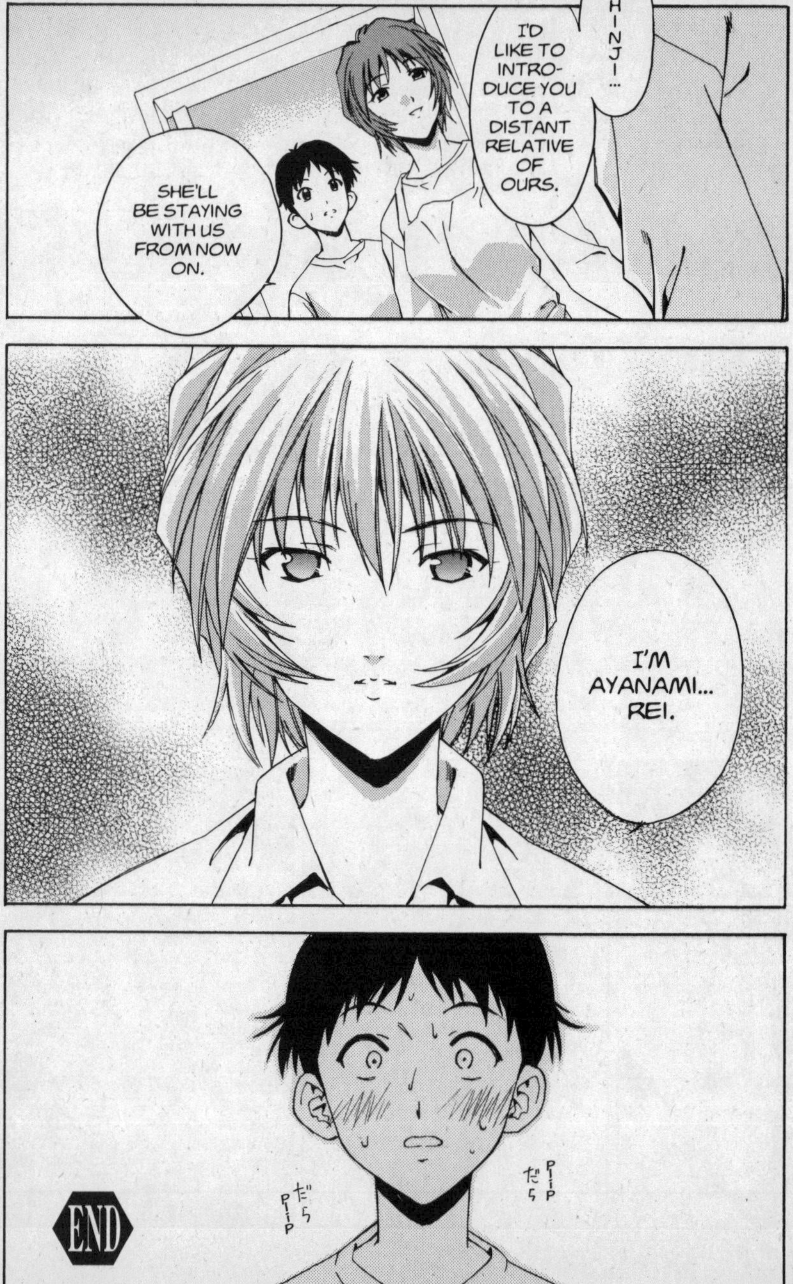
SHINJI...
I'D LIKE TO INTRODUCE YOU TO A DISTANT RELATIVE OF OURS.
SHE'LL BE STAYING WITH US FROM NOW ON.
I'M AYANAMI... REI.
だら PLIP
だら PLIP
END

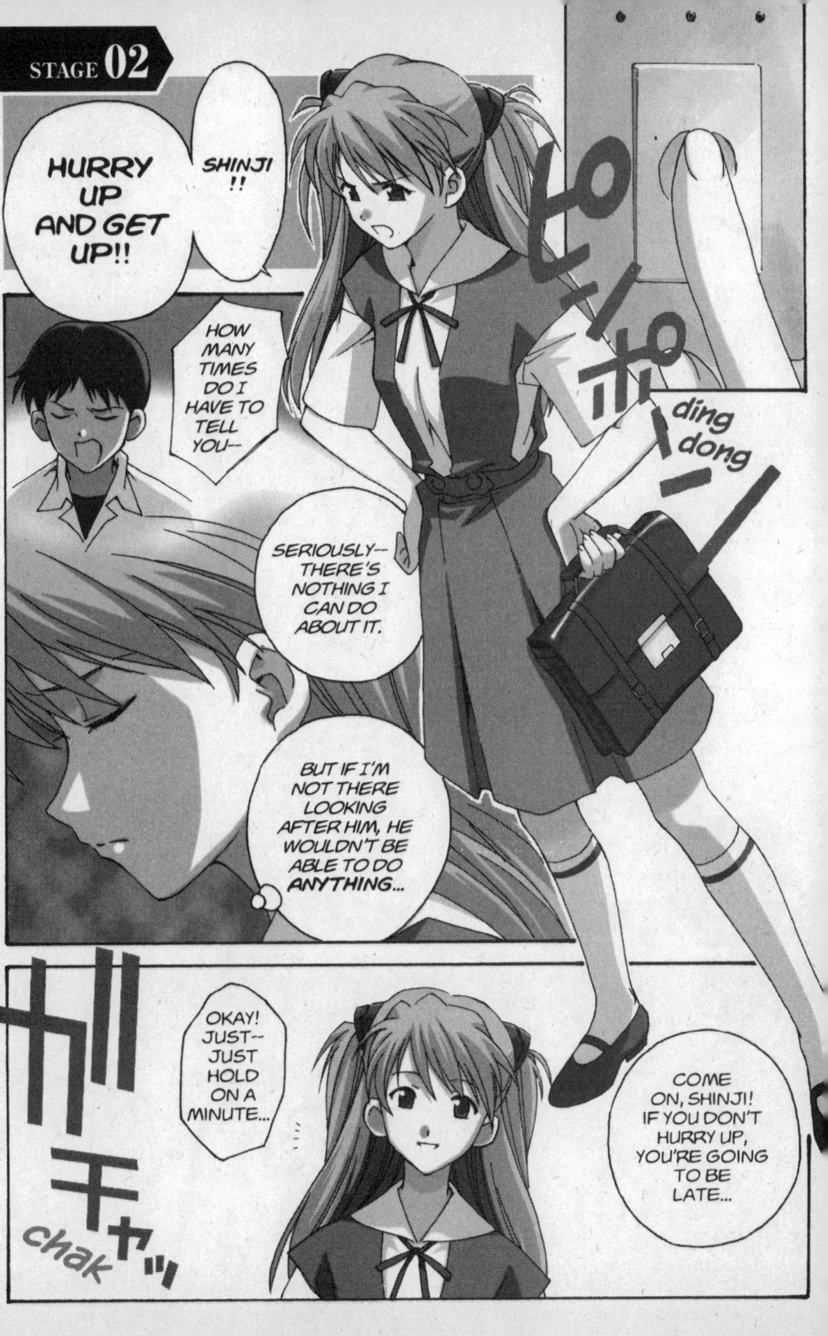
ding dong
SHINJI!!
HURRY UP AND GET UP!!
HOW MANY TIMES DO I HAVE TO TELL YOU--
SERIOUSLY-- THERE'S NOTHING I CAN DO ABOUT IT.
BUT IF I'M NOT THERE LOOKING AFTER HIM, HE WOULDN'T BE ABLE TO DO ANYTHING...
COME ON, SHINJI! IF YOU DON'T HURRY UP, YOU'RE GOING TO BE LATE...
OKAY! JUST-- JUST HOLD ON A MINUTE...
chak

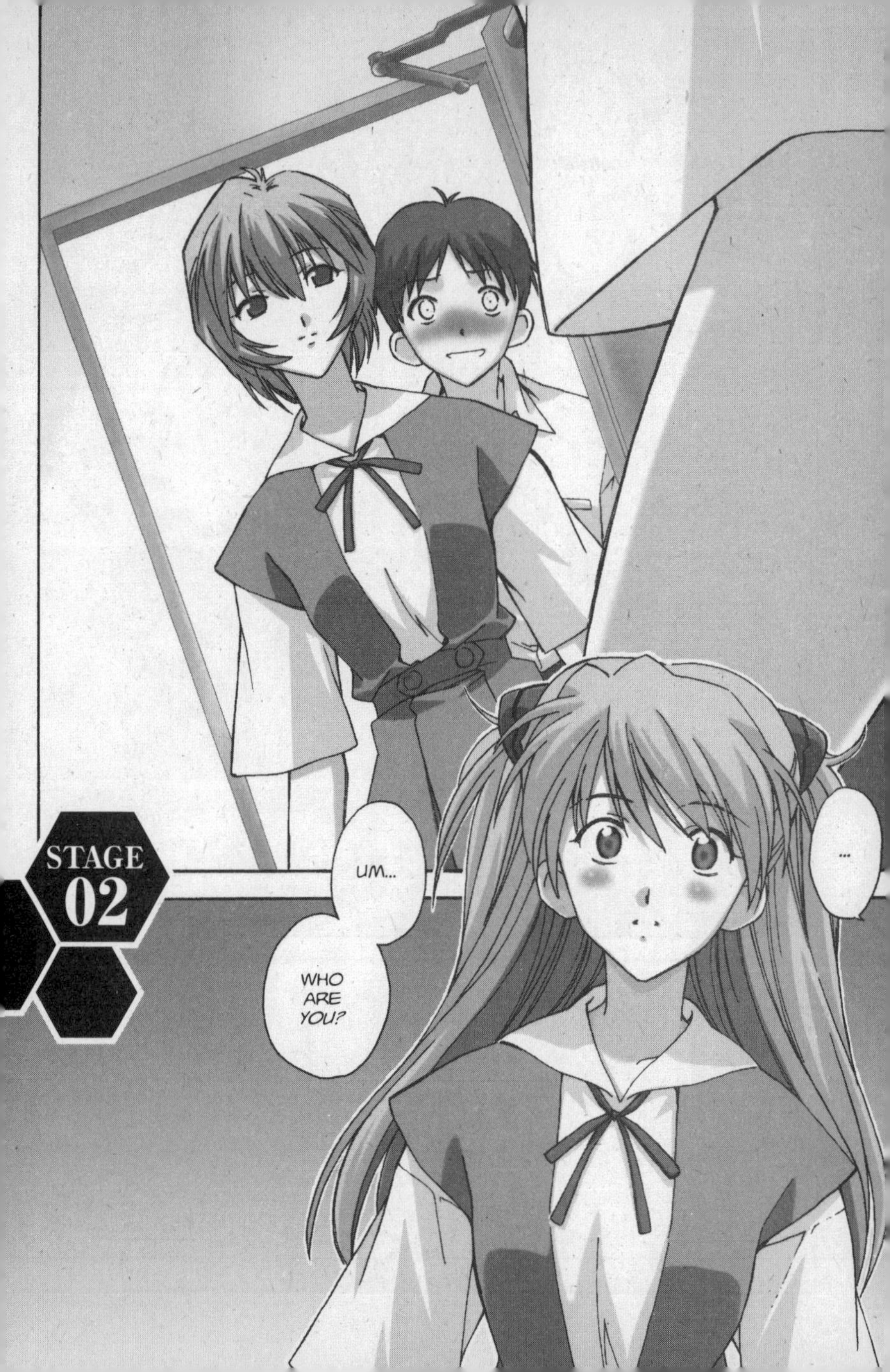
STAGE 02
...
UM...
WHO ARE YOU?

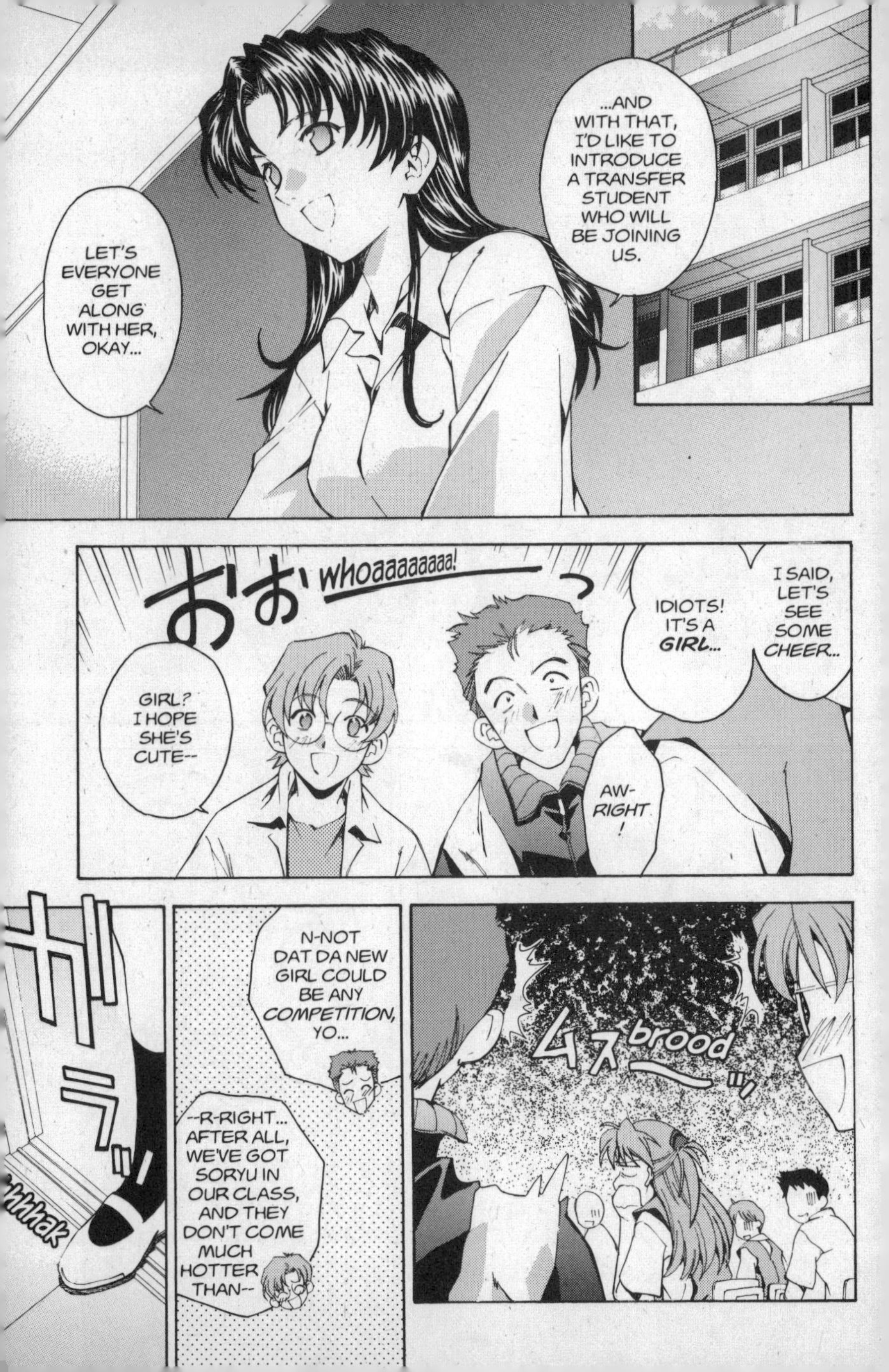
...AND WITH THAT, I'D LIKE TO INTRODUCE A TRANSFER STUDENT WHO WILL BE JOINING US.
LET'S EVERYONE GET ALONG WITH HER, OKAY...
I SAID, LET'S SEE SOME CHEER...
IDIOTS! IT'S A GIRL...
おお whoaaaaaaaa!
GIRL? I HOPE SHE'S CUTE--
AW-RIGHT!
ムスー brood
N-NOT DAT DA NEW GIRL COULD BE ANY COMPETITION, YO...
--R-RIGHT... AFTER ALL, WE'VE GOT SORYU IN OUR CLASS, AND THEY DON'T COME MUCH HOTTER THAN--
ガラッ
hhhak

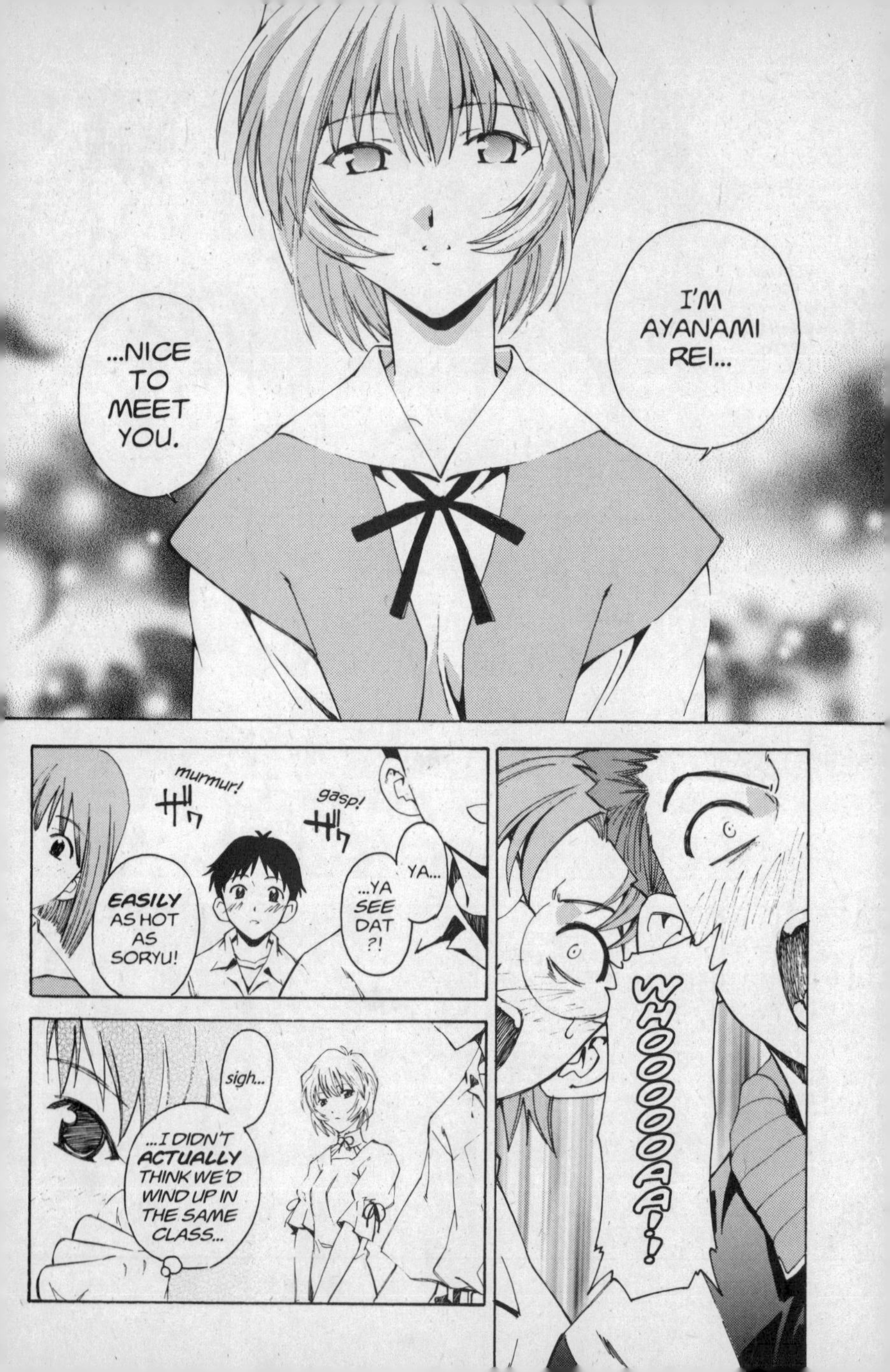
I'M AYANAMI REI...
...NICE TO MEET YOU.
WHOOOOOOAA!!
gasp!
murmur!
YA...
...YA SEE DAT?!
EASILY AS HOT AS SORYU!
sigh...
...I DIDN'T ACTUALLY THINK WE'D WIND UP IN THE SAME CLASS...

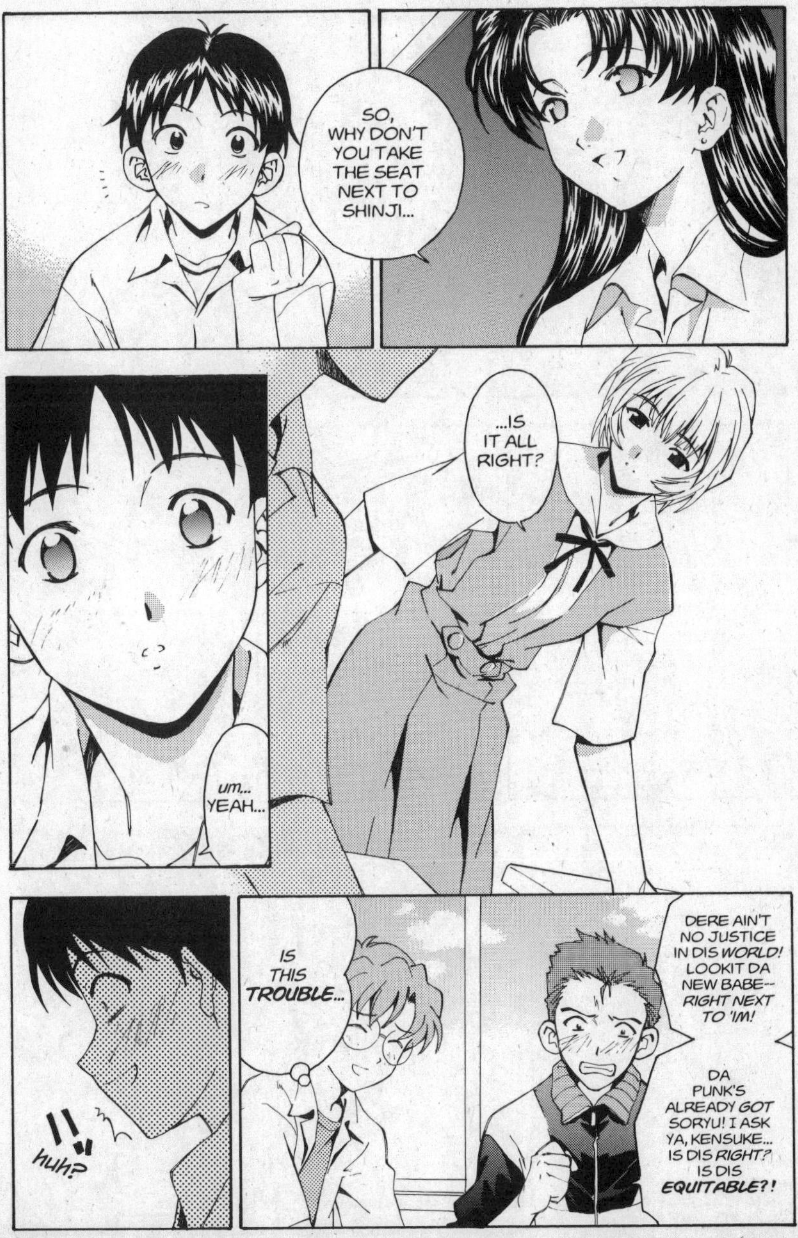
SO, WHY DON'T YOU TAKE THE SEAT NEXT TO SHINJI...
...IS IT ALL RIGHT?
um... YEAH...
DERE AIN'T NO JUSTICE IN DIS *WORLD!* LOOKIT DA NEW BABE-- *RIGHT NEXT TO 'IM!*
DA PUNK'S ALREADY *GOT* SORYU! I ASK YA, KENSUKE... IS DIS *RIGHT?* IS DIS ***EQUITABLE?!***
IS THIS ***TROUBLE...***
!!
huh?

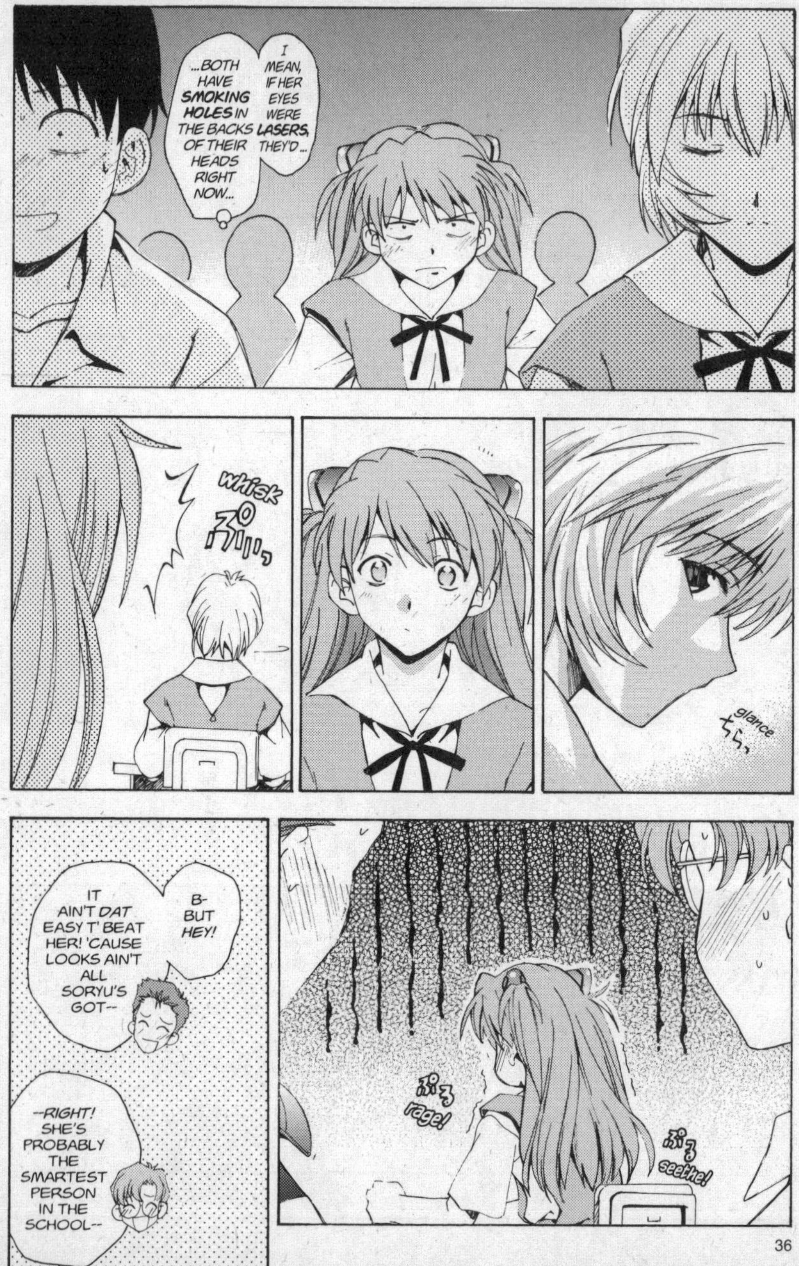
I MEAN, IF HER EYES WERE LASERS, THEY'D...
...BOTH HAVE SMOKING HOLES IN THE BACKS OF THEIR HEADS RIGHT NOW...
glance
whisk
ぷる
rage!
ぷる
seethe!
B- BUT HEY!
IT AIN'T DAT EASY T' BEAT HER! 'CAUSE LOOKS AIN'T ALL SORYU'S GOT--
--RIGHT! SHE'S PROBABLY THE SMARTEST PERSON IN THE SCHOOL--

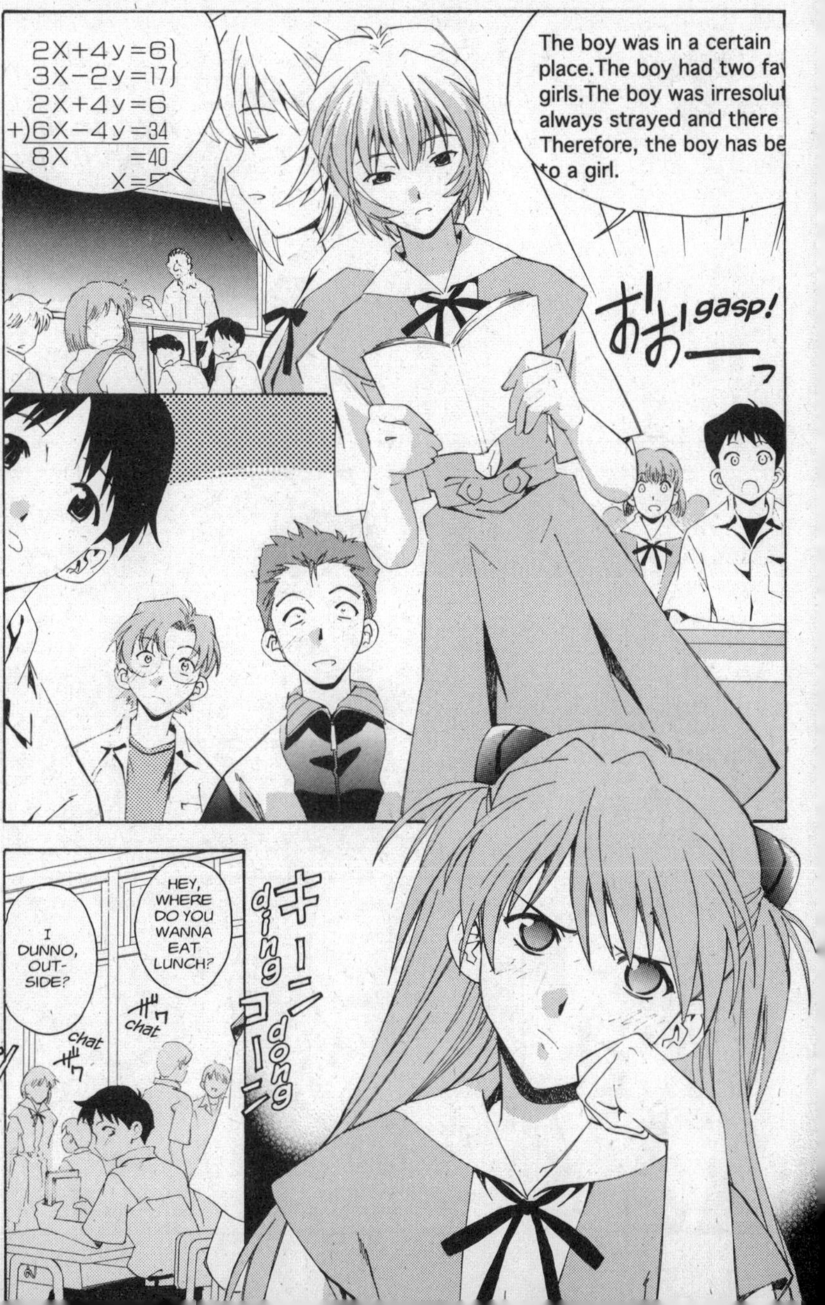

The boy was in a certain place.The boy had two fa girls.The boy was irresolut always strayed and there Therefore, the boy has be to a girl.
おおーっ gasp!
2X+4y=6
3X−2y=17
2X+4y=6
+) 6X−4y=34
8X =40
X=5
キーンコーン ding dong
HEY, WHERE DO YOU WANNA EAT LUNCH?
I DUNNO, OUT-SIDE?
ザワ chat
ザワ chat
カーン ding dong

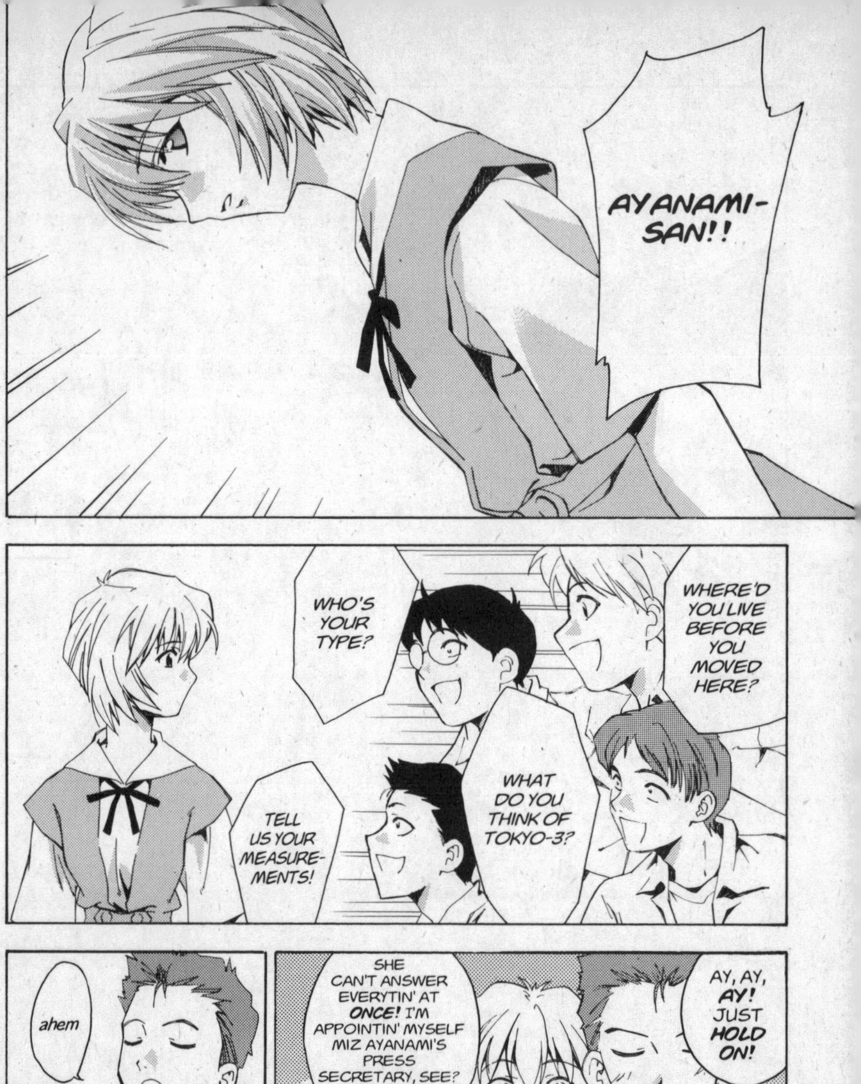
AYANAMI-SAN!!
WHERE'D YOU LIVE BEFORE YOU MOVED HERE?
WHO'S YOUR TYPE?
WHAT DO YOU THINK OF TOKYO-3?
TELL US YOUR MEASUREMENTS!
AY, AY, **AY!** JUST **HOLD ON!**
SHE CAN'T ANSWER EVERYTIN' AT **ONCE!** I'M APPOINTIN' MYSELF MIZ AYANAMI'S PRESS SECRETARY, SEE? WE'LL TAKE **TOINS!**
RIGHT. FOIST QUESTION--
ahem
koff

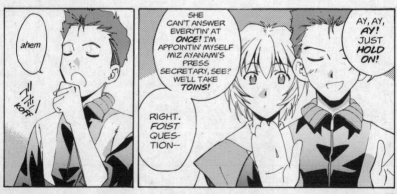

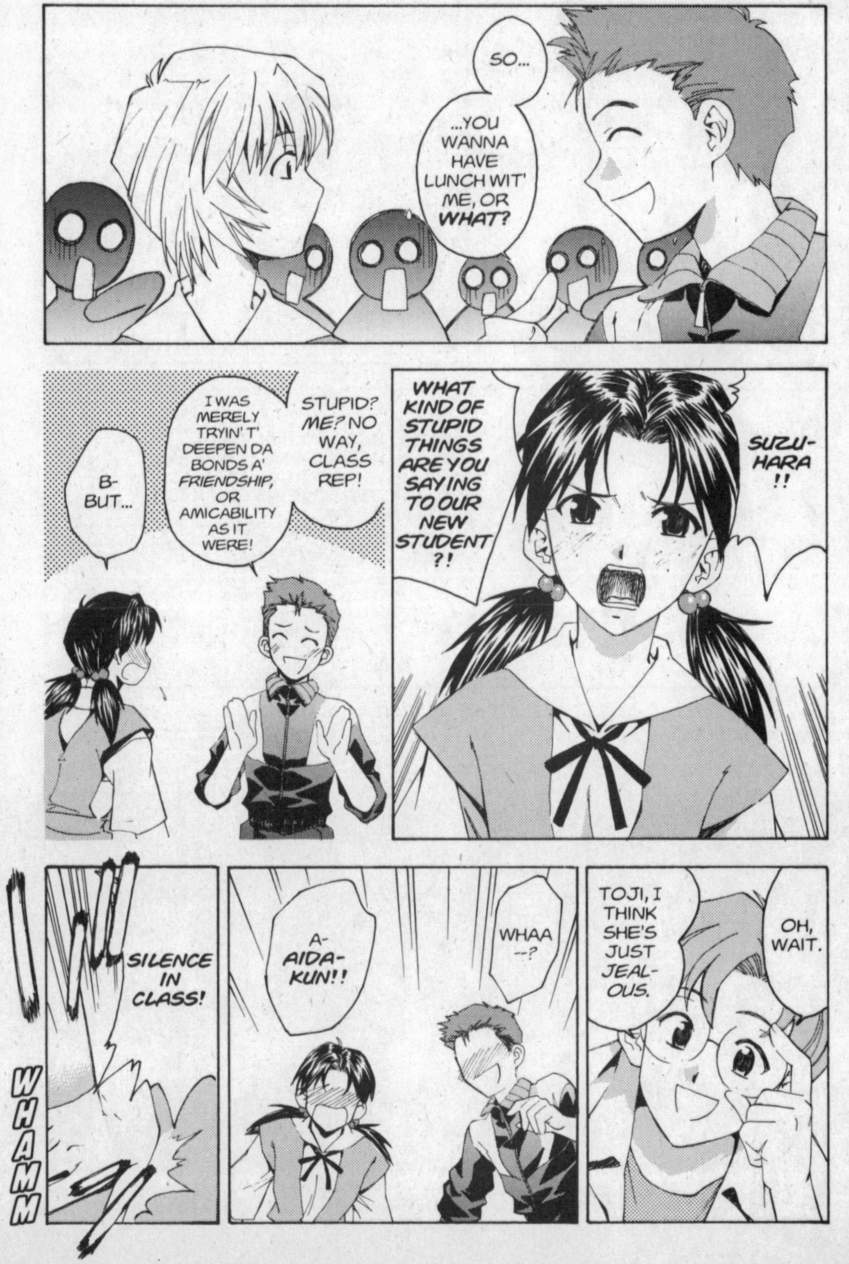
SO...
...YOU WANNA HAVE LUNCH WIT' ME, OR WHAT?
SUZU-HARA!!
WHAT KIND OF STUPID THINGS ARE YOU SAYING TO OUR NEW STUDENT?!
STUPID? ME? NO WAY, CLASS REP!
I WAS MERELY TRYIN' T' DEEPEN DA BONDS A' FRIENDSHIP, OR AMICABILITY AS IT WERE!
B-BUT...
OH, WAIT.
TOJI, I THINK SHE'S JUST JEAL-OUS.
WHAA--?
A-AIDA-KUN!!
SILENCE IN CLASS!
WHAMM

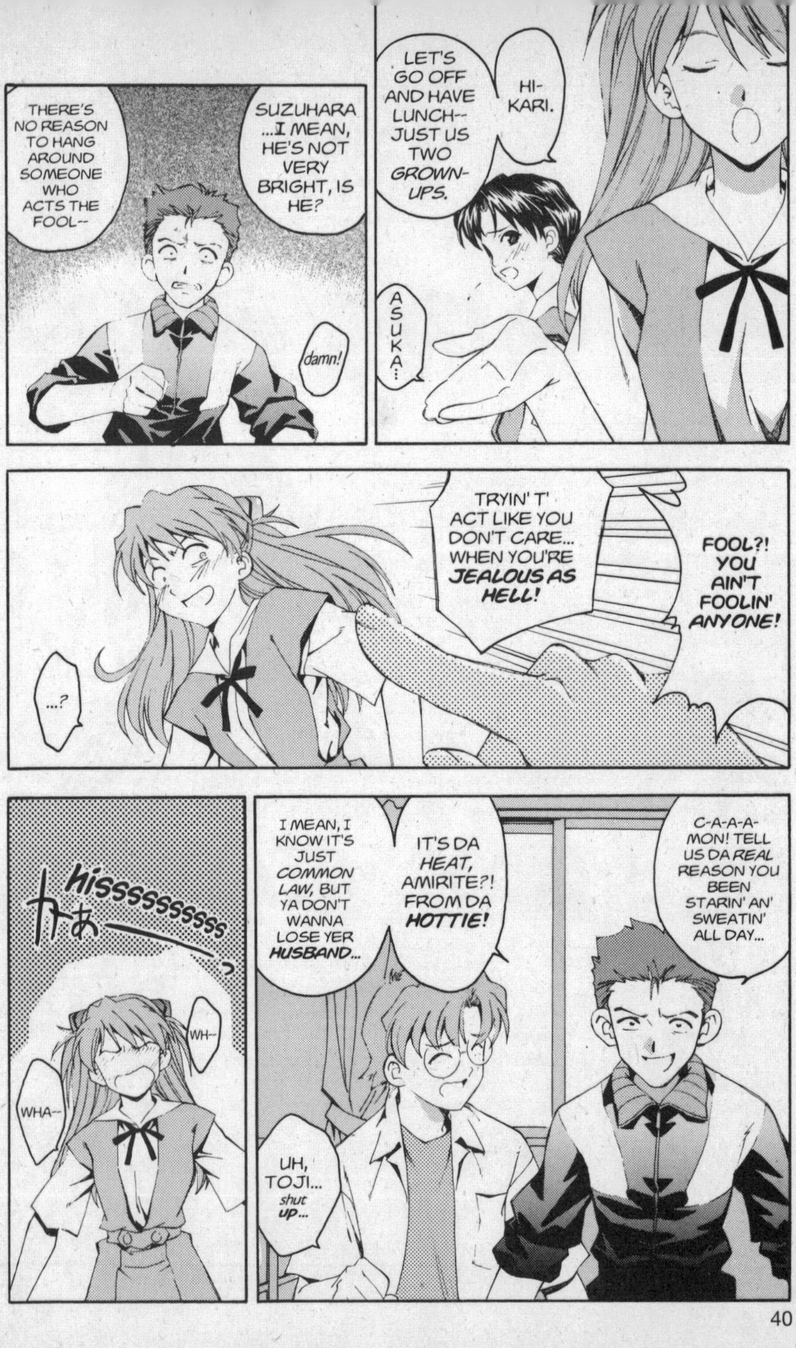
HI-KARI.
LET'S GO OFF AND HAVE LUNCH-- JUST US TWO GROWN-UPS.
ASUKA...
SUZUHARA ...I MEAN, HE'S NOT VERY BRIGHT, IS HE?
THERE'S NO REASON TO HANG AROUND SOMEONE WHO ACTS THE FOOL--
damn!
FOOL?! YOU AIN'T FOOLIN' ANYONE!
TRYIN' T' ACT LIKE YOU DON'T CARE... WHEN YOU'RE JEALOUS AS HELL!
...?
C-A-A-A-MON! TELL US DA REAL REASON YOU BEEN STARIN' AN' SWEATIN' ALL DAY...
IT'S DA HEAT, AMIRITE?! FROM DA HOTTIE!
I MEAN, I KNOW IT'S JUST COMMON LAW, BUT YA DON'T WANNA LOSE YER HUSBAND...
UH, TOJI... shut up...
kissssssssss
かあ——
WH--
WHA--

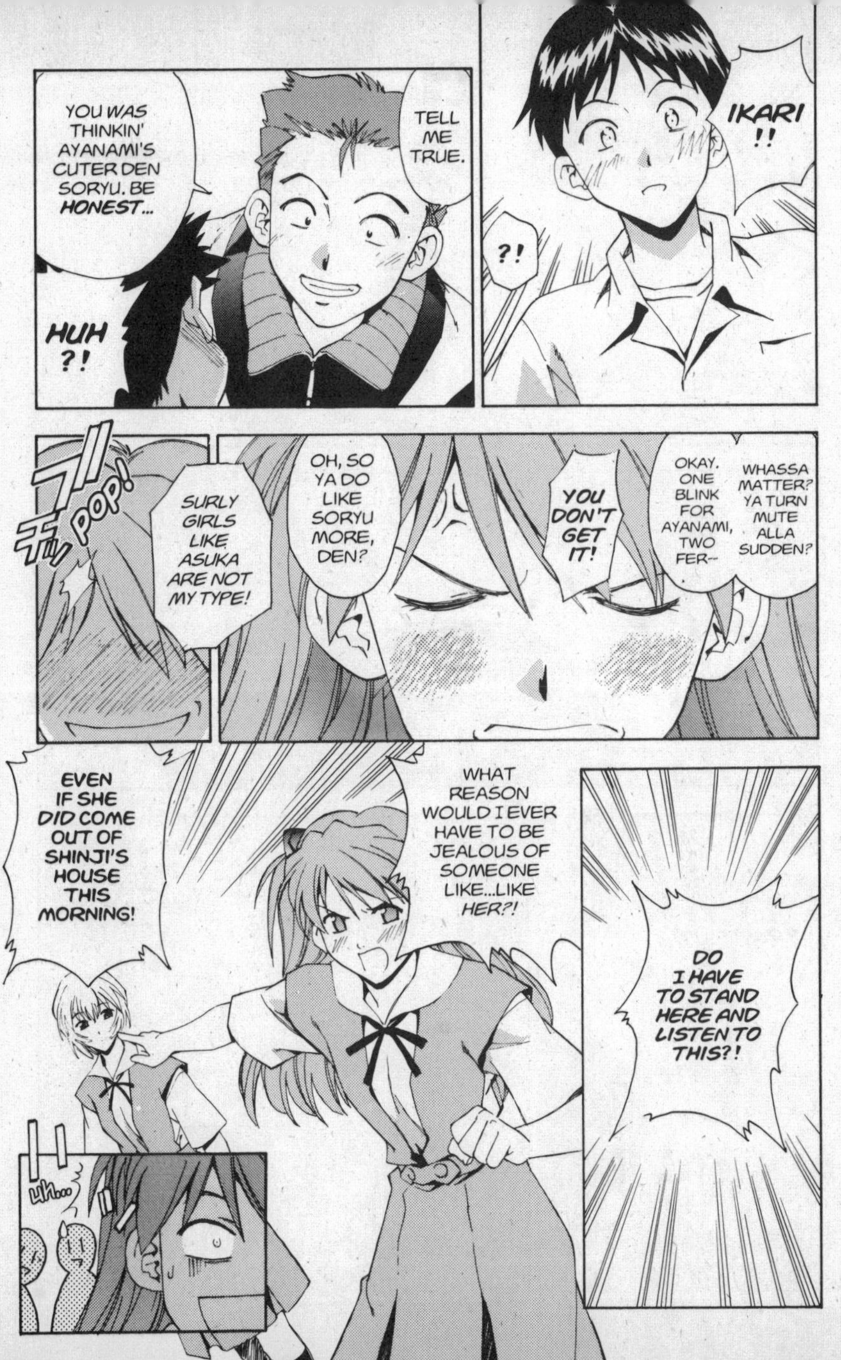
IKARI !!
?!
TELL ME TRUE.
YOU WAS THINKIN' AYANAMI'S CUTER DEN SORYU. BE HONEST...
HUH ?!
WHASSA MATTER? YA TURN MUTE ALLA SUDDEN?
OKAY. ONE BLINK FOR AYANAMI, TWO FER--
YOU DON'T GET IT!
OH, SO YA DO LIKE SORYU MORE, DEN?
POP!
SURLY GIRLS LIKE ASUKA ARE NOT MY TYPE!
DO I HAVE TO STAND HERE AND LISTEN TO THIS?!
WHAT REASON WOULD I EVER HAVE TO BE JEALOUS OF SOMEONE LIKE...LIKE HER?!
EVEN IF SHE DID COME OUT OF SHINJI'S HOUSE THIS MORNING!
uh...

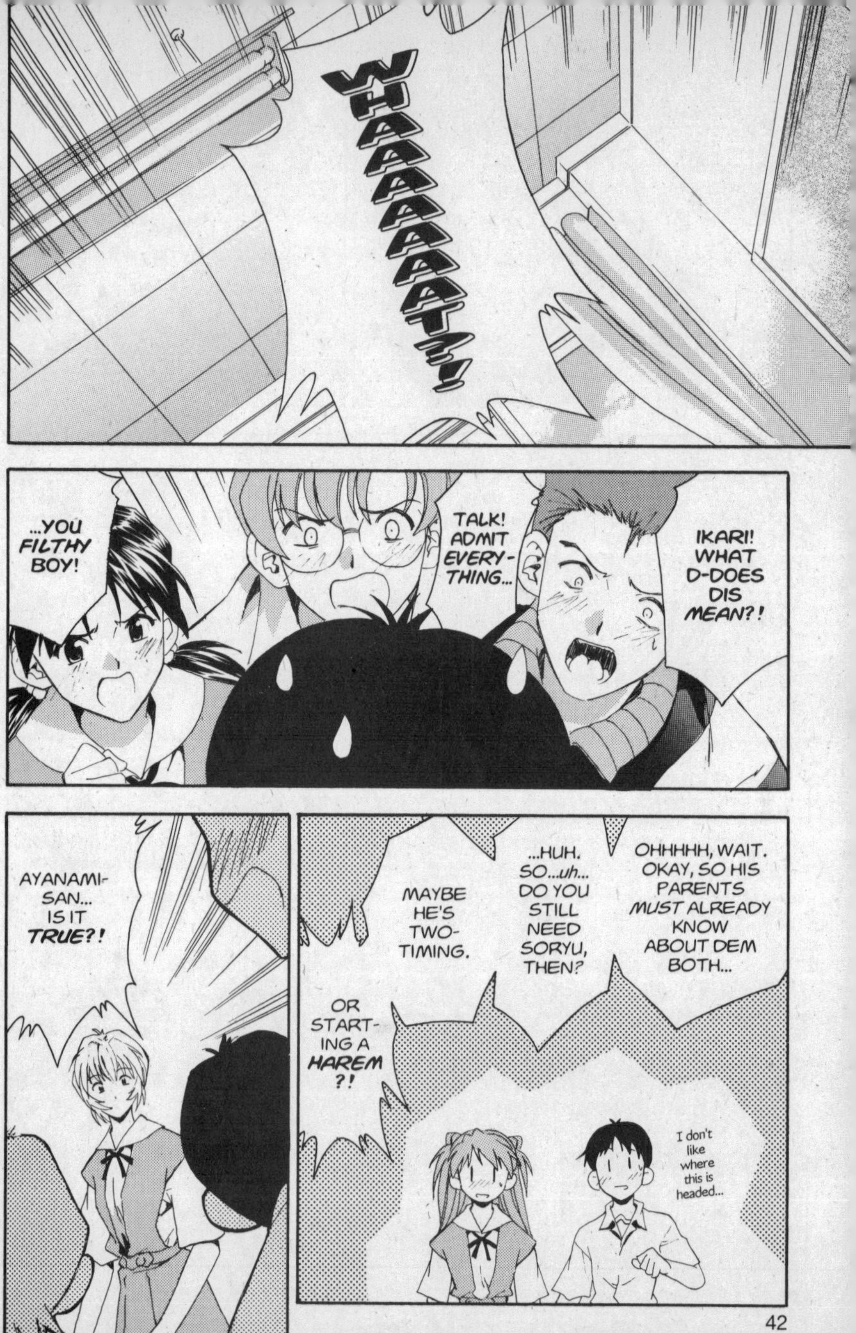
WHAAAAAAAAAT?!
IKARI! WHAT D-DOES DIS MEAN?!
TALK! ADMIT EVERY-THING...
...YOU FILTHY BOY!
OHHHHH, WAIT. OKAY, SO HIS PARENTS MUST ALREADY KNOW ABOUT DEM BOTH...
...HUH. SO...uh... DO YOU STILL NEED SORYU, THEN?
MAYBE HE'S TWO-TIMING.
OR STARTING A HAREM?!
I don't like where this is headed...
AYANAMI-SAN... IS IT TRUE?!

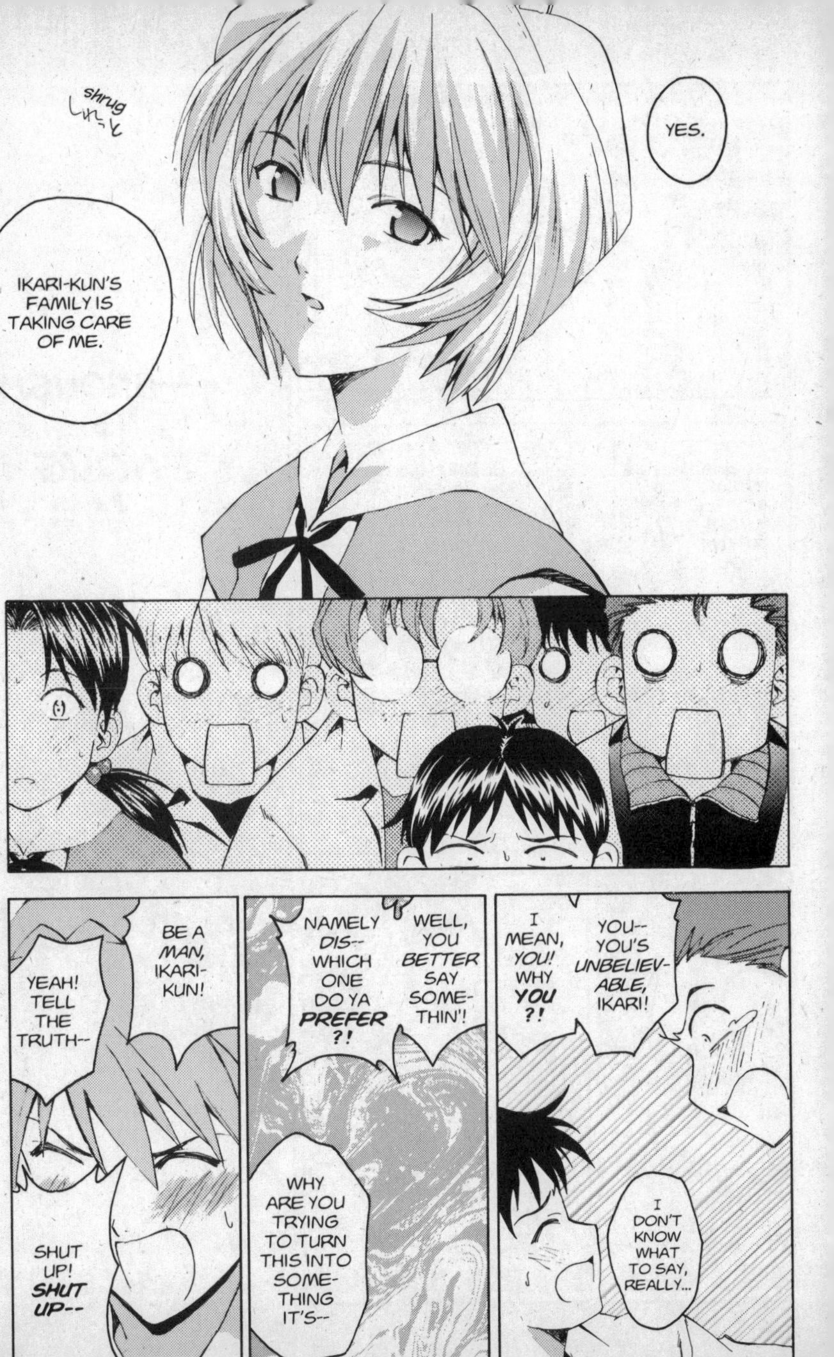
YES.
shrug
しれっと
IKARI-KUN'S FAMILY IS TAKING CARE OF ME.
YOU-- YOU'S *UNBELIEVABLE*, IKARI!
I MEAN, *YOU!* WHY ***YOU*** ?!
I DON'T KNOW WHAT TO SAY, REALLY...
WELL, YOU *BETTER* SAY SOMETHIN'!
NAMELY *DIS*-- WHICH ONE DO YA ***PREFER*** ?!
WHY ARE YOU TRYING TO TURN THIS INTO SOMETHING IT'S--
BE A *MAN*, IKARI-KUN!
YEAH! TELL THE TRUTH--
SHUT UP! ***SHUT UP--***

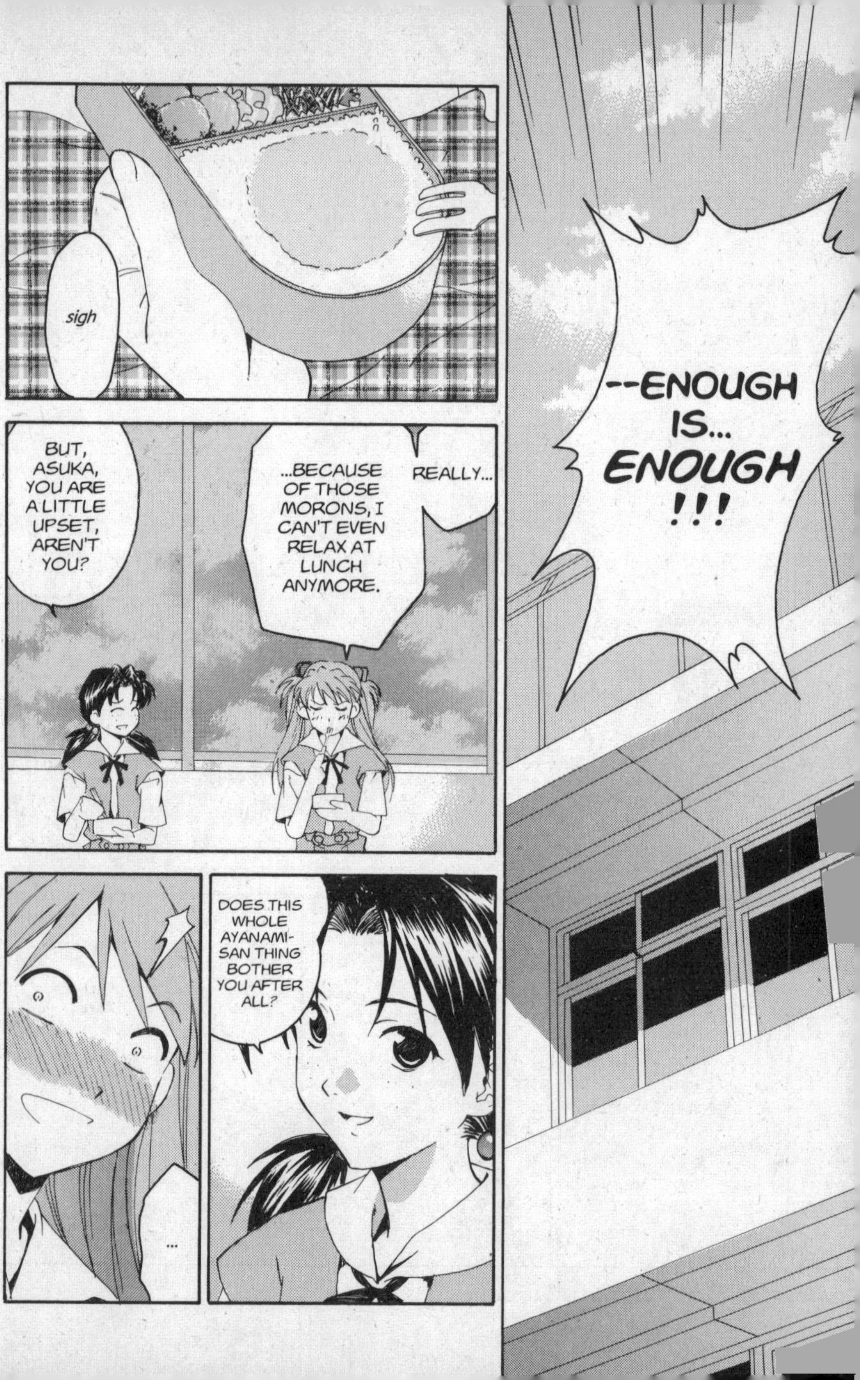
--ENOUGH IS... ENOUGH!!!
sigh
REALLY...
...BECAUSE OF THOSE MORONS, I CAN'T EVEN RELAX AT LUNCH ANYMORE.
BUT, ASUKA, YOU ARE A LITTLE UPSET, AREN'T YOU?
DOES THIS WHOLE AYANAMI-SAN THING BOTHER YOU AFTER ALL?
...

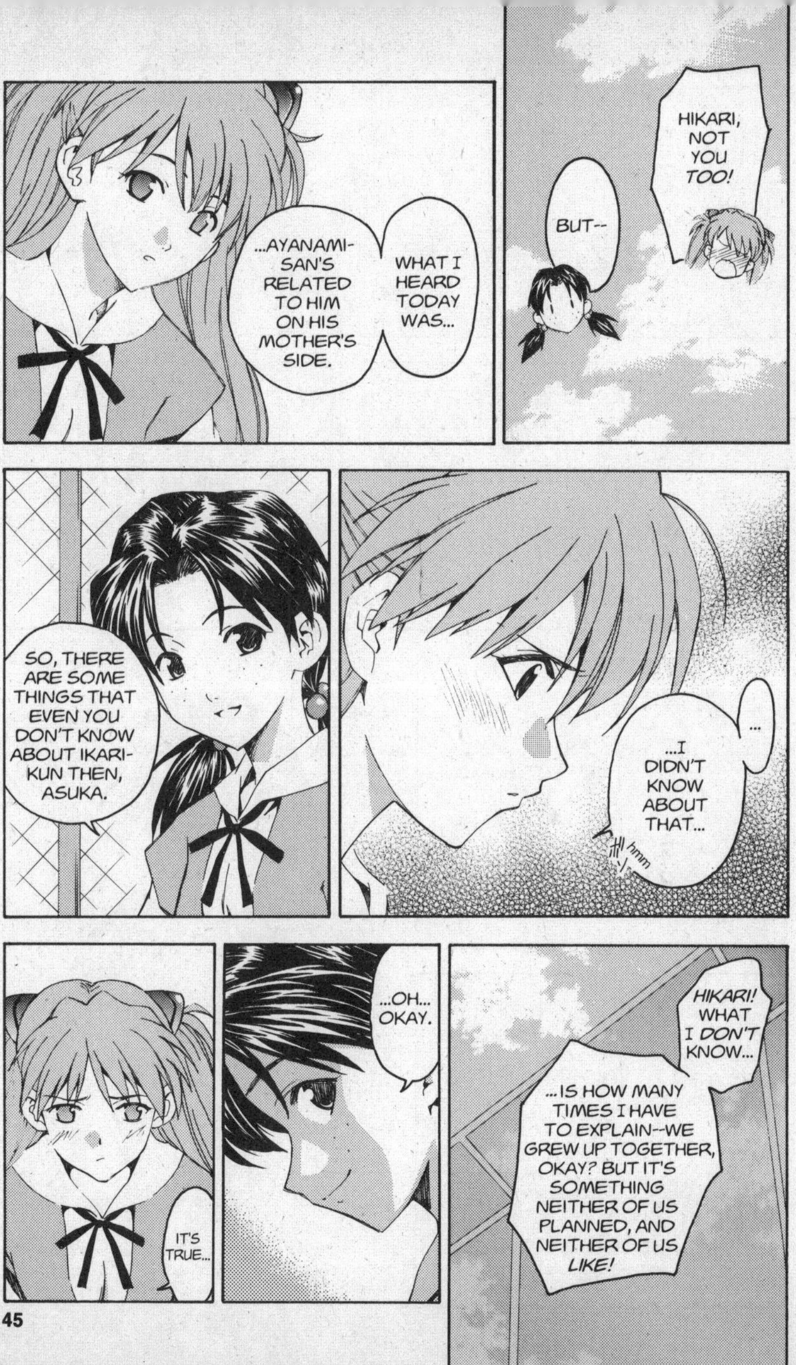
HIKARI, NOT YOU TOO!
BUT--
WHAT I HEARD TODAY WAS...
...AYANAMI-SAN'S RELATED TO HIM ON HIS MOTHER'S SIDE.
...
...I DIDN'T KNOW ABOUT THAT...
hmm
SO, THERE ARE SOME THINGS THAT EVEN YOU DON'T KNOW ABOUT IKARI-KUN THEN, ASUKA.
HIKARI! WHAT I DON'T KNOW...
...IS HOW MANY TIMES I HAVE TO EXPLAIN--WE GREW UP TOGETHER, OKAY? BUT IT'S SOMETHING NEITHER OF US PLANNED, AND NEITHER OF US LIKE!
...OH... OKAY.
IT'S TRUE...

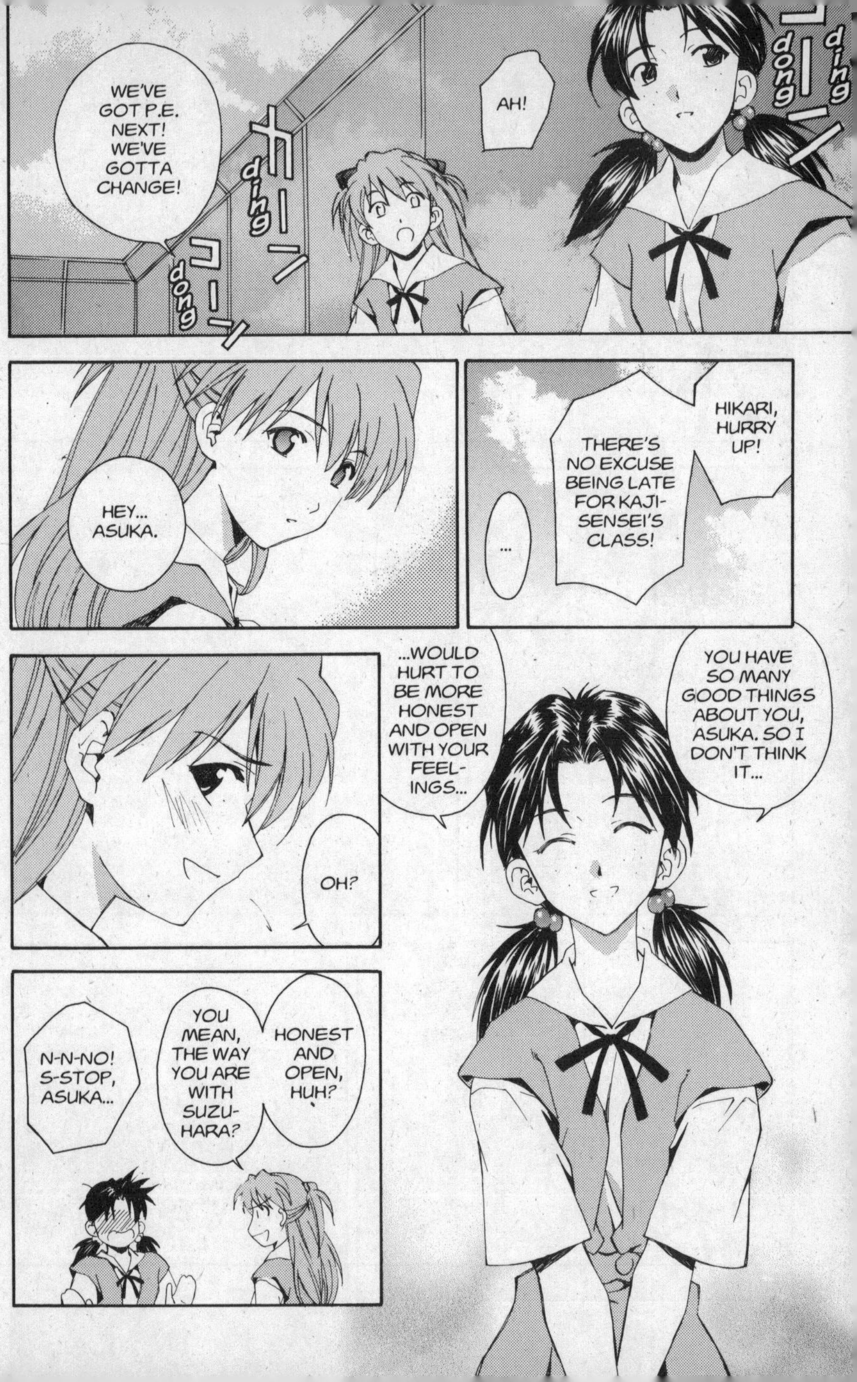
ding dong
AH!
WE'VE GOT P.E. NEXT! WE'VE GOTTA CHANGE!
ding dong
HIKARI, HURRY UP!
THERE'S NO EXCUSE BEING LATE FOR KAJI-SENSEI'S CLASS!
...
HEY... ASUKA.
YOU HAVE SO MANY GOOD THINGS ABOUT YOU, ASUKA. SO I DON'T THINK IT...
...WOULD HURT TO BE MORE HONEST AND OPEN WITH YOUR FEEL-INGS...
OH?
HONEST AND OPEN, HUH?
YOU MEAN, THE WAY YOU ARE WITH SUZU-HARA?
N-N-NO! S-STOP, ASUKA...

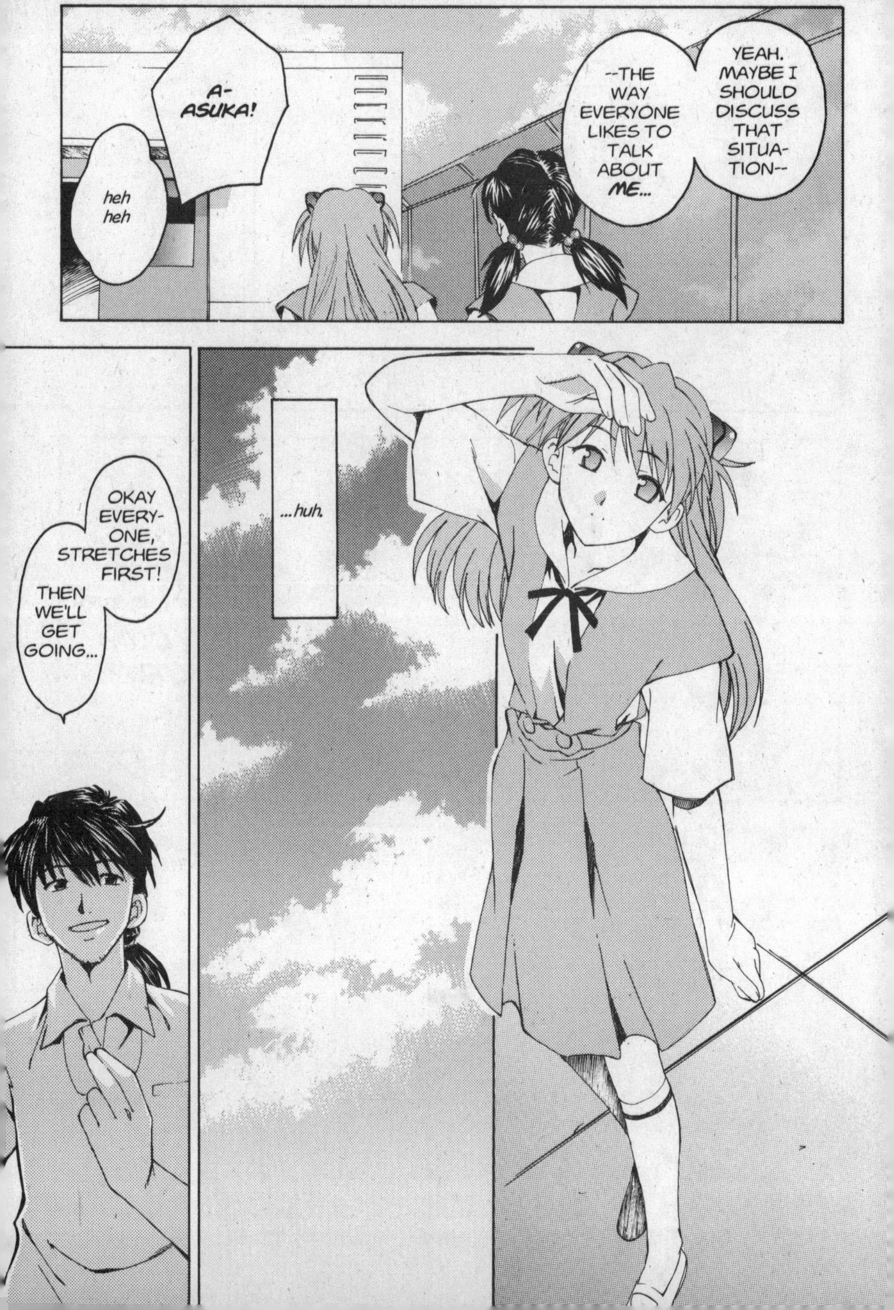
YEAH. MAYBE I SHOULD DISCUSS THAT SITUATION--
--THE WAY EVERYONE LIKES TO TALK ABOUT ME...
A-ASUKA!
heh heh
...huh.
OKAY EVERYONE, STRETCHES FIRST!
THEN WE'LL GET GOING...

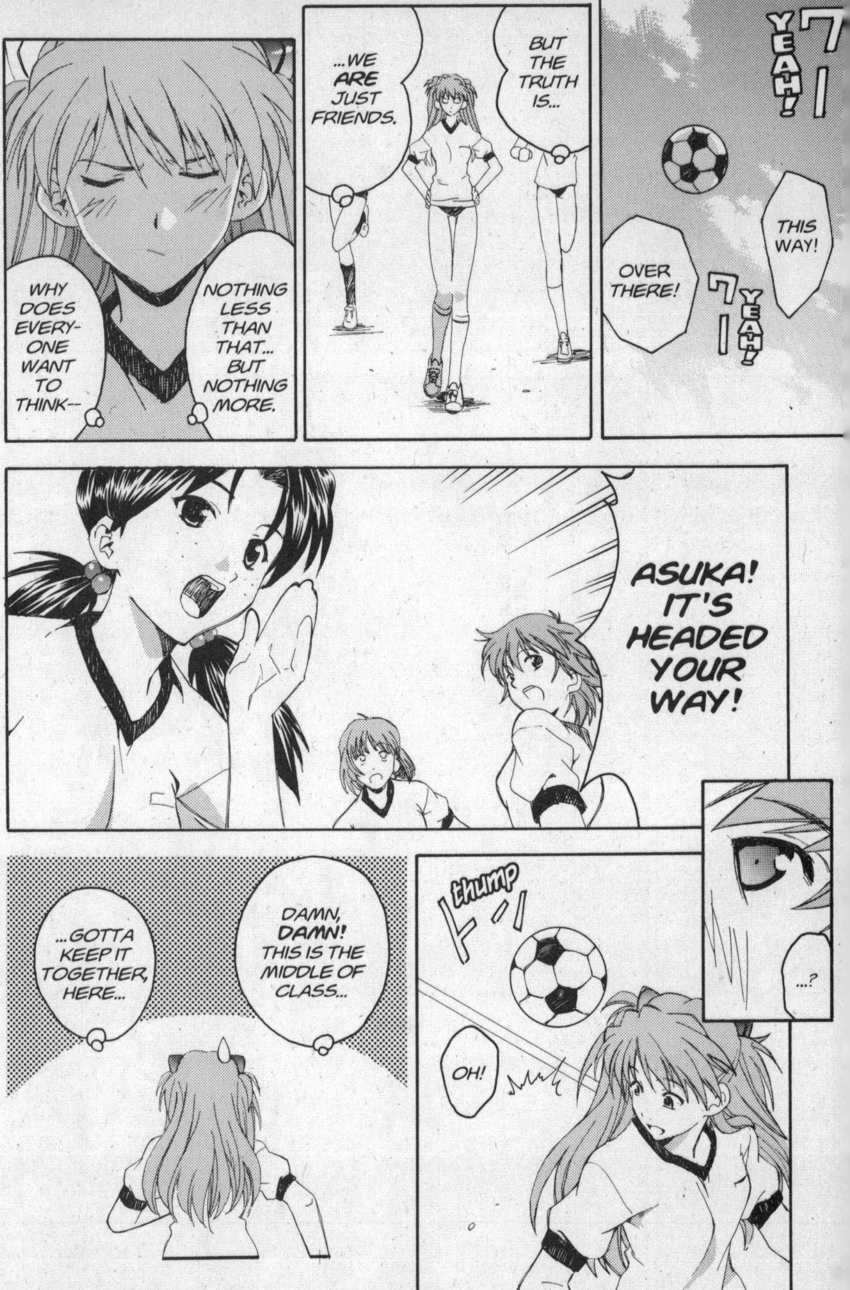
YEAH!
THIS WAY!
OVER THERE!
YEAH!
BUT THE TRUTH IS...
...WE ARE JUST FRIENDS.
NOTHING LESS THAN THAT... BUT NOTHING MORE.
WHY DOES EVERY-ONE WANT TO THINK--
ASUKA! IT'S HEADED YOUR WAY!
...?
thump
OH!
DAMN, DAMN! THIS IS THE MIDDLE OF CLASS...
...GOTTA KEEP IT TOGETHER, HERE...

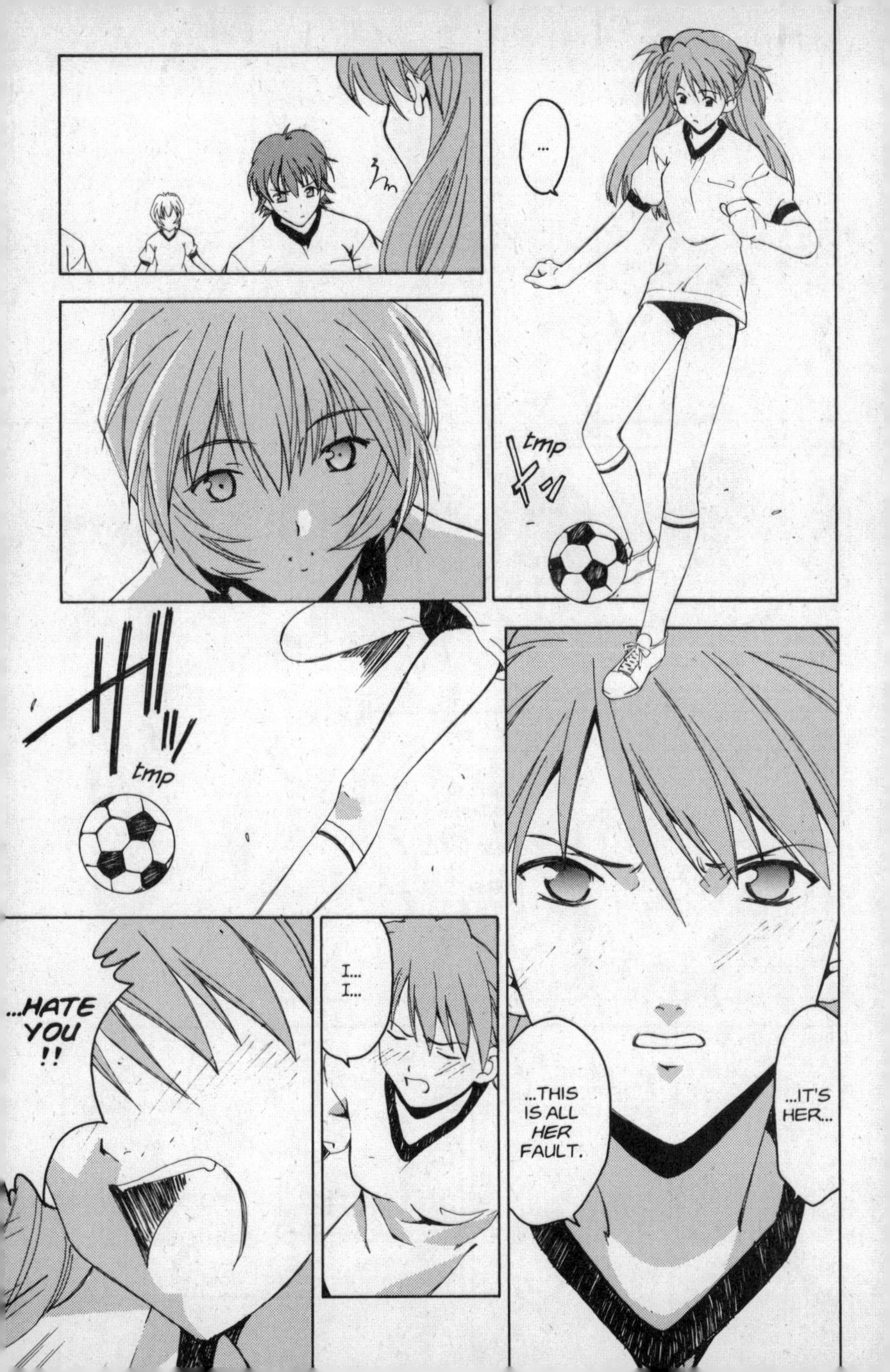
...
tmp
tmp
...IT'S HER...
...THIS IS ALL HER FAULT.
I... I...
...HATE YOU !!

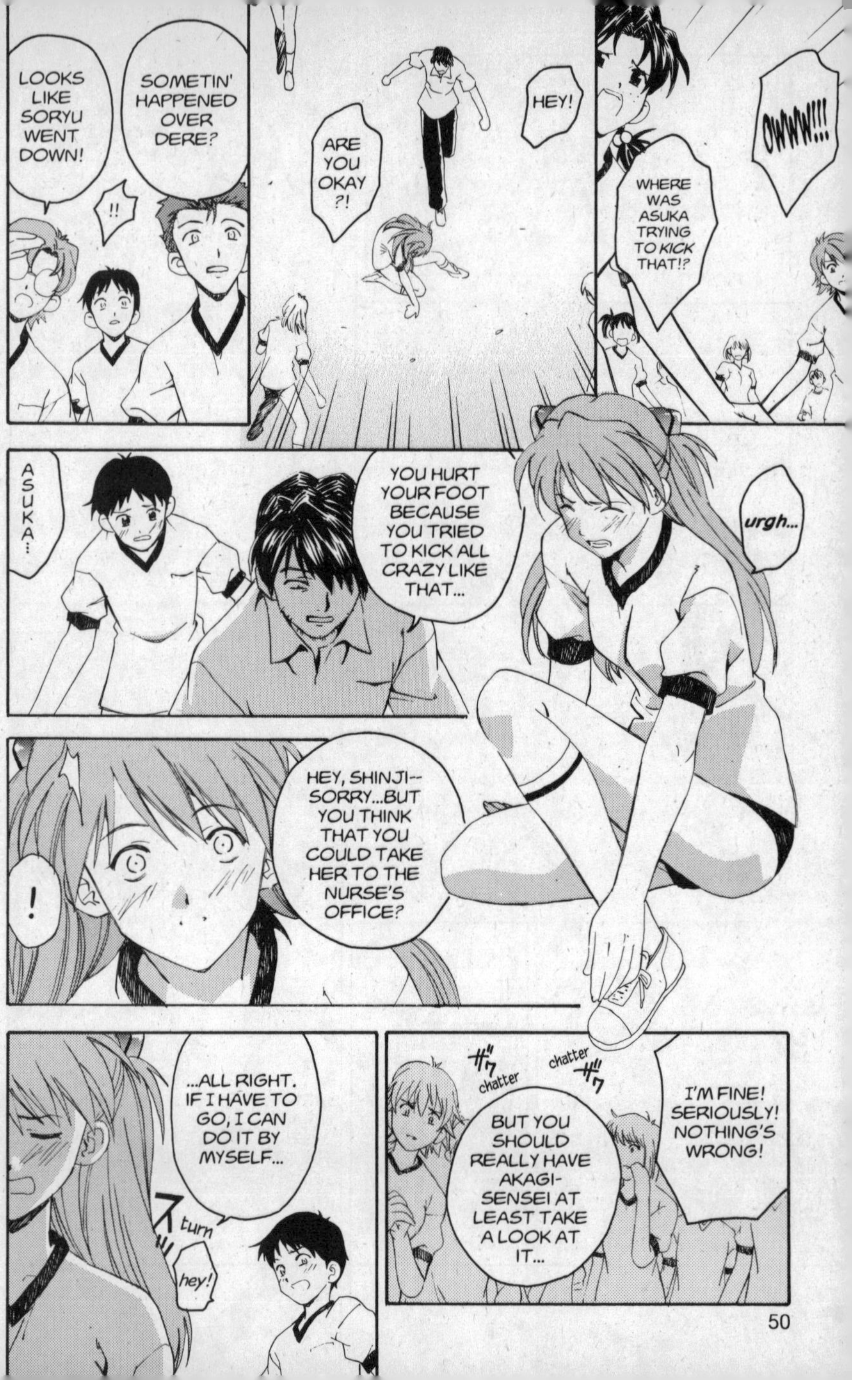
OWWW!!!
WHERE WAS ASUKA TRYING TO KICK THAT!?
HEY!
ARE YOU OKAY ?!
SOMETIN' HAPPENED OVER DERE?
LOOKS LIKE SORYU WENT DOWN!
!!
urgh...
YOU HURT YOUR FOOT BECAUSE YOU TRIED TO KICK ALL CRAZY LIKE THAT...
ASUKA...
HEY, SHINJI-- SORRY...BUT YOU THINK THAT YOU COULD TAKE HER TO THE NURSE'S OFFICE?
!
I'M FINE! SERIOUSLY! NOTHING'S WRONG!
chatter
chatter
BUT YOU SHOULD REALLY HAVE AKAGI-SENSEI AT LEAST TAKE A LOOK AT IT...
...ALL RIGHT. IF I HAVE TO GO, I CAN DO IT BY MYSELF...
turn
hey!

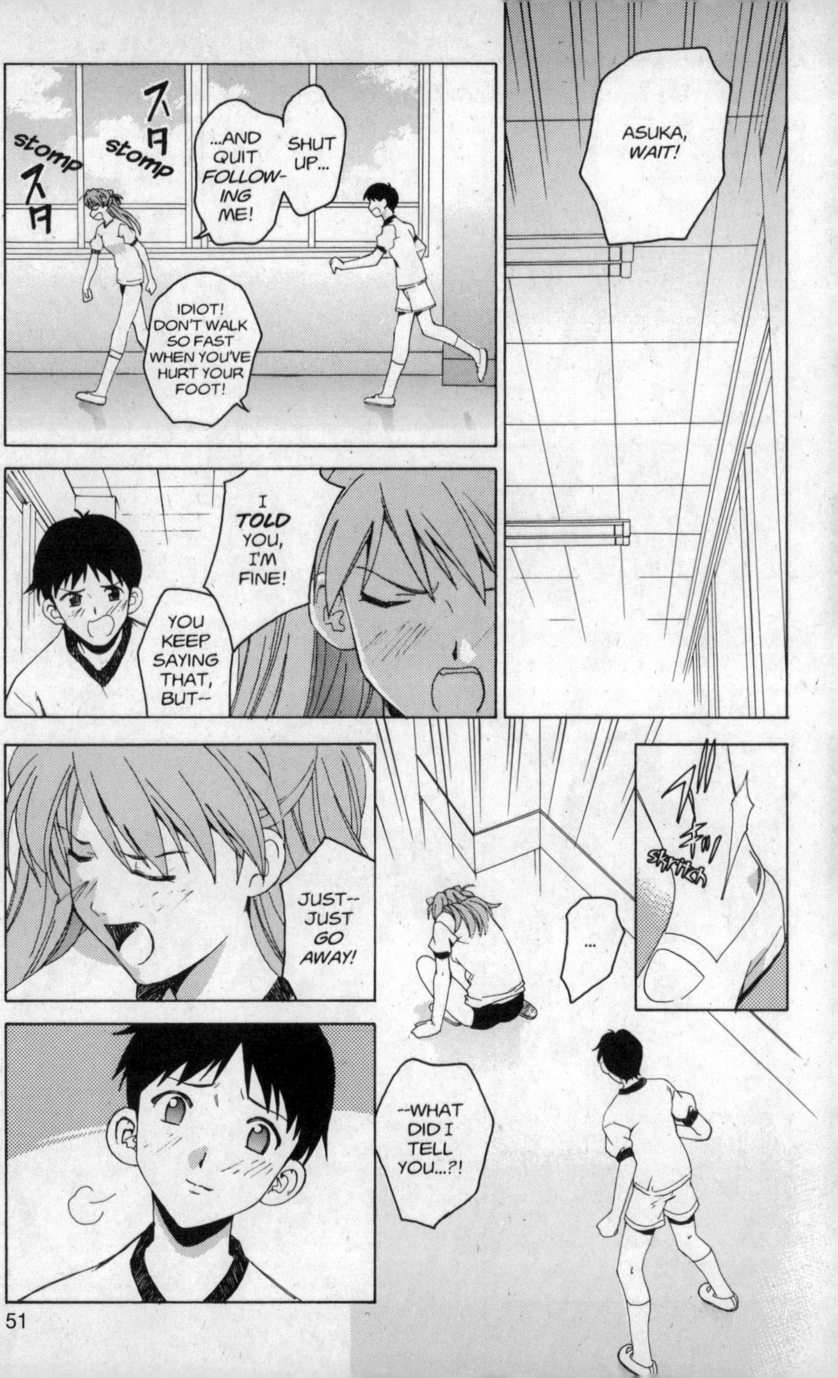
ASUKA, WAIT!
SHUT UP...
...AND QUIT FOLLOWING ME!
stomp
stomp
IDIOT! DON'T WALK SO FAST WHEN YOU'VE HURT YOUR FOOT!
I TOLD YOU, I'M FINE!
YOU KEEP SAYING THAT, BUT--
skritch
...
--WHAT DID I TELL YOU...?!
JUST-- JUST GO AWAY!

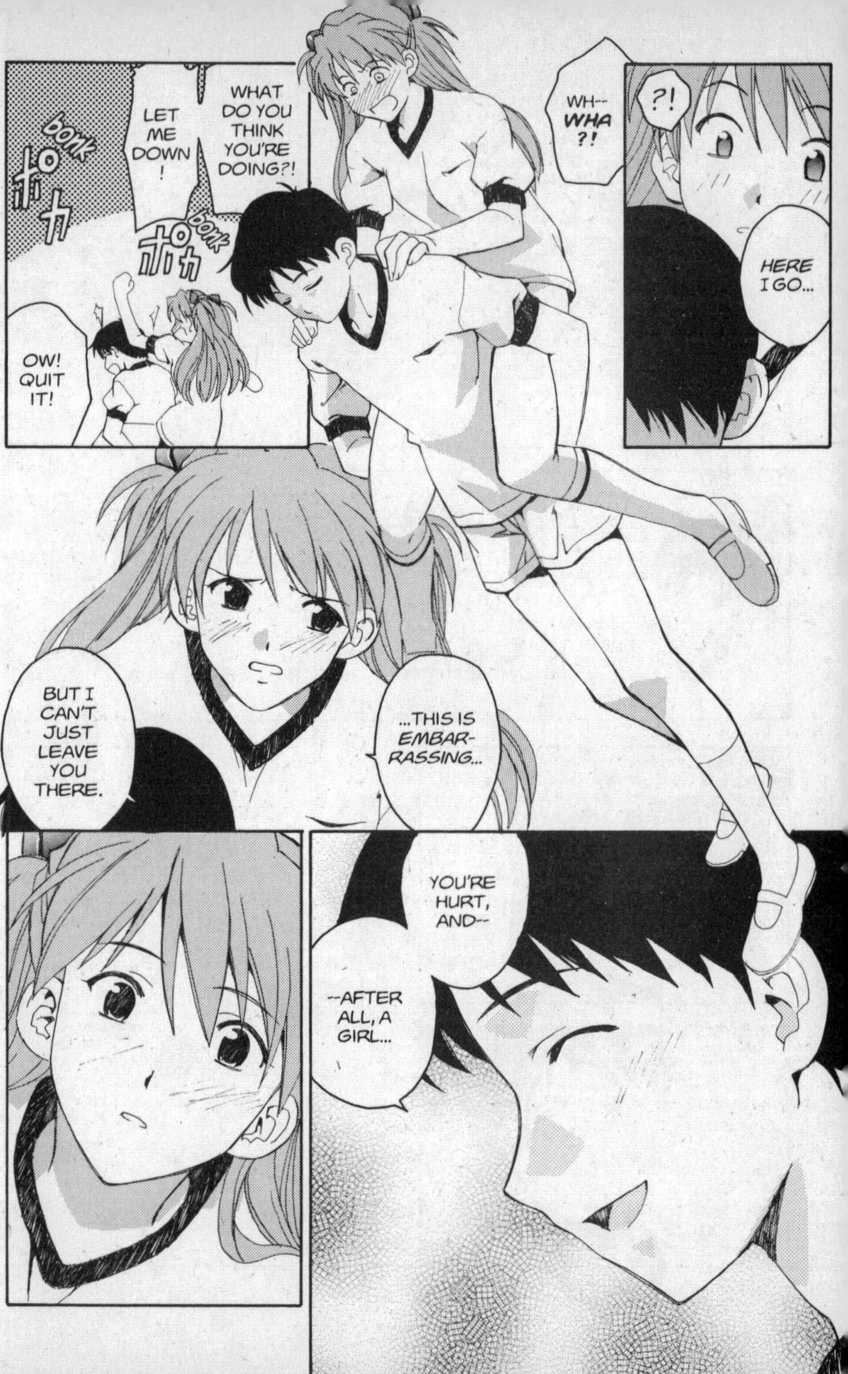
?!
HERE I GO...
WH-- WHA ?!
WHAT DO YOU THINK YOU'RE DOING?!
LET ME DOWN!
bonk
ポカ
bonk
ポカ
OW! QUIT IT!
...THIS IS EMBARRASSING...
BUT I CAN'T JUST LEAVE YOU THERE.
YOU'RE HURT, AND--
--AFTER ALL, A GIRL...

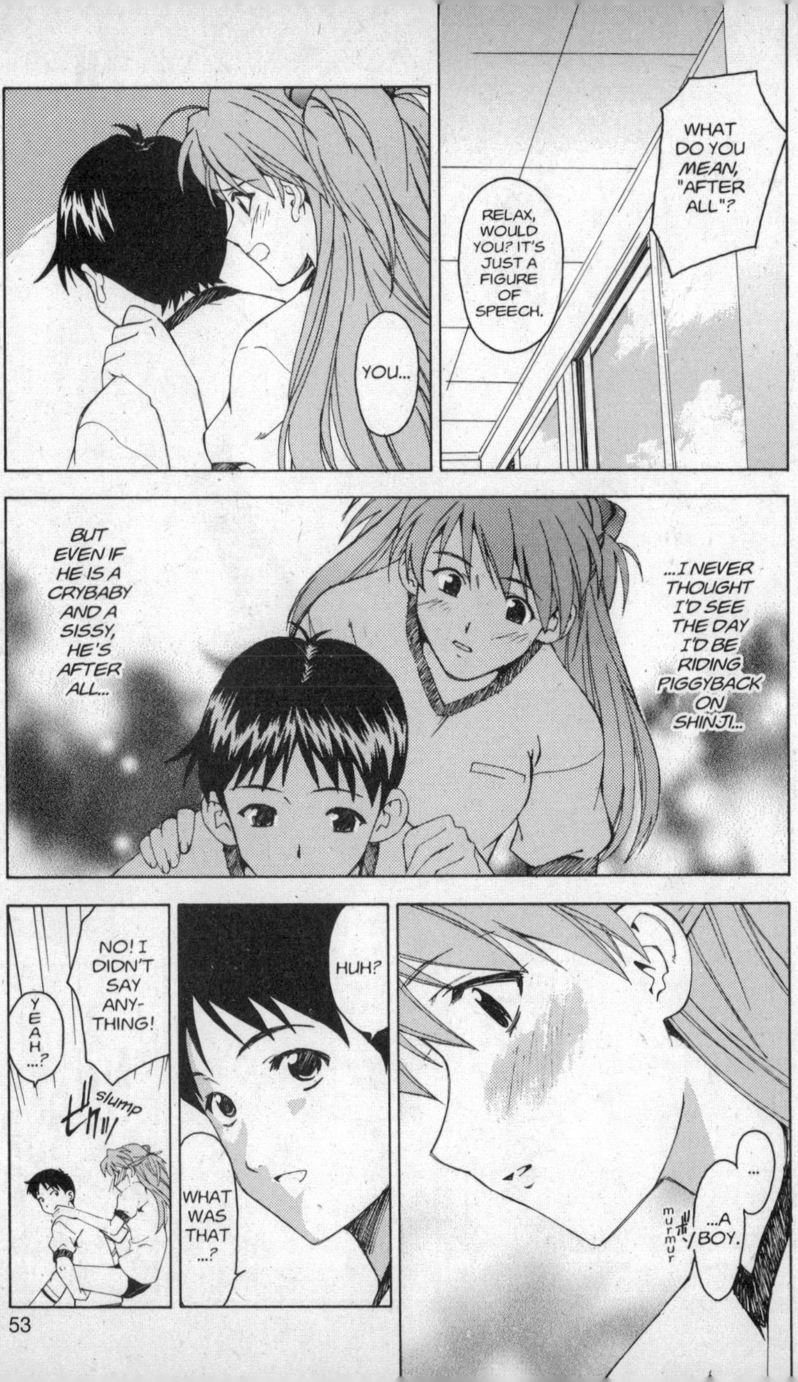
WHAT DO YOU MEAN, "AFTER ALL"?
RELAX, WOULD YOU? IT'S JUST A FIGURE OF SPEECH.
YOU...
...I NEVER THOUGHT I'D SEE THE DAY I'D BE RIDING PIGGYBACK ON SHINJI...
BUT EVEN IF HE IS A CRYBABY AND A SISSY, HE'S AFTER ALL...
...
...A BOY.
murmur
HUH?
WHAT WAS THAT ...?
NO! I DIDN'T SAY ANYTHING!
YEAH ...?
slump

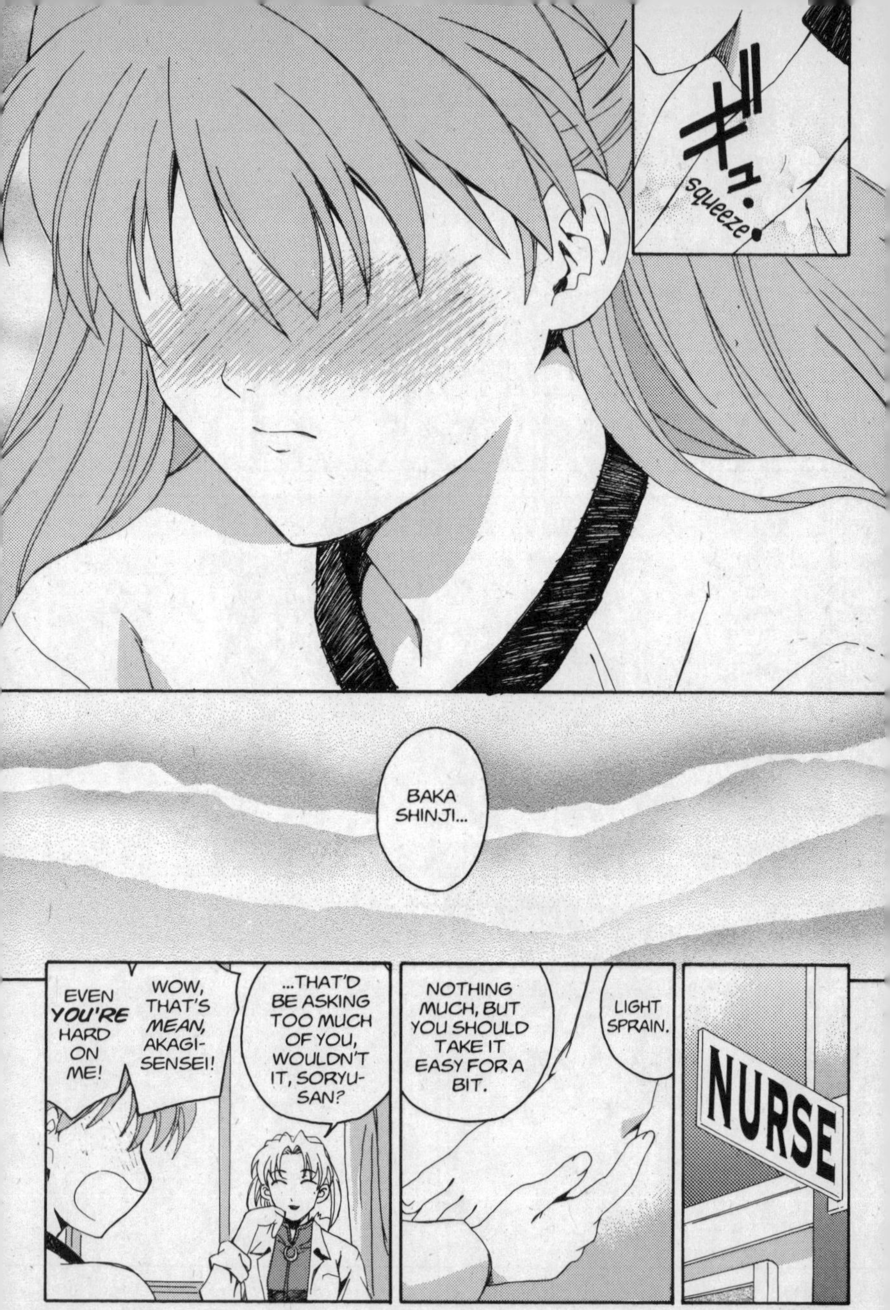
ギュ
squeeze
BAKA SHINJI...
NURSE
LIGHT SPRAIN.
NOTHING MUCH, BUT YOU SHOULD TAKE IT EASY FOR A BIT.
...THAT'D BE ASKING TOO MUCH OF YOU, WOULDN'T IT, SORYU-SAN?
WOW, THAT'S *MEAN*, AKAGI-SENSEI!
EVEN ***YOU'RE*** HARD ON ME!

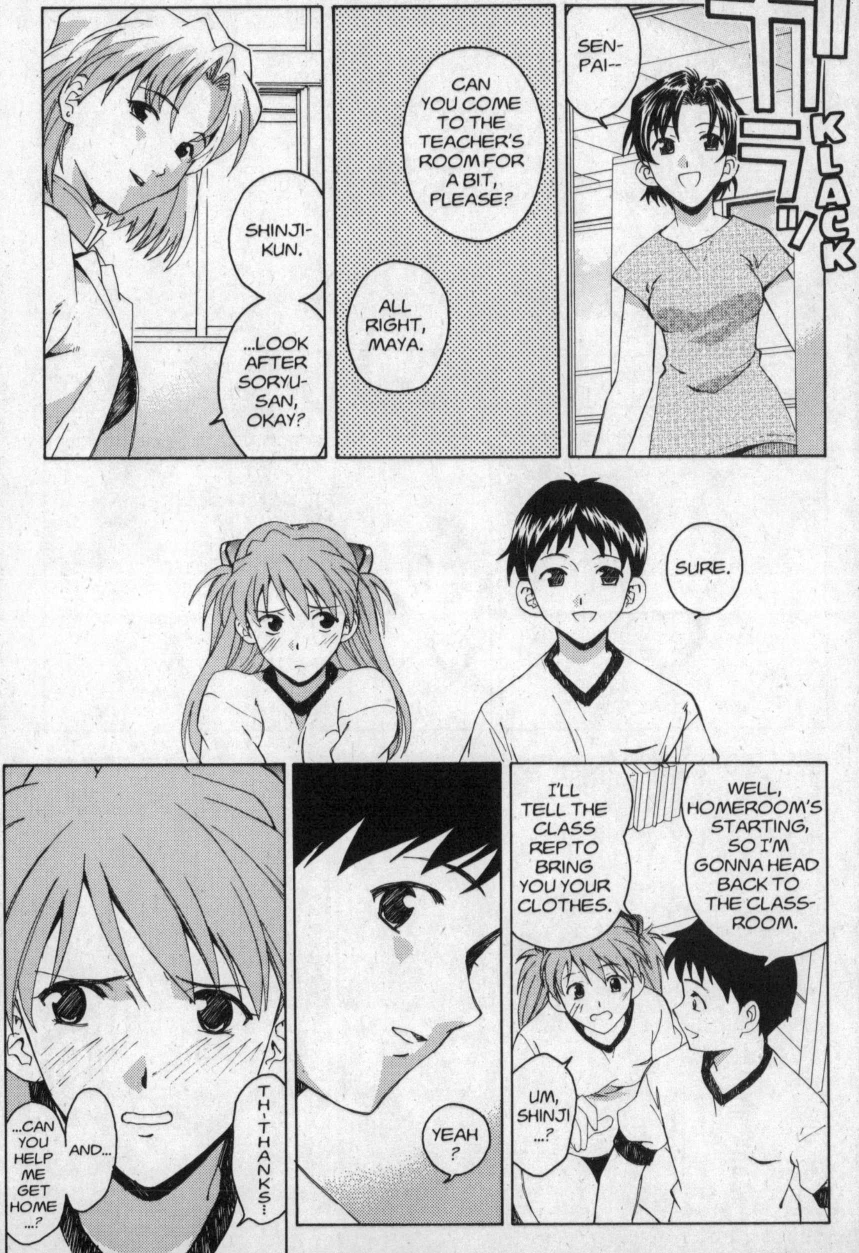
ガラッ
KLACK
SEN-PAI--
CAN YOU COME TO THE TEACHER'S ROOM FOR A BIT, PLEASE?
ALL RIGHT, MAYA.
SHINJI-KUN.
...LOOK AFTER SORYU-SAN, OKAY?
SURE.
WELL, HOMEROOM'S STARTING, SO I'M GONNA HEAD BACK TO THE CLASS-ROOM.
I'LL TELL THE CLASS REP TO BRING YOU YOUR CLOTHES.
UM, SHINJI ...?
YEAH ?
TH-THANKS...
AND...
...CAN YOU HELP ME GET HOME ...?

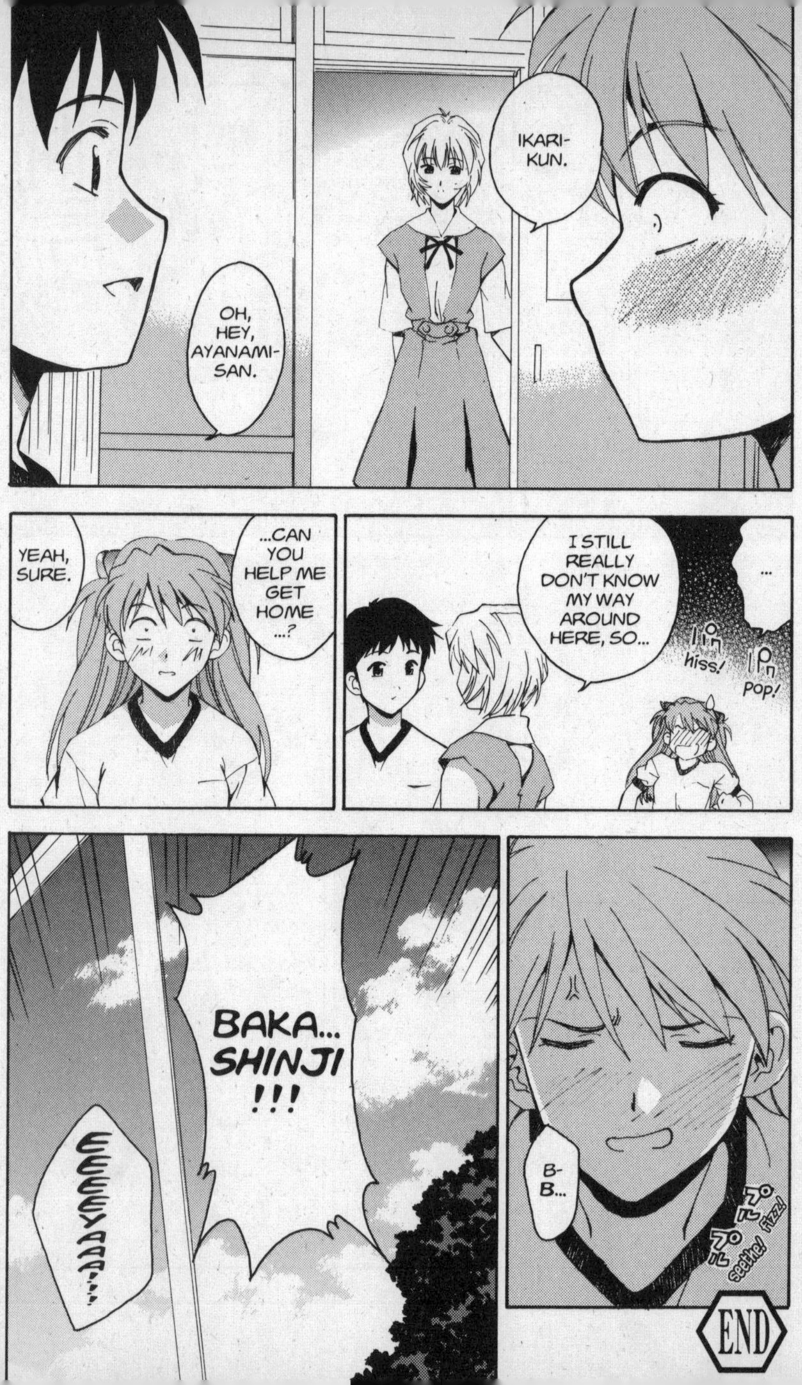
IKARI-KUN.
OH, HEY, AYANAMI-SAN.
I STILL REALLY DON'T KNOW MY WAY AROUND HERE, SO...
...
kiss!
pop!
...CAN YOU HELP ME GET HOME ...?
YEAH, SURE.
B-B...
seethe! fizz!
BAKA... SHINJI !!!
EEEEYAAA!!!
END

STAGE
03

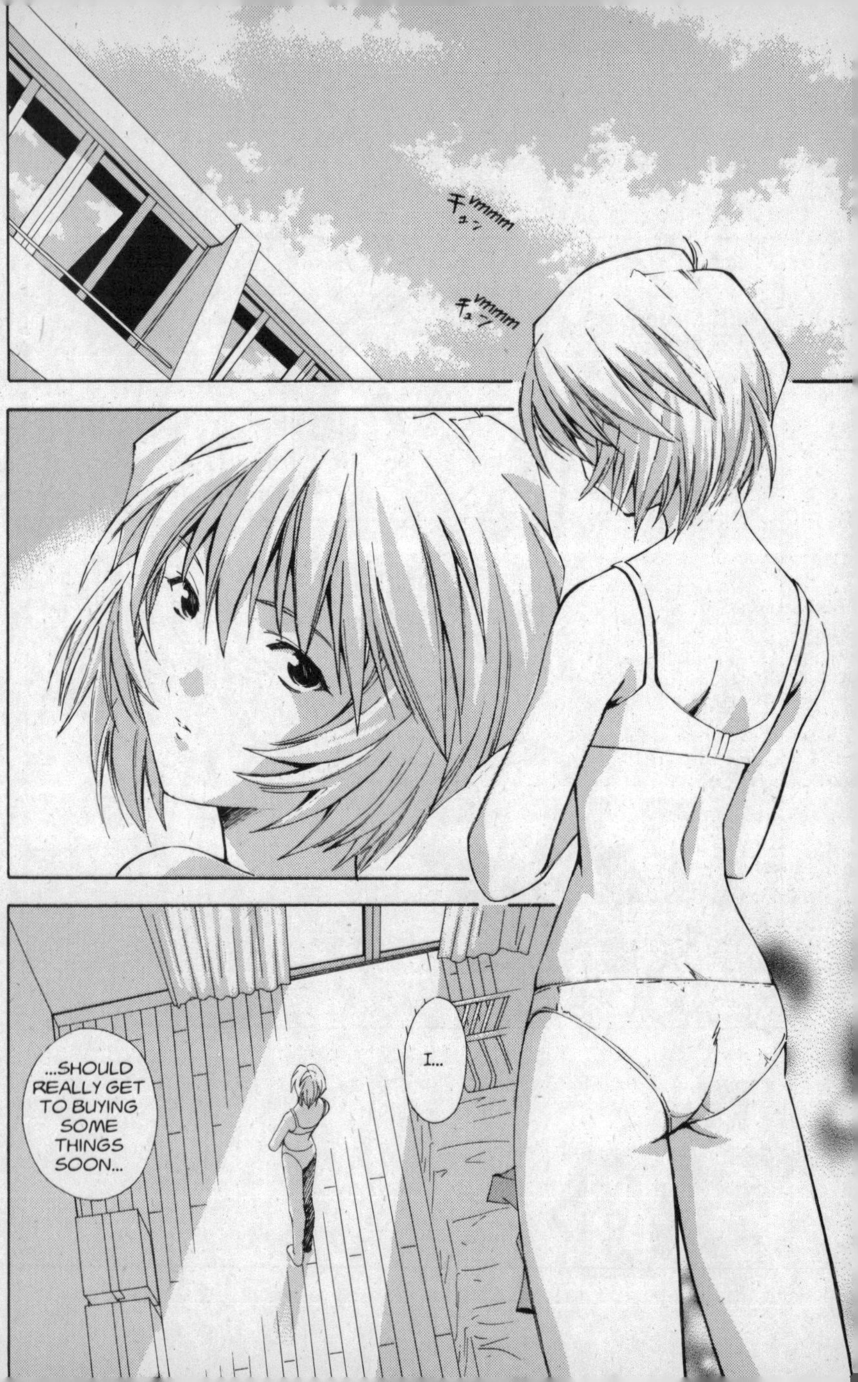
vmmm
vmmm
I...
...SHOULD REALLY GET TO BUYING SOME THINGS SOON...

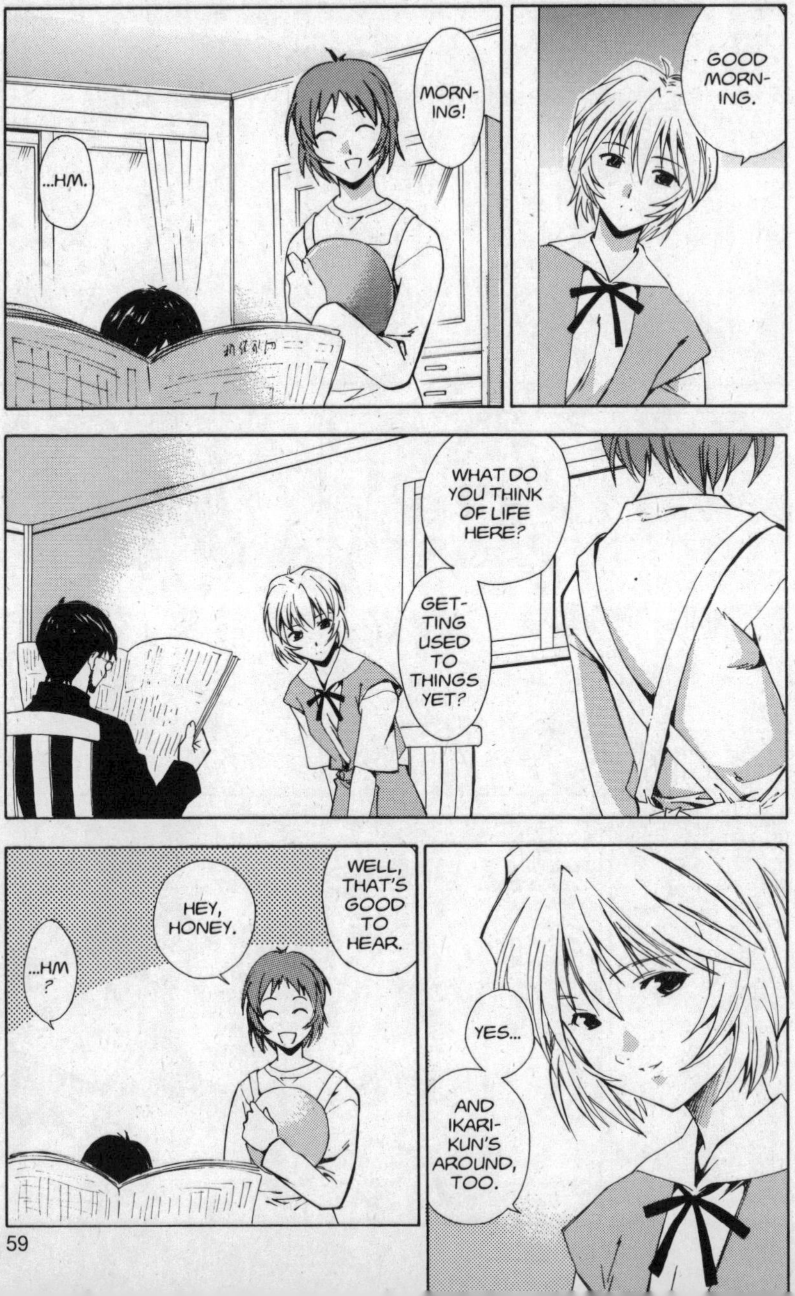
GOOD MORNING.
MORNING!
...HM.
WHAT DO YOU THINK OF LIFE HERE?
GETTING USED TO THINGS YET?
YES...
AND IKARI-KUN'S AROUND, TOO.
WELL, THAT'S GOOD TO HEAR.
HEY, HONEY.
...HM?

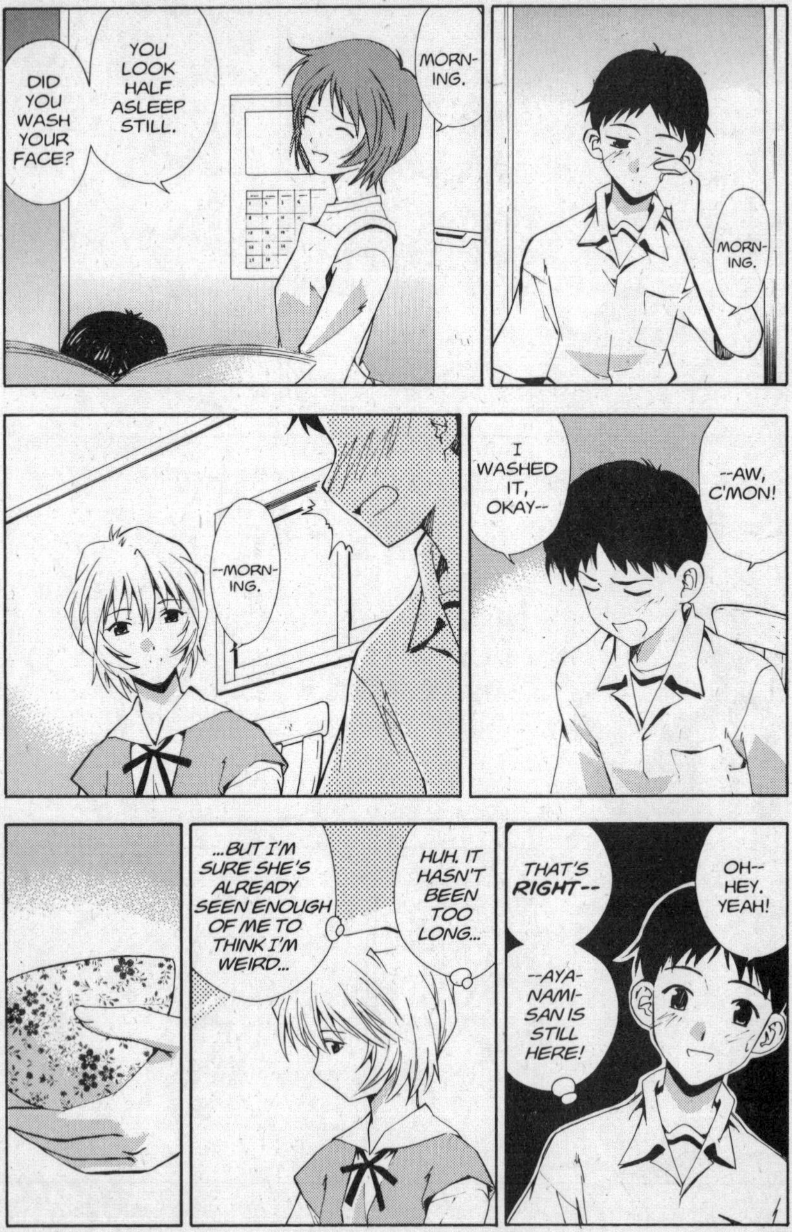
MORN-ING.
MORN-ING.
YOU LOOK HALF ASLEEP STILL.
DID YOU WASH YOUR FACE?
--AW, C'MON!
I WASHED IT, OKAY--
--MORN-ING.
OH-- HEY. YEAH!
THAT'S **RIGHT**--
--AYA-NAMI-SAN IS STILL HERE!
HUH. IT HASN'T BEEN TOO LONG...
...BUT I'M SURE SHE'S ALREADY SEEN ENOUGH OF ME TO THINK I'M WEIRD...

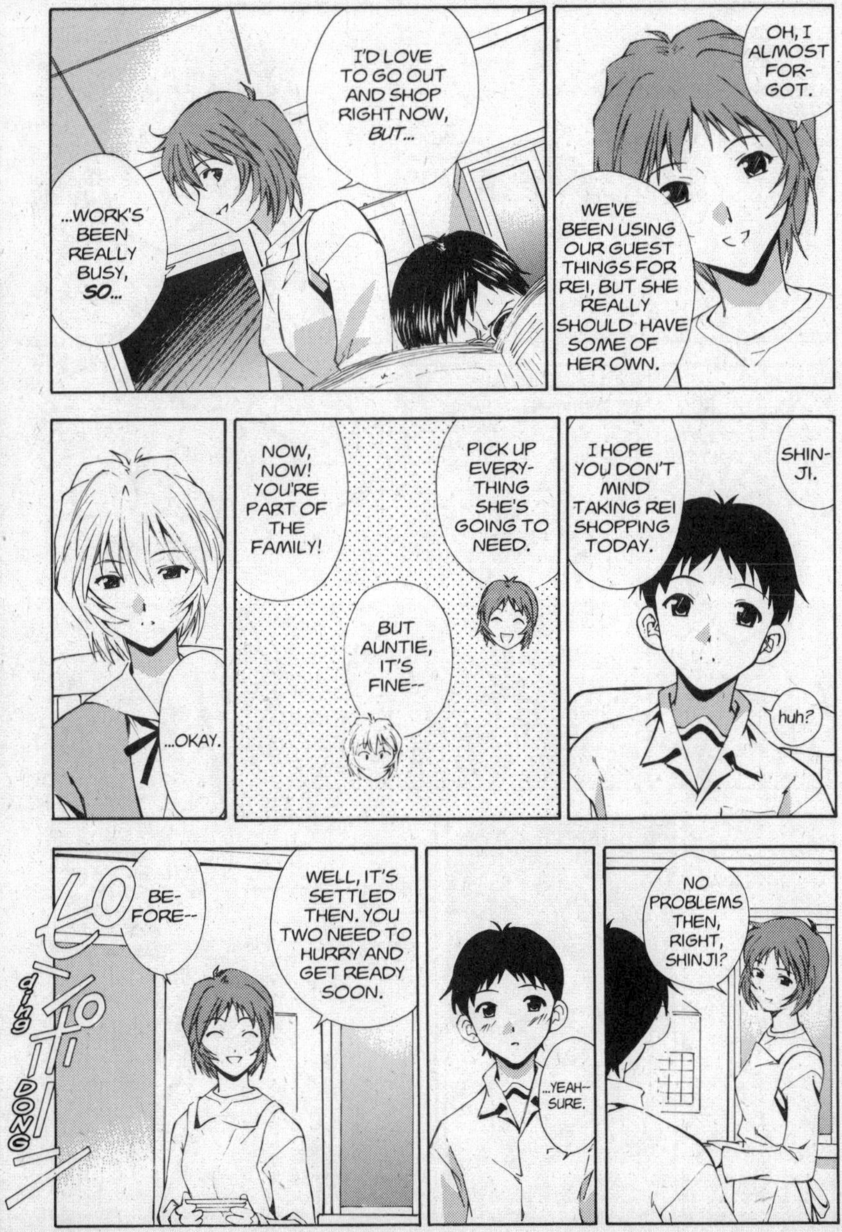

OH, I ALMOST FORGOT.
WE'VE BEEN USING OUR GUEST THINGS FOR REI, BUT SHE REALLY SHOULD HAVE SOME OF HER OWN.
I'D LOVE TO GO OUT AND SHOP RIGHT NOW, *BUT*...
...WORK'S BEEN REALLY BUSY, ***SO***...
SHINJI.
I HOPE YOU DON'T MIND TAKING REI SHOPPING TODAY.
huh?
PICK UP EVERYTHING SHE'S GOING TO NEED.
NOW, NOW! YOU'RE PART OF THE FAMILY!
BUT AUNTIE, IT'S FINE--
...OKAY.
NO PROBLEMS THEN, RIGHT, SHINJI?
...YEAH--SURE.
WELL, IT'S SETTLED THEN. YOU TWO NEED TO HURRY AND GET READY SOON.
BEFORE--
ding DONG

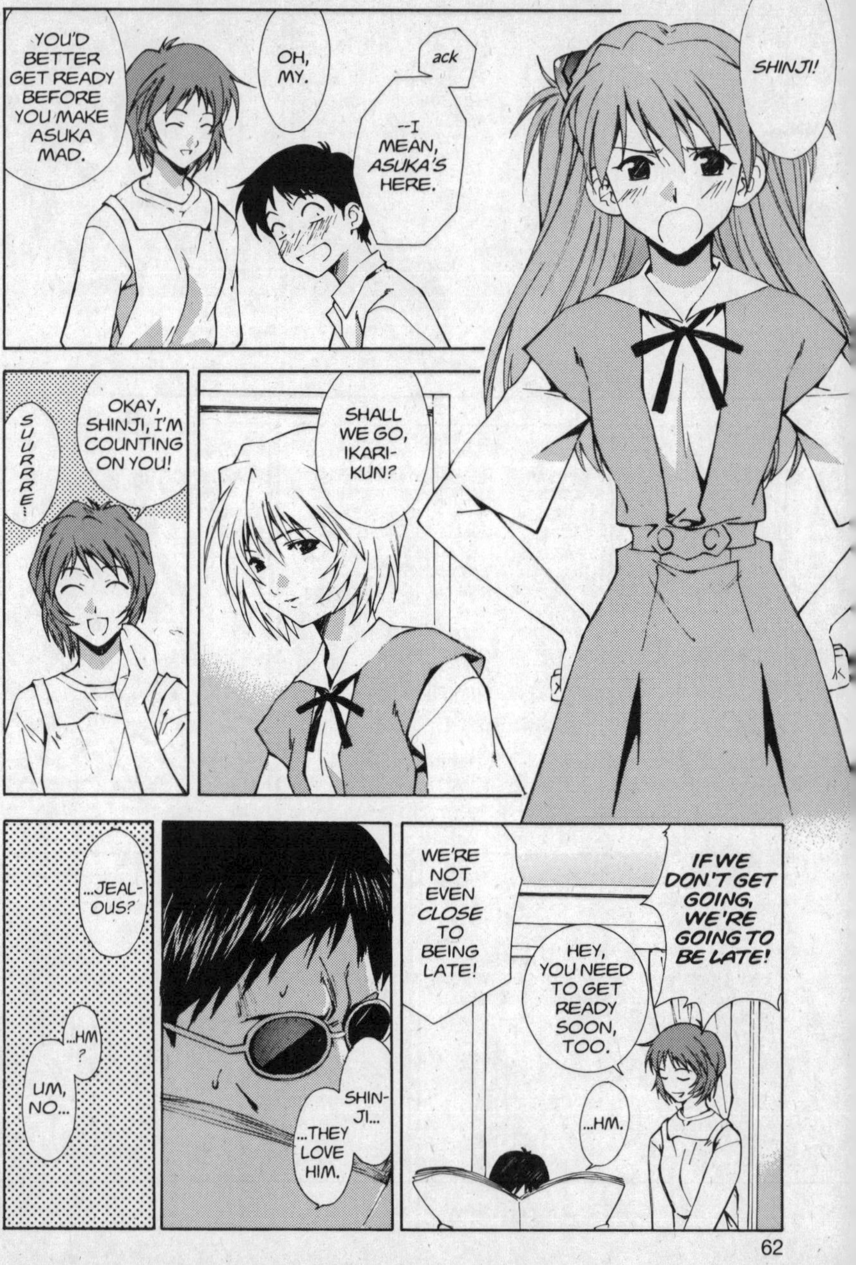
SHINJI!
ack
--I MEAN, ASUKA'S HERE.
OH, MY.
YOU'D BETTER GET READY BEFORE YOU MAKE ASUKA MAD.
SHALL WE GO, IKARI-KUN?
OKAY, SHINJI, I'M COUNTING ON YOU!
SUURRRE...
IF WE DON'T GET GOING, WE'RE GOING TO BE LATE!
WE'RE NOT EVEN CLOSE TO BEING LATE!
HEY, YOU NEED TO GET READY SOON, TOO.
...HM.
SHIN-JI...
...THEY LOVE HIM.
...JEAL-OUS?
...HM?
UM, NO...

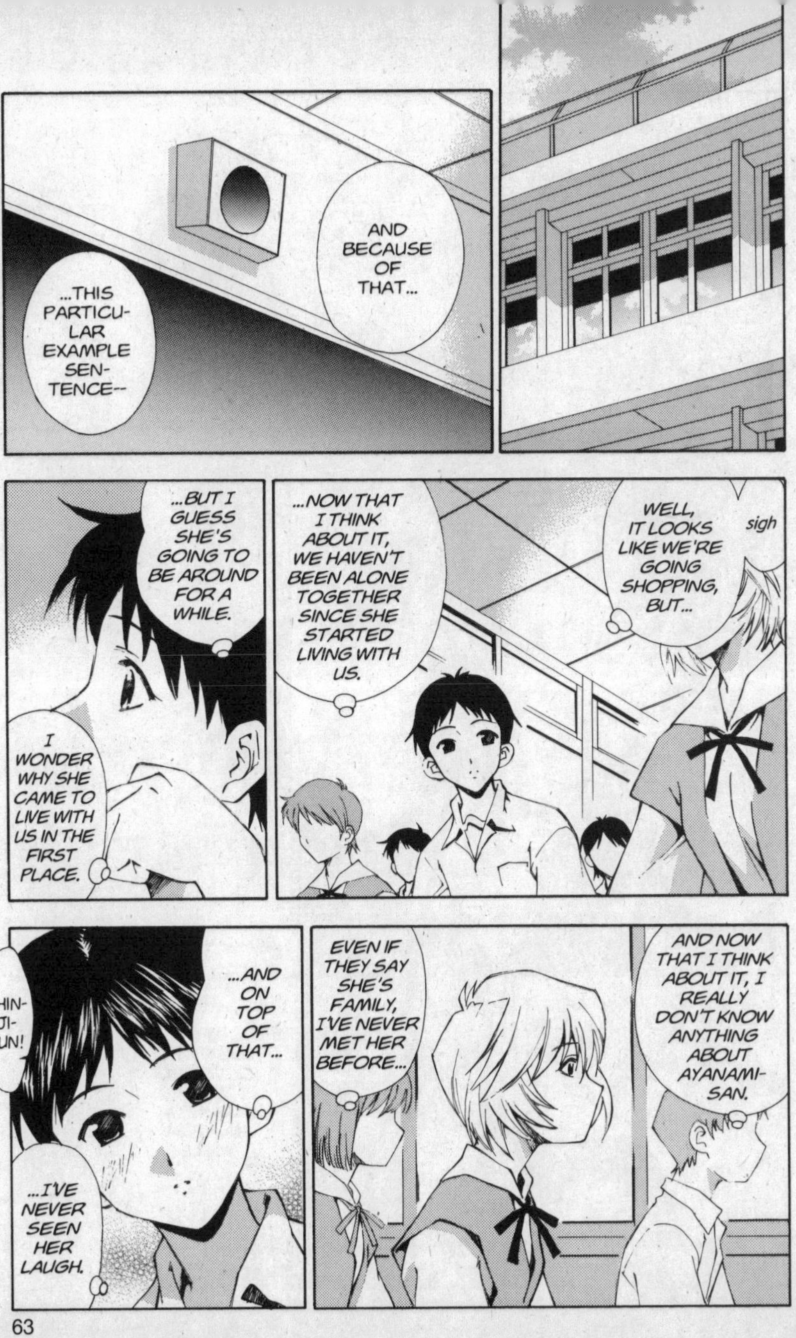
AND BECAUSE OF THAT...
...THIS PARTICU-LAR EXAMPLE SEN-TENCE--
WELL, IT LOOKS LIKE WE'RE GOING SHOPPING, BUT...
sigh
...NOW THAT I THINK ABOUT IT, WE HAVEN'T BEEN ALONE TOGETHER SINCE SHE STARTED LIVING WITH US.
...BUT I GUESS SHE'S GOING TO BE AROUND FOR A WHILE.
I WONDER WHY SHE CAME TO LIVE WITH US IN THE FIRST PLACE.
AND NOW THAT I THINK ABOUT IT, I REALLY DON'T KNOW ANYTHING ABOUT AYANAMI-SAN.
EVEN IF THEY SAY SHE'S FAMILY, I'VE NEVER MET HER BEFORE...
...AND ON TOP OF THAT...
SHIN-JI-KUN!
...I'VE NEVER SEEN HER LAUGH.

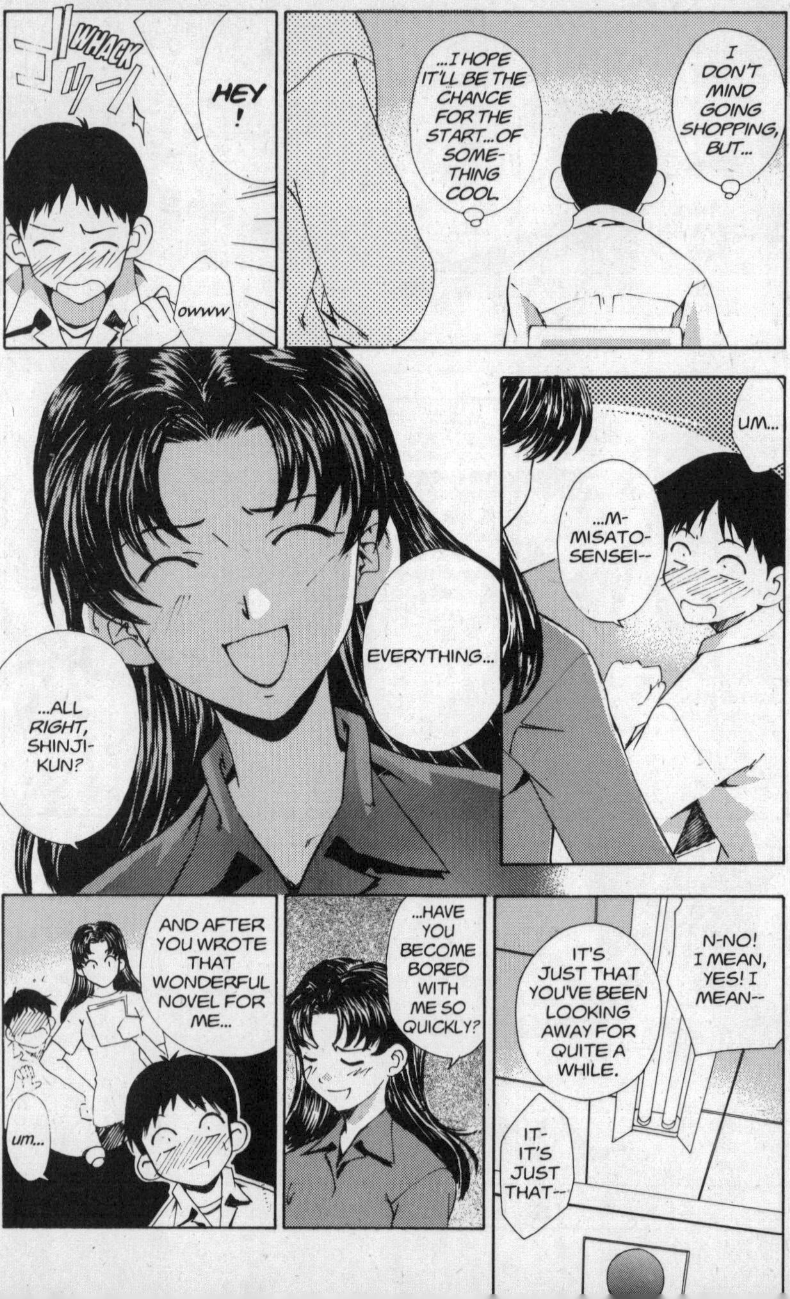
I DON'T MIND GOING SHOPPING, BUT...
...I HOPE IT'LL BE THE CHANCE FOR THE START...OF SOME-THING COOL.
WHACK
HEY!
owww
UM...
...M-MISATO-SENSEI--
EVERYTHING...
...ALL RIGHT, SHINJI-KUN?
N-NO! I MEAN, YES! I MEAN--
IT'S JUST THAT YOU'VE BEEN LOOKING AWAY FOR QUITE A WHILE.
IT- IT'S JUST THAT--
...HAVE YOU BECOME BORED WITH ME SO QUICKLY?
AND AFTER YOU WROTE THAT WONDERFUL NOVEL FOR ME...
um...

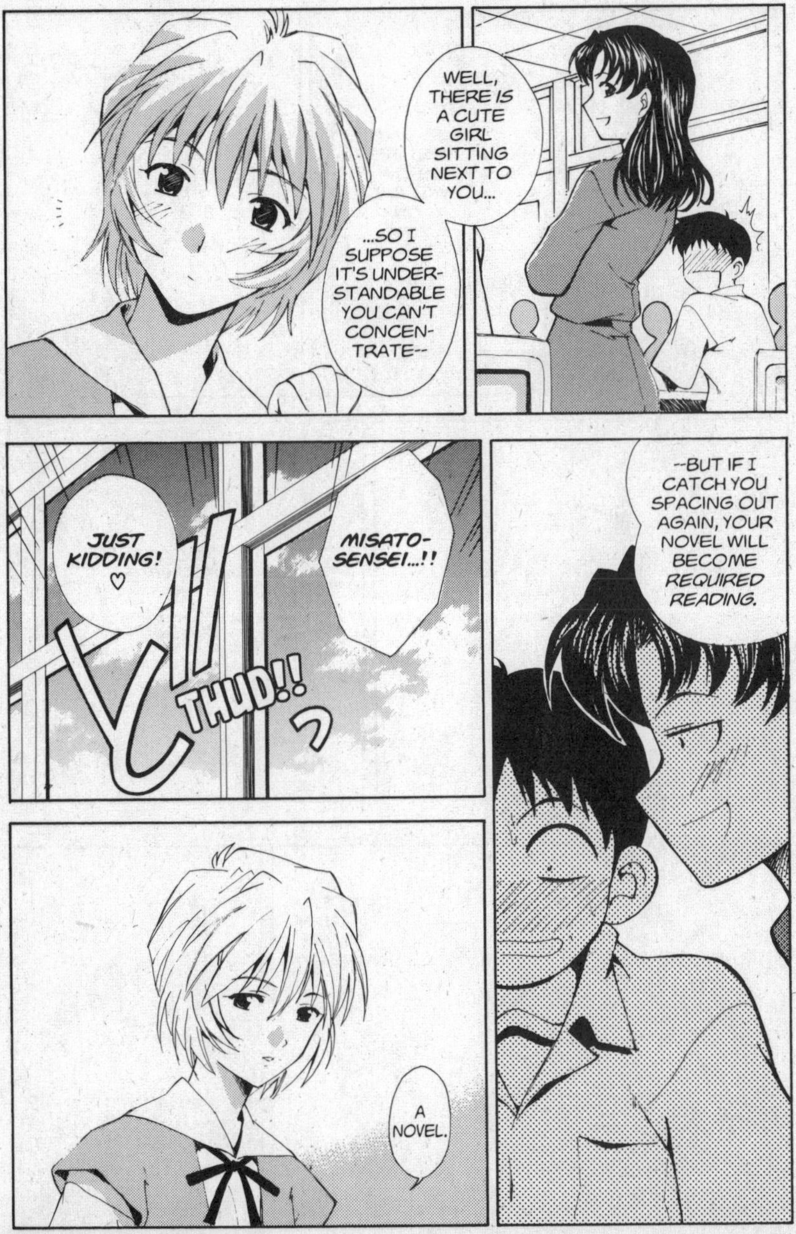
WELL, THERE IS A CUTE GIRL SITTING NEXT TO YOU...
...SO I SUPPOSE IT'S UNDER-STANDABLE YOU CAN'T CONCEN-TRATE--
--BUT IF I CATCH YOU SPACING OUT AGAIN, YOUR NOVEL WILL BECOME *REQUIRED READING.*
MISATO-SENSEI...!!
JUST KIDDING! ♡
THUD!!
A NOVEL.

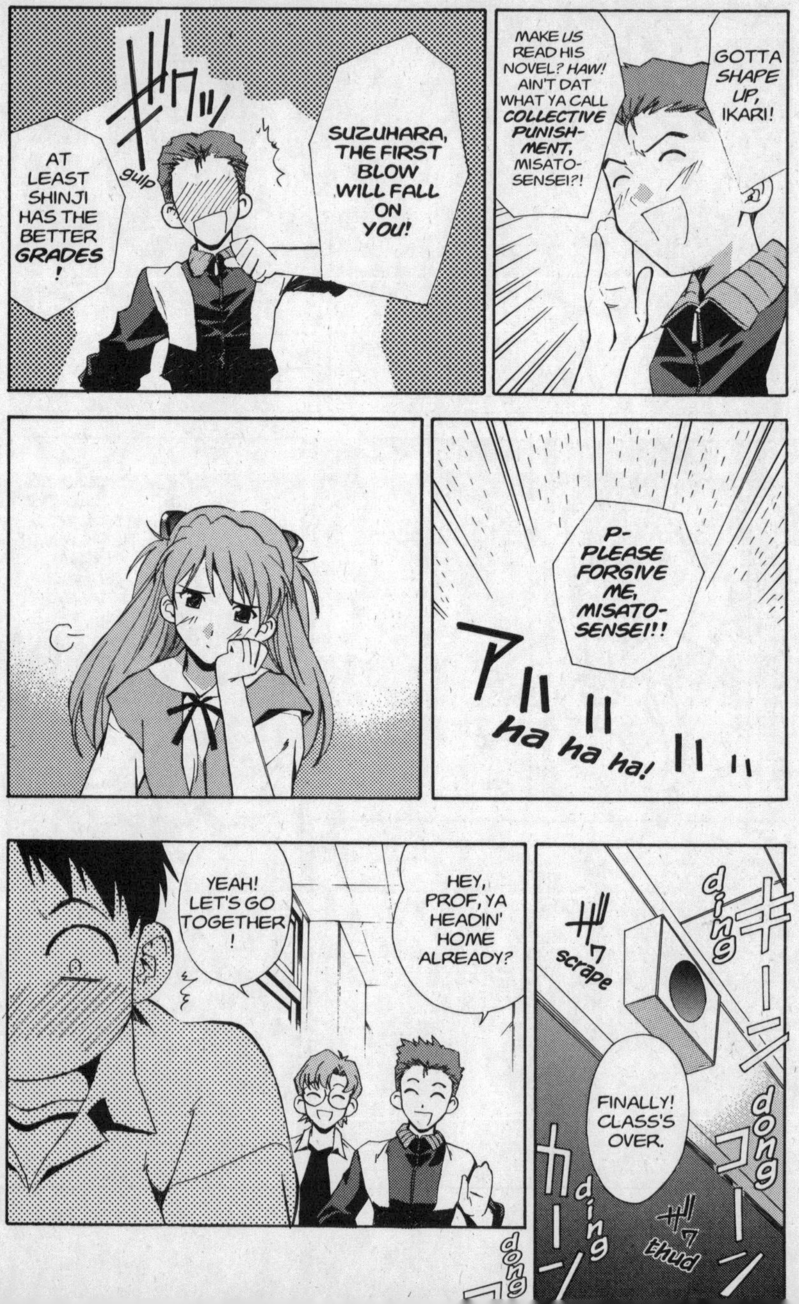
GOTTA SHAPE UP, IKARI!
MAKE US READ HIS NOVEL? HAW! AIN'T DAT WHAT YA CALL COLLECTIVE PUNISHMENT, MISATO-SENSEI?!
SUZUHARA, THE FIRST BLOW WILL FALL ON YOU!
gulp
AT LEAST SHINJI HAS THE BETTER GRADES!
P-PLEASE FORGIVE ME, MISATO-SENSEI!!
ha ha ha!
ding
dong
scrape
FINALLY! CLASS'S OVER.
ding
thud
dong
HEY, PROF, YA HEADIN' HOME ALREADY?
YEAH! LET'S GO TOGETHER!

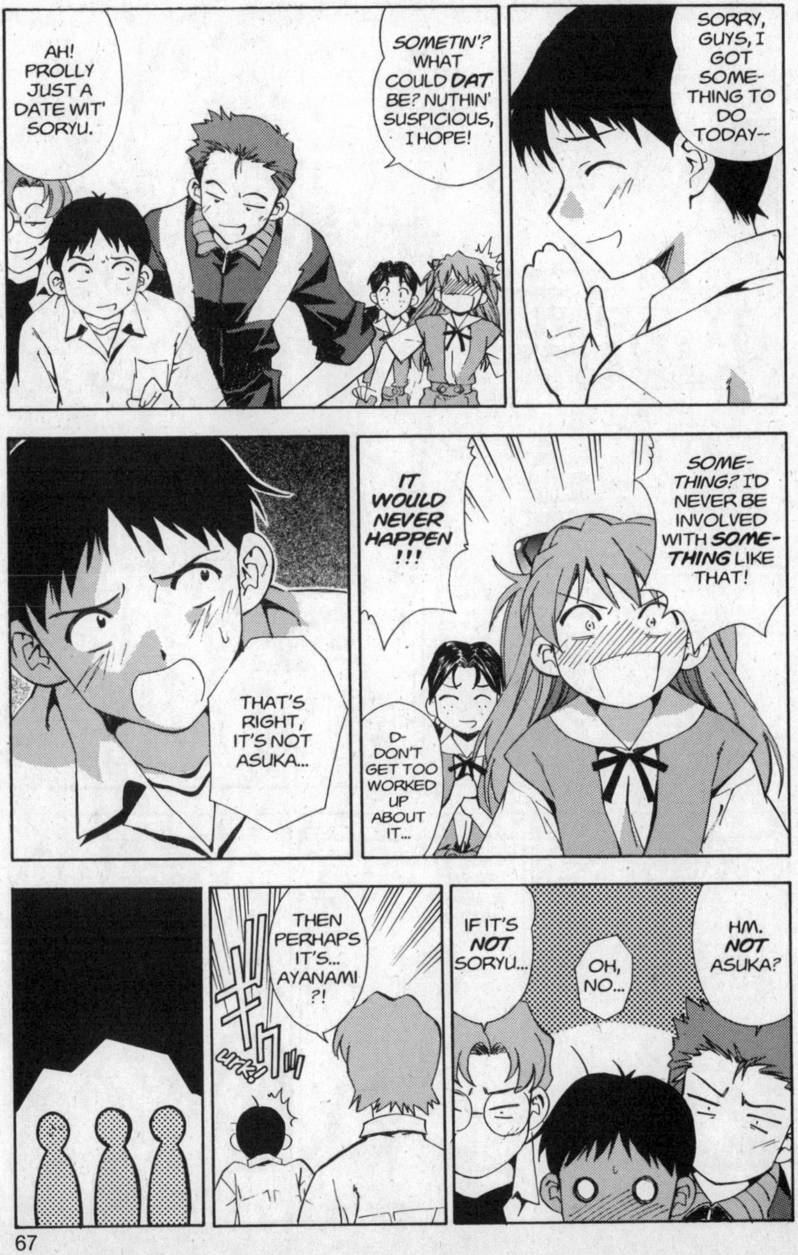
SORRY, GUYS, I GOT SOME-THING TO DO TODAY--
SOMETIN'? WHAT COULD **DAT** BE? NUTHIN' SUSPICIOUS, I HOPE!
AH! PROLLY JUST A DATE WIT' SORYU.
SOME-THING? I'D NEVER BE INVOLVED WITH **SOME-THING** LIKE THAT!
IT WOULD NEVER HAPPEN!!!
D-DON'T GET TOO WORKED UP ABOUT IT...
THAT'S RIGHT, IT'S NOT ASUKA...
HM. ***NOT*** ASUKA?
OH, NO...
IF IT'S ***NOT*** SORYU...
THEN PERHAPS IT'S... AYANAMI?!
URK!

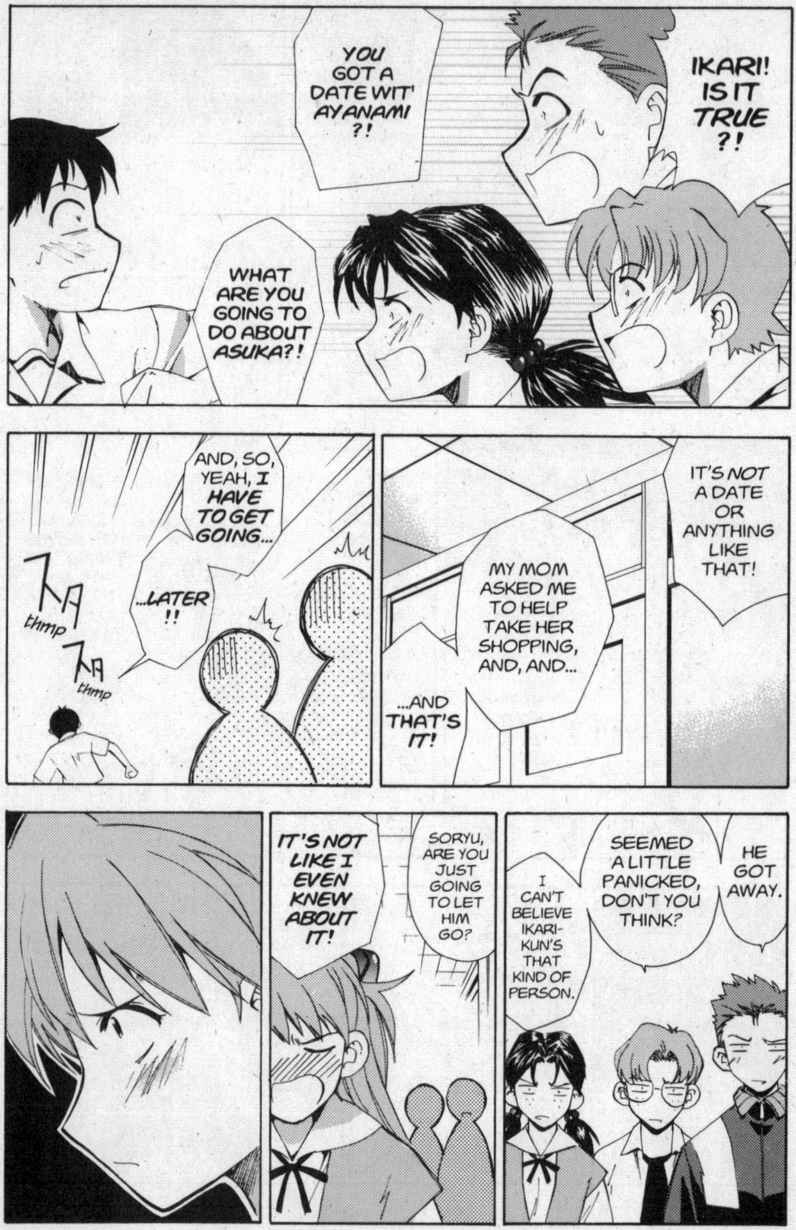
IKARI! IS IT TRUE?!
YOU GOT A DATE WIT' AYANAMI?!
WHAT ARE YOU GOING TO DO ABOUT ASUKA?!
IT'S NOT A DATE OR ANYTHING LIKE THAT!
MY MOM ASKED ME TO HELP TAKE HER SHOPPING, AND, AND...
...AND THAT'S IT!
AND, SO, YEAH, I HAVE TO GET GOING...
...LATER!!
thmp
thmp
HE GOT AWAY.
SEEMED A LITTLE PANICKED, DON'T YOU THINK?
I CAN'T BELIEVE IKARI-KUN'S THAT KIND OF PERSON.
SORYU, ARE YOU JUST GOING TO LET HIM GO?
IT'S NOT LIKE I EVEN KNEW ABOUT IT!

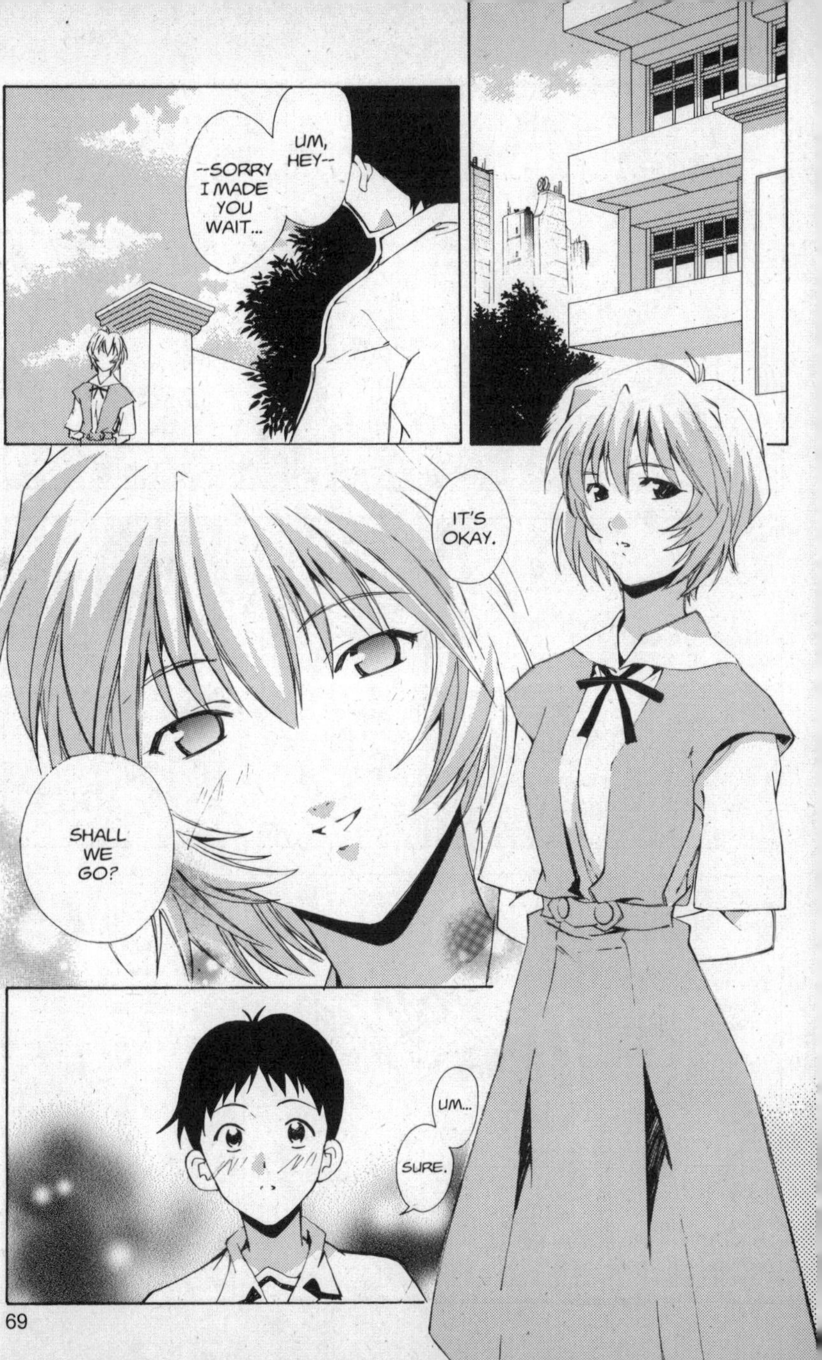
UM, HEY--
--SORRY I MADE YOU WAIT...
IT'S OKAY.
SHALL WE GO?
UM...
SURE.

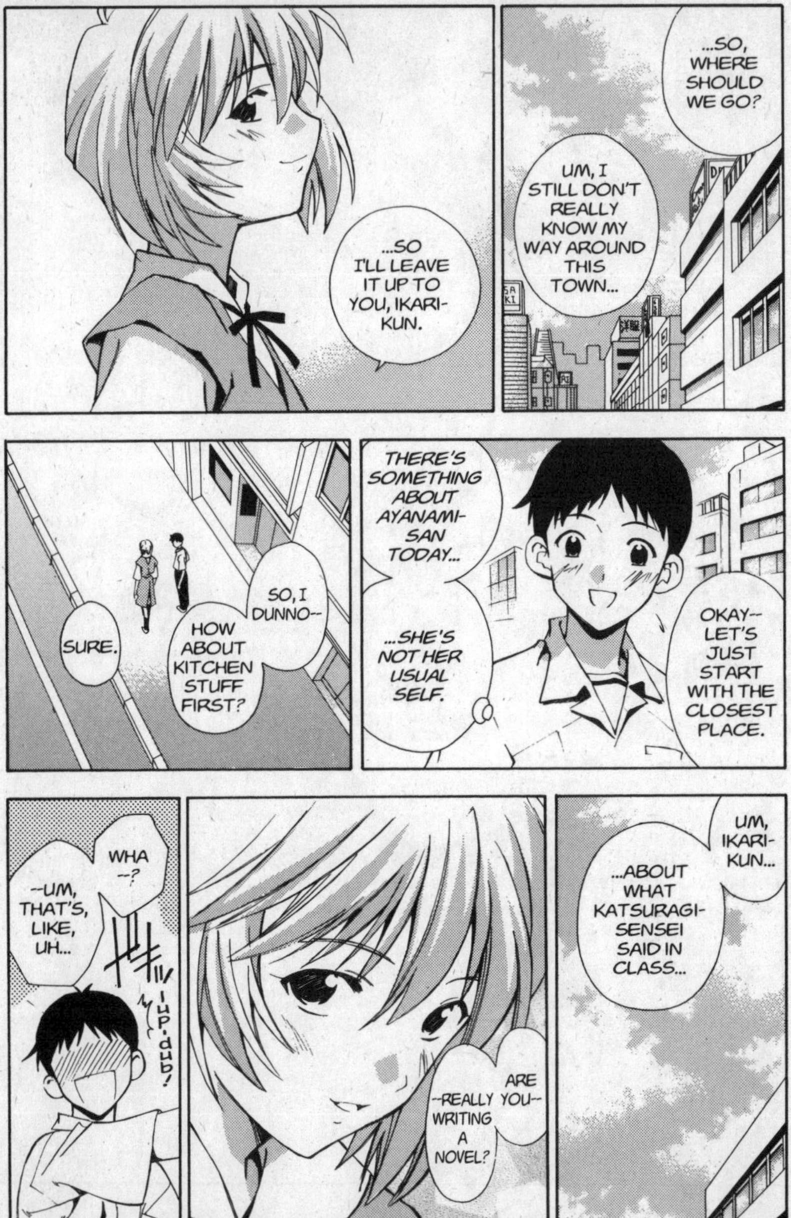
...SO, WHERE SHOULD WE GO?
UM, I STILL DON'T REALLY KNOW MY WAY AROUND THIS TOWN...
...SO I'LL LEAVE IT UP TO YOU, IKARI-KUN.
THERE'S SOMETHING ABOUT AYANAMI-SAN TODAY...
...SHE'S NOT HER USUAL SELF.
OKAY-- LET'S JUST START WITH THE CLOSEST PLACE.
SO, I DUNNO--
HOW ABOUT KITCHEN STUFF FIRST?
SURE.
UM, IKARI-KUN...
...ABOUT WHAT KATSURAGI-SENSEI SAID IN CLASS...
ARE YOU--
--REALLY WRITING A NOVEL?
WHA --?
--UM, THAT'S, LIKE, UH...

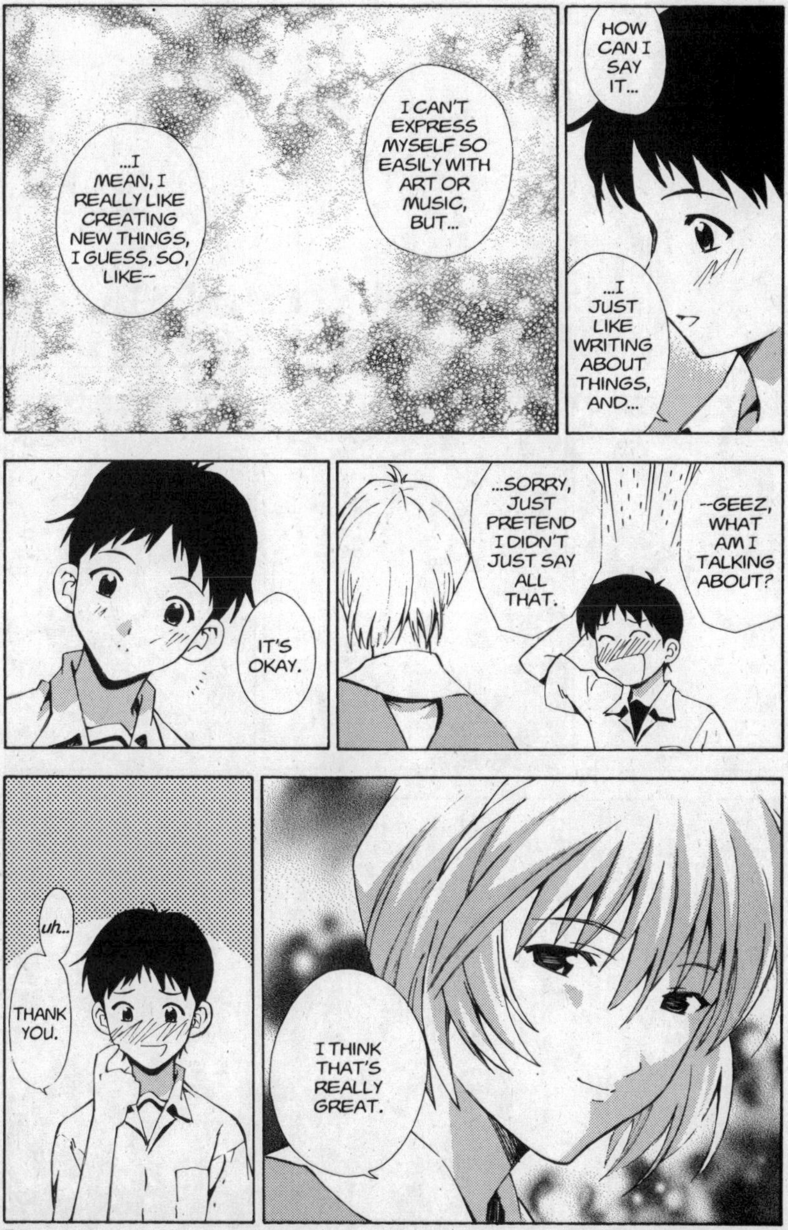
HOW CAN I SAY IT...
...I JUST LIKE WRITING ABOUT THINGS, AND...
I CAN'T EXPRESS MYSELF SO EASILY WITH ART OR MUSIC, BUT...
...I MEAN, I REALLY LIKE CREATING NEW THINGS, I GUESS, SO, LIKE--
--GEEZ, WHAT AM I TALKING ABOUT?
...SORRY, JUST PRETEND I DIDN'T JUST SAY ALL THAT.
IT'S OKAY.
I THINK THAT'S REALLY GREAT.
uh...
THANK YOU.

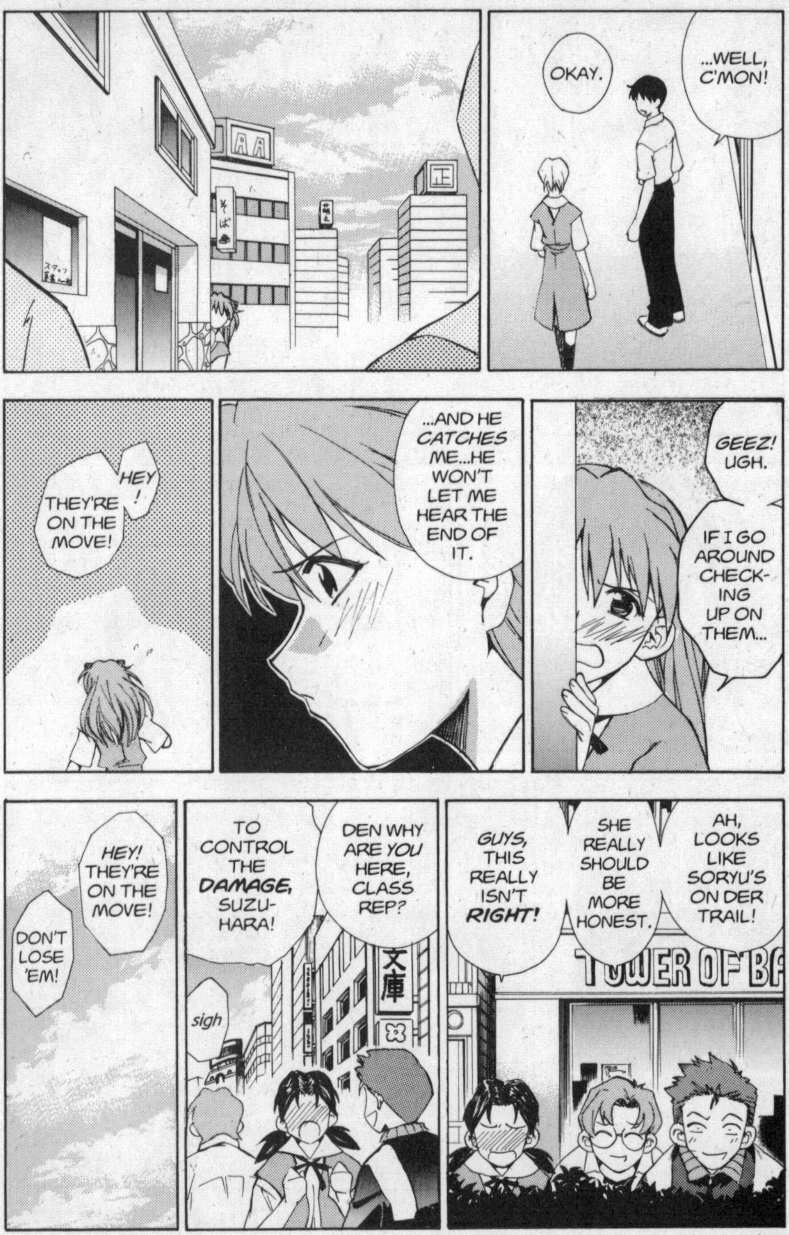
...WELL, C'MON!
OKAY.
GEEZ! UGH.
IF I GO AROUND CHECKING UP ON THEM...
...AND HE CATCHES ME...HE WON'T LET ME HEAR THE END OF IT.
HEY! THEY'RE ON THE MOVE!
AH, LOOKS LIKE SORYU'S ON DER TRAIL!
SHE REALLY SHOULD BE MORE HONEST.
GUYS, THIS REALLY ISN'T RIGHT!
TOWER OF BA
DEN WHY ARE YOU HERE, CLASS REP?
TO CONTROL THE DAMAGE, SUZUHARA!
文庫
sigh
HEY! THEY'RE ON THE MOVE!
DON'T LOSE 'EM!

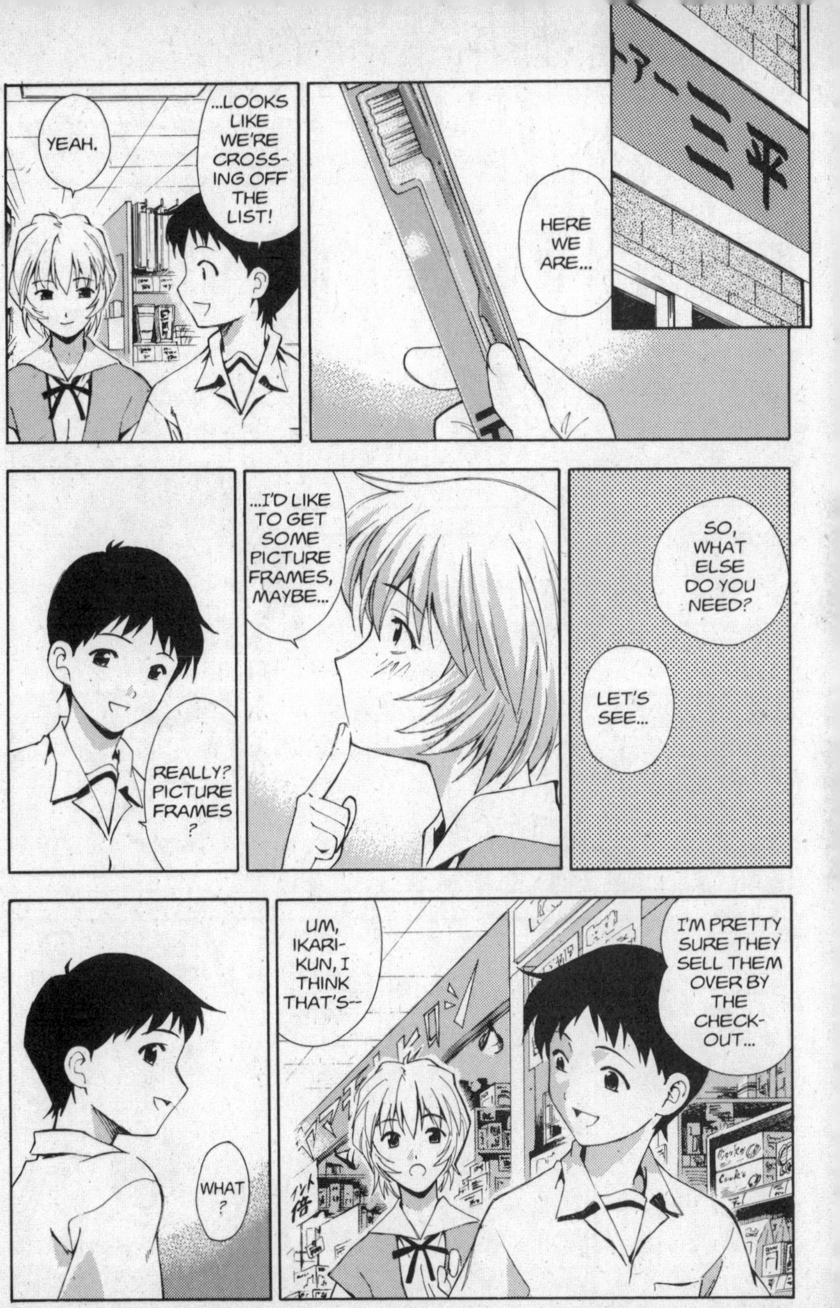
HERE WE ARE...
...LOOKS LIKE WE'RE CROSSING OFF THE LIST!
YEAH.
SO, WHAT ELSE DO YOU NEED?
LET'S SEE...
...I'D LIKE TO GET SOME PICTURE FRAMES, MAYBE...
REALLY? PICTURE FRAMES?
I'M PRETTY SURE THEY SELL THEM OVER BY THE CHECK-OUT...
UM, IKARI-KUN, I THINK THAT'S--
WHAT?

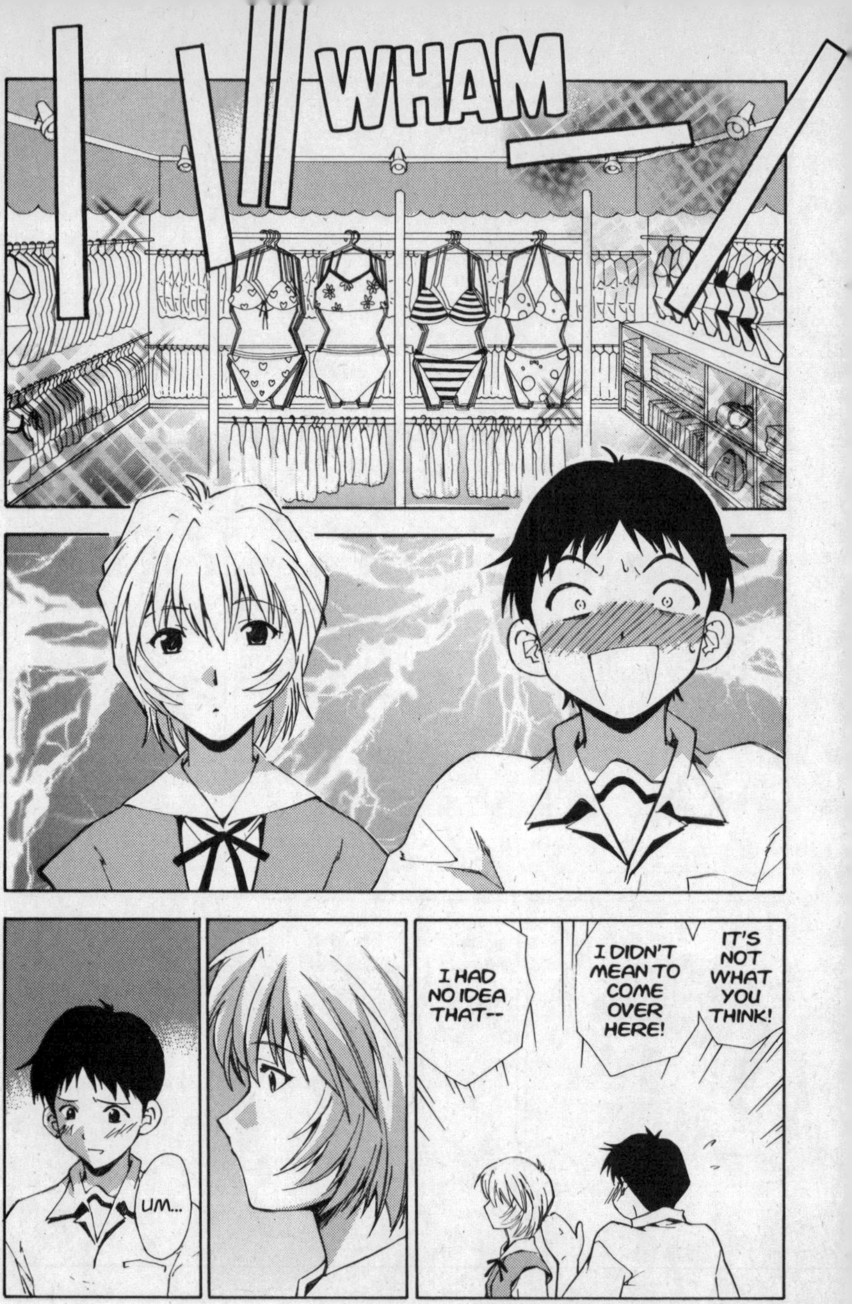
WHAM
IT'S NOT WHAT YOU THINK!
I DIDN'T MEAN TO COME OVER HERE!
I HAD NO IDEA THAT--
UM...

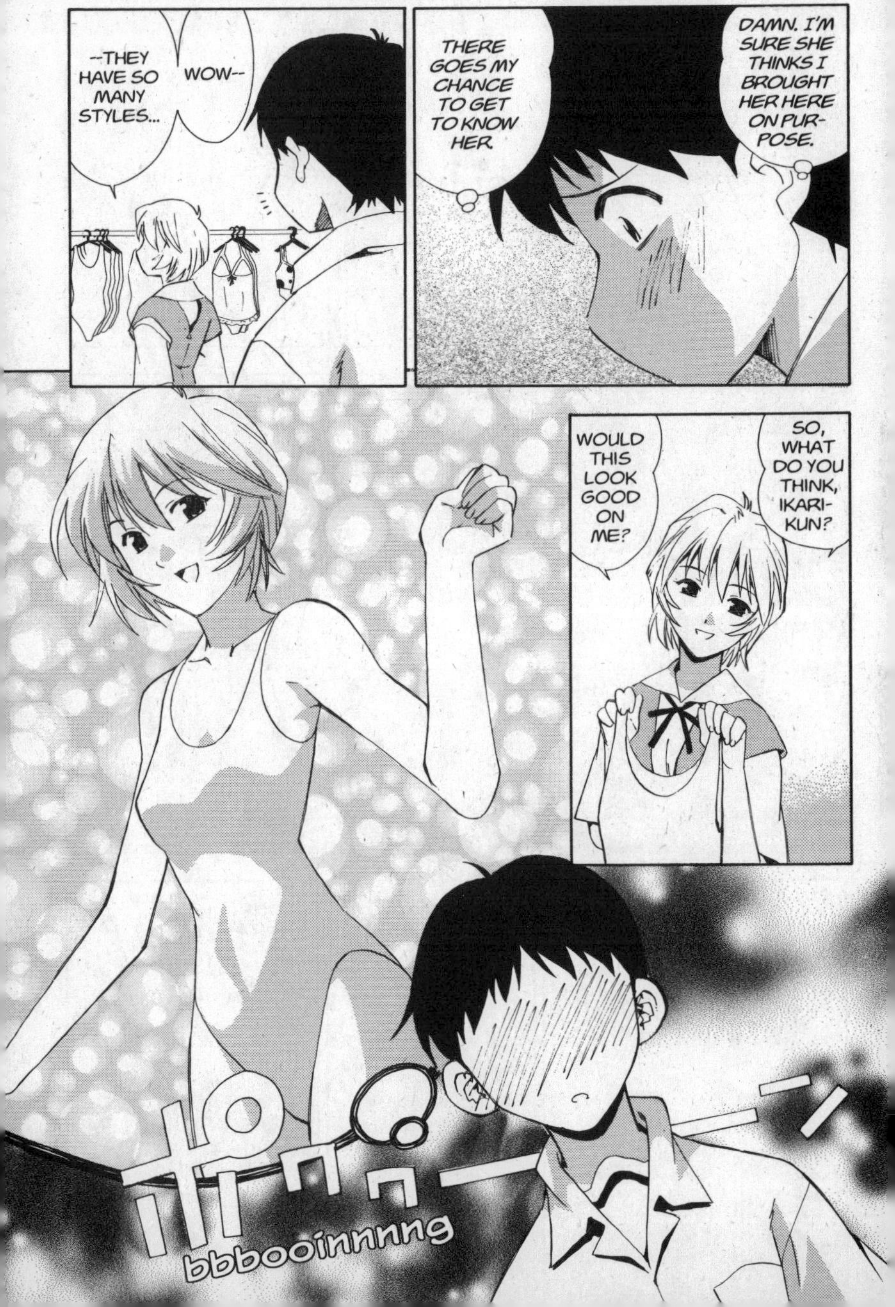
DAMN. I'M SURE SHE THINKS I BROUGHT HER HERE ON PURPOSE.
THERE GOES MY CHANCE TO GET TO KNOW HER.
WOW--
--THEY HAVE SO MANY STYLES...
SO, WHAT DO YOU THINK, IKARI-KUN?
WOULD THIS LOOK GOOD ON ME?
bbbooinnnng

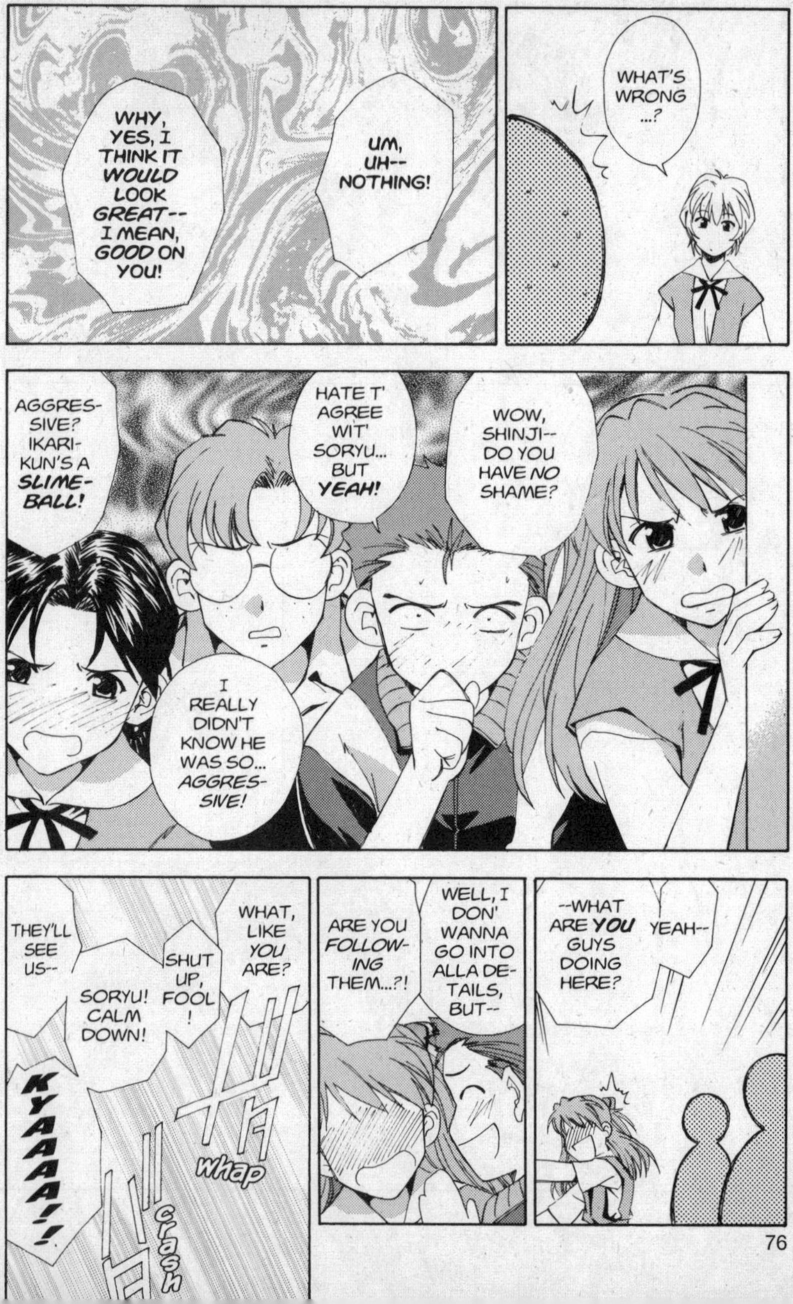
WHAT'S WRONG ...?
UM, UH-- NOTHING!
WHY, YES, I THINK IT *WOULD* LOOK *GREAT*-- I MEAN, *GOOD* ON YOU!
WOW, SHINJI-- DO YOU HAVE *NO* SHAME?
HATE T' AGREE WIT' SORYU... BUT ***YEAH!***
I REALLY DIDN'T KNOW HE WAS SO... *AGGRES-SIVE!*
AGGRES-SIVE? IKARI-KUN'S A ***SLIME-BALL!***
YEAH--
--WHAT ARE ***YOU*** GUYS DOING HERE?
WELL, I DON' WANNA GO INTO ALLA DE-TAILS, BUT--
ARE YOU *FOLLOW-ING* THEM...?!
WHAT, LIKE *YOU* ARE?
SHUT UP, FOOL!
THEY'LL SEE US--
SORYU! CALM DOWN!
whap
KYAAAAI!
crash

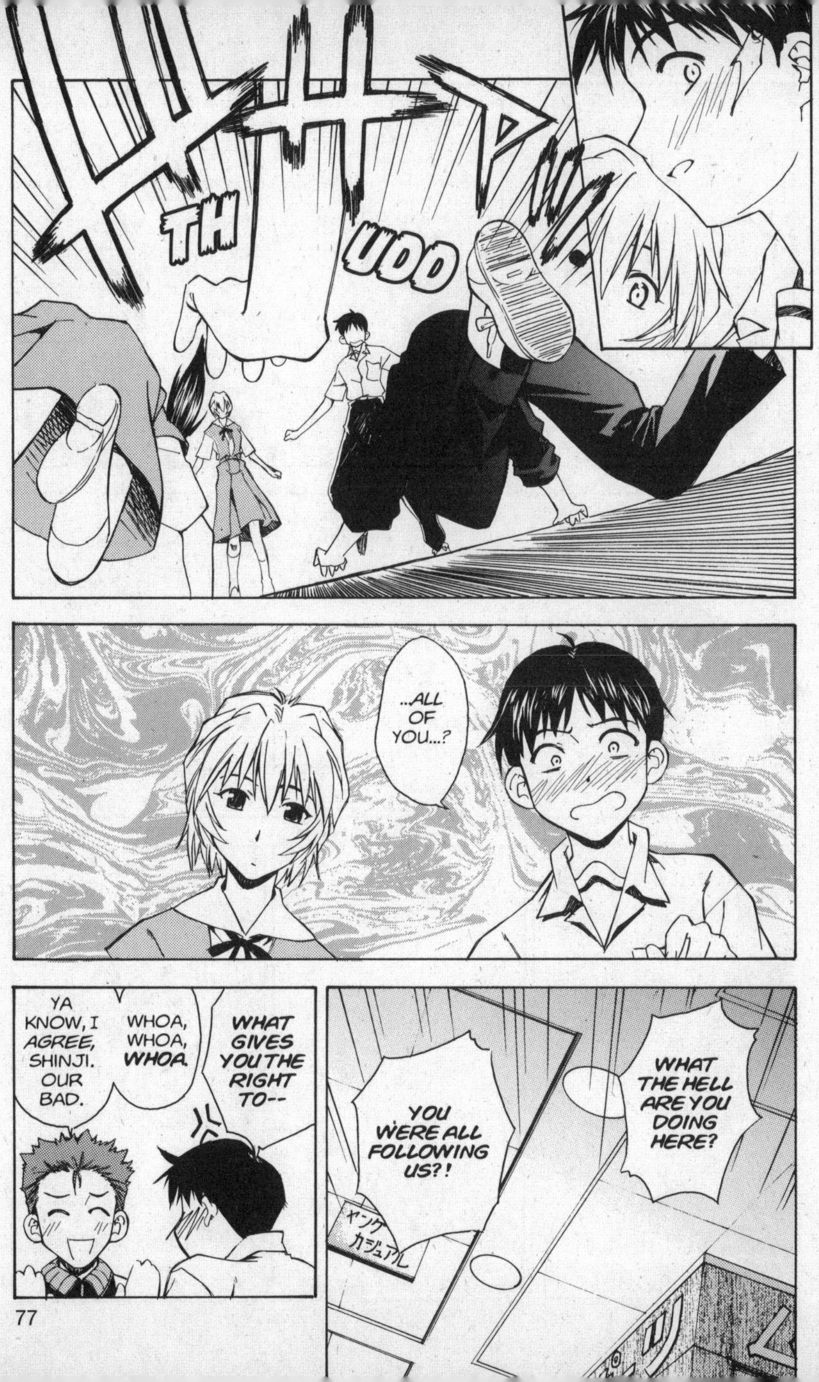
THUDD
...ALL OF YOU...?
WHAT THE HELL ARE YOU DOING HERE?
YOU WERE ALL FOLLOWING US?!
ヤング カジュアル
WHAT GIVES YOU THE RIGHT TO--
WHOA, WHOA, WHOA.
YA KNOW, I AGREE, SHINJI. OUR BAD.

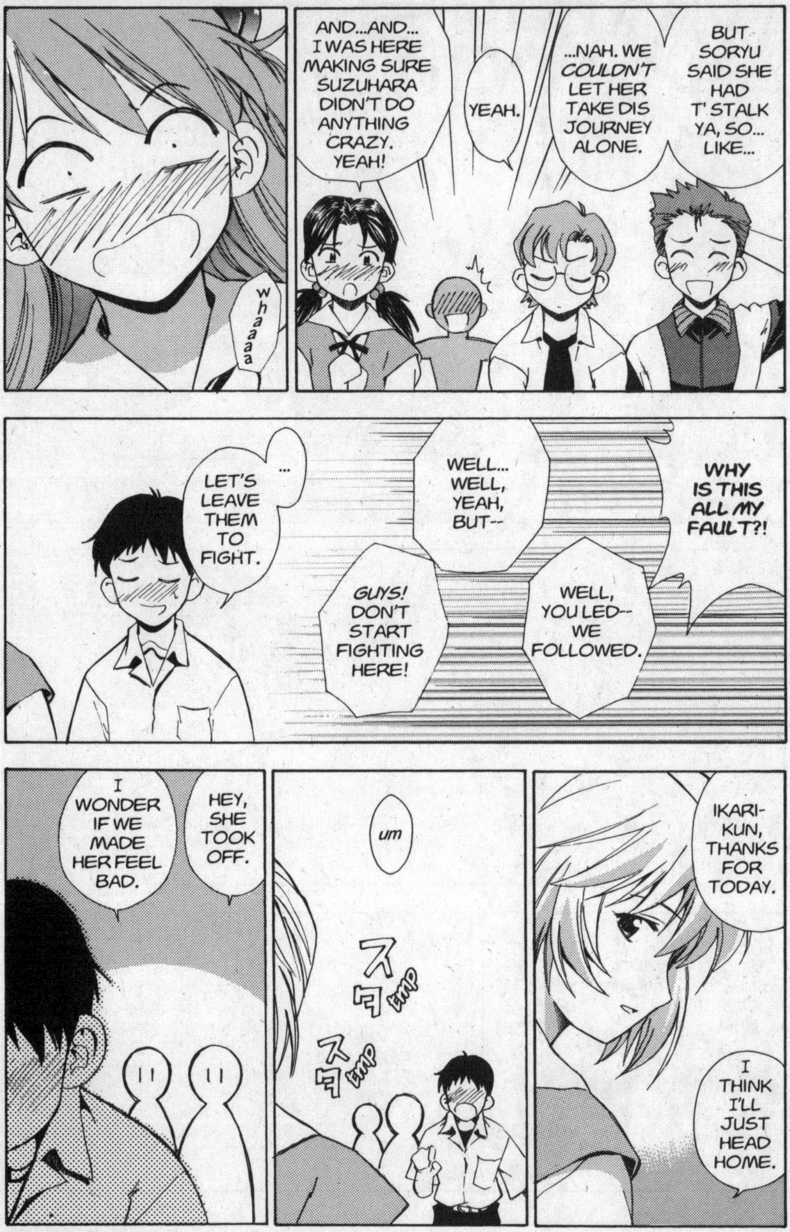
BUT SORYU SAID SHE HAD T' STALK YA, SO... LIKE...
...NAH. WE *COULDN'T* LET HER TAKE DIS JOURNEY ALONE.
YEAH.
AND...AND... I WAS HERE MAKING SURE SUZUHARA DIDN'T DO ANYTHING CRAZY. YEAH!
whaaaa
WHY IS THIS ALL MY FAULT?!
WELL... WELL, YEAH, BUT--
WELL, YOU LED-- WE FOLLOWED.
GUYS! DON'T START FIGHTING HERE!
...
LET'S LEAVE THEM TO FIGHT.
IKARI-KUN, THANKS FOR TODAY.
I THINK I'LL JUST HEAD HOME.
um
スタ tmp
スタ tmp
HEY, SHE TOOK OFF.
I WONDER IF WE MADE HER FEEL BAD.

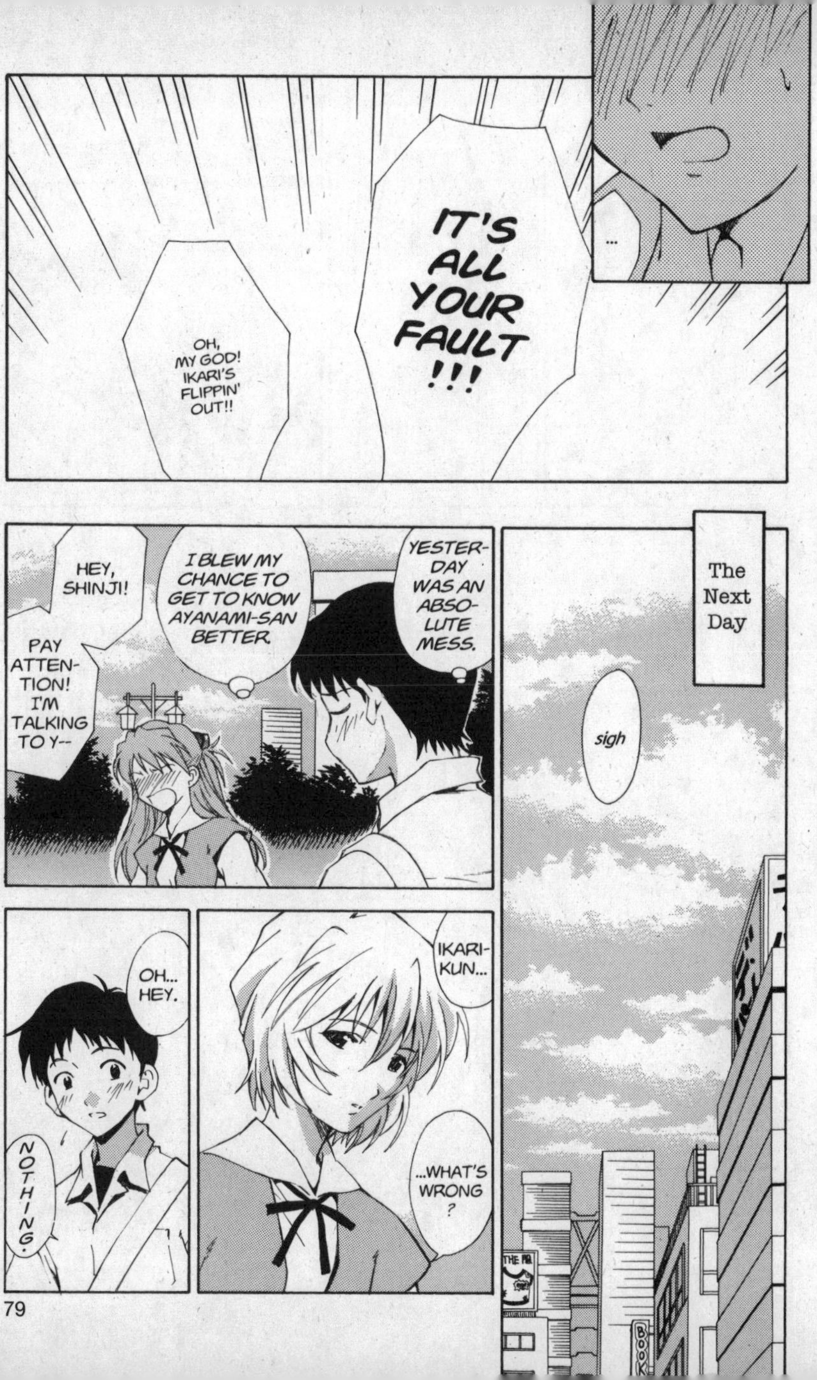
...
IT'S ALL YOUR FAULT!!!
OH, MY GOD! IKARI'S FLIPPIN' OUT!!
The Next Day
sigh
YESTERDAY WAS AN ABSOLUTE MESS.
I BLEW MY CHANCE TO GET TO KNOW AYANAMI-SAN BETTER.
HEY, SHINJI!
PAY ATTENTION! I'M TALKING TO Y--
IKARI-KUN...
...WHAT'S WRONG?
OH... HEY.
NOTHING.
THE PA
BOOK

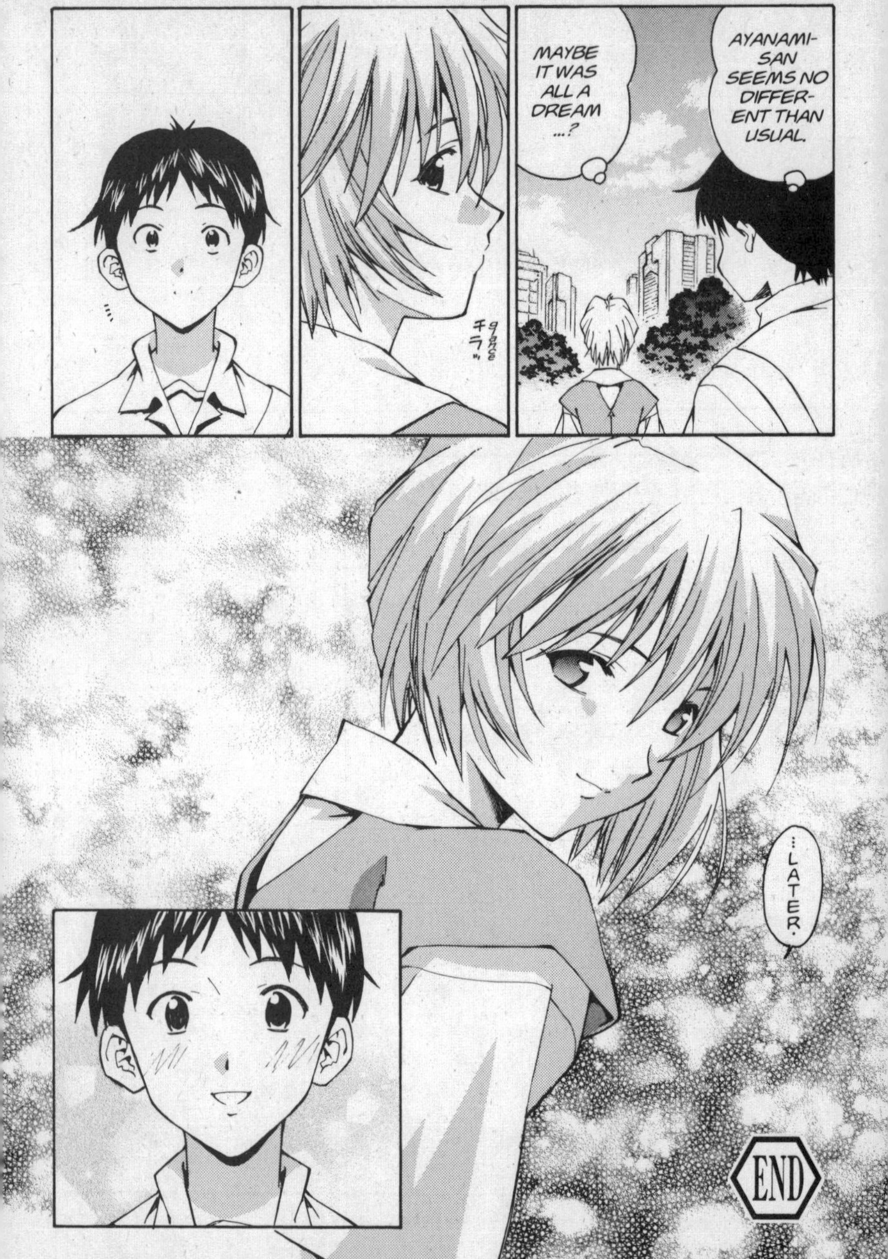
AYANAMI-SAN SEEMS NO DIFFERENT THAN USUAL.
MAYBE IT WAS ALL A DREAM ...?
チラ
glance
...
...LATER.
END

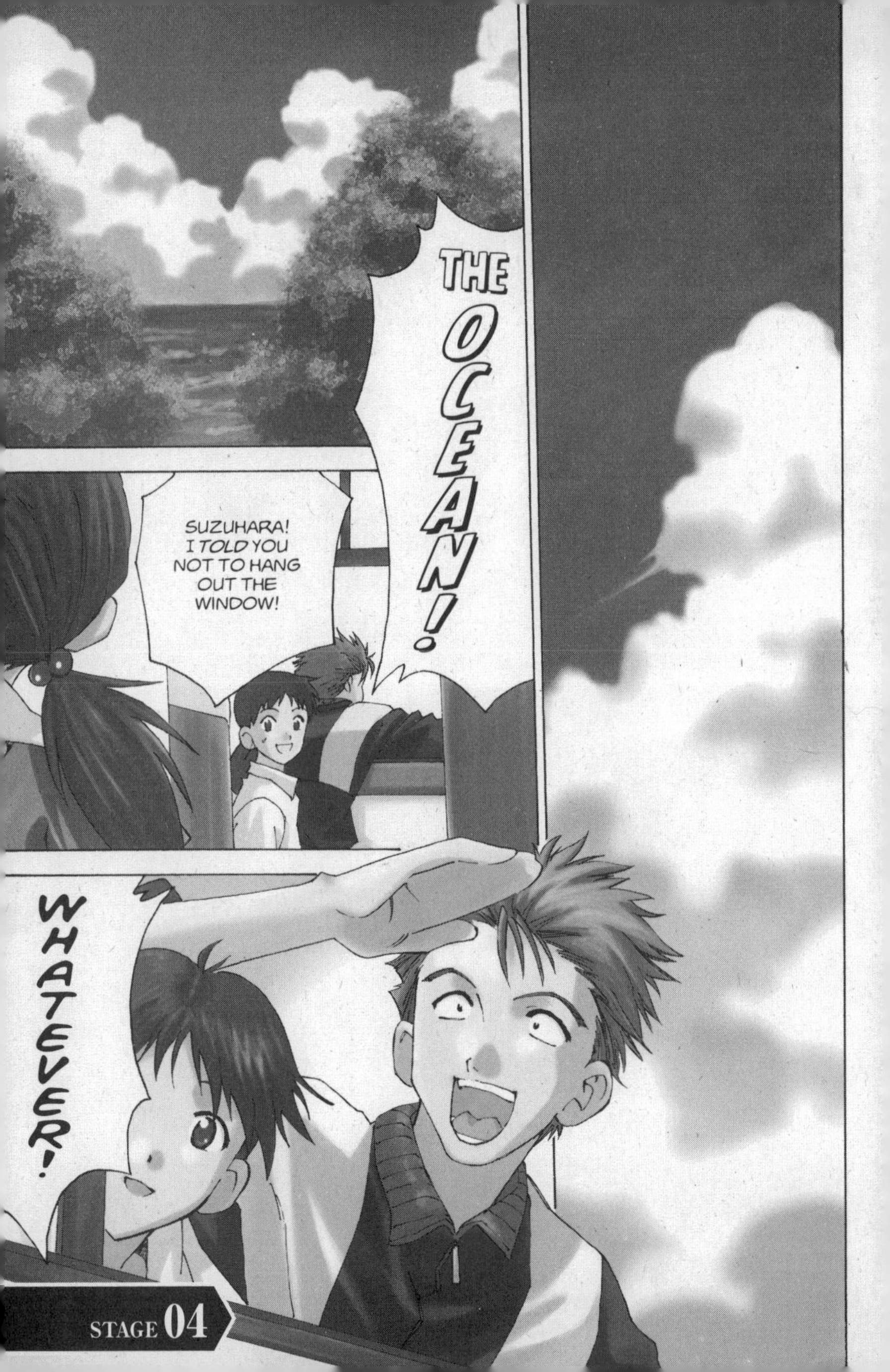
THE OCEAN!
SUZUHARA! I TOLD YOU NOT TO HANG OUT THE WINDOW!
WHATEVER!
STAGE 04

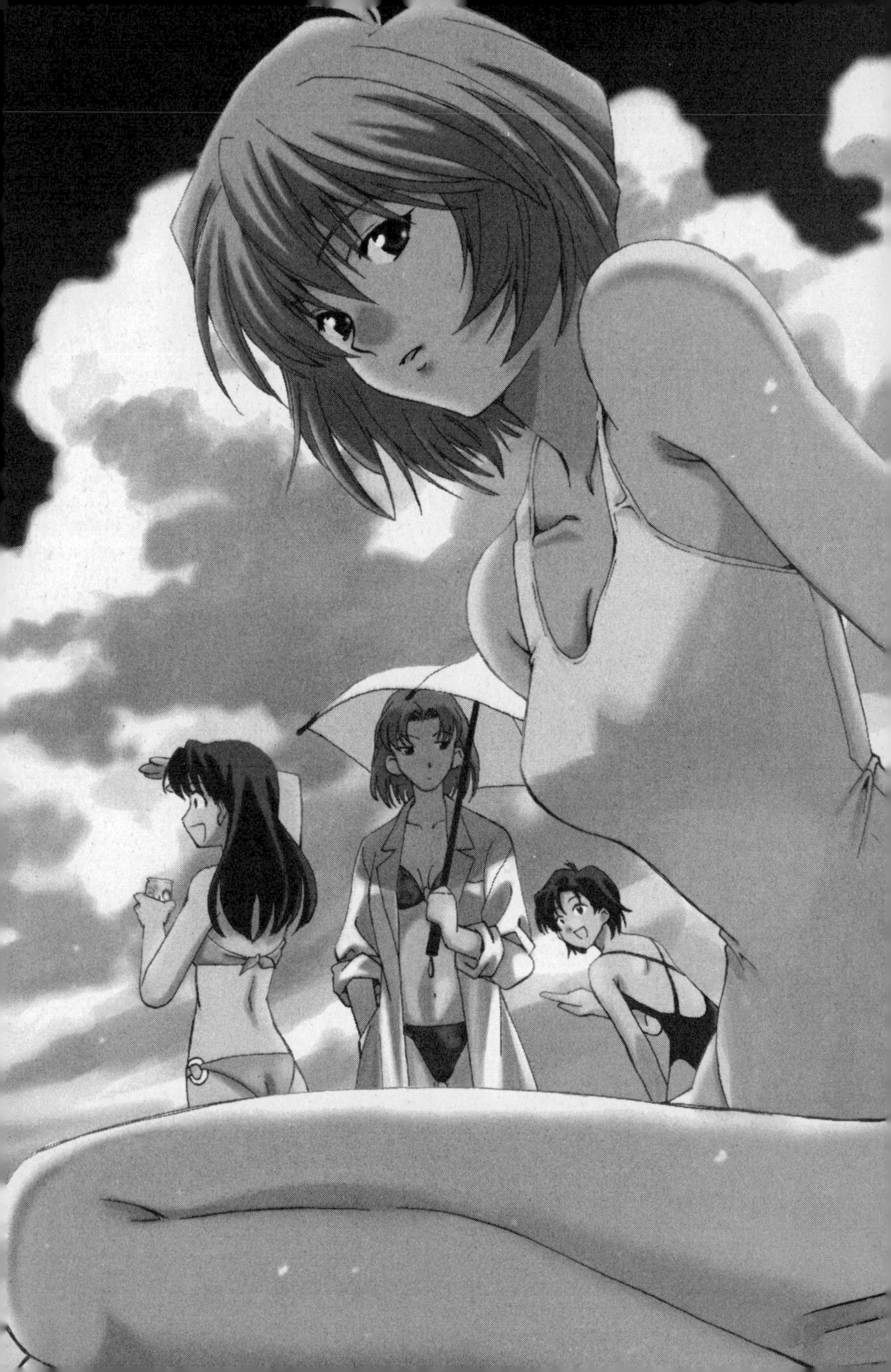

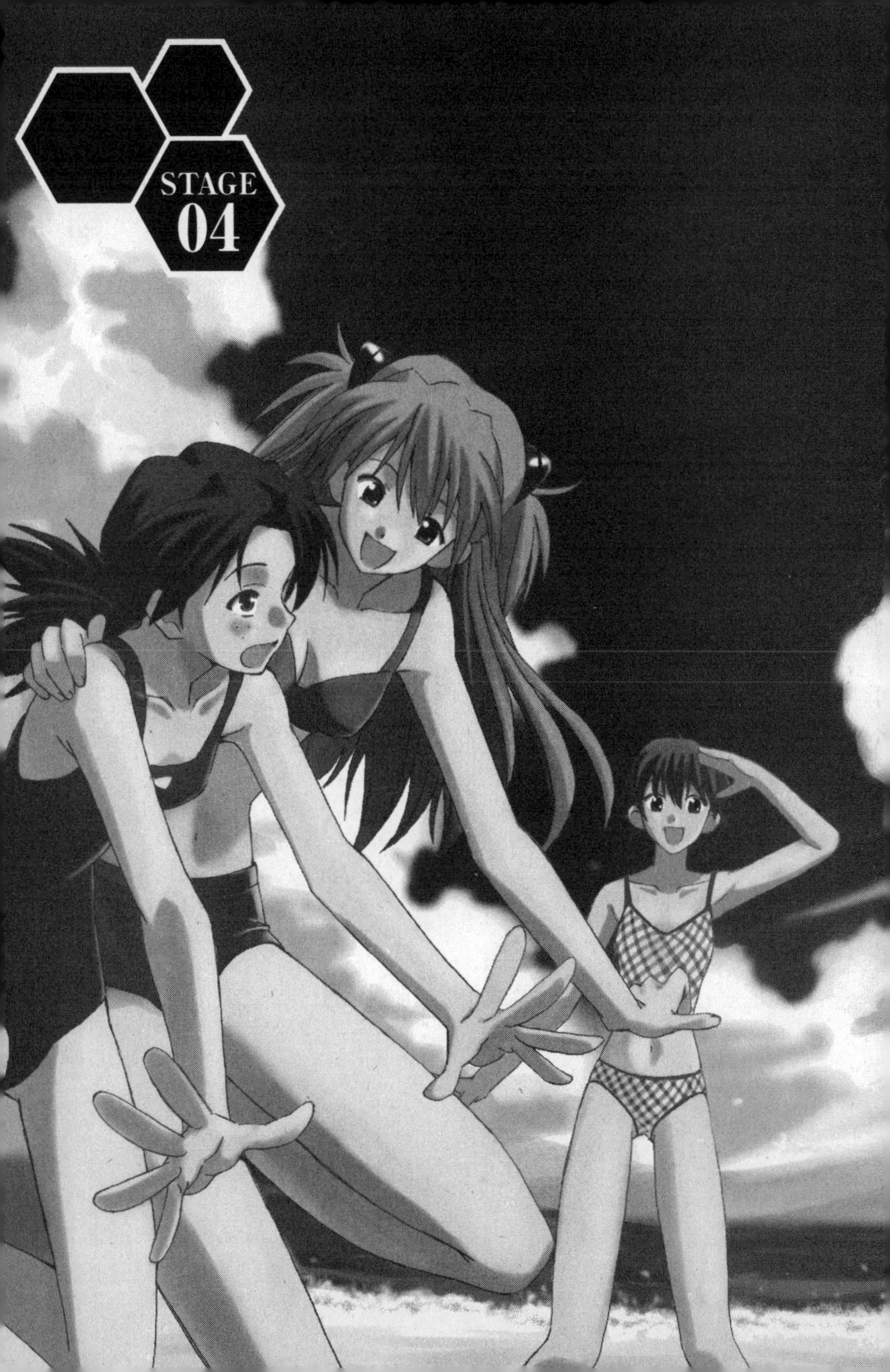
STAGE
04

NEON GENESIS
EVANGELION
THE SHINJI IKARI RAISING PROJECT

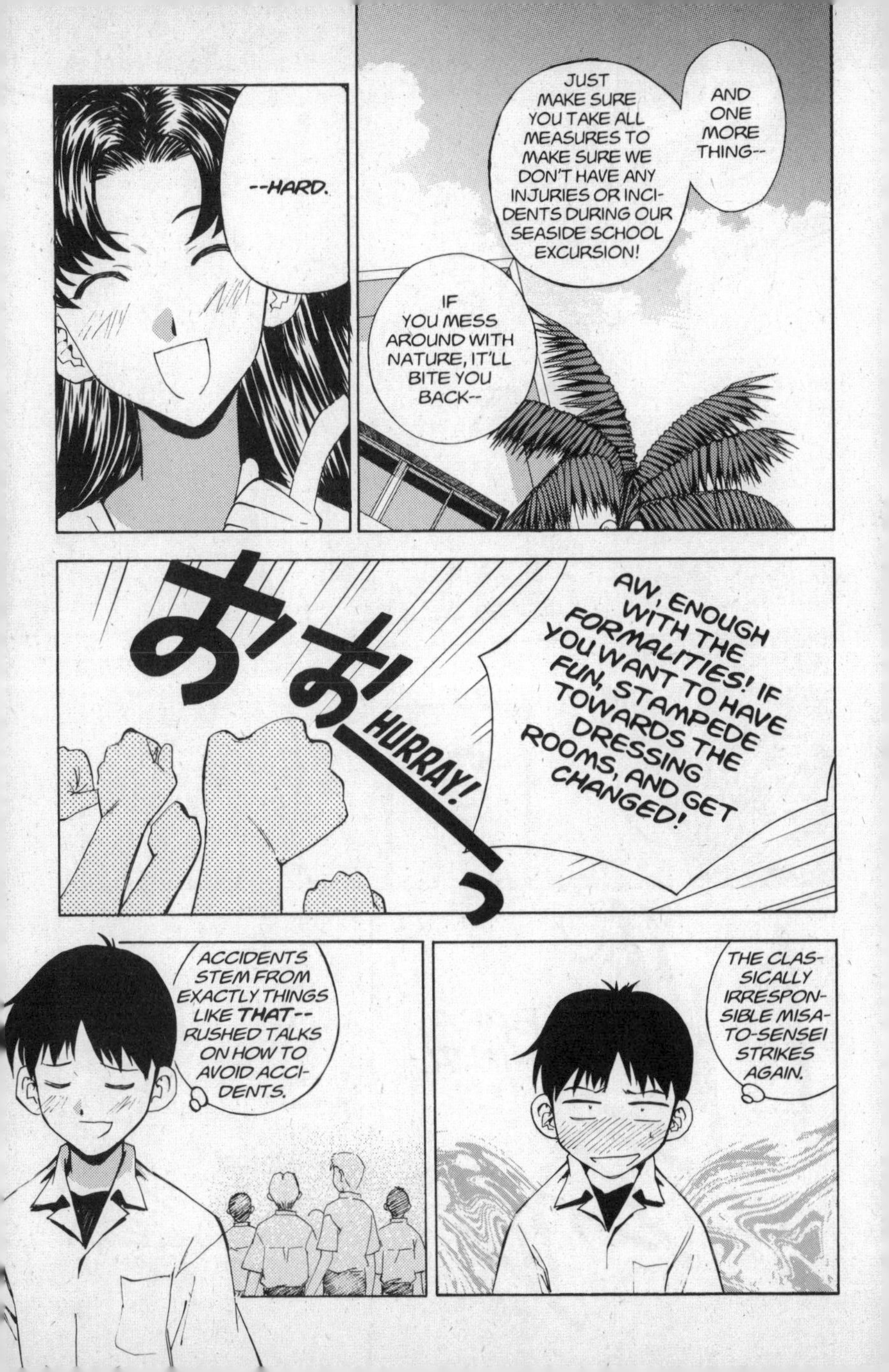
AND ONE MORE THING--
JUST MAKE SURE YOU TAKE ALL MEASURES TO MAKE SURE WE DON'T HAVE ANY INJURIES OR INCIDENTS DURING OUR SEASIDE SCHOOL EXCURSION!
IF YOU MESS AROUND WITH NATURE, IT'LL BITE YOU BACK--
--HARD.
AW, ENOUGH WITH THE FORMALITIES! IF YOU WANT TO HAVE FUN, STAMPEDE TOWARDS THE DRESSING ROOMS, AND GET CHANGED!
おお
HURRAY!
THE CLASSICALLY IRRESPONSIBLE MISATO-SENSEI STRIKES AGAIN.
ACCIDENTS STEM FROM EXACTLY THINGS LIKE THAT-- RUSHED TALKS ON HOW TO AVOID ACCIDENTS.

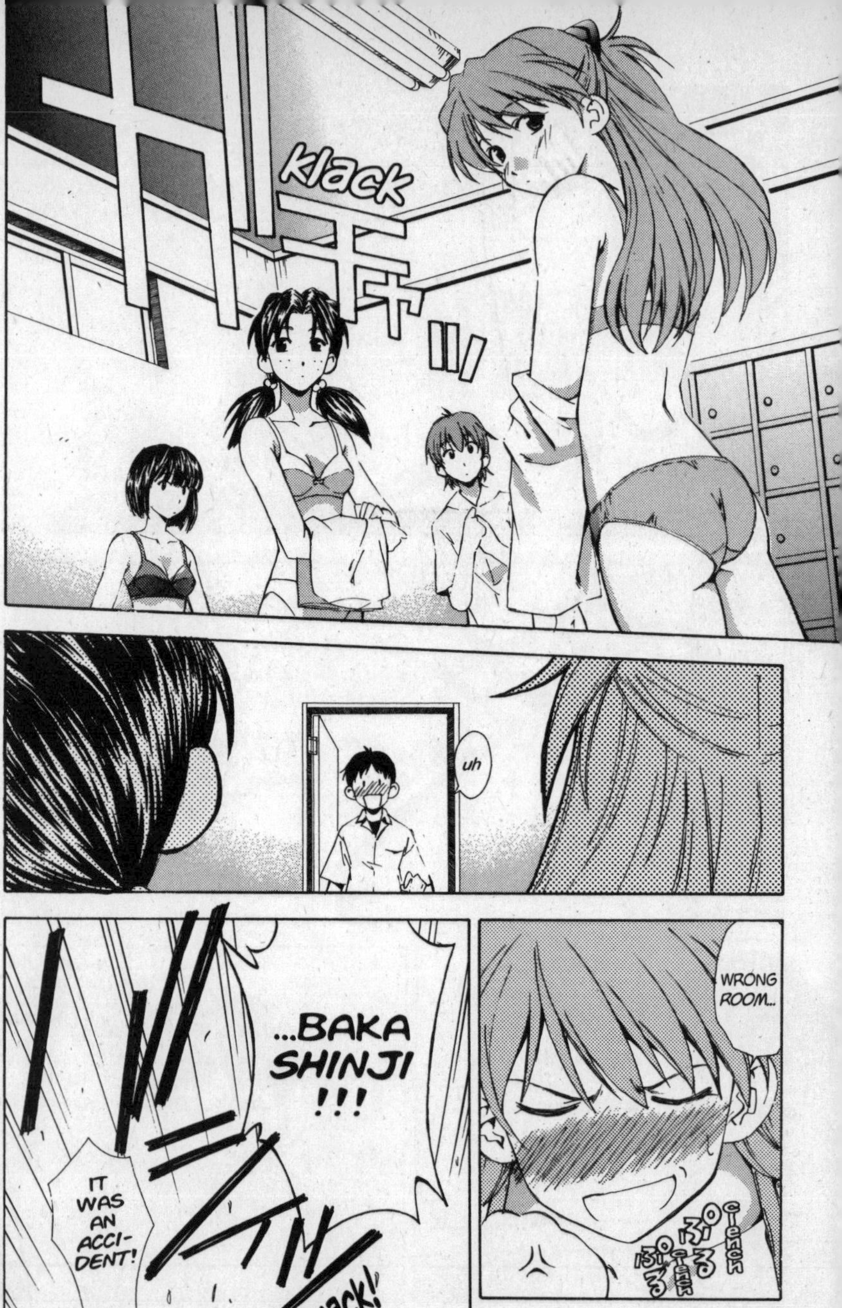
klack
uh
WRONG ROOM...
clench
...BAKA SHINJI !!!
IT WAS AN ACCI-DENT!
smack!

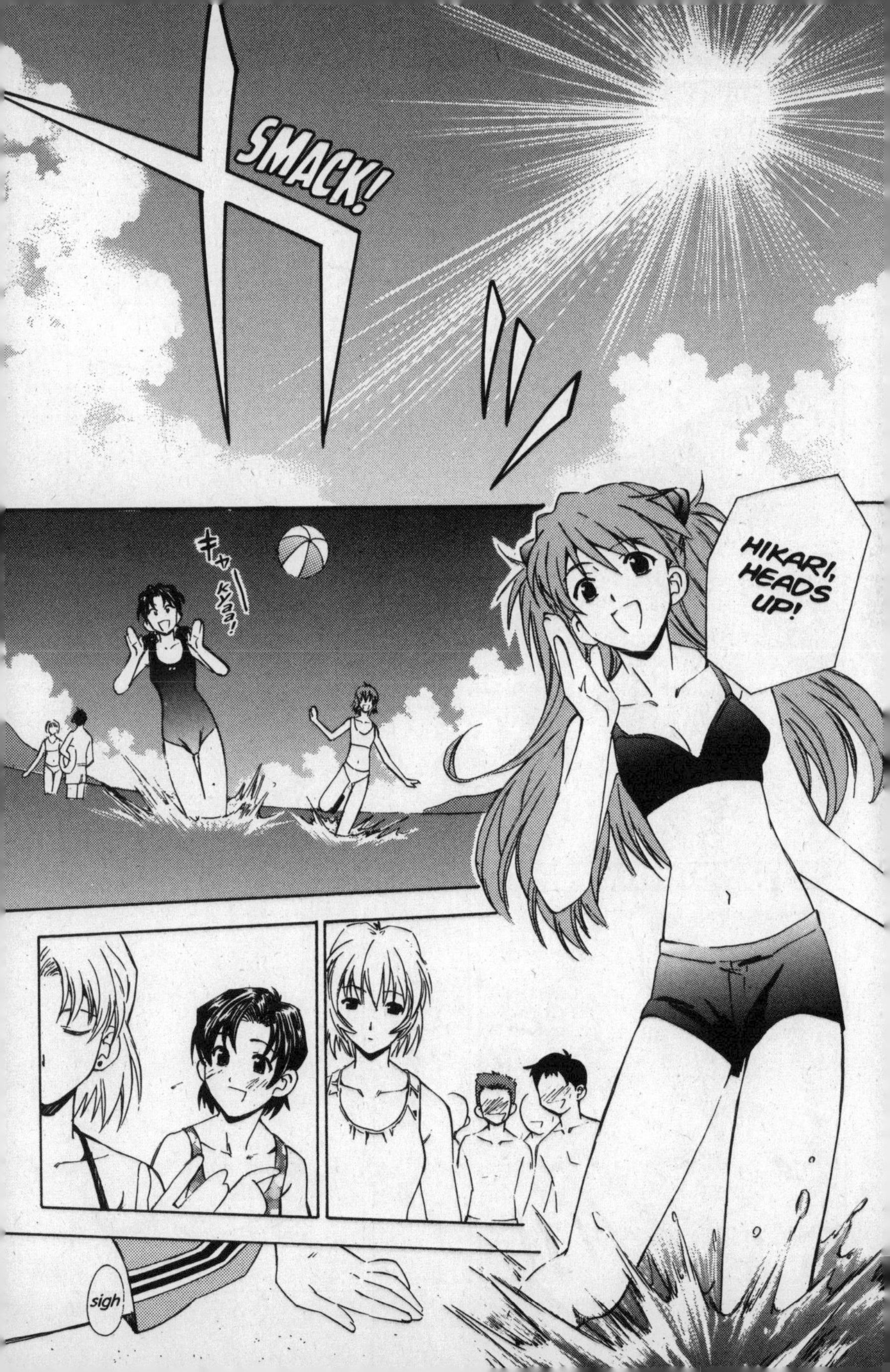
SMACK!
HIKARI, HEADS UP!
キャー
kyaa!
sigh

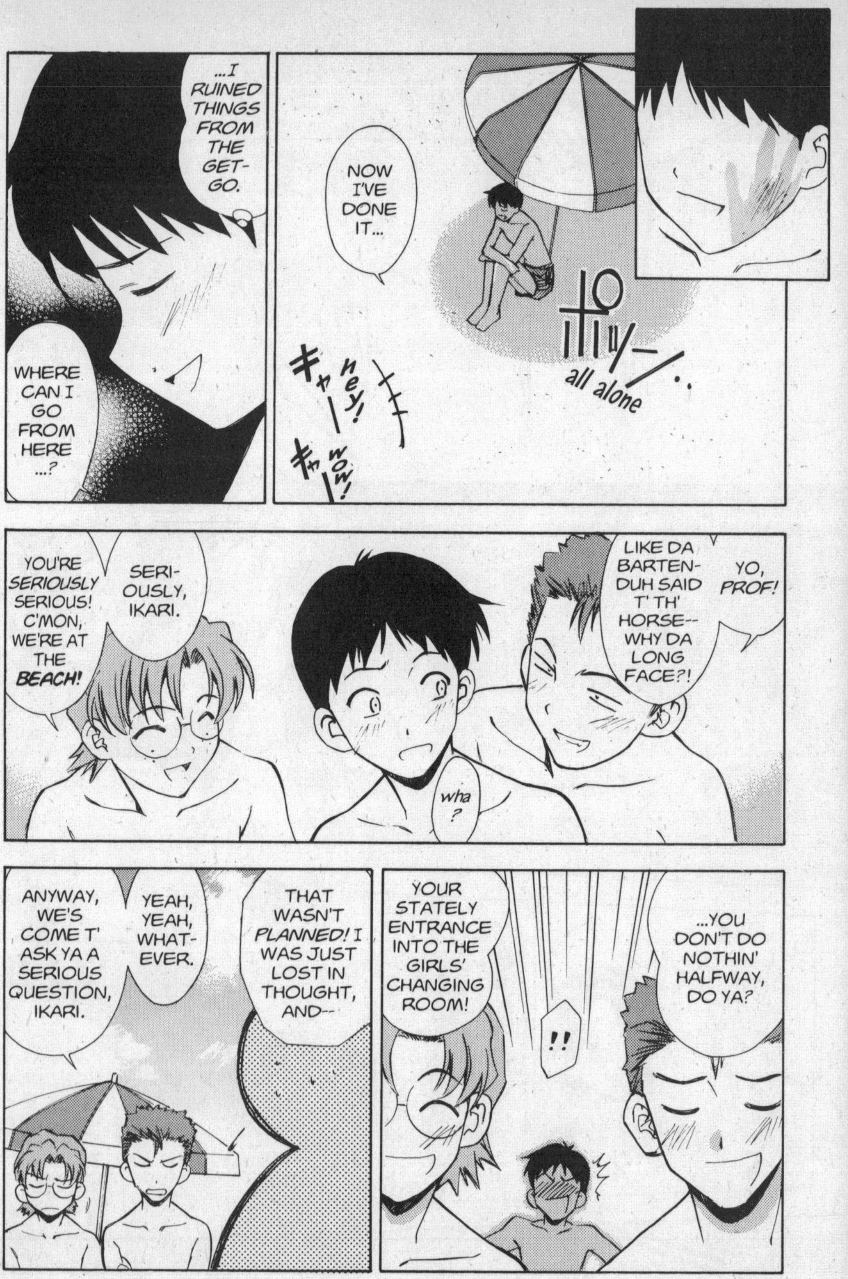

NOW I'VE DONE IT...
all alone
hey!
wow!
...I RUINED THINGS FROM THE GET-GO.
WHERE CAN I GO FROM HERE ...?
YO, *PROF!*
LIKE DA BARTEN-DUH SAID T' TH' HORSE-- WHY DA LONG FACE?!
wha ?
SERI-OUSLY, IKARI.
YOU'RE *SERIOUSLY* SERIOUS! C'MON, WE'RE AT THE ***BEACH!***
...YOU DON'T DO NOTHIN' HALFWAY, DO YA?
YOUR STATELY ENTRANCE INTO THE GIRLS' CHANGING ROOM!
!!
THAT WASN'T *PLANNED!* I WAS JUST LOST IN THOUGHT, AND--
YEAH, YEAH, WHAT-EVER.
ANYWAY, WE'S COME T' ASK YA A SERIOUS QUESTION, IKARI.

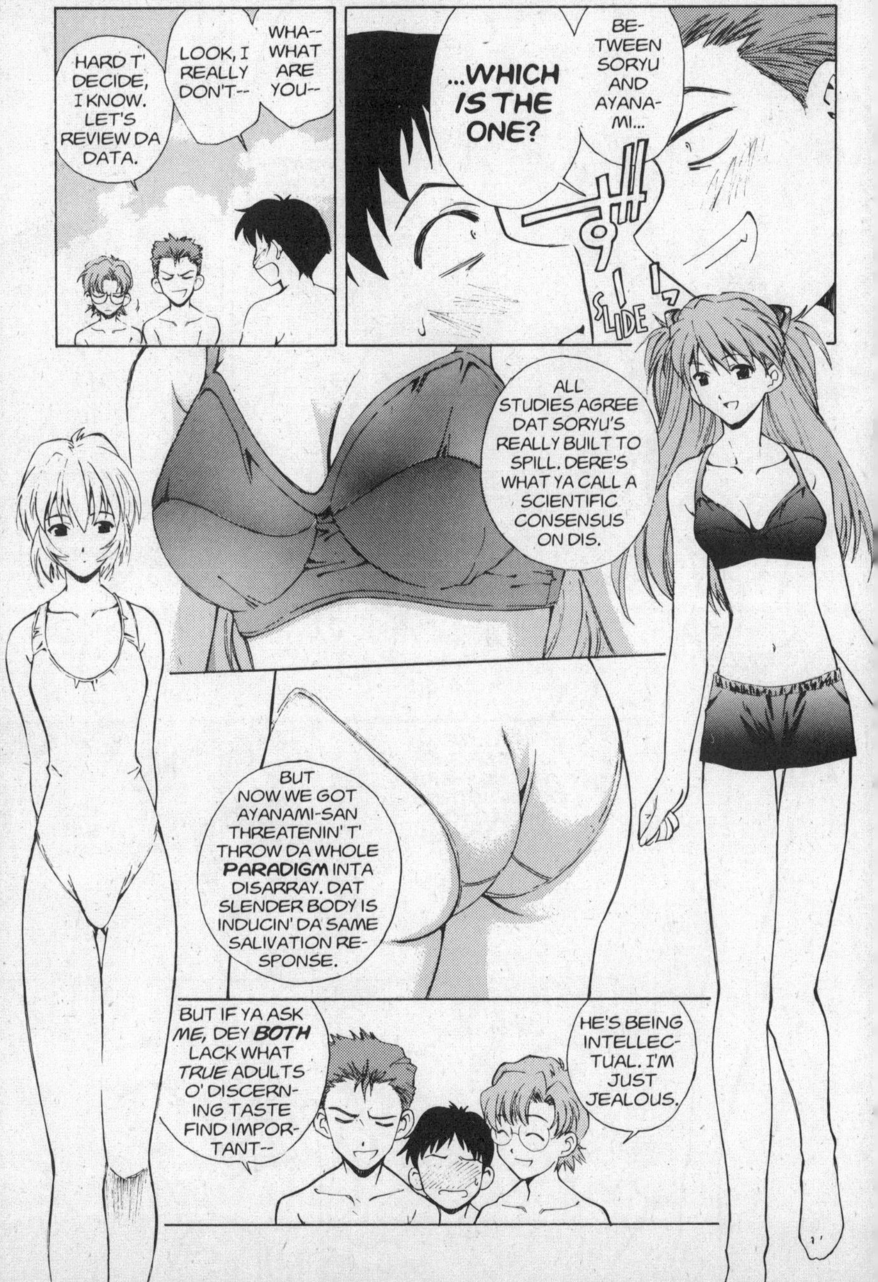
BE-TWEEN SORYU AND AYANA-MI...
...WHICH IS THE ONE?
SLIDE
WHA-- WHAT ARE YOU--
LOOK, I REALLY DON'T--
HARD T' DECIDE, I KNOW. LET'S REVIEW DA DATA.
ALL STUDIES AGREE DAT SORYU'S REALLY BUILT TO SPILL. DERE'S WHAT YA CALL A SCIENTIFIC CONSENSUS ON DIS.
BUT NOW WE GOT AYANAMI-SAN THREATENIN' T' THROW DA WHOLE PARADIGM INTA DISARRAY. DAT SLENDER BODY IS INDUCIN' DA SAME SALIVATION RE-SPONSE.
BUT IF YA ASK ME, DEY BOTH LACK WHAT TRUE ADULTS O' DISCERN-ING TASTE FIND IMPOR-TANT--
HE'S BEING INTELLEC-TUAL. I'M JUST JEALOUS.

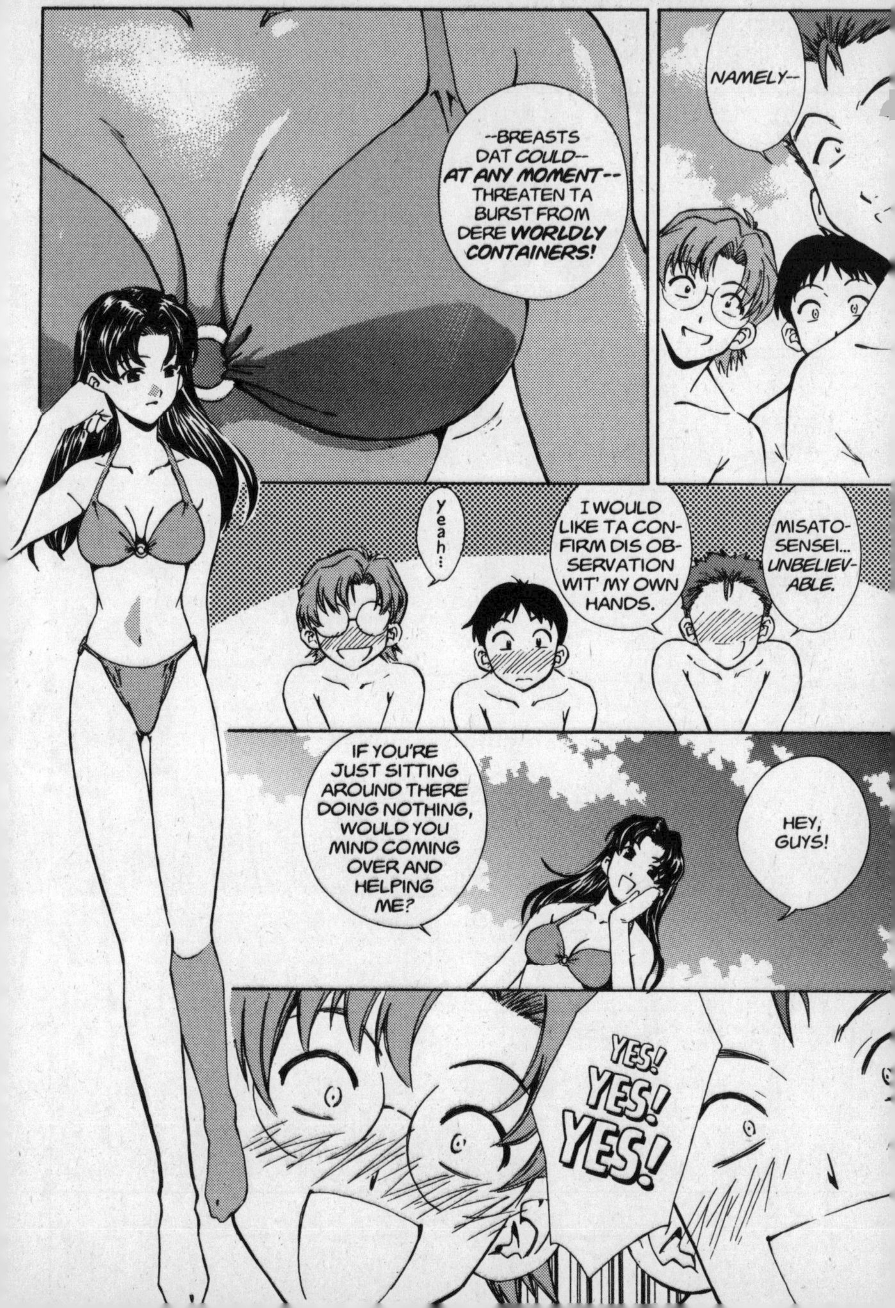
NAMELY--
--BREASTS DAT COULD-- AT ANY MOMENT-- THREATEN TA BURST FROM DERE WORLDLY CONTAINERS!
MISATO-SENSEI... UNBELIEVABLE.
I WOULD LIKE TA CONFIRM DIS OBSERVATION WIT' MY OWN HANDS.
Yeah...
HEY, GUYS!
IF YOU'RE JUST SITTING AROUND THERE DOING NOTHING, WOULD YOU MIND COMING OVER AND HELPING ME?
YES! YES! YES!

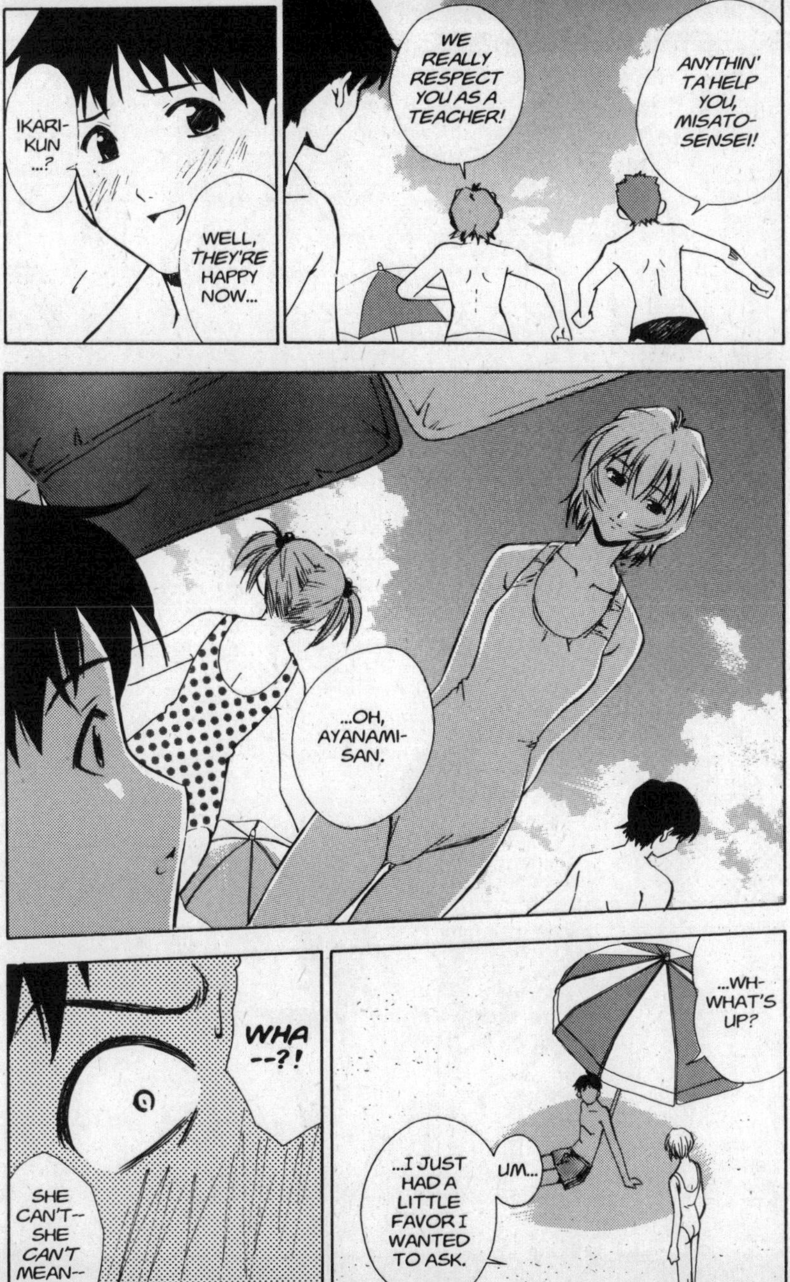
ANYTHIN' TA HELP YOU, MISATO-SENSEI!
WE REALLY RESPECT YOU AS A TEACHER!
IKARI-KUN ...?
WELL, THEY'RE HAPPY NOW...
...OH, AYANAMI-SAN.
...WH-WHAT'S UP?
UM...
...I JUST HAD A LITTLE FAVOR I WANTED TO ASK.
WHA--?!
SHE CAN'T-- SHE CAN'T MEAN--

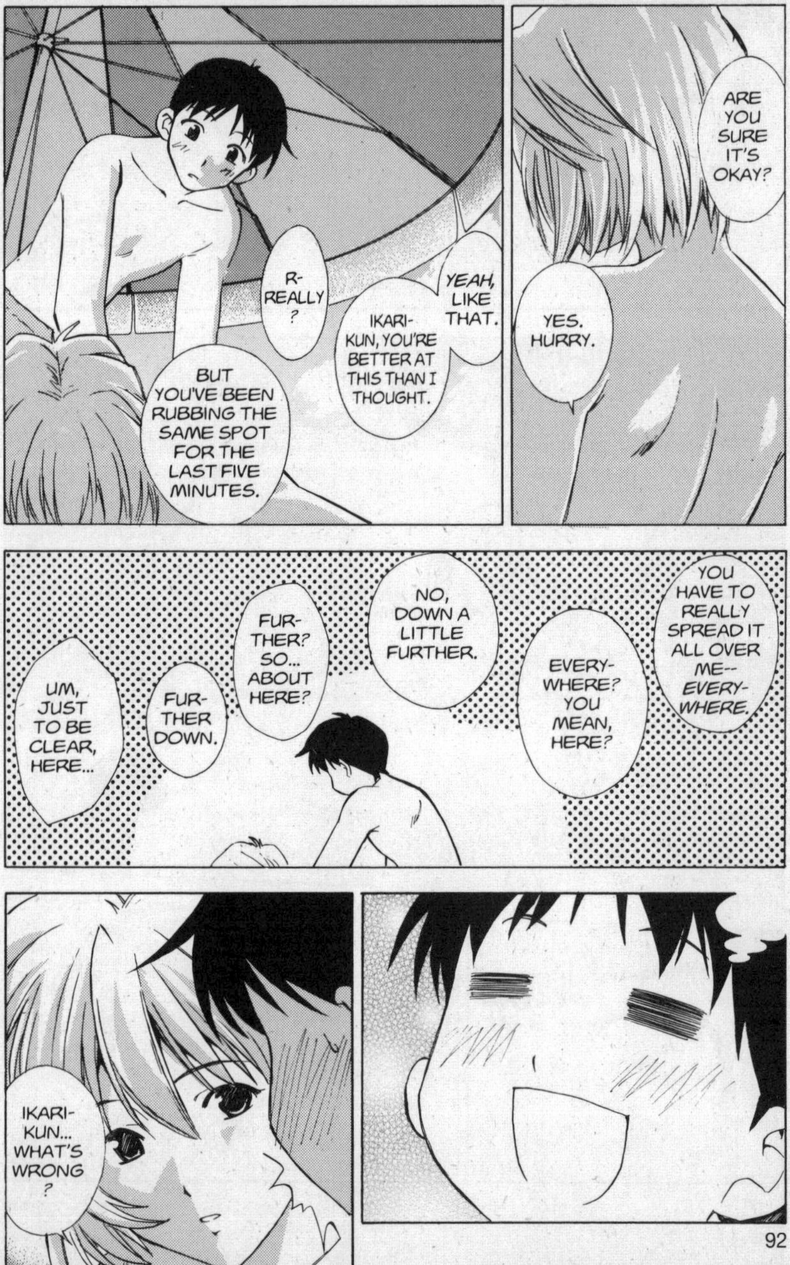
ARE YOU SURE IT'S OKAY?
YES. HURRY.
YEAH, LIKE THAT.
IKARI-KUN, YOU'RE BETTER AT THIS THAN I THOUGHT.
R-REALLY?
BUT YOU'VE BEEN RUBBING THE SAME SPOT FOR THE LAST FIVE MINUTES.
YOU HAVE TO REALLY SPREAD IT ALL OVER ME-- *EVERYWHERE.*
EVERY-WHERE? YOU MEAN, HERE?
NO, DOWN A LITTLE FURTHER.
FUR-THER? SO... ABOUT HERE?
FUR-THER DOWN.
UM, JUST TO BE CLEAR, HERE...
IKARI-KUN... WHAT'S WRONG?

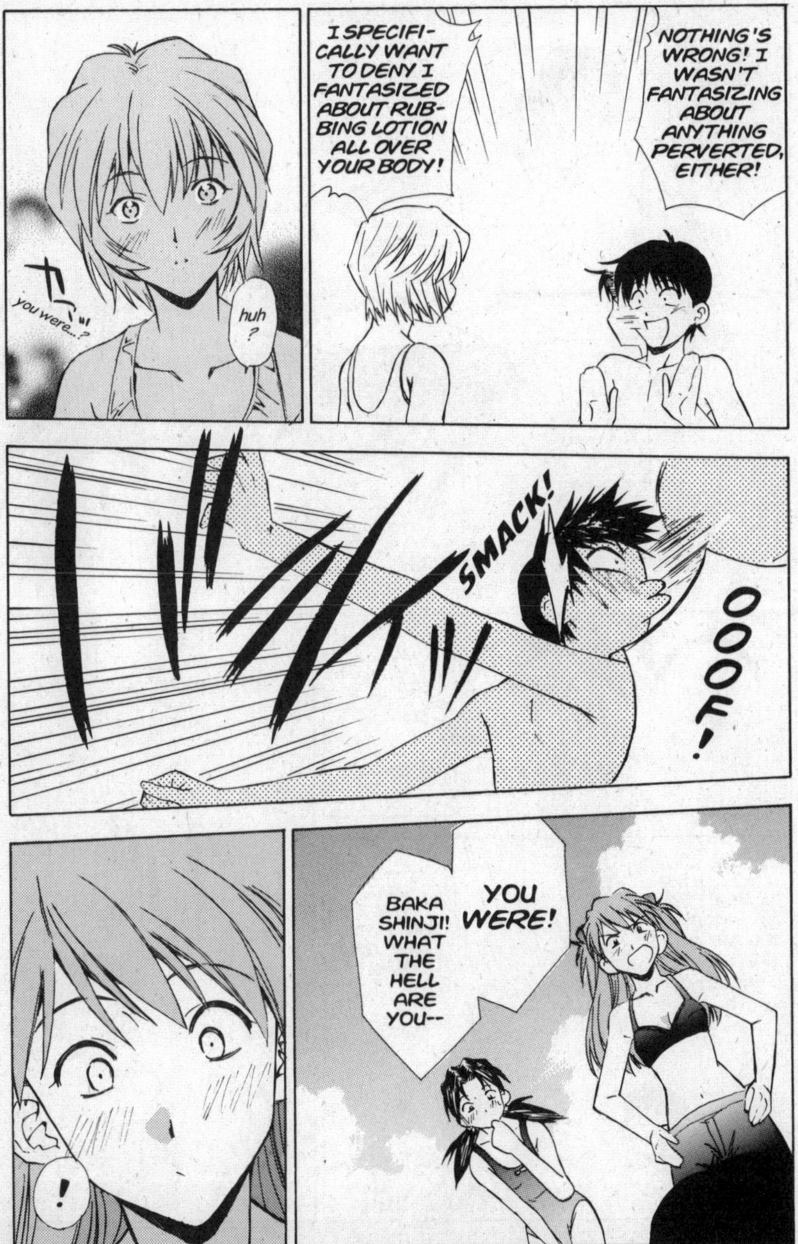
NOTHING'S WRONG! I WASN'T FANTASIZING ABOUT ANYTHING PERVERTED, EITHER!
I SPECIFI-CALLY WANT TO DENY I FANTASIZED ABOUT RUB-BING LOTION ALL OVER YOUR BODY!
huh ?
you were...?
SMACK!
OOOOF!
YOU WERE!
BAKA SHINJI! WHAT THE HELL ARE YOU--
!

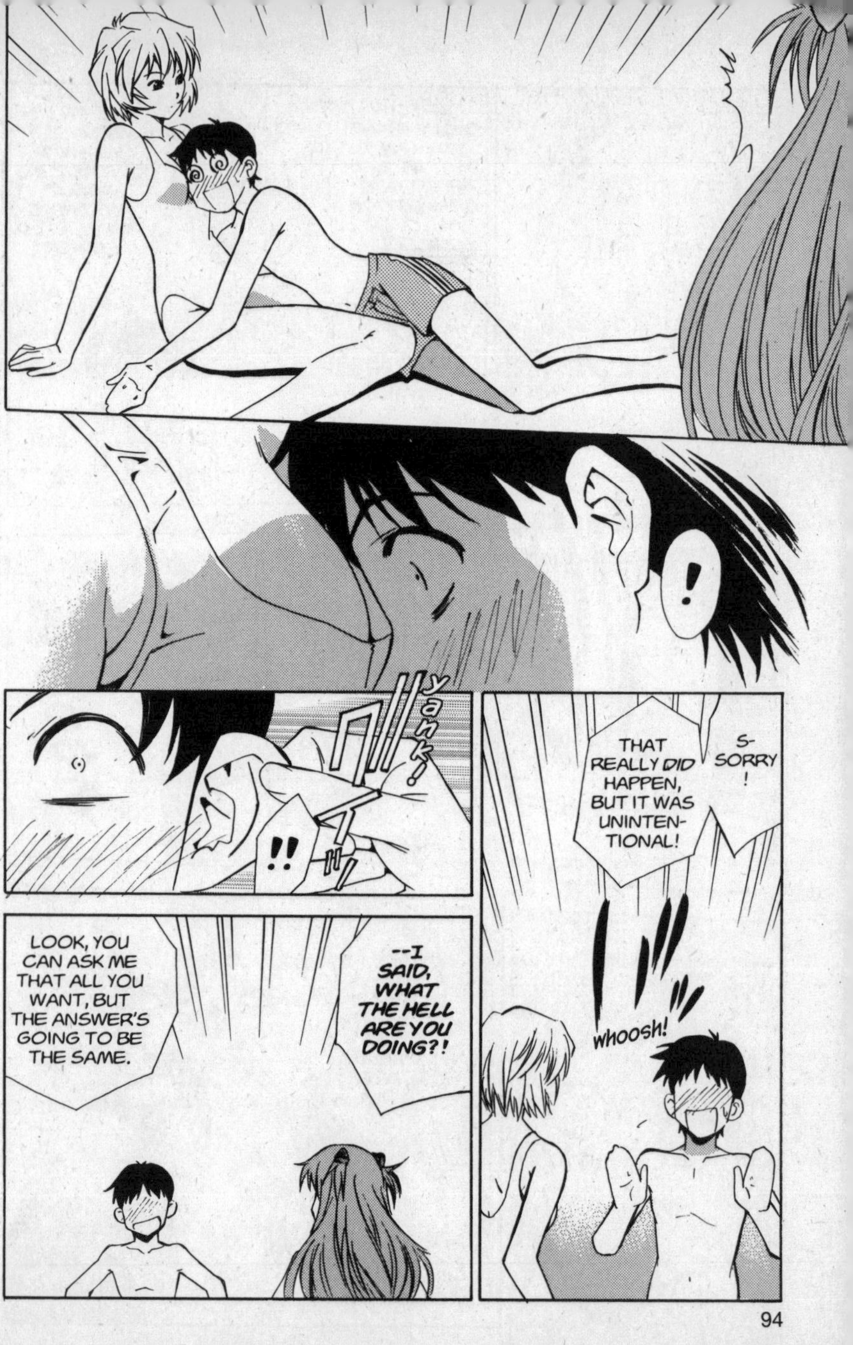
!
S-SORRY!
THAT REALLY DID HAPPEN, BUT IT WAS UNINTENTIONAL!
whoosh!
yank!
!!
--I SAID, WHAT THE HELL ARE YOU DOING?!
LOOK, YOU CAN ASK ME THAT ALL YOU WANT, BUT THE ANSWER'S GOING TO BE THE SAME.

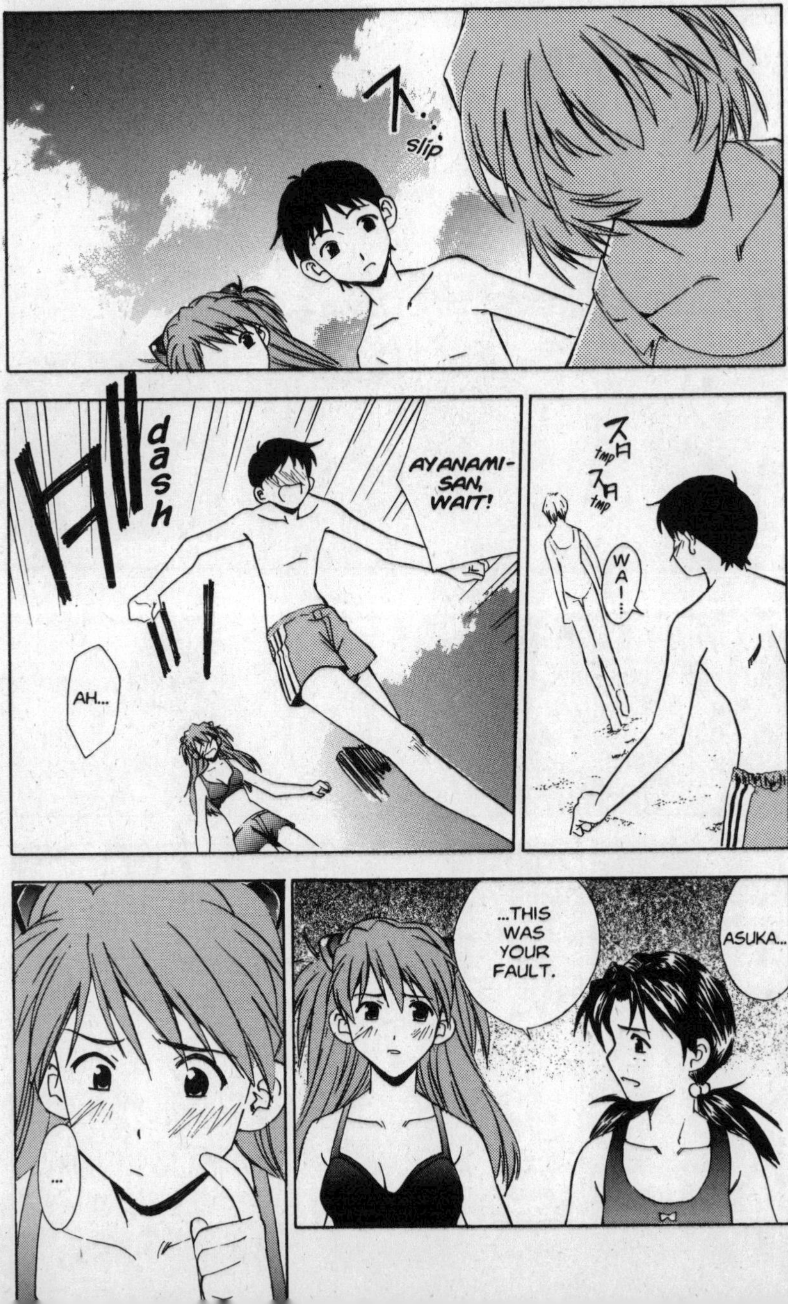
slip
tmp
tmp
WA!...
AYANAMI-SAN, WAIT!
dash
AH...
ASUKA...
...THIS WAS YOUR FAULT.
...

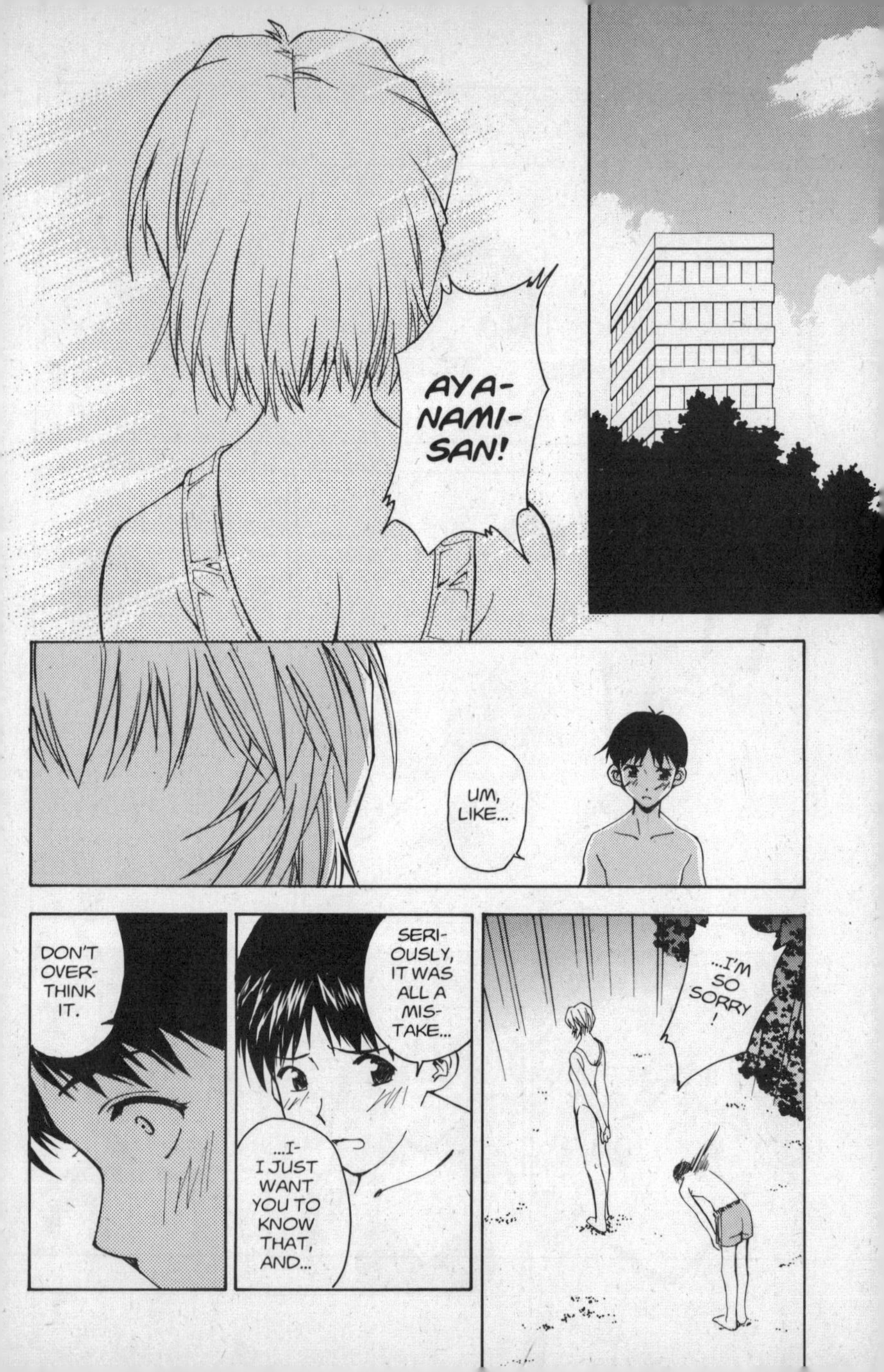
AYA-NAMI-SAN!
UM, LIKE...
...I'M SO SORRY!
SERI-OUSLY, IT WAS ALL A MIS-TAKE...
...I- I JUST WANT YOU TO KNOW THAT, AND...
DON'T OVER-THINK IT.

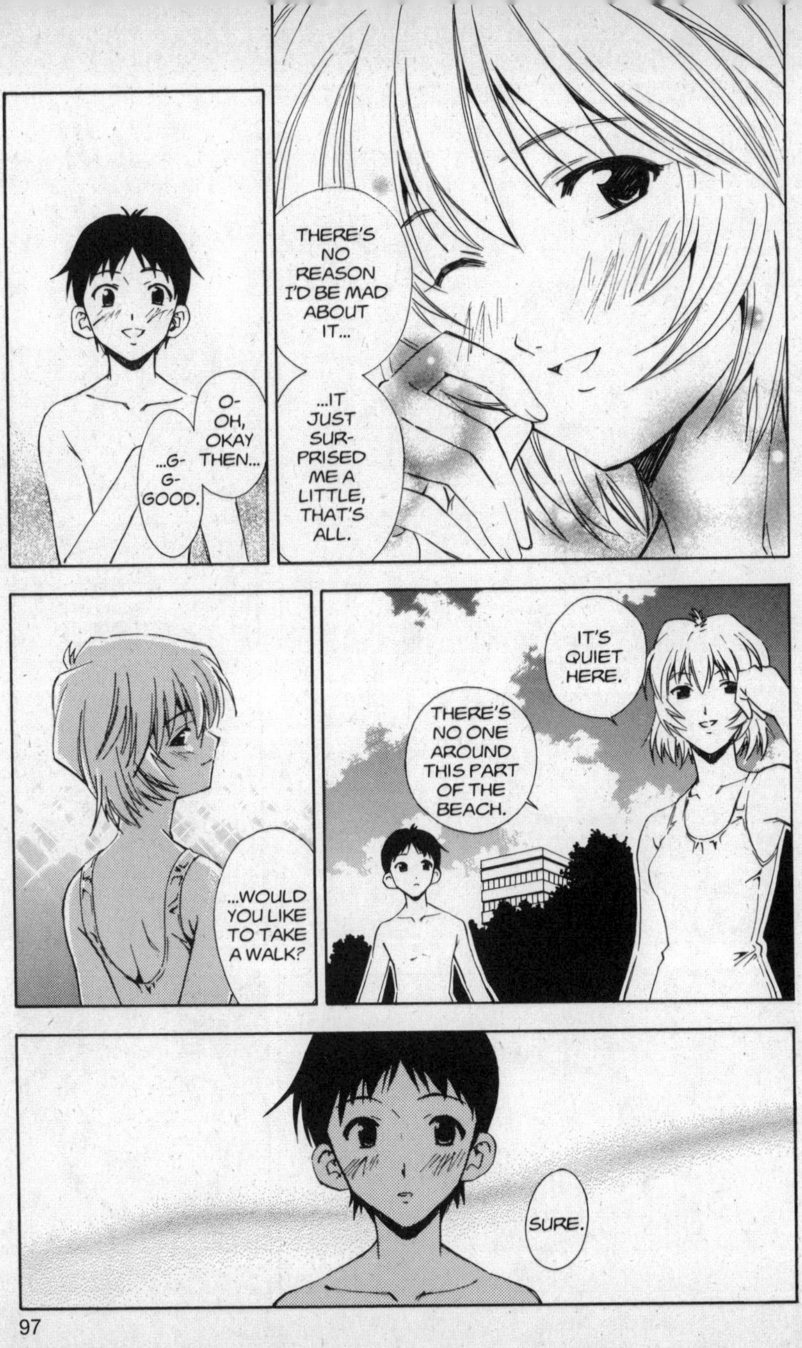
THERE'S NO REASON I'D BE MAD ABOUT IT...
...IT JUST SUR-PRISED ME A LITTLE, THAT'S ALL.
O-OH, OKAY THEN...
...G-G-GOOD.
IT'S QUIET HERE.
THERE'S NO ONE AROUND THIS PART OF THE BEACH.
...WOULD YOU LIKE TO TAKE A WALK?
SURE.

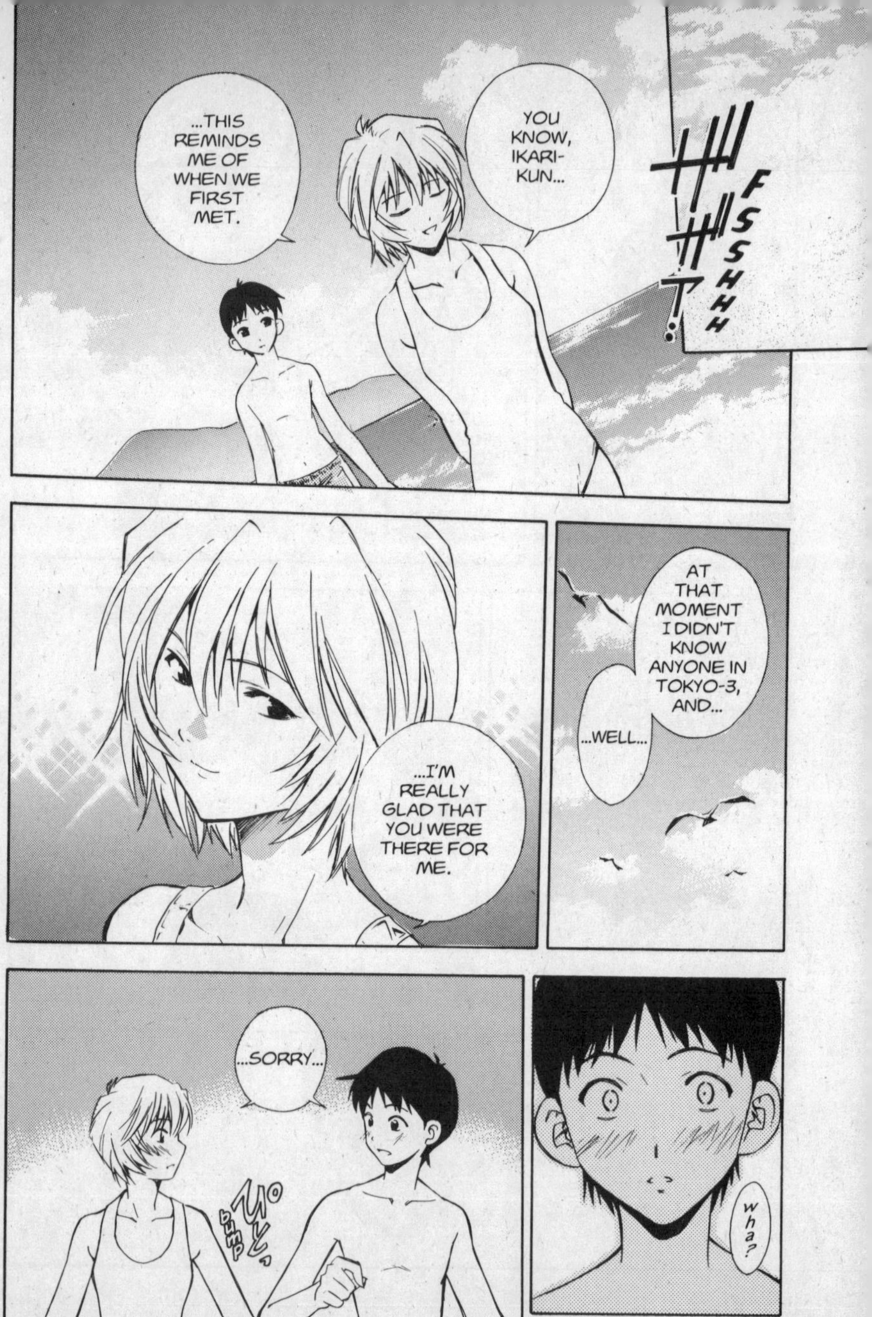
FSSHHH
YOU KNOW, IKARI-KUN...
...THIS REMINDS ME OF WHEN WE FIRST MET.
AT THAT MOMENT I DIDN'T KNOW ANYONE IN TOKYO-3, AND...
...WELL...
...I'M REALLY GLAD THAT YOU WERE THERE FOR ME.
wha?
...SORRY...
bump

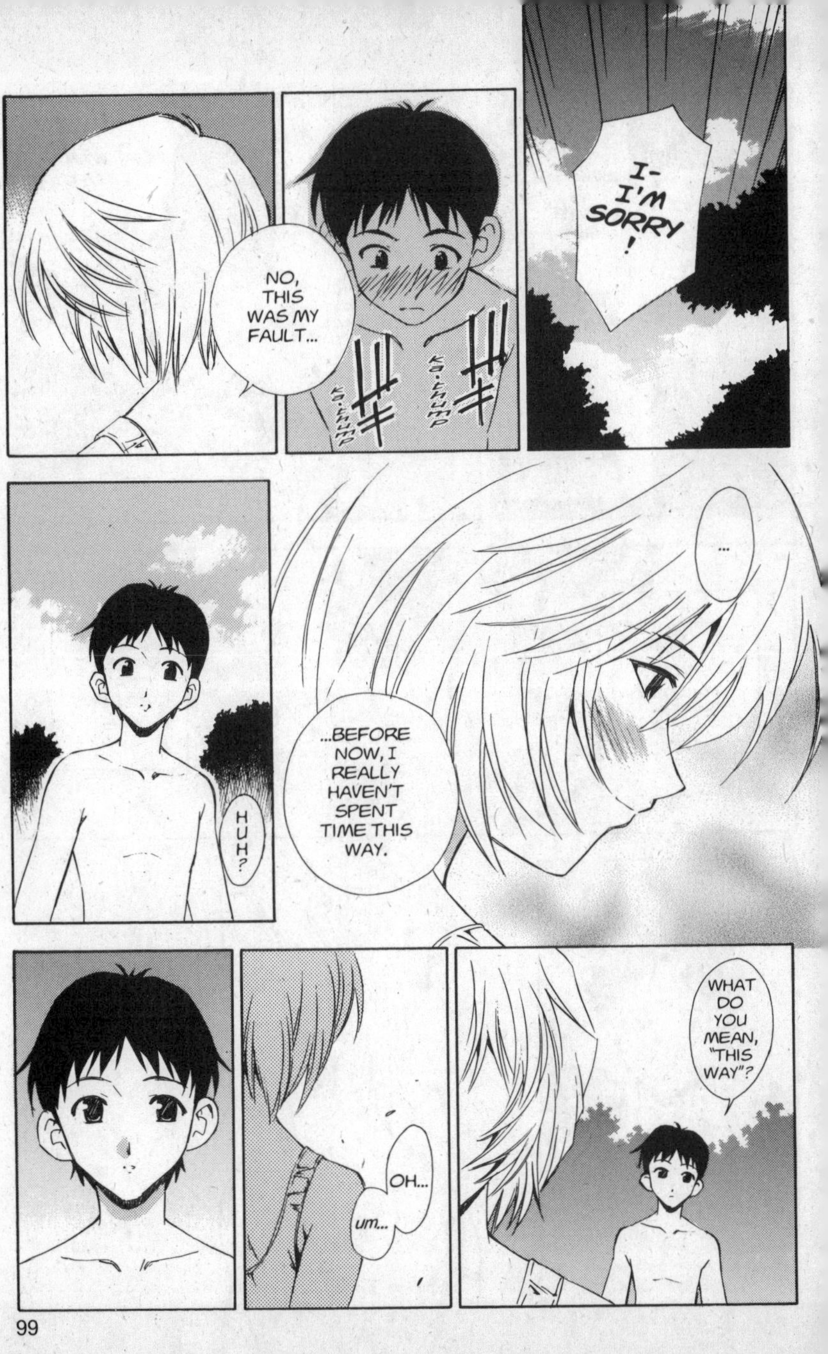
I- I'M SORRY!
NO, THIS WAS MY FAULT...
ka-thump
ka-thump
...
...BEFORE NOW, I REALLY HAVEN'T SPENT TIME THIS WAY.
HUH?
WHAT DO YOU MEAN, "THIS WAY"?
OH...
um...

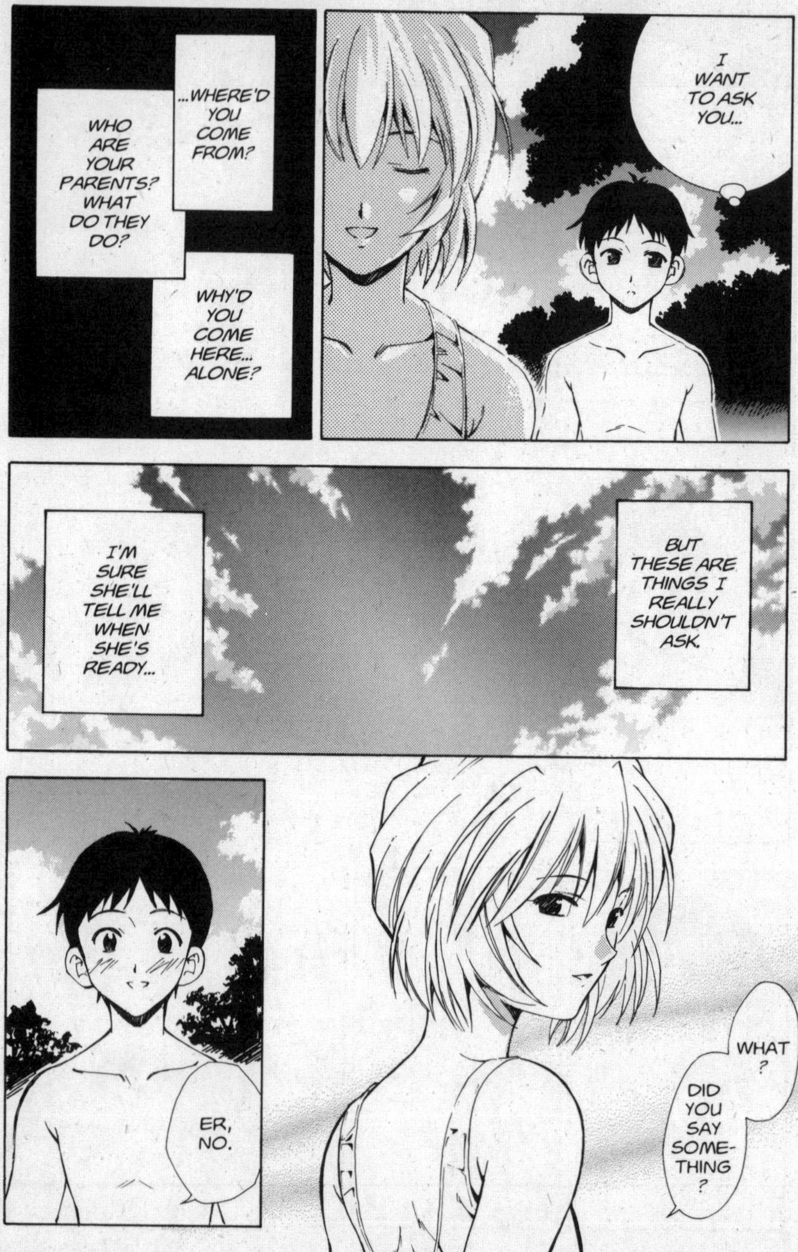
I WANT TO ASK YOU...
...WHERE'D YOU COME FROM?
WHO ARE YOUR PARENTS? WHAT DO THEY DO?
WHY'D YOU COME HERE... ALONE?
BUT THESE ARE THINGS I REALLY SHOULDN'T ASK.
I'M SURE SHE'LL TELL ME WHEN SHE'S READY...
WHAT? DID YOU SAY SOME-THING?
ER, NO.

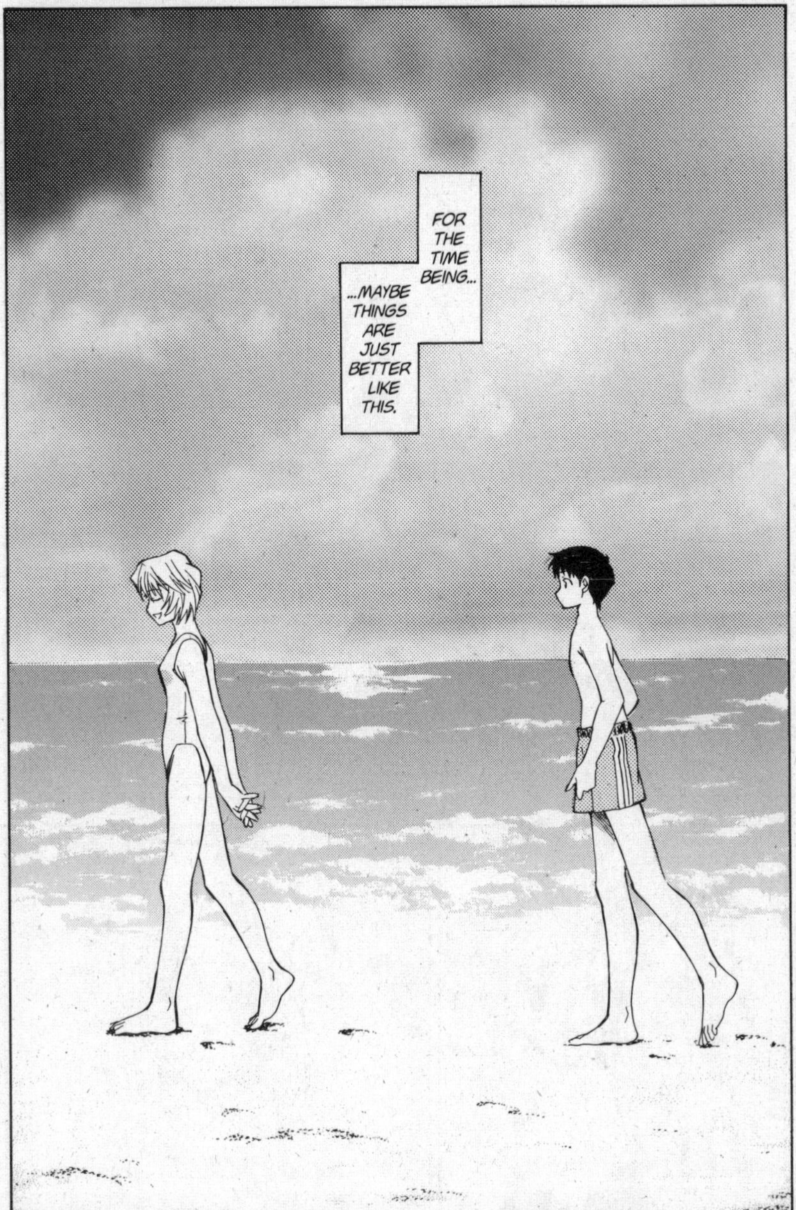
FOR THE TIME BEING...
...MAYBE THINGS ARE JUST BETTER LIKE THIS.

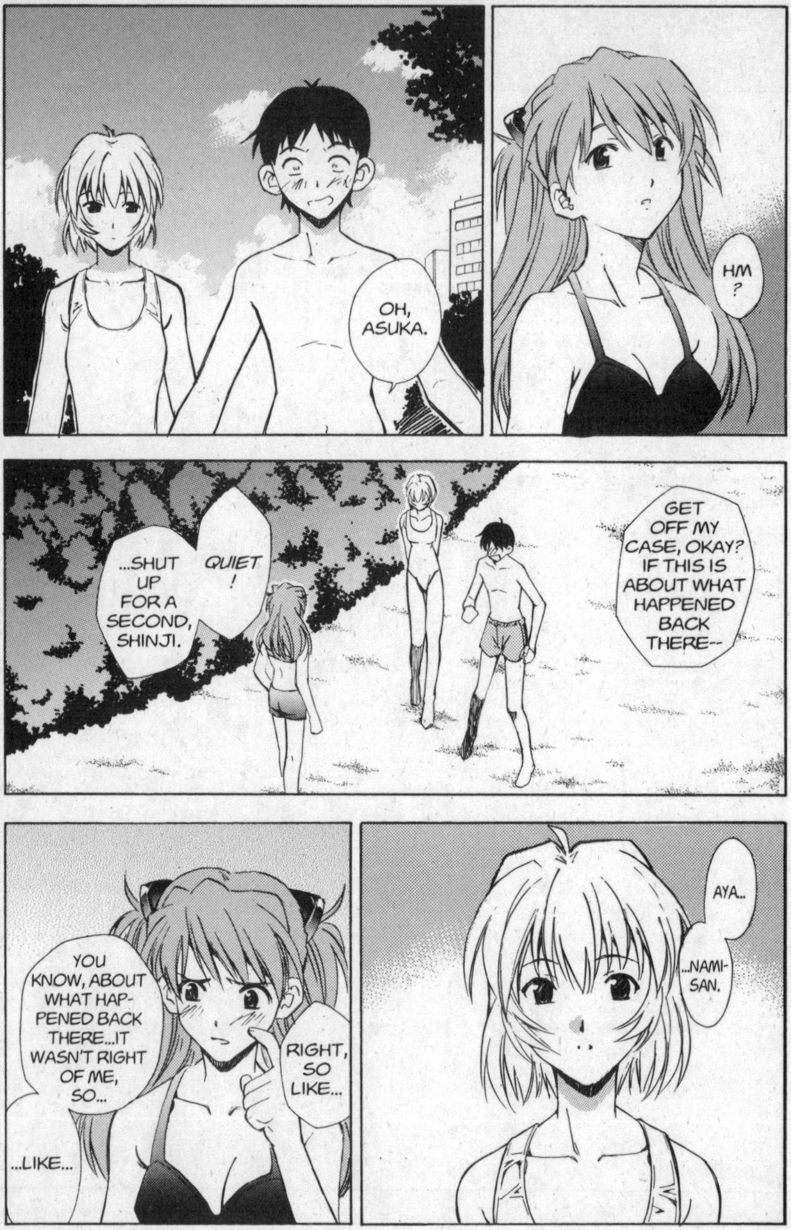
HM ?
OH, ASUKA.
GET OFF MY CASE, OKAY? IF THIS IS ABOUT WHAT HAPPENED BACK THERE--
QUIET !
...SHUT UP FOR A SECOND, SHINJI.
AYA...
...NAMI-SAN.
RIGHT, SO LIKE...
YOU KNOW, ABOUT WHAT HAP-PENED BACK THERE...IT WASN'T RIGHT OF ME, SO...
...LIKE...

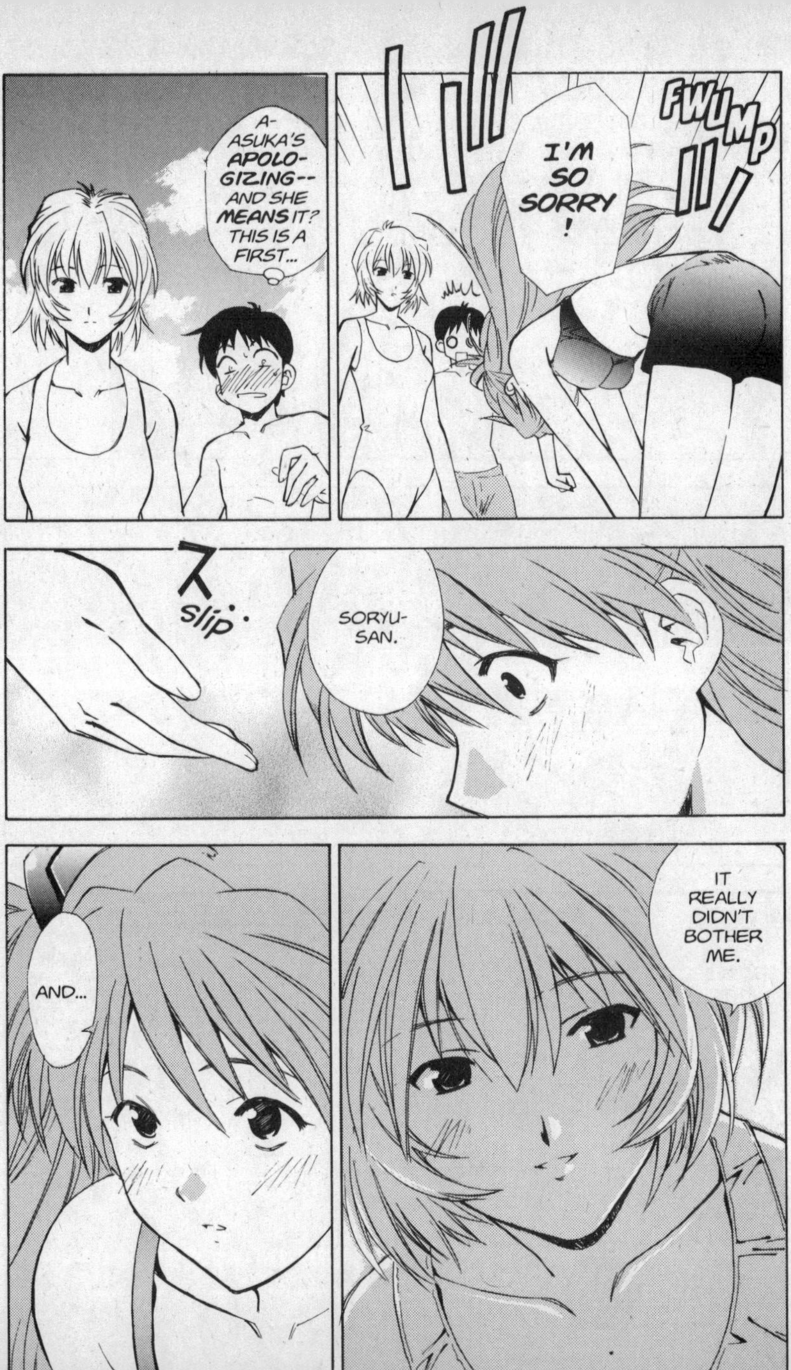
FWUMP
I'M SO SORRY!
A-ASUKA'S APOLOGIZING-- AND SHE MEANS IT? THIS IS A FIRST...
slip
SORYU-SAN.
IT REALLY DIDN'T BOTHER ME.
AND...

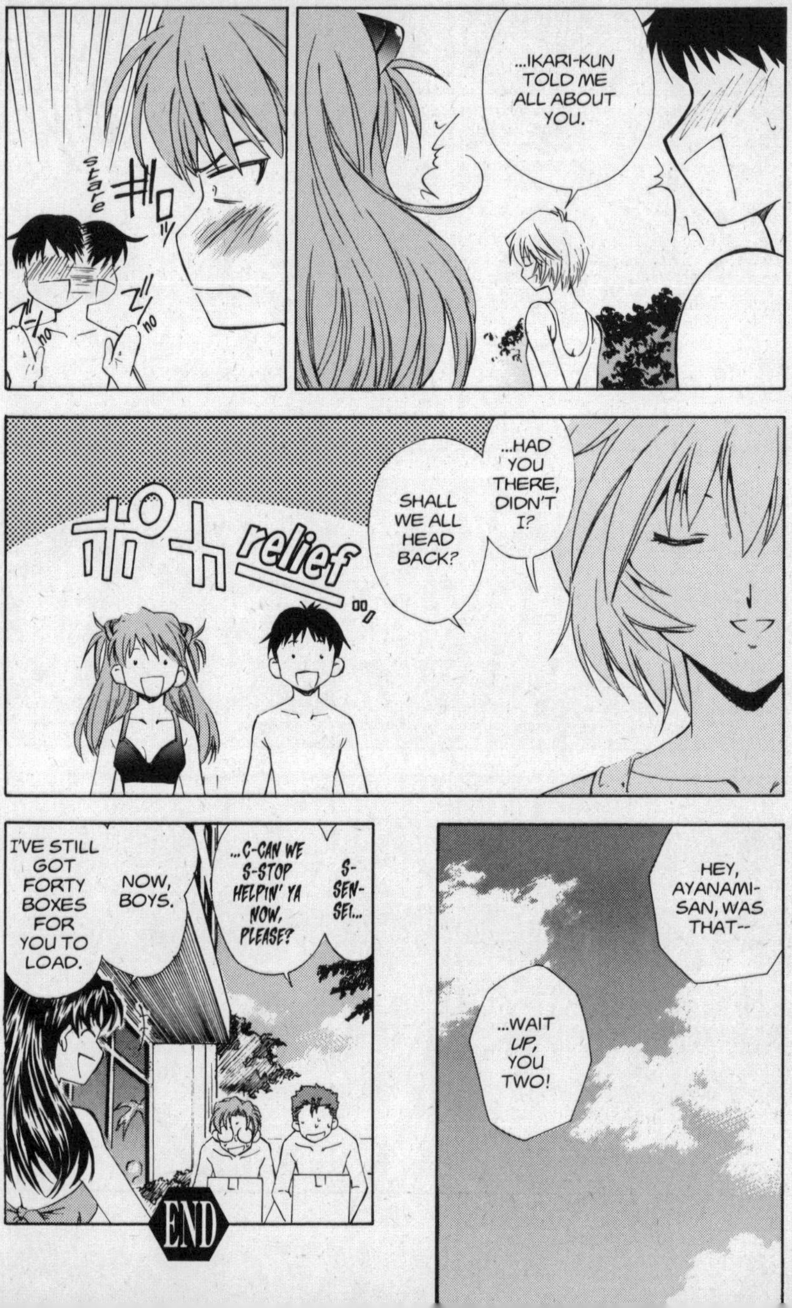
...IKARI-KUN TOLD ME ALL ABOUT YOU.
stare
no
no
...HAD YOU THERE, DIDN'T I?
SHALL WE ALL HEAD BACK?
relief
HEY, AYANAMI-SAN, WAS THAT--
...WAIT UP, YOU TWO!
S-SEN-SEI...
...C-CAN WE S-STOP HELPIN' YA NOW, PLEASE?
NOW, BOYS.
I'VE STILL GOT FORTY BOXES FOR YOU TO LOAD.
END

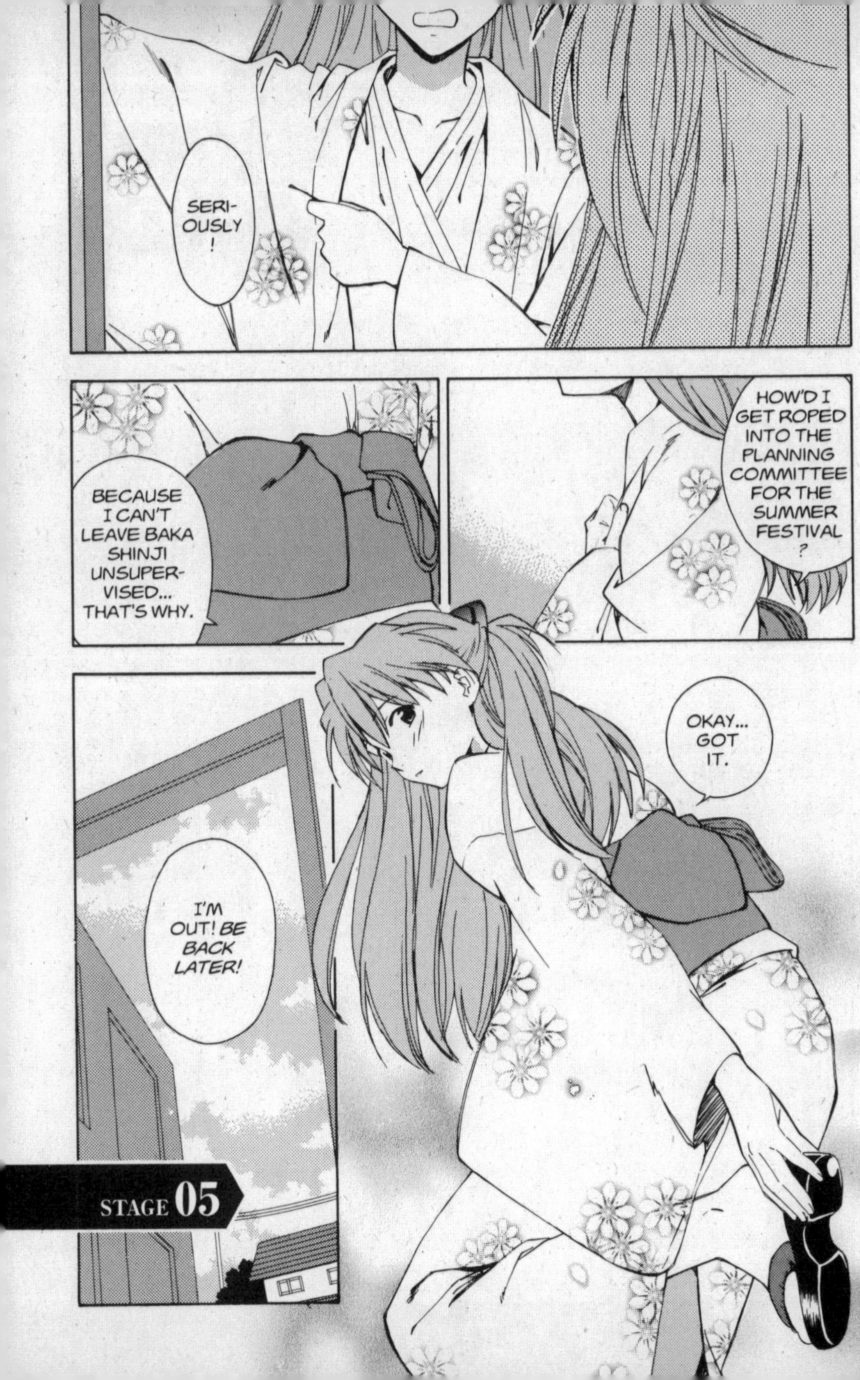
SERI-OUSLY!
HOW'D I GET ROPED INTO THE PLANNING COMMITTEE FOR THE SUMMER FESTIVAL?
BECAUSE I CAN'T LEAVE BAKA SHINJI UNSUPER-VISED... THAT'S WHY.
OKAY... GOT IT.
I'M OUT! *BE BACK LATER!*
STAGE 05

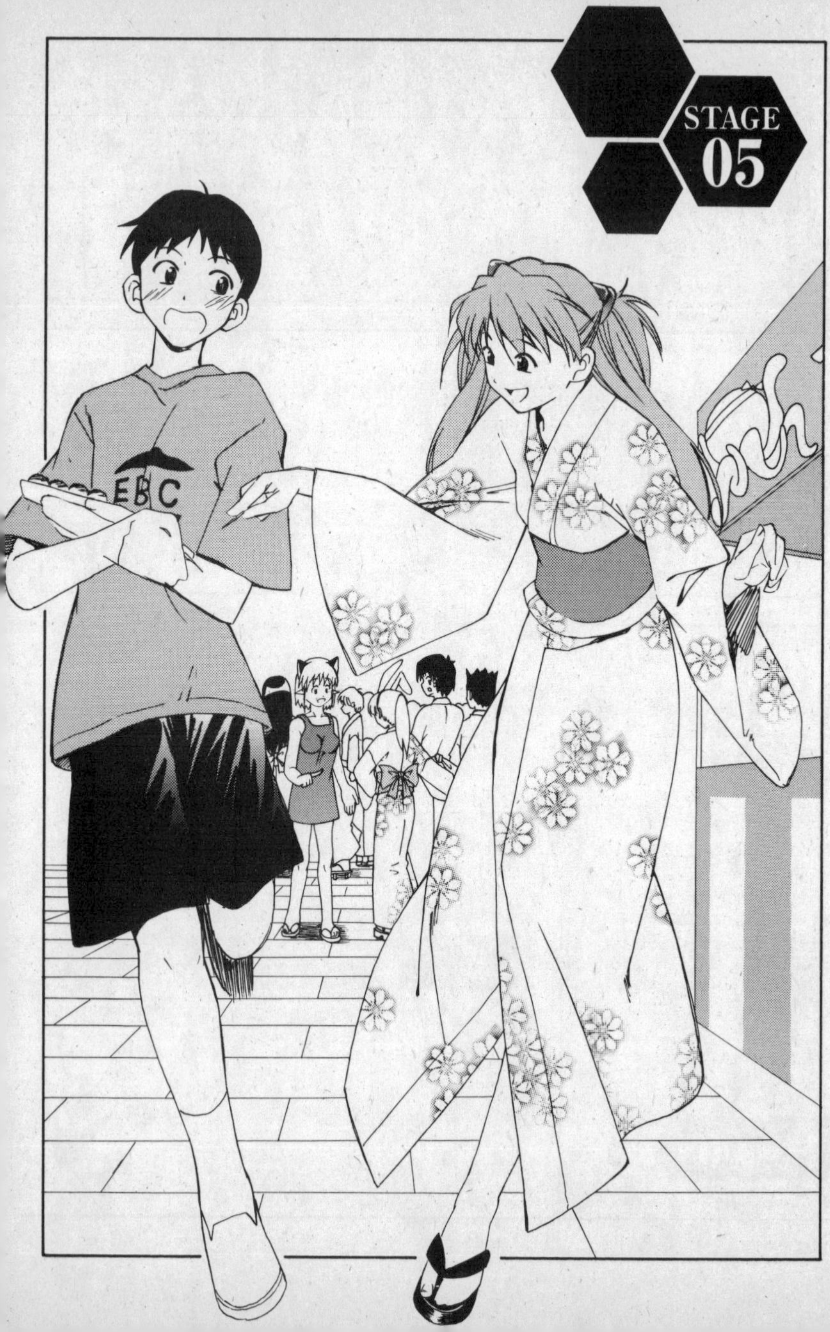
STAGE
05
EBC

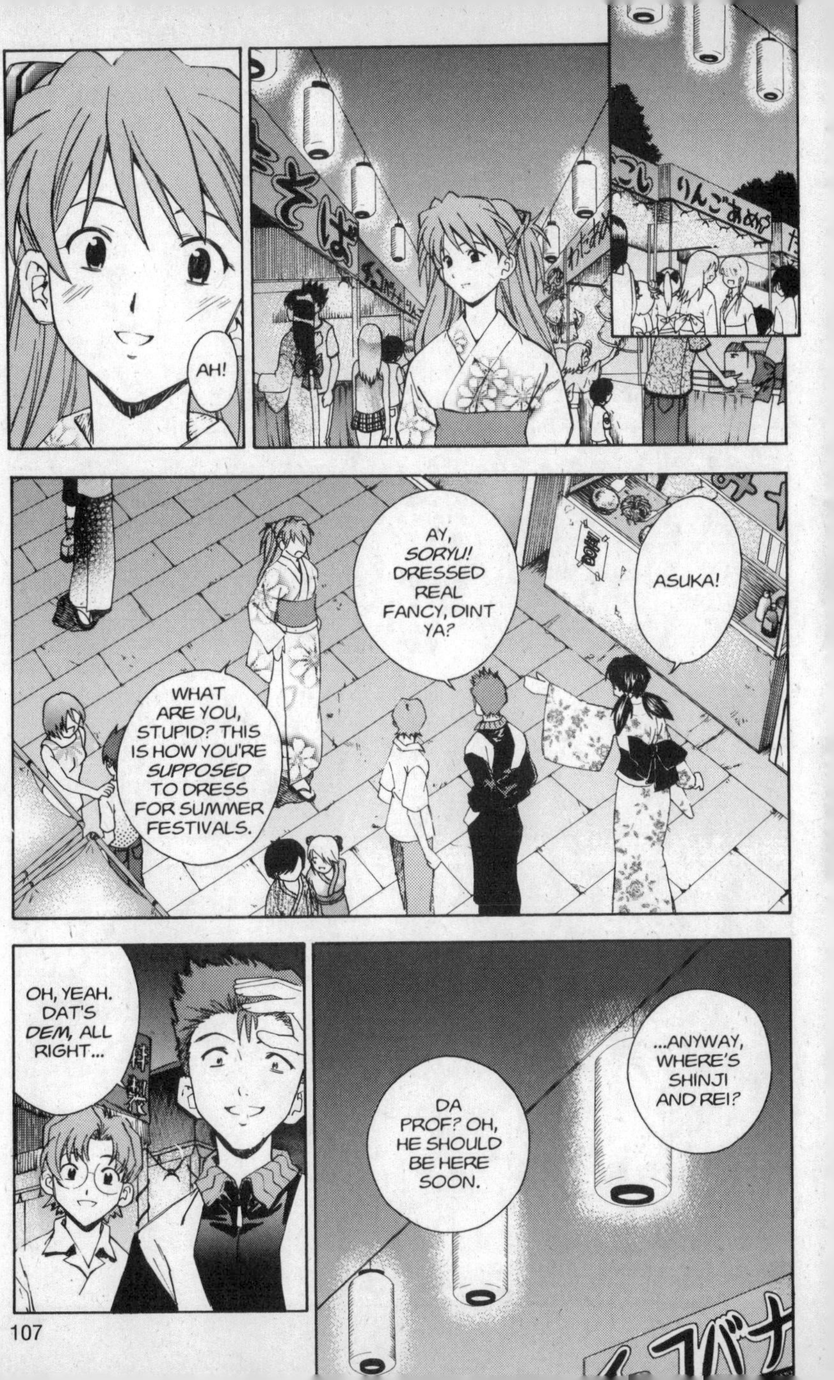
AH!
ASUKA!
AY, SORYU! DRESSED REAL FANCY, DINT YA?
WHAT ARE YOU, STUPID? THIS IS HOW YOU'RE SUPPOSED TO DRESS FOR SUMMER FESTIVALS.
...ANYWAY, WHERE'S SHINJI AND REI?
DA PROF? OH, HE SHOULD BE HERE SOON.
OH, YEAH. DAT'S DEM, ALL RIGHT...

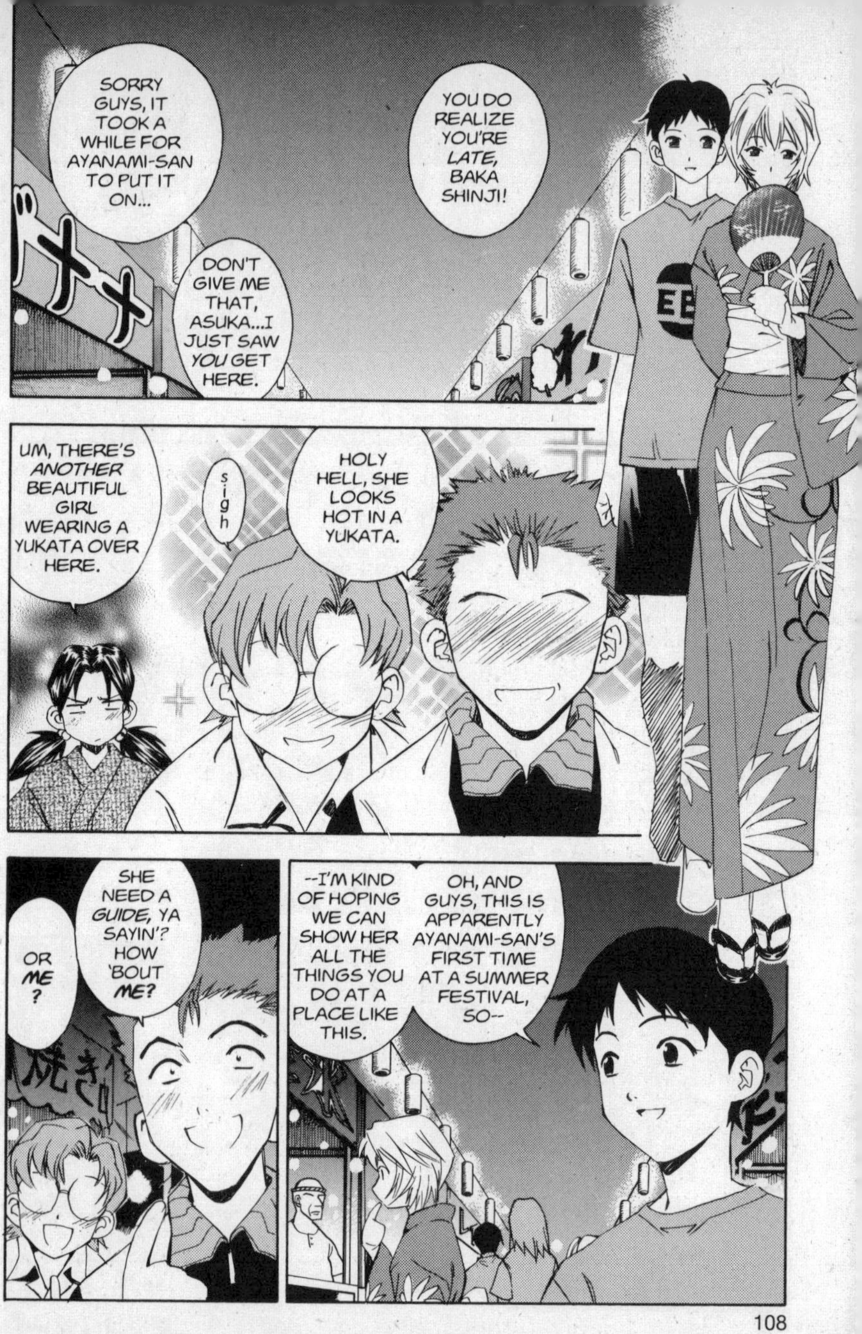
YOU DO REALIZE YOU'RE *LATE*, BAKA SHINJI!
SORRY GUYS, IT TOOK A WHILE FOR AYANAMI-SAN TO PUT IT ON...
DON'T GIVE ME THAT, ASUKA...I JUST SAW *YOU* GET HERE.
HOLY HELL, SHE LOOKS HOT IN A YUKATA.
sigh
UM, THERE'S *ANOTHER* BEAUTIFUL GIRL WEARING A YUKATA OVER HERE.
OH, AND GUYS, THIS IS APPARENTLY AYANAMI-SAN'S FIRST TIME AT A SUMMER FESTIVAL, SO--
--I'M KIND OF HOPING WE CAN SHOW HER ALL THE THINGS YOU DO AT A PLACE LIKE THIS.
SHE NEED A *GUIDE*, YA SAYIN'? HOW 'BOUT **ME?**
OR **ME**?

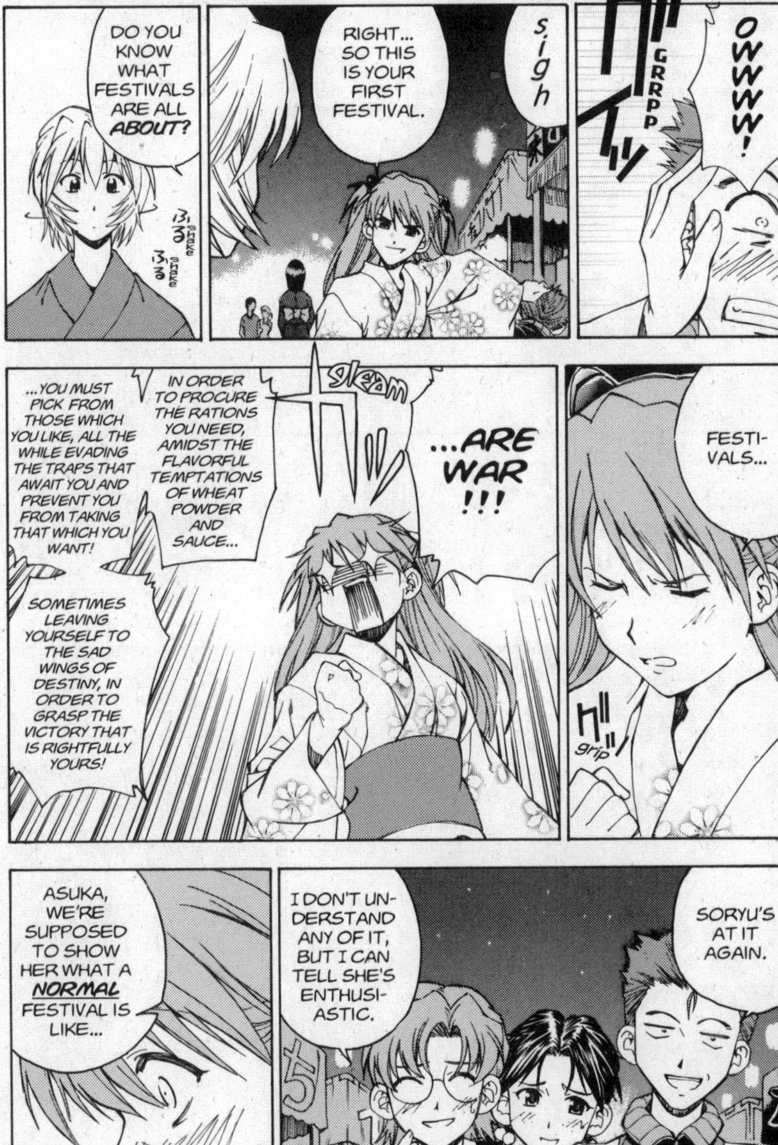
OWWWWW!
GRRPP
sigh
RIGHT... SO THIS IS YOUR FIRST FESTIVAL.
DO YOU KNOW WHAT FESTIVALS ARE ALL ABOUT?
shake
shake
FESTI-VALS...
grip
...ARE WAR!!!
gleam
IN ORDER TO PROCURE THE RATIONS YOU NEED, AMIDST THE FLAVORFUL TEMPTATIONS OF WHEAT POWDER AND SAUCE...
...YOU MUST PICK FROM THOSE WHICH YOU LIKE, ALL THE WHILE EVADING THE TRAPS THAT AWAIT YOU AND PREVENT YOU FROM TAKING THAT WHICH YOU WANT!
SOMETIMES LEAVING YOURSELF TO THE SAD WINGS OF DESTINY, IN ORDER TO GRASP THE VICTORY THAT IS RIGHTFULLY YOURS!
SORYU'S AT IT AGAIN.
I DON'T UN-DERSTAND ANY OF IT, BUT I CAN TELL SHE'S ENTHUSI-ASTIC.
ASUKA, WE'RE SUPPOSED TO SHOW HER WHAT A NORMAL FESTIVAL IS LIKE...

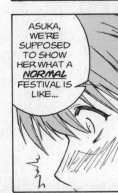

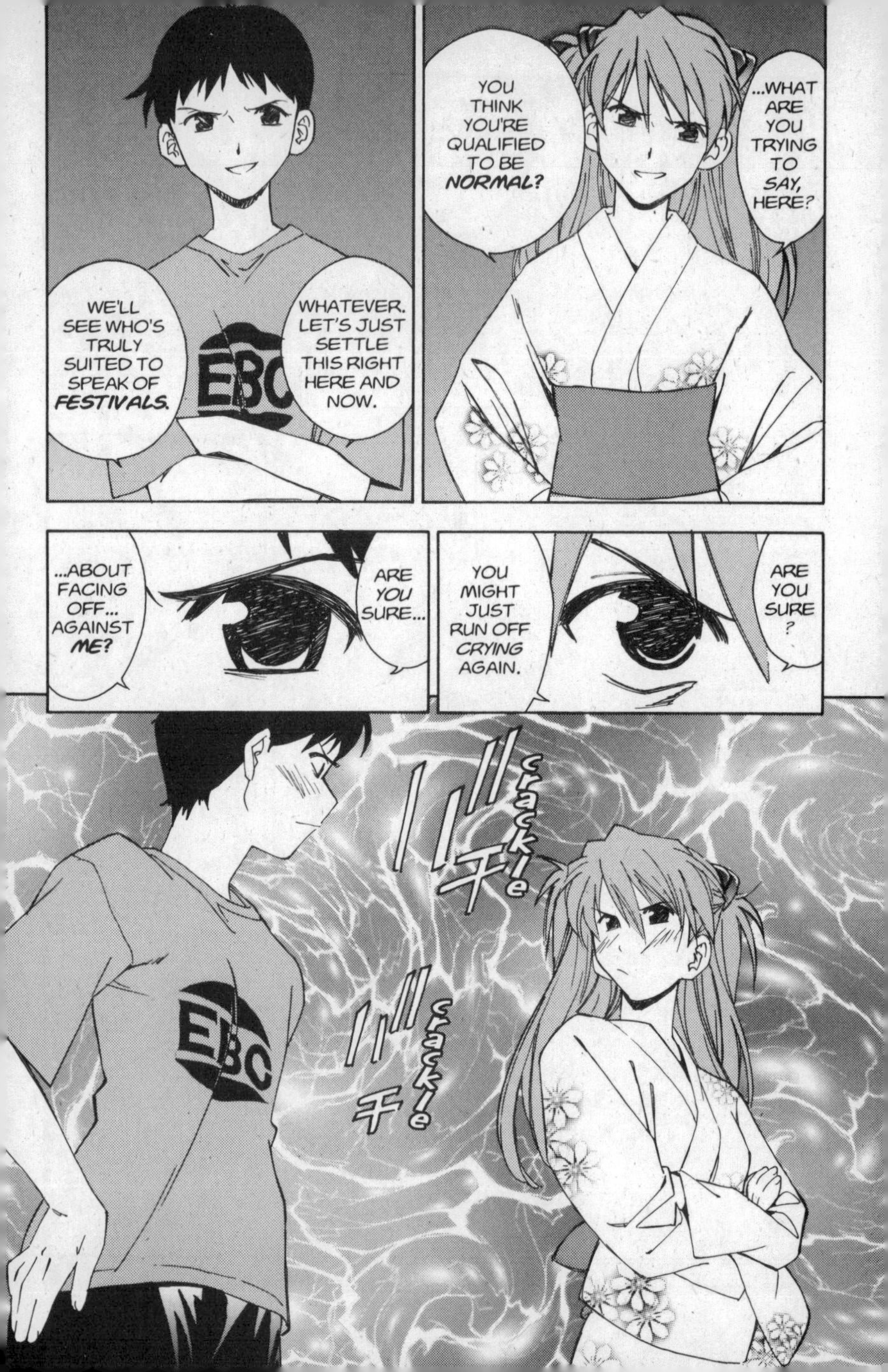
...WHAT ARE YOU TRYING TO SAY, HERE?
YOU THINK YOU'RE QUALIFIED TO BE NORMAL?
WHATEVER. LET'S JUST SETTLE THIS RIGHT HERE AND NOW.
WE'LL SEE WHO'S TRULY SUITED TO SPEAK OF FESTIVALS.
ARE YOU SURE ?
YOU MIGHT JUST RUN OFF CRYING AGAIN.
ARE YOU SURE...
...ABOUT FACING OFF... AGAINST ME?
チ
crackle
チ
crackle

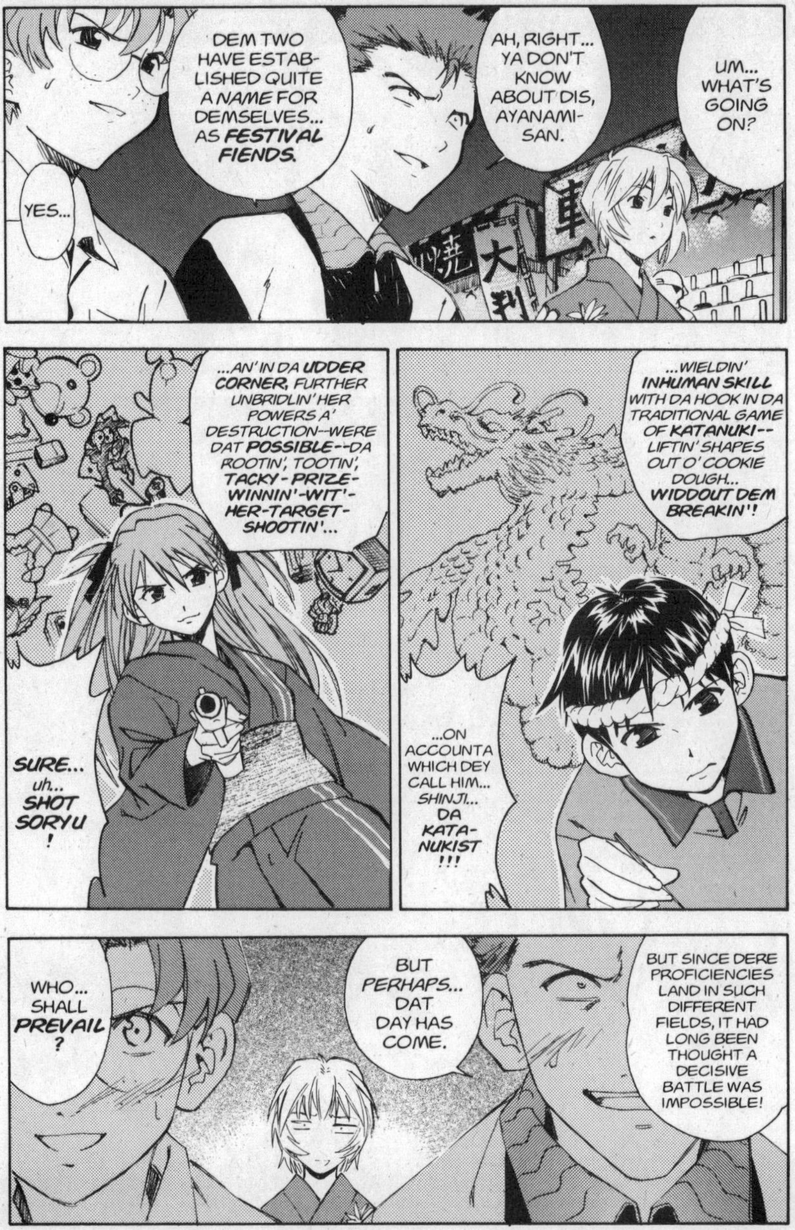
UM... WHAT'S GOING ON?
AH, RIGHT... YA DON'T KNOW ABOUT DIS, AYANAMI-SAN.
DEM TWO HAVE ESTABLISHED QUITE A NAME FOR DEMSELVES... AS FESTIVAL FIENDS.
YES...
...WIELDIN' INHUMAN SKILL WITH DA HOOK IN DA TRADITIONAL GAME OF KATANUKI-- LIFTIN' SHAPES OUT O' COOKIE DOUGH... WIDDOUT DEM BREAKIN'!
...ON ACCOUNTA WHICH DEY CALL HIM... SHINJI... DA KATA-NUKIST!!!
...AN' IN DA UDDER CORNER, FURTHER UNBRIDLIN' HER POWERS A' DESTRUCTION--WERE DAT POSSIBLE--DA ROOTIN', TOOTIN', TACKY-PRIZE-WINNIN'-WIT'-HER-TARGET-SHOOTIN'...
SURE... uh... SHOT SORYU!
BUT SINCE DERE PROFICIENCIES LAND IN SUCH DIFFERENT FIELDS, IT HAD LONG BEEN THOUGHT A DECISIVE BATTLE WAS IMPOSSIBLE!
BUT PERHAPS... DAT DAY HAS COME.
WHO... SHALL PREVAIL?

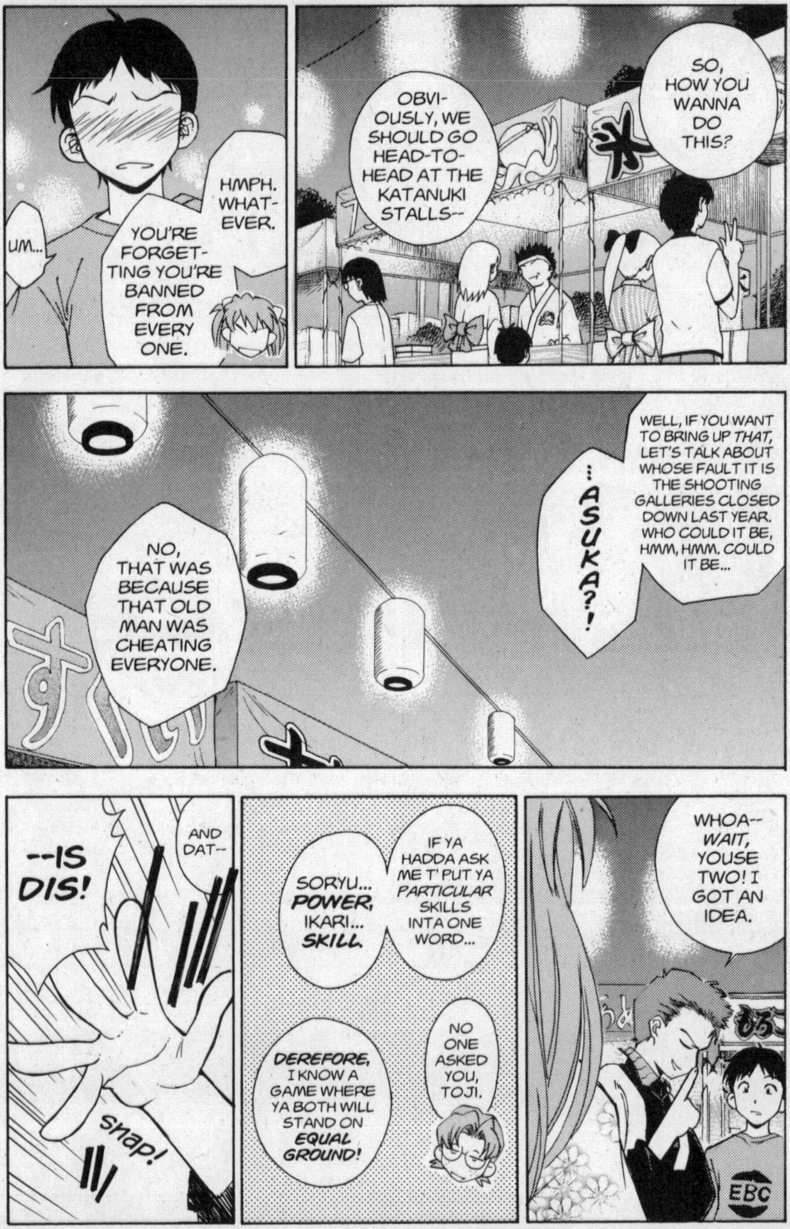
SO, HOW YOU WANNA DO THIS?
OBVI-OUSLY, WE SHOULD GO HEAD-TO-HEAD AT THE KATANUKI STALLS--
HMPH. WHAT-EVER.
YOU'RE FORGET-TING YOU'RE BANNED FROM EVERY ONE.
UM...
WELL, IF YOU WANT TO BRING UP *THAT*, LET'S TALK ABOUT WHOSE FAULT IT IS THE SHOOTING GALLERIES CLOSED DOWN LAST YEAR. WHO COULD IT BE, HMM, HMM. COULD IT BE...
...ASUKA?!
NO, THAT WAS BECAUSE THAT OLD MAN WAS CHEATING EVERYONE.
WHOA-- *WAIT*, YOUSE TWO! I GOT AN IDEA.
EBC
IF YA HADDA ASK ME T' PUT YA *PARTICULAR* SKILLS INTA ONE WORD...
SORYU... **POWER**, IKARI... **SKILL**.
NO ONE ASKED YOU, TOJI.
DEREFORE, I KNOW A GAME WHERE YA BOTH WILL STAND ON **EQUAL GROUND**!
AND DAT--
--IS **DIS**!
snap!

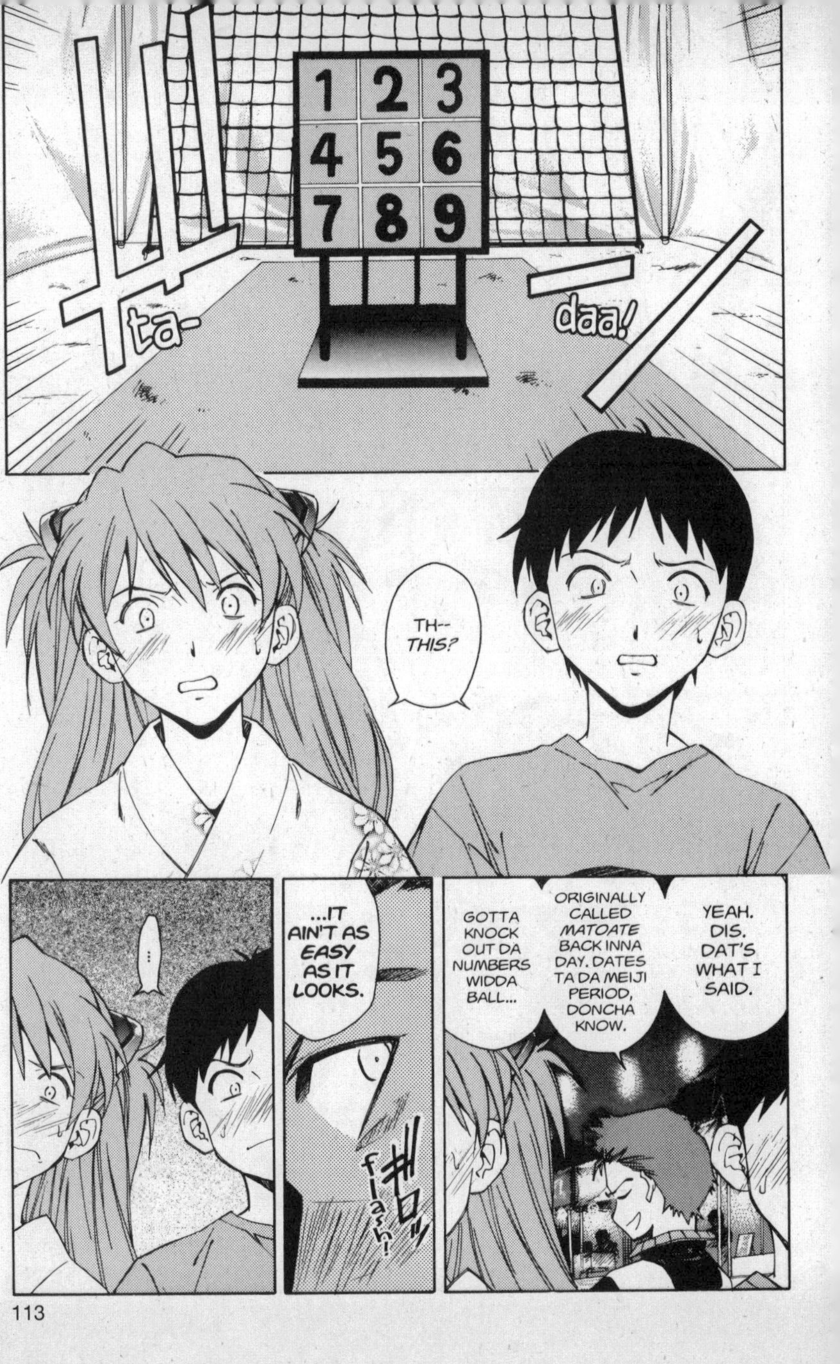

ta-
daa!
1 2 3 4 5 6 7 8 9
TH-- THIS?
YEAH. DIS. DAT'S WHAT I SAID.
ORIGINALLY CALLED MATOATE BACK INNA DAY. DATES TA DA MEIJI PERIOD, DONCHA KNOW.
GOTTA KNOCK OUT DA NUMBERS WIDDA BALL...
...IT AIN'T AS EASY AS IT LOOKS.
flash!
...

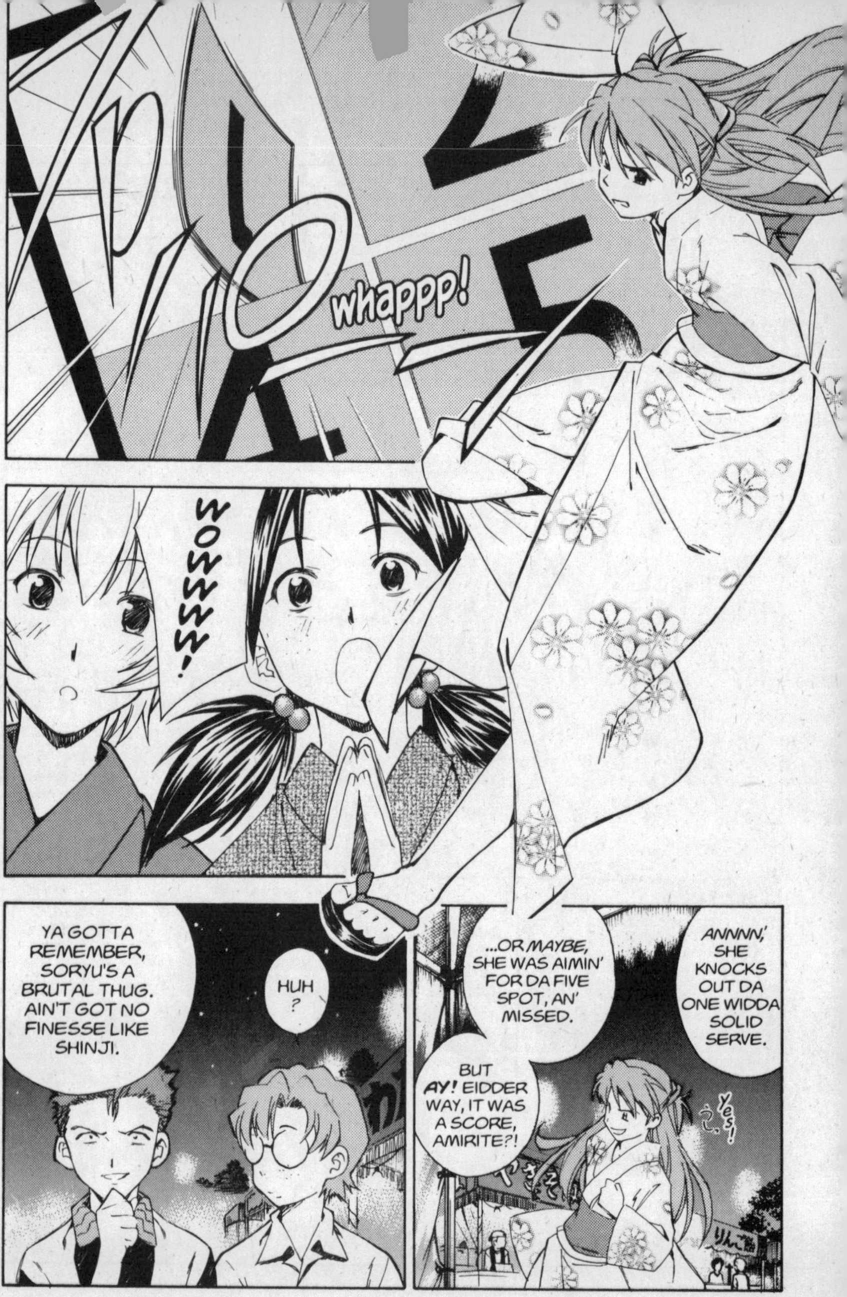
whappp!
WOWWWW!
ANNNN', SHE KNOCKS OUT DA ONE WIDDA SOLID SERVE.
...OR MAYBE, SHE WAS AIMIN' FOR DA FIVE SPOT, AN' MISSED.
BUT AY! EIDDER WAY, IT WAS A SCORE, AMIRITE?!
Yes!
YA GOTTA REMEMBER, SORYU'S A BRUTAL THUG. AIN'T GOT NO FINESSE LIKE SHINJI.
HUH?

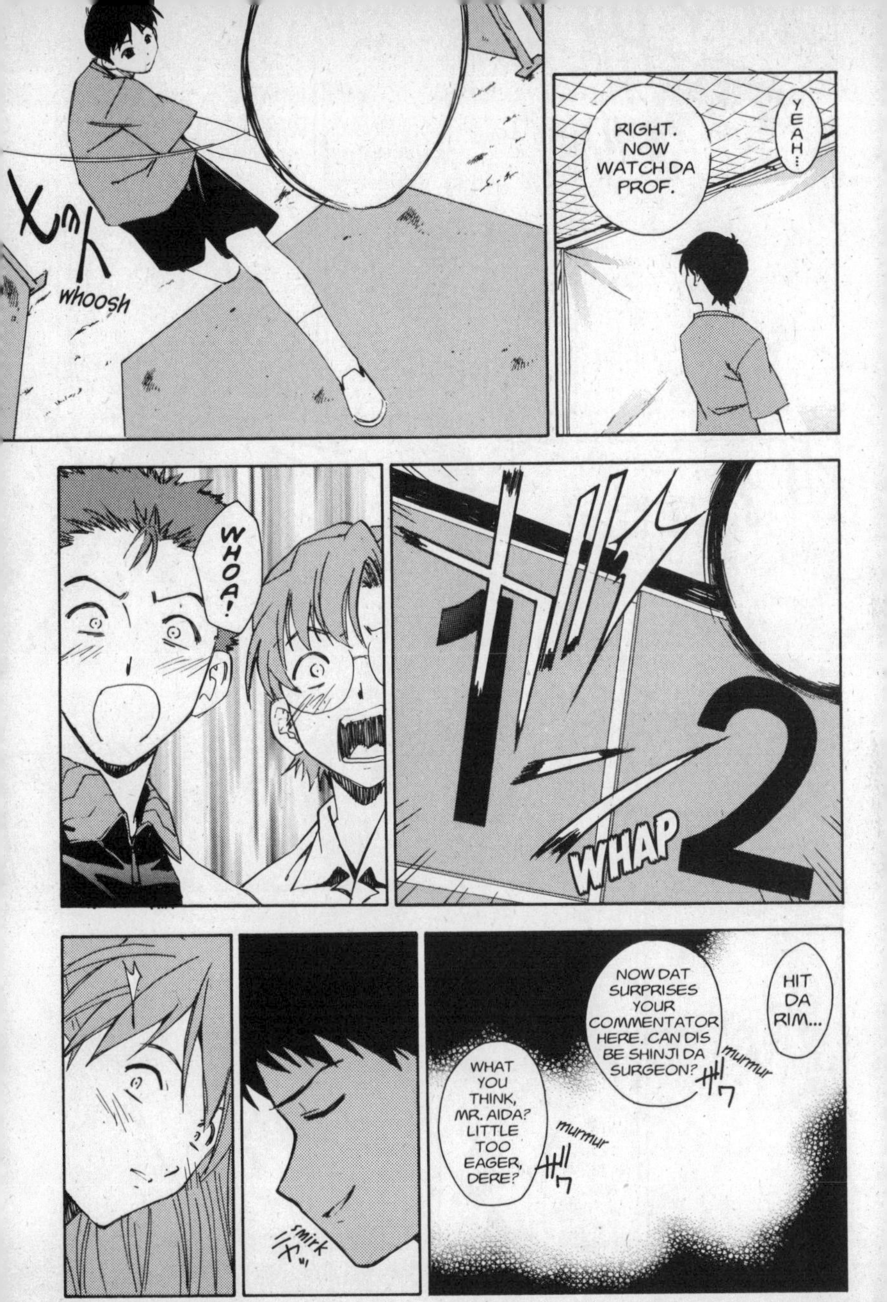
YEAH...
RIGHT. NOW WATCH DA PROF.
whoosh
WHAP
WHOA!
HIT DA RIM...
NOW DAT SURPRISES YOUR COMMENTATOR HERE. CAN DIS BE SHINJI DA SURGEON?
murmur
WHAT YOU THINK, MR. AIDA? LITTLE TOO EAGER, DERE?
murmur
smirk

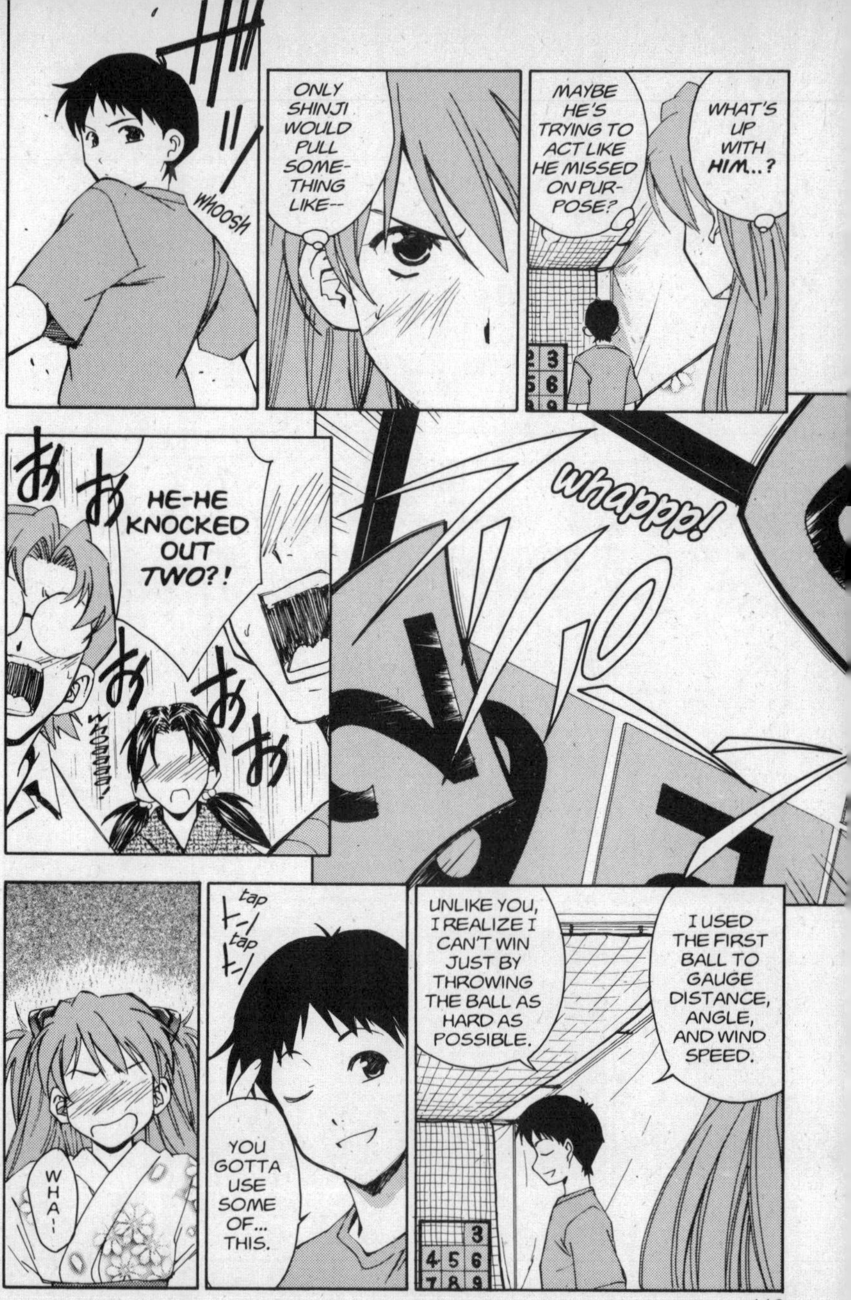

WHAT'S UP WITH HIM..?
MAYBE HE'S TRYING TO ACT LIKE HE MISSED ON PURPOSE?
ONLY SHINJI WOULD PULL SOME-THING LIKE--
whoosh
whappp!
おお
HE-HE KNOCKED OUT TWO?!
おおおお
I USED THE FIRST BALL TO GAUGE DISTANCE, ANGLE, AND WIND SPEED.
UNLIKE YOU, I REALIZE I CAN'T WIN JUST BY THROWING THE BALL AS HARD AS POSSIBLE.
tap
tap
YOU GOTTA USE SOME OF... THIS.
WHA-!

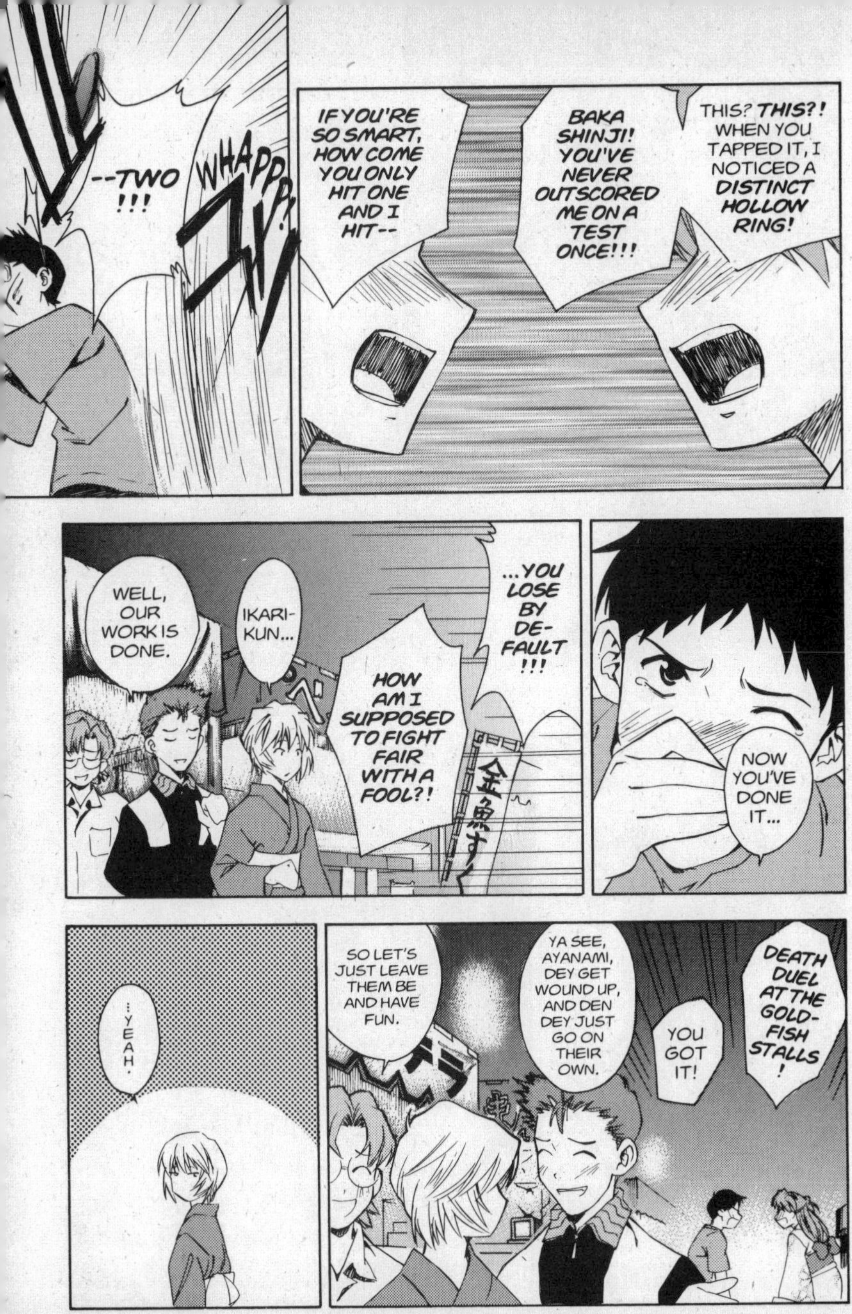
THIS? THIS?! WHEN YOU TAPPED IT, I NOTICED A DISTINCT HOLLOW RING!
BAKA SHINJI! YOU'VE NEVER OUTSCORED ME ON A TEST ONCE!!!
IF YOU'RE SO SMART, HOW COME YOU ONLY HIT ONE AND I HIT--
WHAPPP
--TWO !!!
NOW YOU'VE DONE IT...
...YOU LOSE BY DE-FAULT !!!
HOW AM I SUPPOSED TO FIGHT FAIR WITH A FOOL?!
金魚すく
IKARI-KUN...
WELL, OUR WORK IS DONE.
DEATH DUEL AT THE GOLD-FISH STALLS!
YOU GOT IT!
YA SEE, AYANAMI, DEY GET WOUND UP, AND DEN DEY JUST GO ON THEIR OWN.
SO LET'S JUST LEAVE THEM BE AND HAVE FUN.
...YEAH.

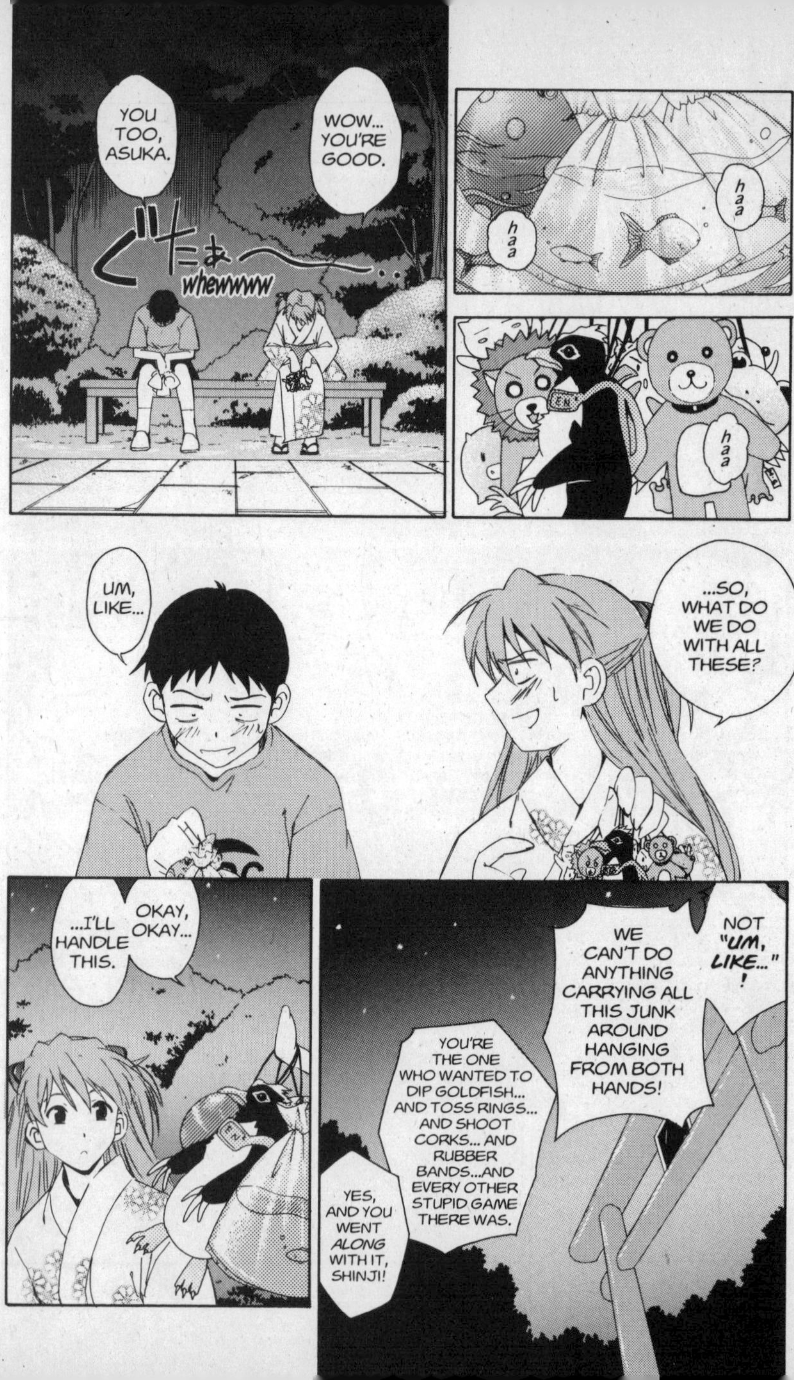
haa
haa
haa
WOW... YOU'RE GOOD.
YOU TOO, ASUKA.
ぐたぁ〜〜…
whewwww
...SO, WHAT DO WE DO WITH ALL THESE?
UM, LIKE...
NOT "UM, LIKE..."!
WE CAN'T DO ANYTHING CARRYING ALL THIS JUNK AROUND HANGING FROM BOTH HANDS!
YOU'RE THE ONE WHO WANTED TO DIP GOLDFISH... AND TOSS RINGS... AND SHOOT CORKS... AND RUBBER BANDS...AND EVERY OTHER STUPID GAME THERE WAS.
YES, AND YOU WENT *ALONG* WITH IT, SHINJI!
OKAY, OKAY...
...I'LL HANDLE THIS.

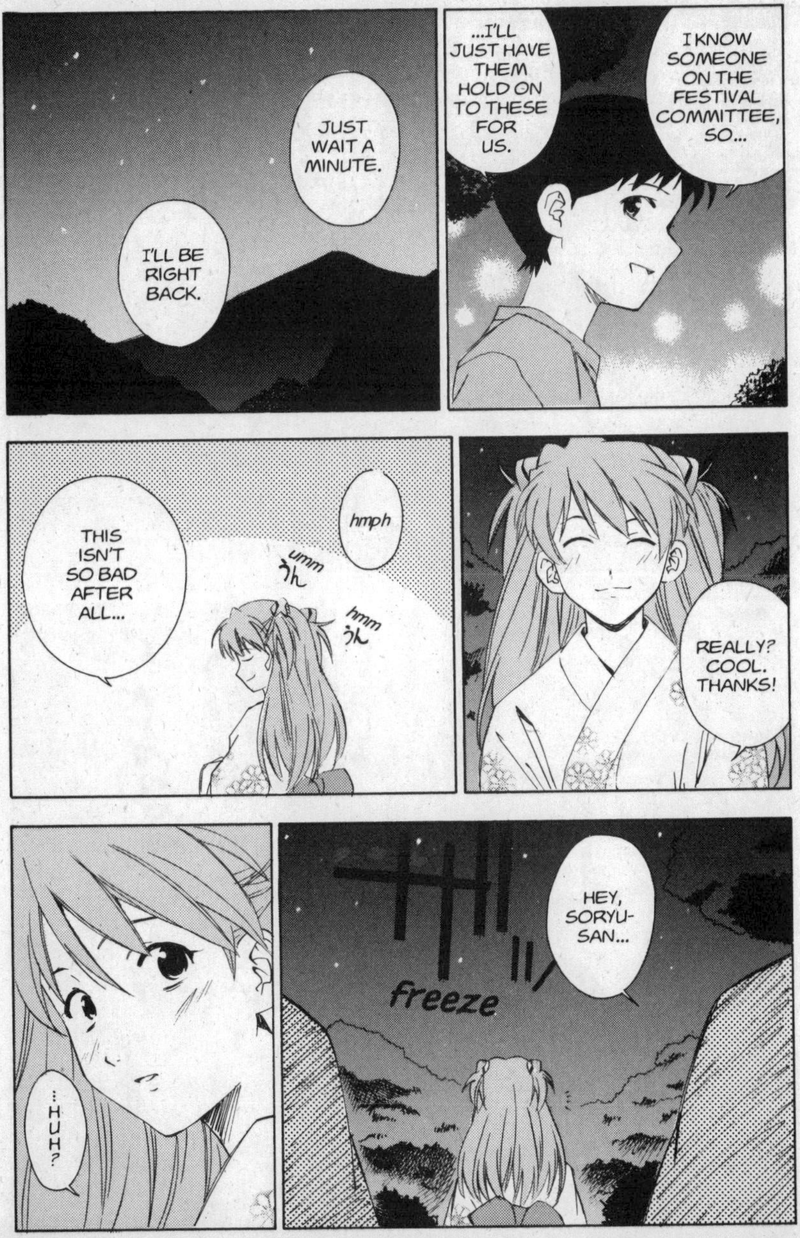
I KNOW SOMEONE ON THE FESTIVAL COMMITTEE, SO...
...I'LL JUST HAVE THEM HOLD ON TO THESE FOR US.
JUST WAIT A MINUTE.
I'LL BE RIGHT BACK.
REALLY? COOL. THANKS!
hmph
umm うん
hmm うん
THIS ISN'T SO BAD AFTER ALL...
HEY, SORYU-SAN...
freeze
...HUH?

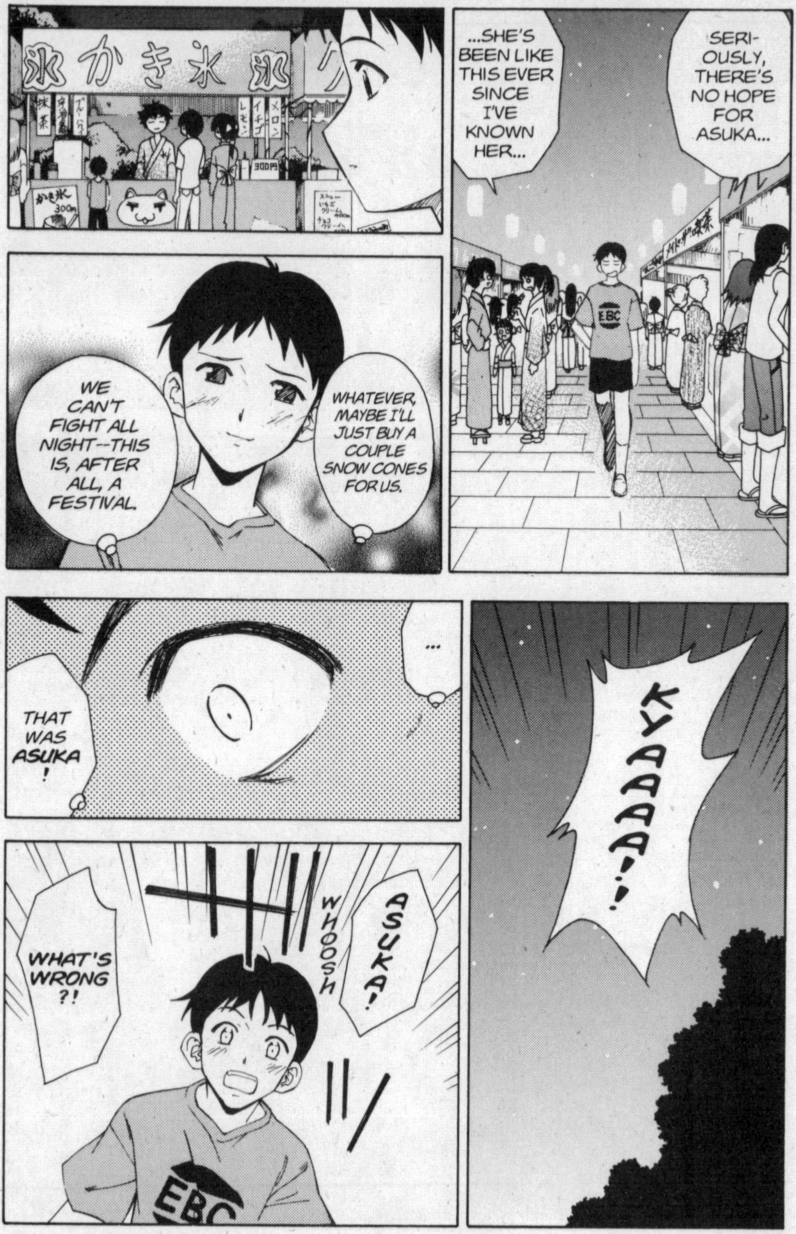
SERIOUSLY, THERE'S NO HOPE FOR ASUKA...
...SHE'S BEEN LIKE THIS EVER SINCE I'VE KNOWN HER...
氷かき氷氷
かき氷 300円
300円
WHATEVER, MAYBE I'LL JUST BUY A COUPLE SNOW CONES FOR US.
WE CAN'T FIGHT ALL NIGHT--THIS IS, AFTER ALL, A FESTIVAL.
KYAAAAA!!
...
THAT WAS ASUKA!
ASUKA!
WHOOSH
WHAT'S WRONG?!

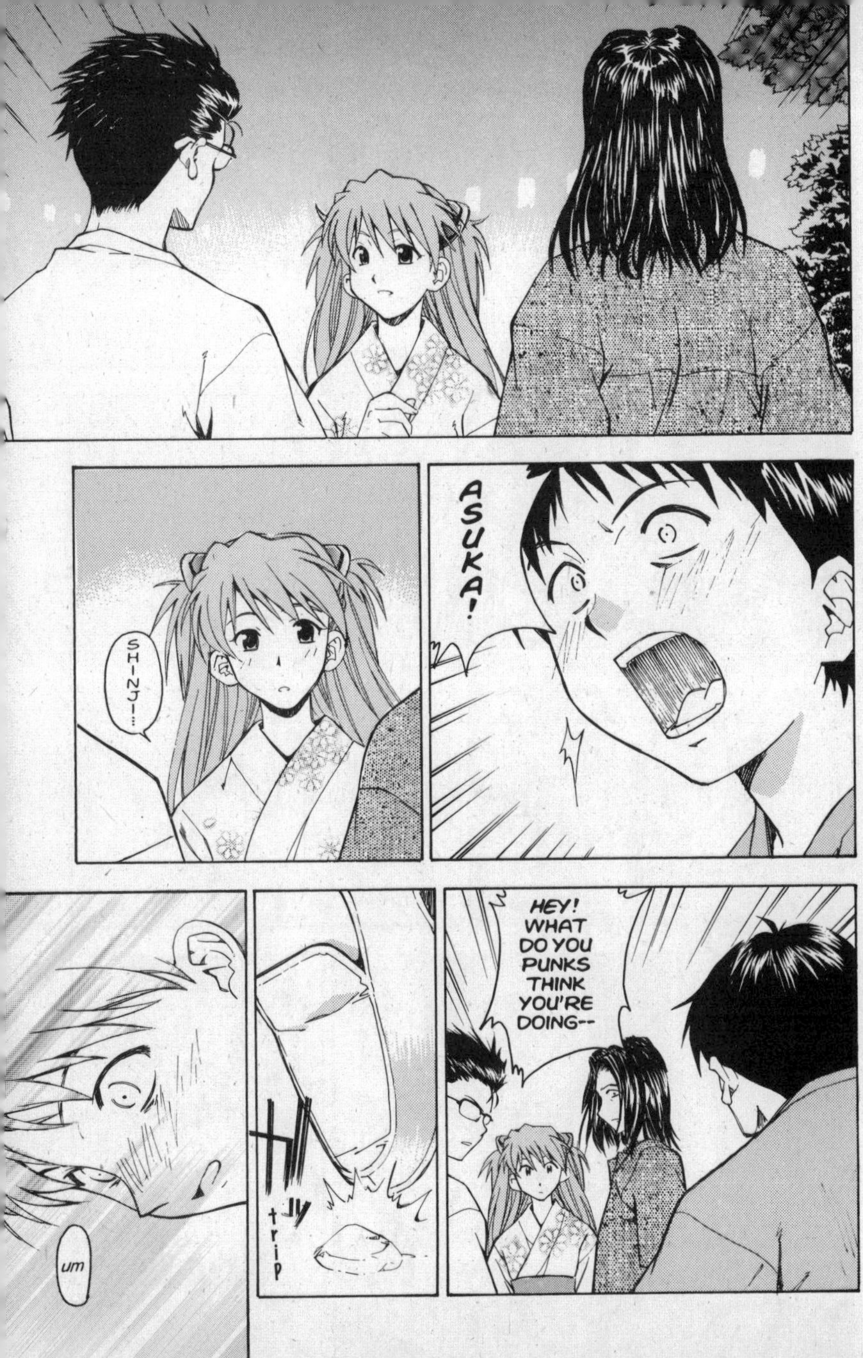
ASUKA!
SHINJI...
HEY! WHAT DO YOU PUNKS THINK YOU'RE DOING--
trip
um

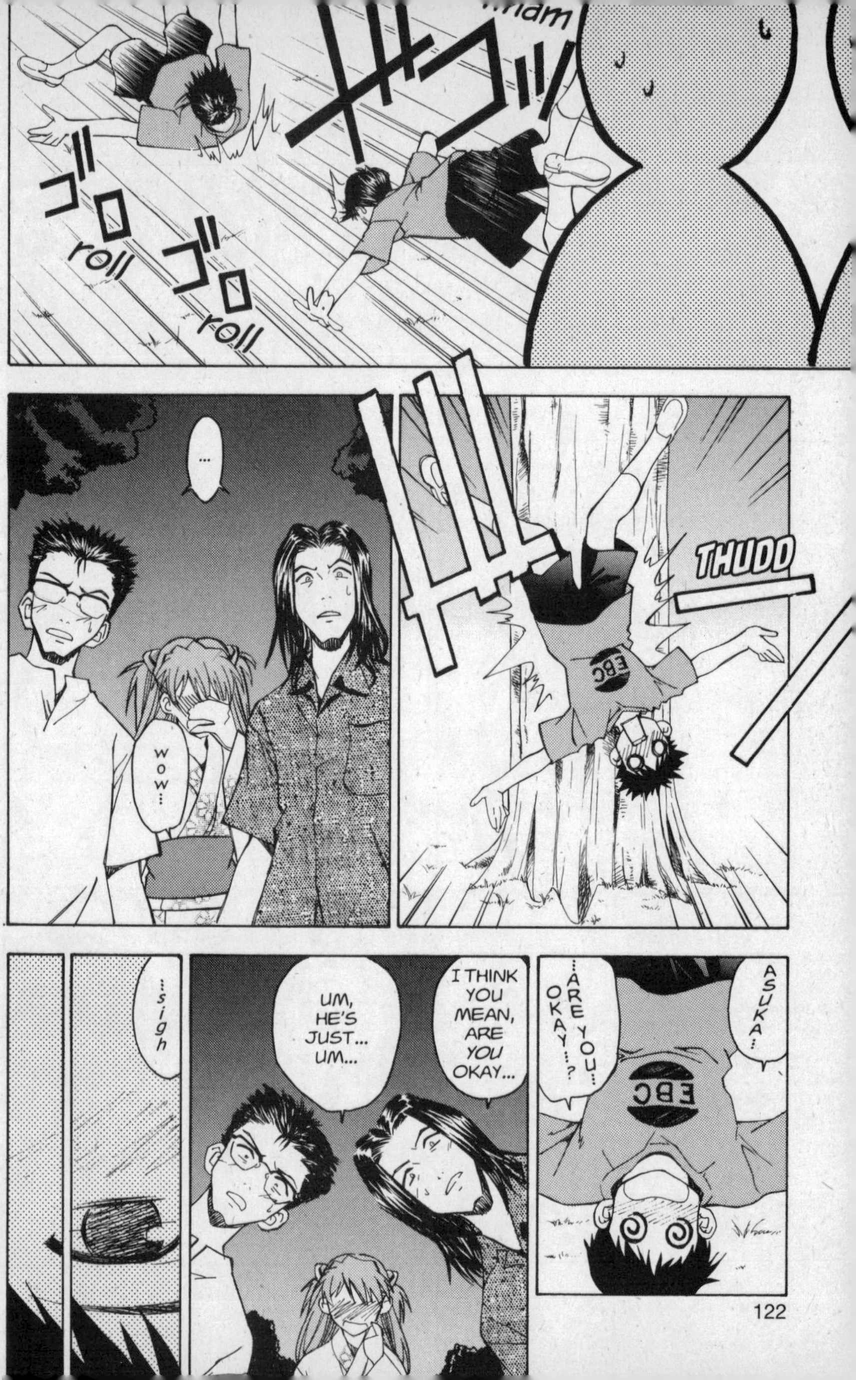

...ham
ゴッ
ゴロ
roll
ゴロ
roll
THUDD
...
WOW...
ASUKA...
...ARE YOU... OKAY...?
I THINK YOU MEAN, ARE YOU OKAY...
UM, HE'S JUST... UM...
...sigh

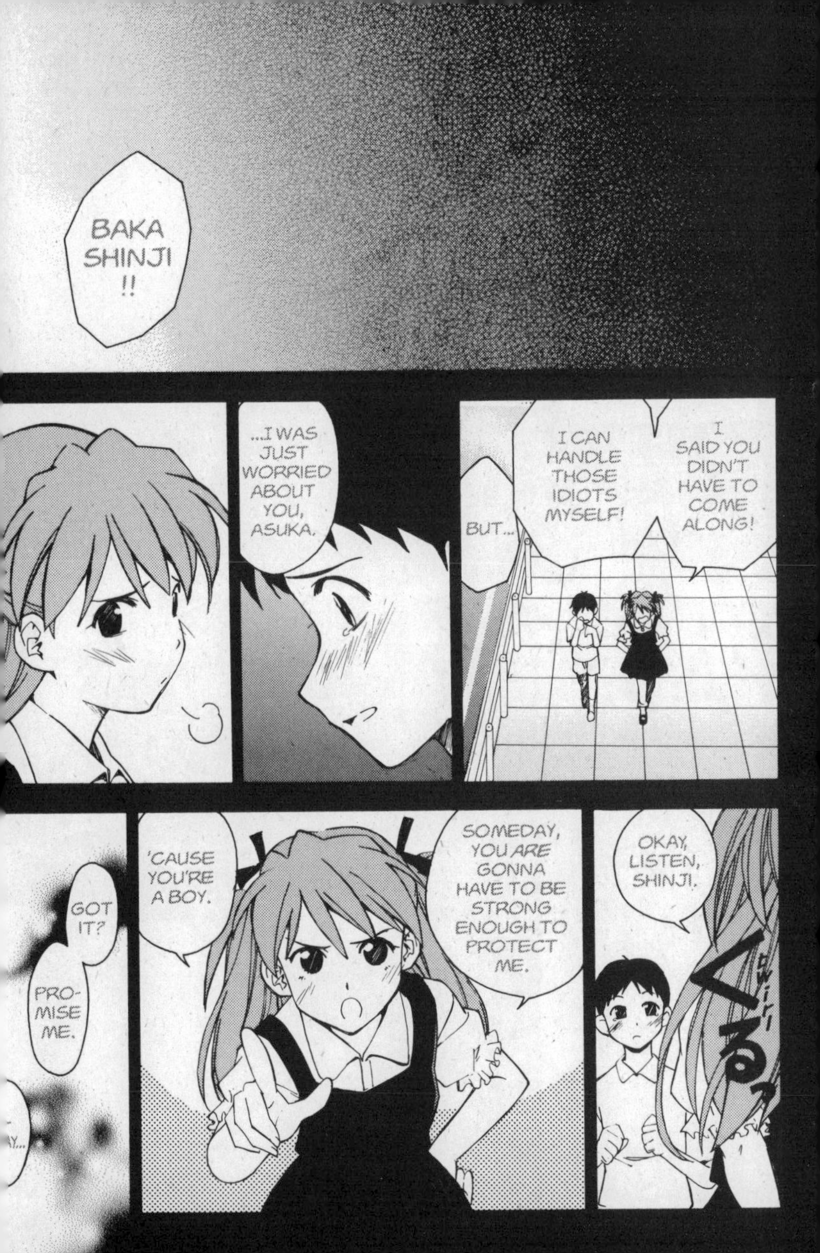
BAKA SHINJI !!
I SAID YOU DIDN'T HAVE TO COME ALONG!
I CAN HANDLE THOSE IDIOTS MYSELF!
BUT...
...I WAS JUST WORRIED ABOUT YOU, ASUKA.
OKAY, LISTEN, SHINJI.
くるっ
twirl
SOMEDAY, YOU *ARE* GONNA HAVE TO BE STRONG ENOUGH TO PROTECT ME.
'CAUSE YOU'RE A BOY.
GOT IT?
PRO-MISE ME.

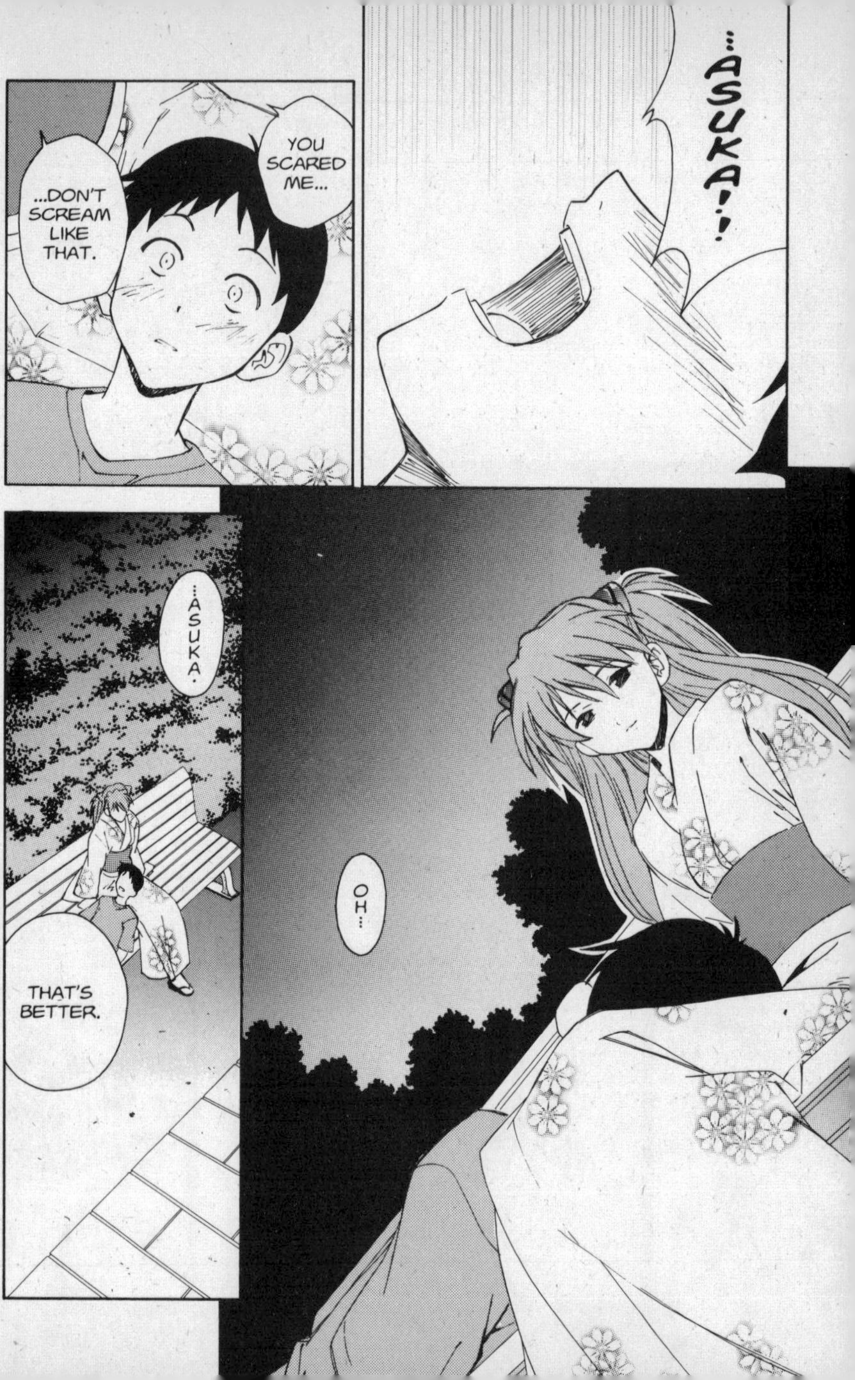
...ASUKA!!
YOU SCARED ME...
...DON'T SCREAM LIKE THAT.
OH...
...ASUKA.
THAT'S BETTER.

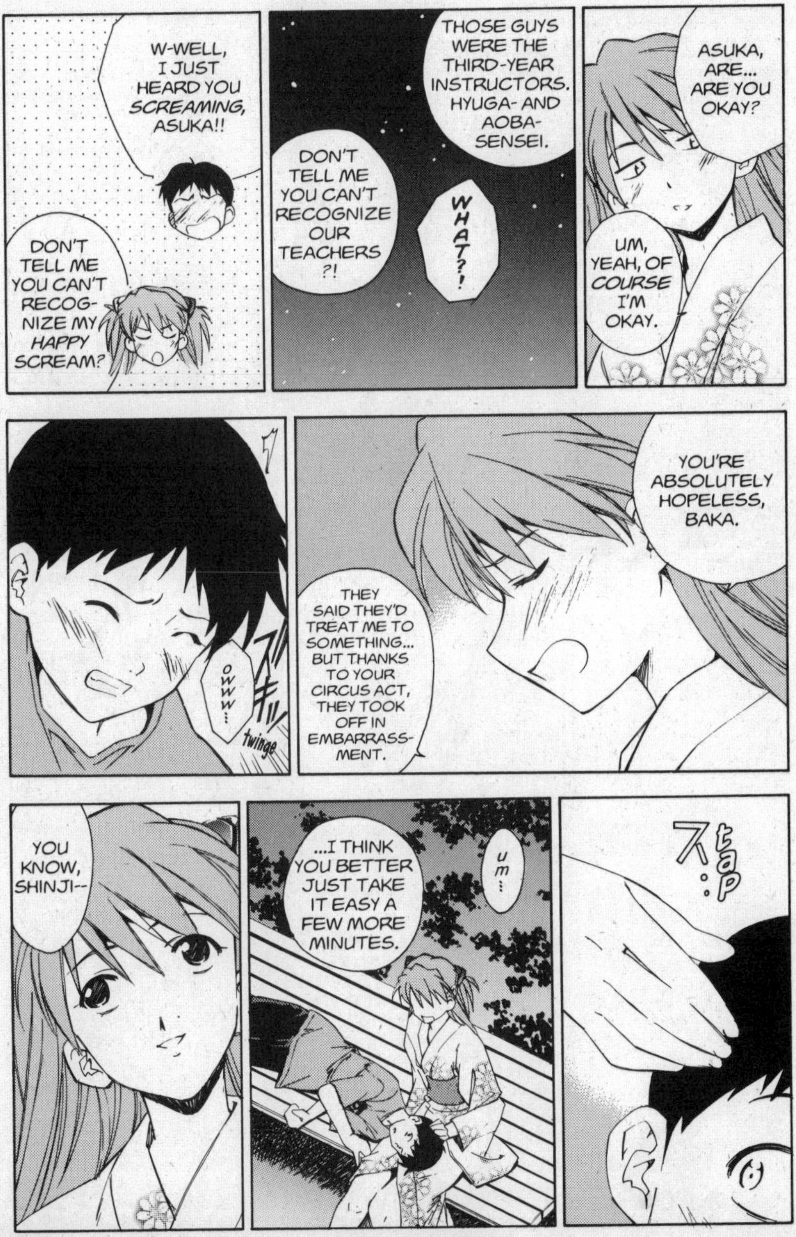
ASUKA, ARE... ARE YOU OKAY?
UM, YEAH, OF COURSE I'M OKAY.
THOSE GUYS WERE THE THIRD-YEAR INSTRUCTORS. HYUGA- AND AOBA-SENSEI.
WHAT?!
DON'T TELL ME YOU CAN'T RECOGNIZE OUR TEACHERS?!
W-WELL, I JUST HEARD YOU SCREAMING, ASUKA!!
DON'T TELL ME YOU CAN'T RECOGNIZE MY HAPPY SCREAM?
YOU'RE ABSOLUTELY HOPELESS, BAKA.
...THEY SAID THEY'D TREAT ME TO SOMETHING... BUT THANKS TO YOUR CIRCUS ACT, THEY TOOK OFF IN EMBARRASSMENT.
OWWW...
twinge
tap
UM...
...I THINK YOU BETTER JUST TAKE IT EASY A FEW MORE MINUTES.
YOU KNOW, SHINJI--

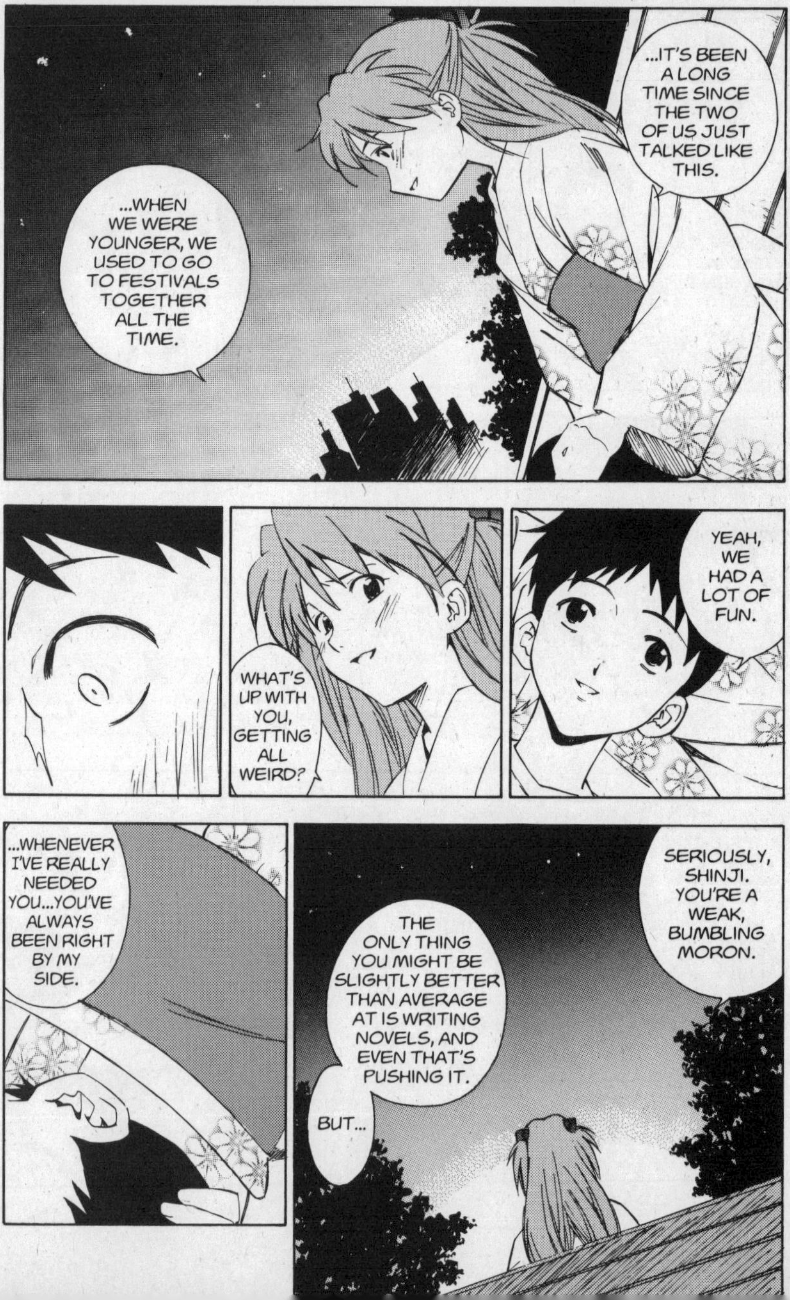
...IT'S BEEN A LONG TIME SINCE THE TWO OF US JUST TALKED LIKE THIS.
...WHEN WE WERE YOUNGER, WE USED TO GO TO FESTIVALS TOGETHER ALL THE TIME.
YEAH, WE HAD A LOT OF FUN.
WHAT'S UP WITH YOU, GETTING ALL WEIRD?
SERIOUSLY, SHINJI. YOU'RE A WEAK, BUMBLING MORON.
THE ONLY THING YOU MIGHT BE SLIGHTLY BETTER THAN AVERAGE AT IS WRITING NOVELS, AND EVEN THAT'S PUSHING IT.
BUT...
...WHENEVER I'VE REALLY NEEDED YOU...YOU'VE ALWAYS BEEN RIGHT BY MY SIDE.

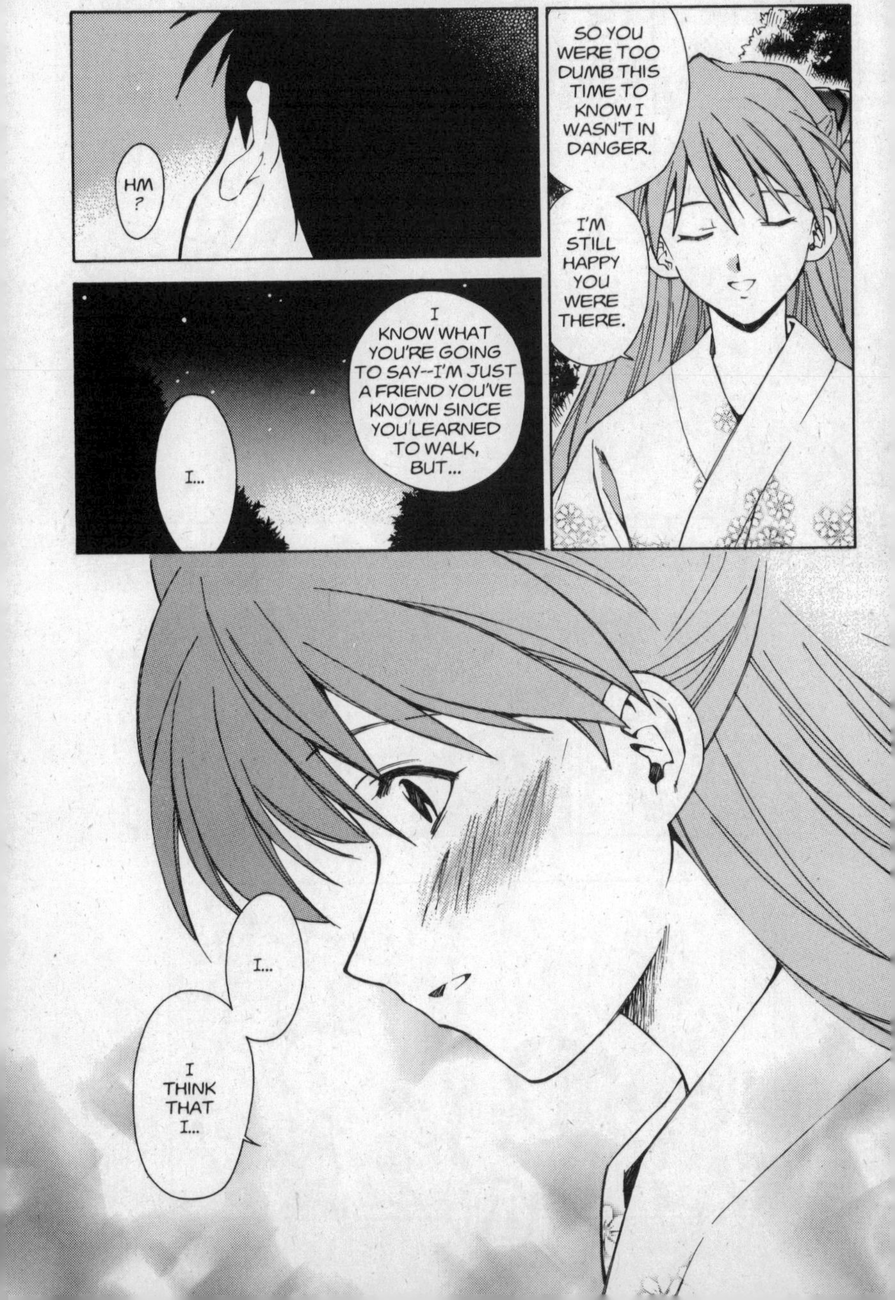
SO YOU WERE TOO DUMB THIS TIME TO KNOW I WASN'T IN DANGER.
I'M STILL HAPPY YOU WERE THERE.
HM?
I KNOW WHAT YOU'RE GOING TO SAY--I'M JUST A FRIEND YOU'VE KNOWN SINCE YOU LEARNED TO WALK, BUT...
I...
I...
I THINK THAT I...

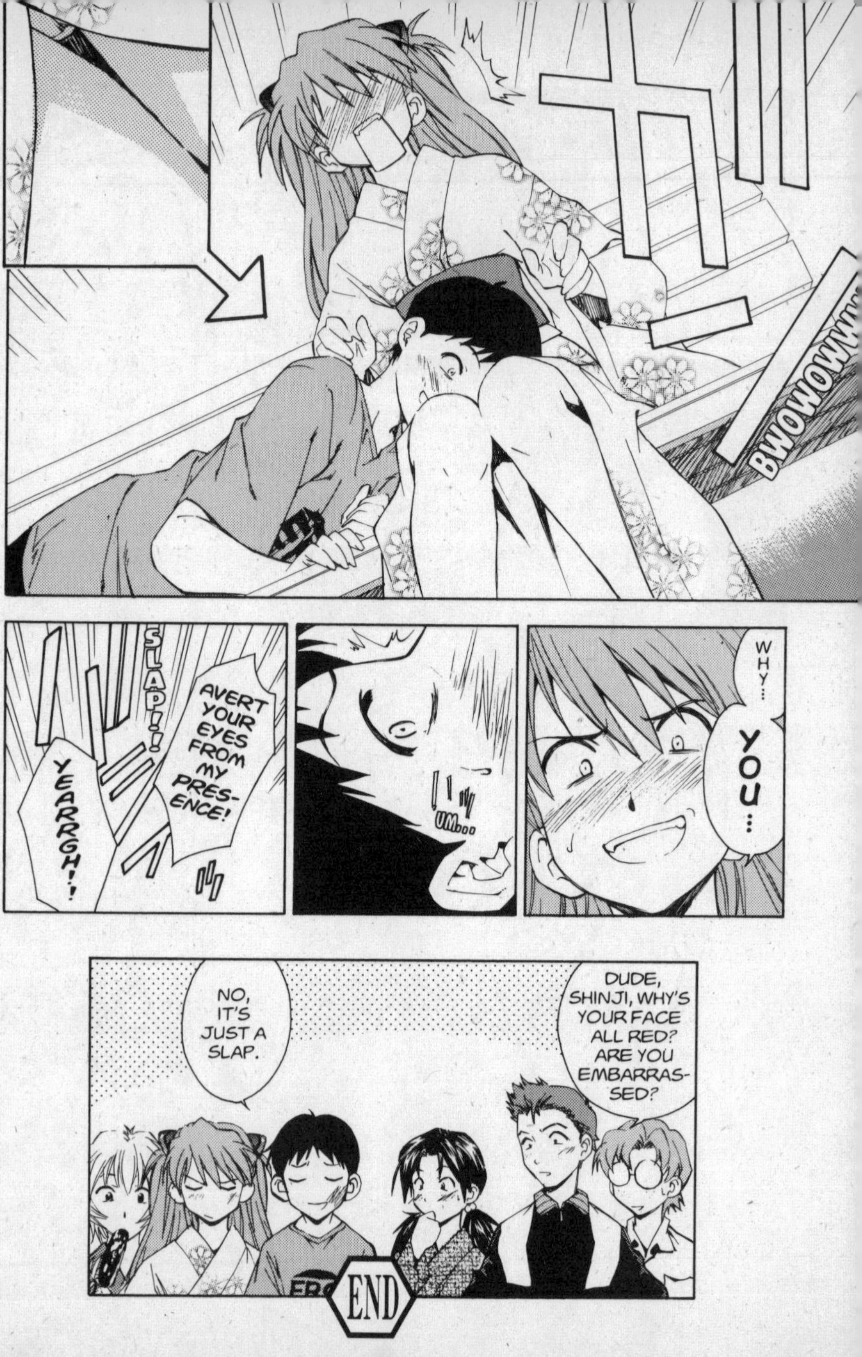
BWOWOWW
WHY...
YOU...
UM...
SLAP!!
AVERT YOUR EYES FROM MY PRESENCE!
YEARRGH!!
DUDE, SHINJI, WHY'S YOUR FACE ALL RED? ARE YOU EMBARRASSED?
NO, IT'S JUST A SLAP.
END

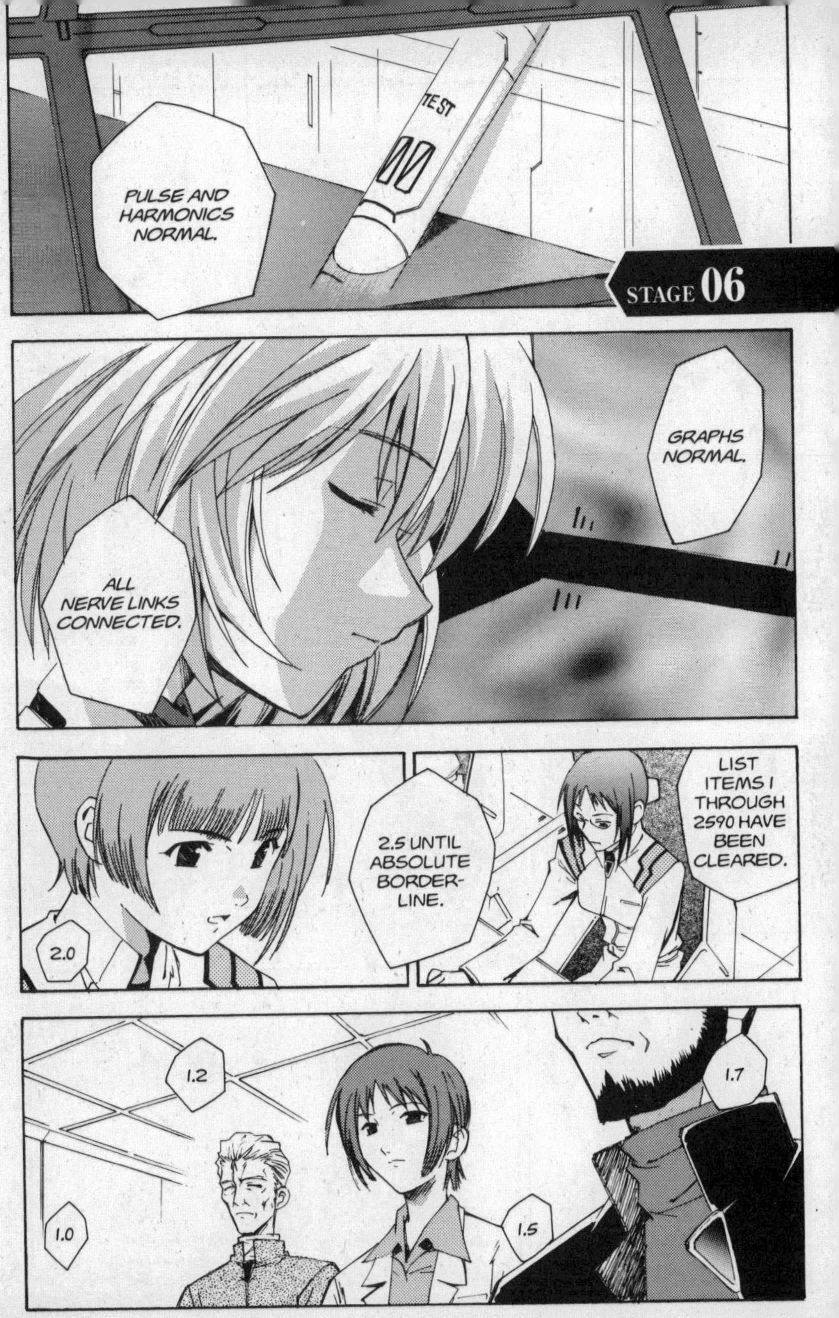

STAGE 06
TE ST
PULSE AND HARMONICS NORMAL.
GRAPHS NORMAL.
ALL NERVE LINKS CONNECTED.
LIST ITEMS 1 THROUGH 2590 HAVE BEEN CLEARED.
2.5 UNTIL ABSOLUTE BORDER-LINE.
2.0
1.7
1.2
1.5
1.0

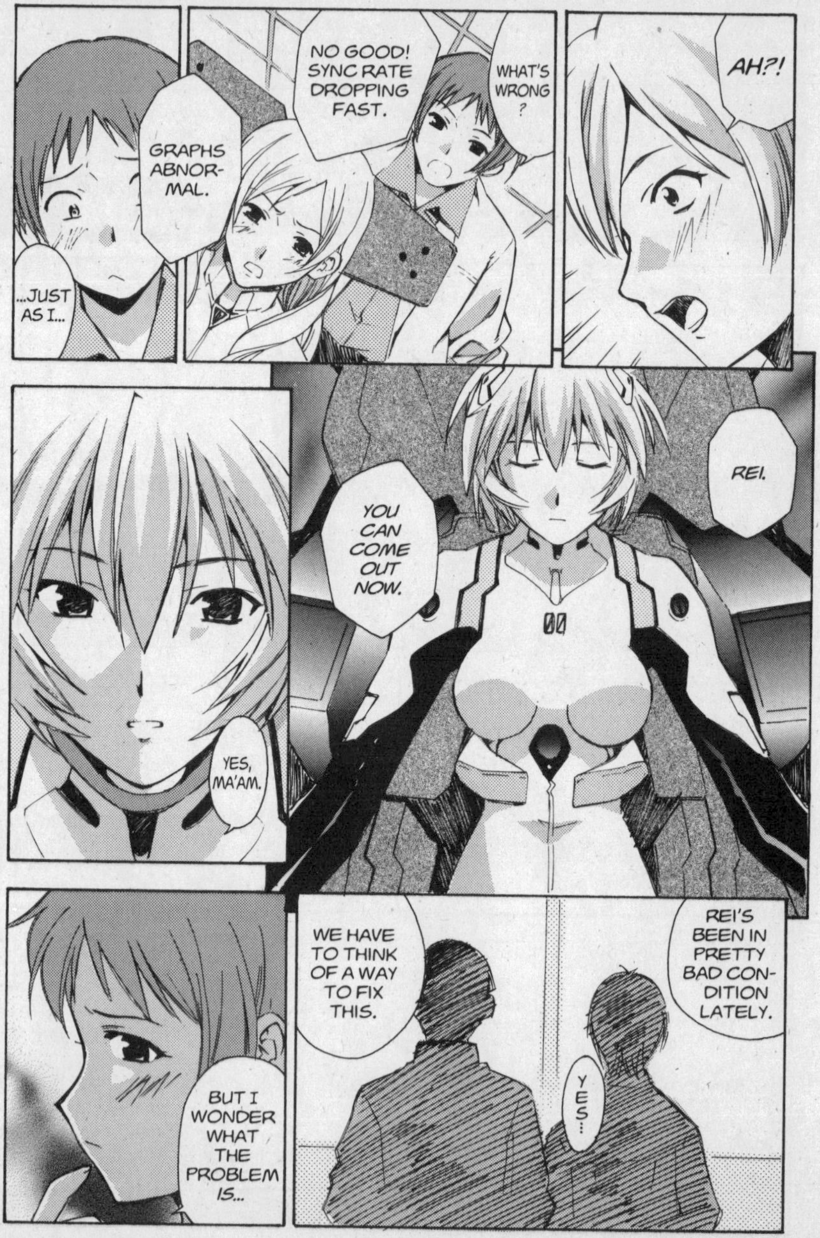
AH?!
WHAT'S WRONG?
NO GOOD! SYNC RATE DROPPING FAST.
GRAPHS ABNOR-MAL.
...JUST AS I...
REI.
YOU CAN COME OUT NOW.
YES, MA'AM.
REI'S BEEN IN PRETTY BAD CON-DITION LATELY.
WE HAVE TO THINK OF A WAY TO FIX THIS.
YES...
BUT I WONDER WHAT THE PROBLEM IS...

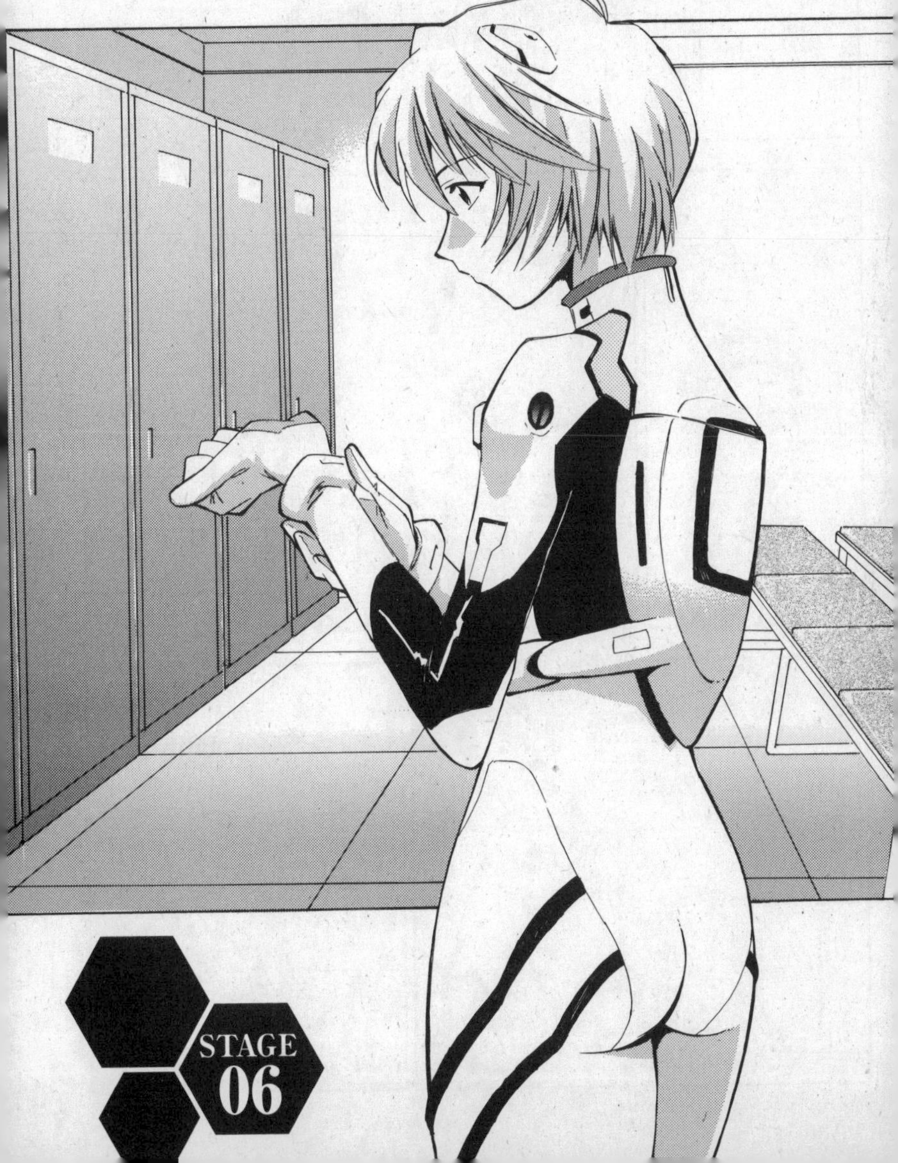
STAGE
06

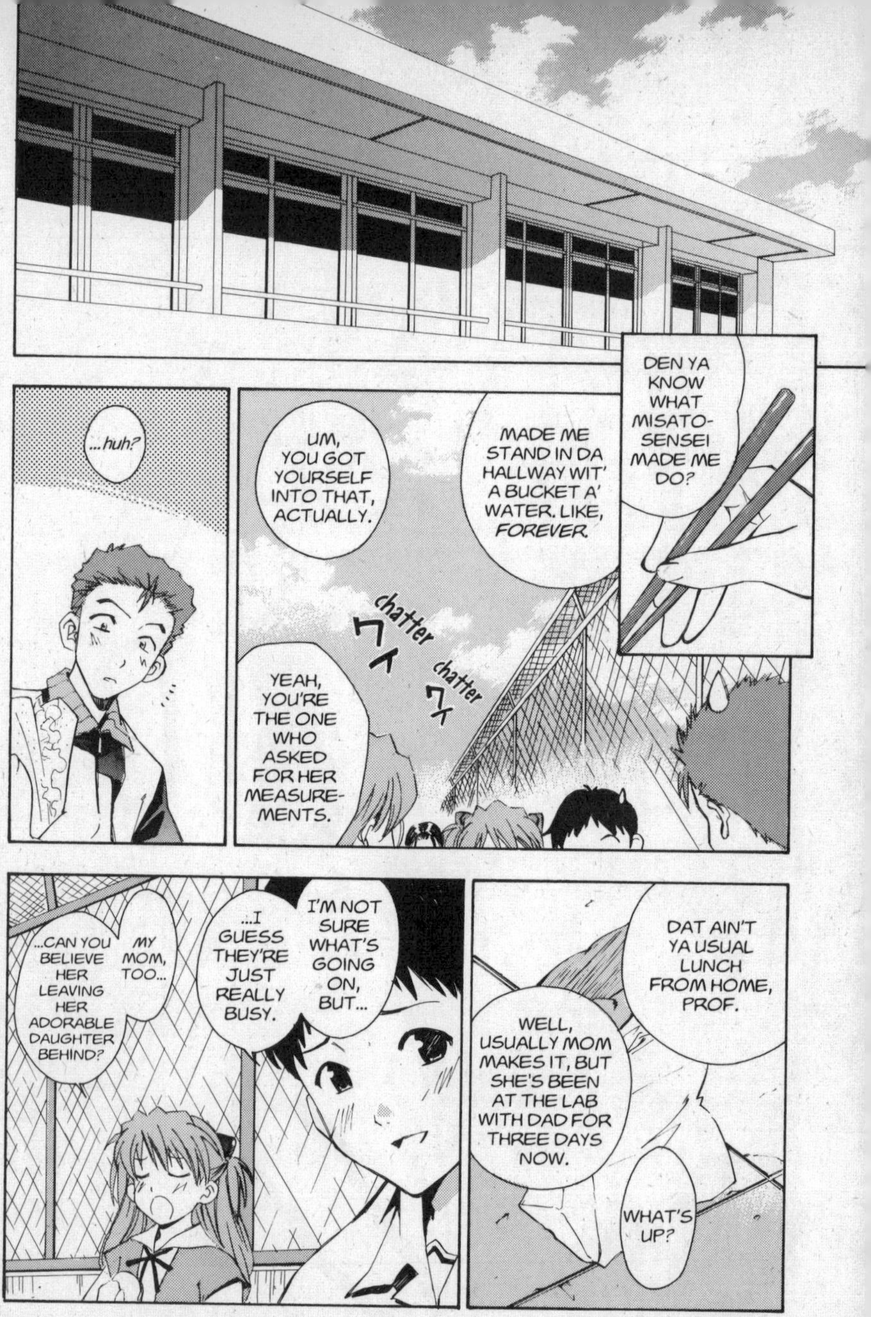
DEN YA KNOW WHAT MISATO-SENSEI MADE ME DO?
MADE ME STAND IN DA HALLWAY WIT' A BUCKET A' WATER. LIKE, FOREVER.
UM, YOU GOT YOURSELF INTO THAT, ACTUALLY.
chatter
ワイ
chatter
ワイ
YEAH, YOU'RE THE ONE WHO ASKED FOR HER MEASUREMENTS.
...huh?
DAT AIN'T YA USUAL LUNCH FROM HOME, PROF.
WHAT'S UP?
WELL, USUALLY MOM MAKES IT, BUT SHE'S BEEN AT THE LAB WITH DAD FOR THREE DAYS NOW.
I'M NOT SURE WHAT'S GOING ON, BUT...
...I GUESS THEY'RE JUST REALLY BUSY.
MY MOM, TOO...
...CAN YOU BELIEVE HER LEAVING HER ADORABLE DAUGHTER BEHIND?

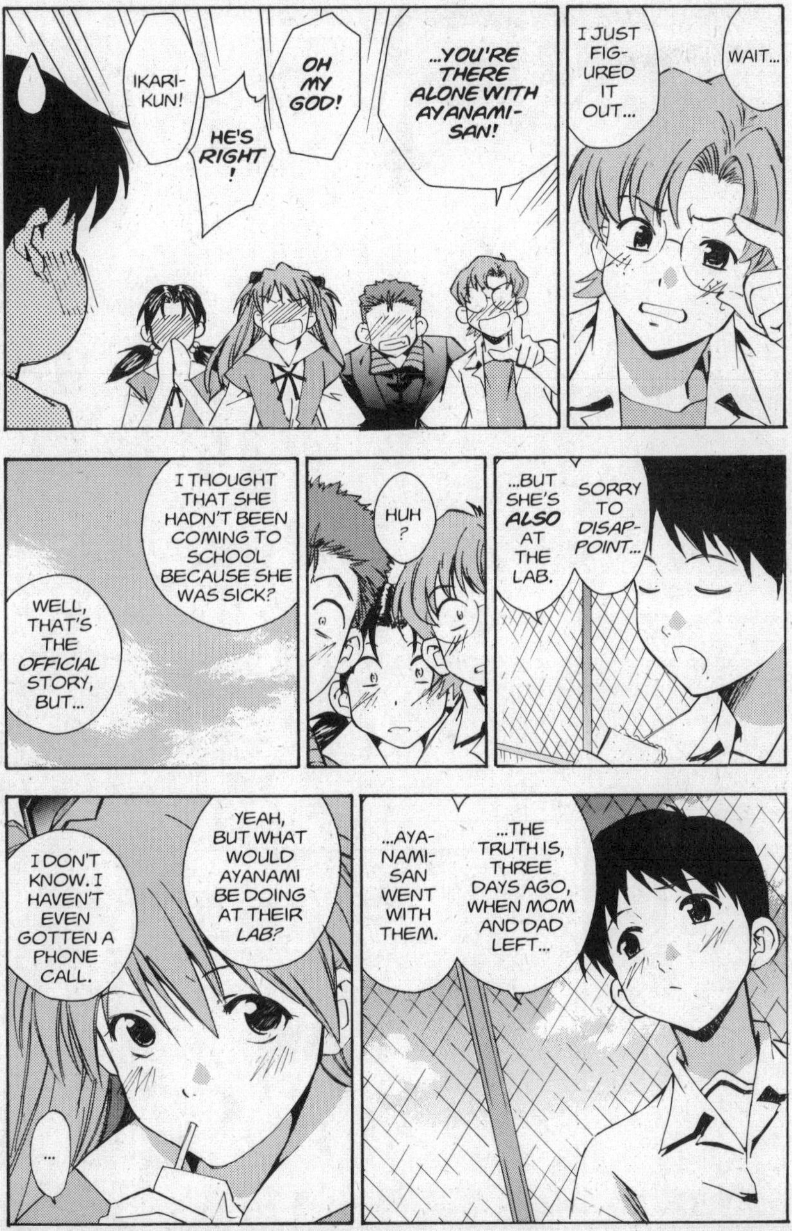
WAIT...
I JUST FIGURED IT OUT...
...YOU'RE THERE ALONE WITH AYANAMI-SAN!
OH MY GOD!
HE'S RIGHT!
IKARI-KUN!
SORRY TO DISAPPOINT...
...BUT SHE'S ALSO AT THE LAB.
HUH?
I THOUGHT THAT SHE HADN'T BEEN COMING TO SCHOOL BECAUSE SHE WAS SICK?
WELL, THAT'S THE OFFICIAL STORY, BUT...
...THE TRUTH IS, THREE DAYS AGO, WHEN MOM AND DAD LEFT...
...AYANAMI-SAN WENT WITH THEM.
YEAH, BUT WHAT WOULD AYANAMI BE DOING AT THEIR LAB?
I DON'T KNOW. I HAVEN'T EVEN GOTTEN A PHONE CALL.
...

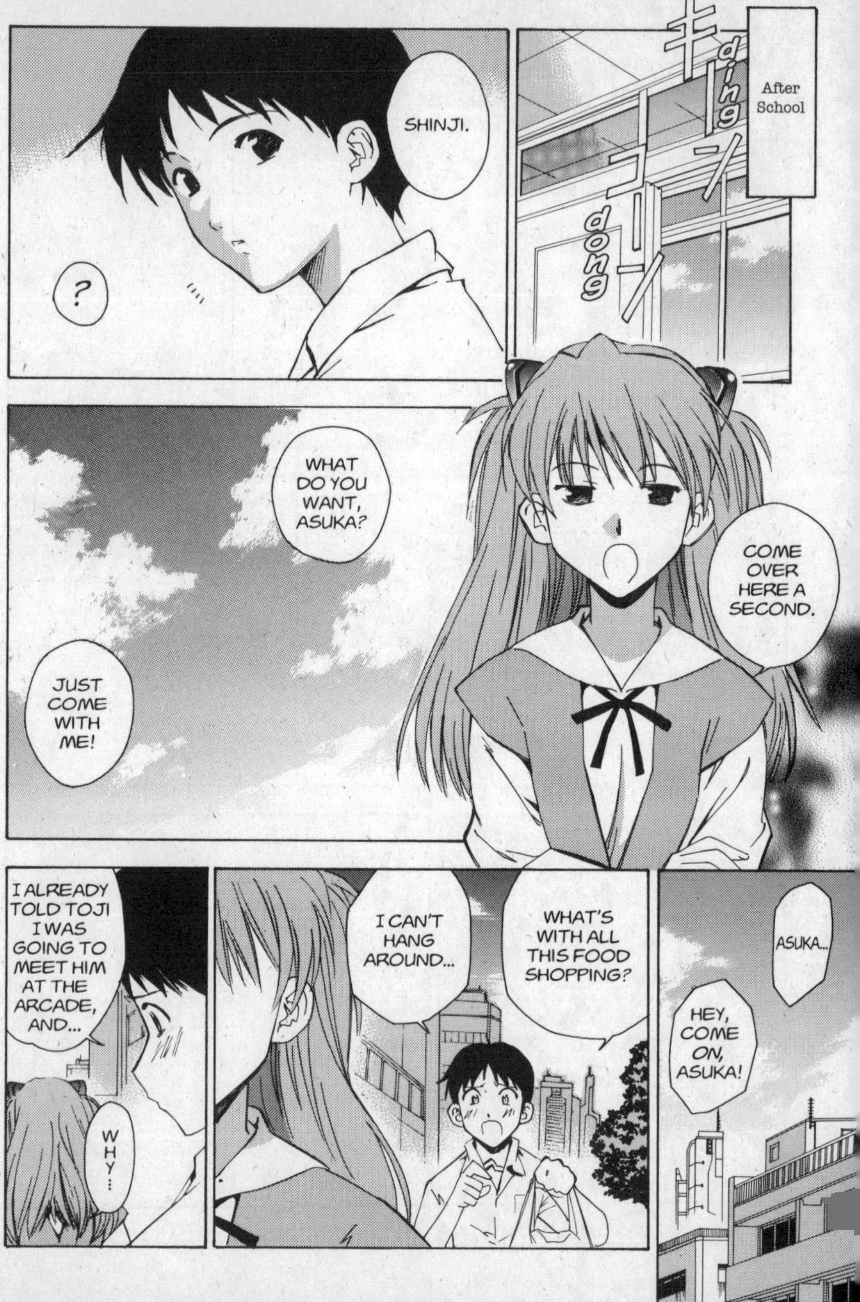
After School
ding dong
SHINJI.
?
COME OVER HERE A SECOND.
WHAT DO YOU WANT, ASUKA?
JUST COME WITH ME!
ASUKA...
HEY, COME ON, ASUKA!
WHAT'S WITH ALL THIS FOOD SHOPPING?
I CAN'T HANG AROUND...
I ALREADY TOLD TOJI I WAS GOING TO MEET HIM AT THE ARCADE, AND...
WHY...

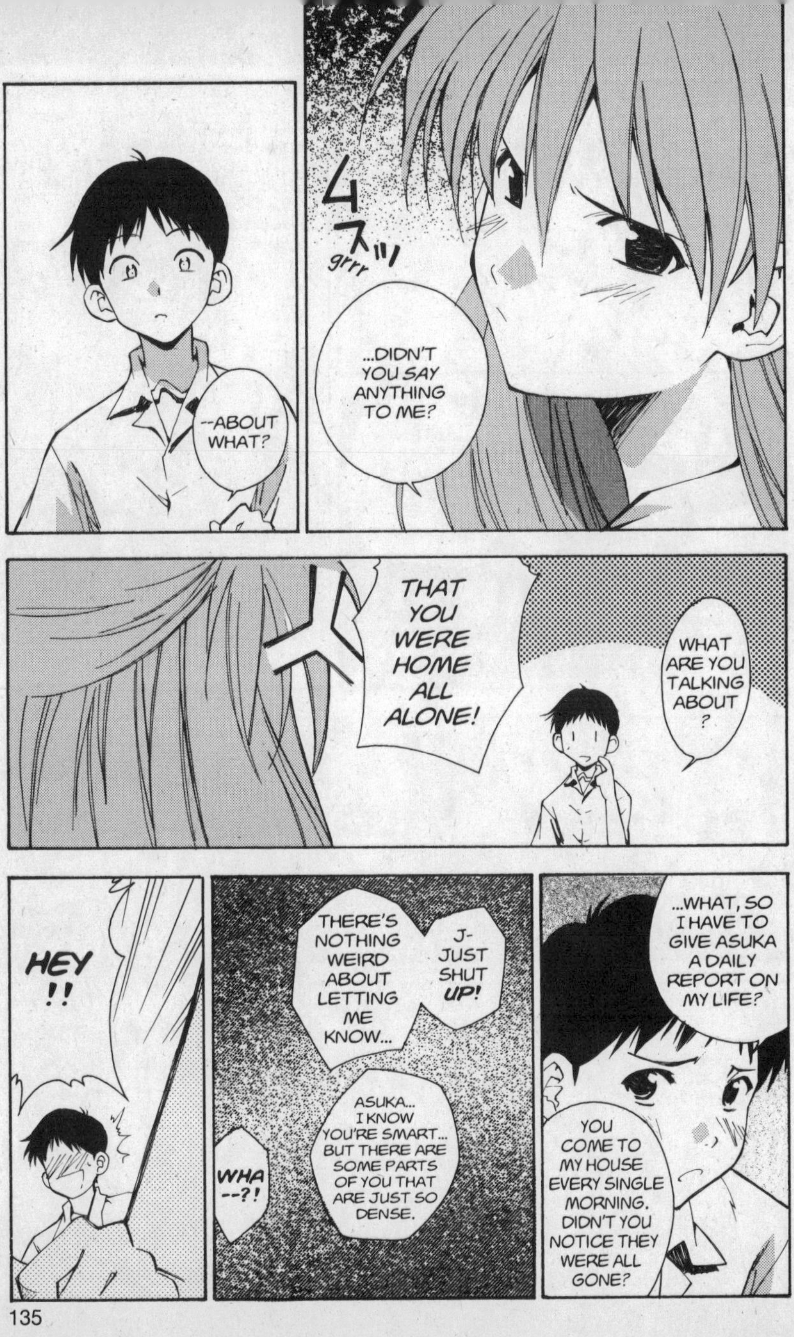
ムスッ
grrr
...DIDN'T YOU SAY ANYTHING TO ME?
--ABOUT WHAT?
THAT YOU WERE HOME ALL ALONE!
WHAT ARE YOU TALKING ABOUT ?
...WHAT, SO I HAVE TO GIVE ASUKA A DAILY REPORT ON MY LIFE?
YOU COME TO MY HOUSE EVERY SINGLE MORNING. DIDN'T YOU NOTICE THEY WERE ALL GONE?
THERE'S NOTHING WEIRD ABOUT LETTING ME KNOW...
J- JUST SHUT UP!
ASUKA... I KNOW YOU'RE SMART... BUT THERE ARE SOME PARTS OF YOU THAT ARE JUST SO DENSE.
WHA --?!
HEY !!

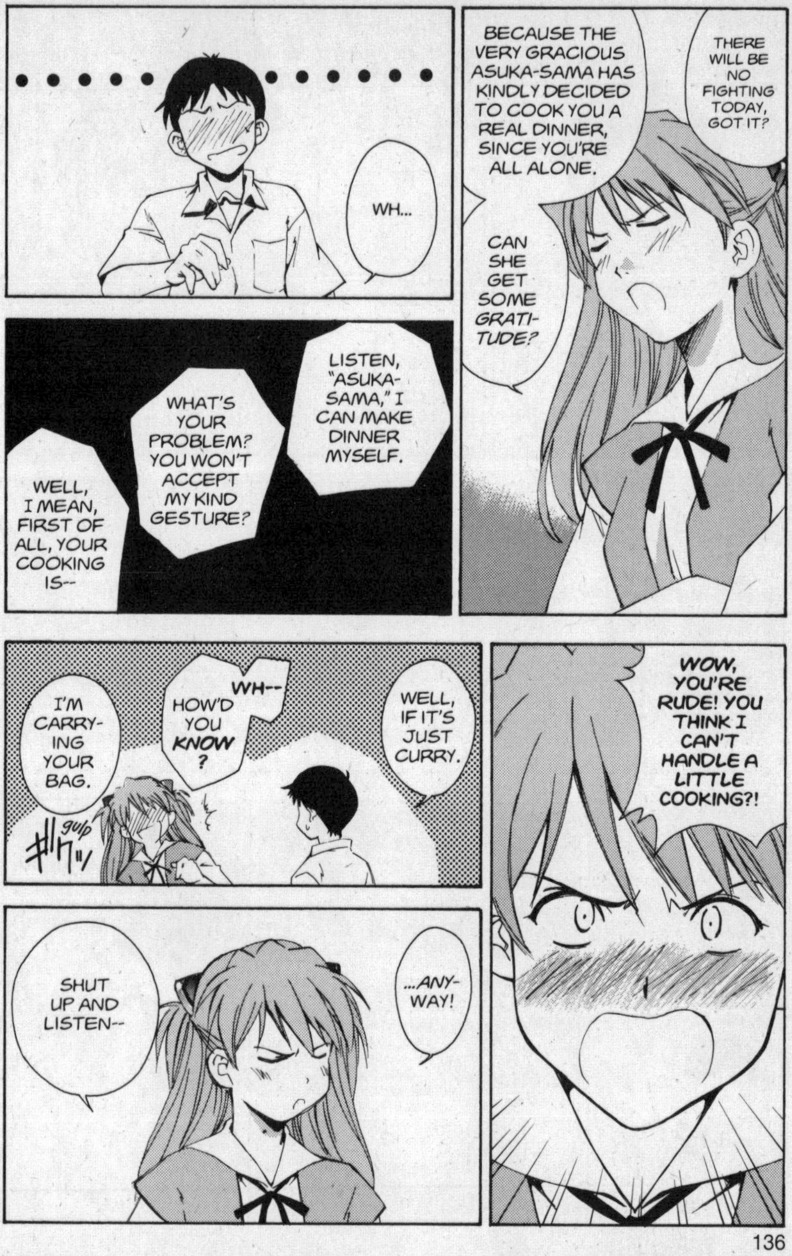
THERE WILL BE NO FIGHTING TODAY, GOT IT?
BECAUSE THE VERY GRACIOUS ASUKA-SAMA HAS KINDLY DECIDED TO COOK YOU A REAL DINNER, SINCE YOU'RE ALL ALONE.
CAN SHE GET SOME *GRATITUDE?*
• • • • • • • • • • •
WH...
LISTEN, "ASUKA-SAMA," I CAN MAKE DINNER MYSELF.
WHAT'S YOUR PROBLEM? YOU WON'T ACCEPT MY KIND GESTURE?
WELL, I MEAN, FIRST OF ALL, YOUR COOKING IS--
WOW, YOU'RE RUDE! YOU THINK I CAN'T HANDLE A LITTLE COOKING?!
WELL, IF IT'S JUST CURRY.
WH-- HOW'D YOU *KNOW*?
I'M CARRYING YOUR BAG.
ギクッ
gulp
...ANYWAY!
SHUT UP AND LISTEN--

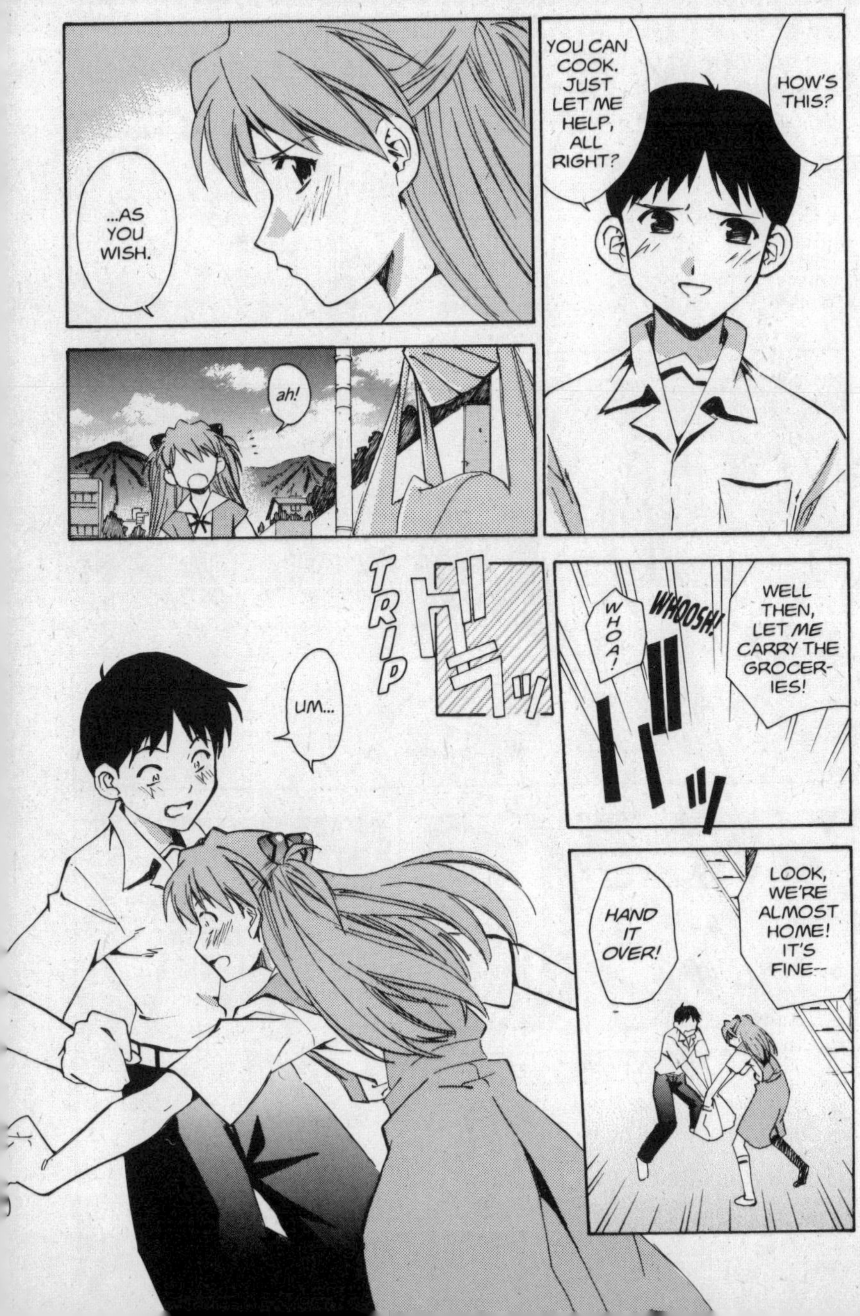
HOW'S THIS?
YOU CAN COOK. JUST LET ME HELP, ALL RIGHT?
...AS YOU WISH.
ah!
WELL THEN, LET ME CARRY THE GROCER-IES!
WHOOSH!
WHOA!
LOOK, WE'RE ALMOST HOME! IT'S FINE--
HAND IT OVER!
TRIP
UM...

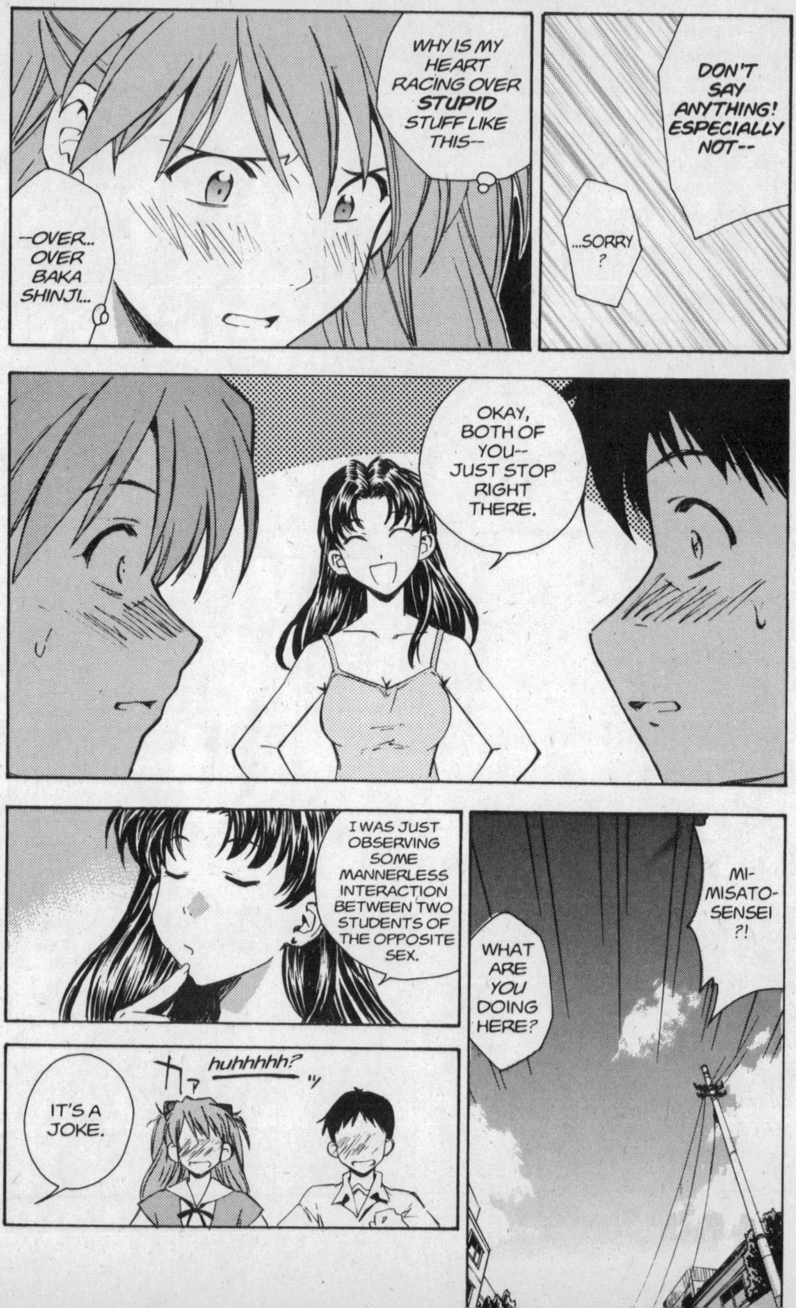
DON'T SAY ANYTHING! ESPECIALLY NOT--
...SORRY?
WHY IS MY HEART RACING OVER STUPID STUFF LIKE THIS--
--OVER.. OVER BAKA SHINJI...
OKAY, BOTH OF YOU-- JUST STOP RIGHT THERE.
MI-MISATO-SENSEI?!
WHAT ARE YOU DOING HERE?
I WAS JUST OBSERVING SOME MANNERLESS INTERACTION BETWEEN TWO STUDENTS OF THE OPPOSITE SEX.
huhhhhh?
カァ
IT'S A JOKE.

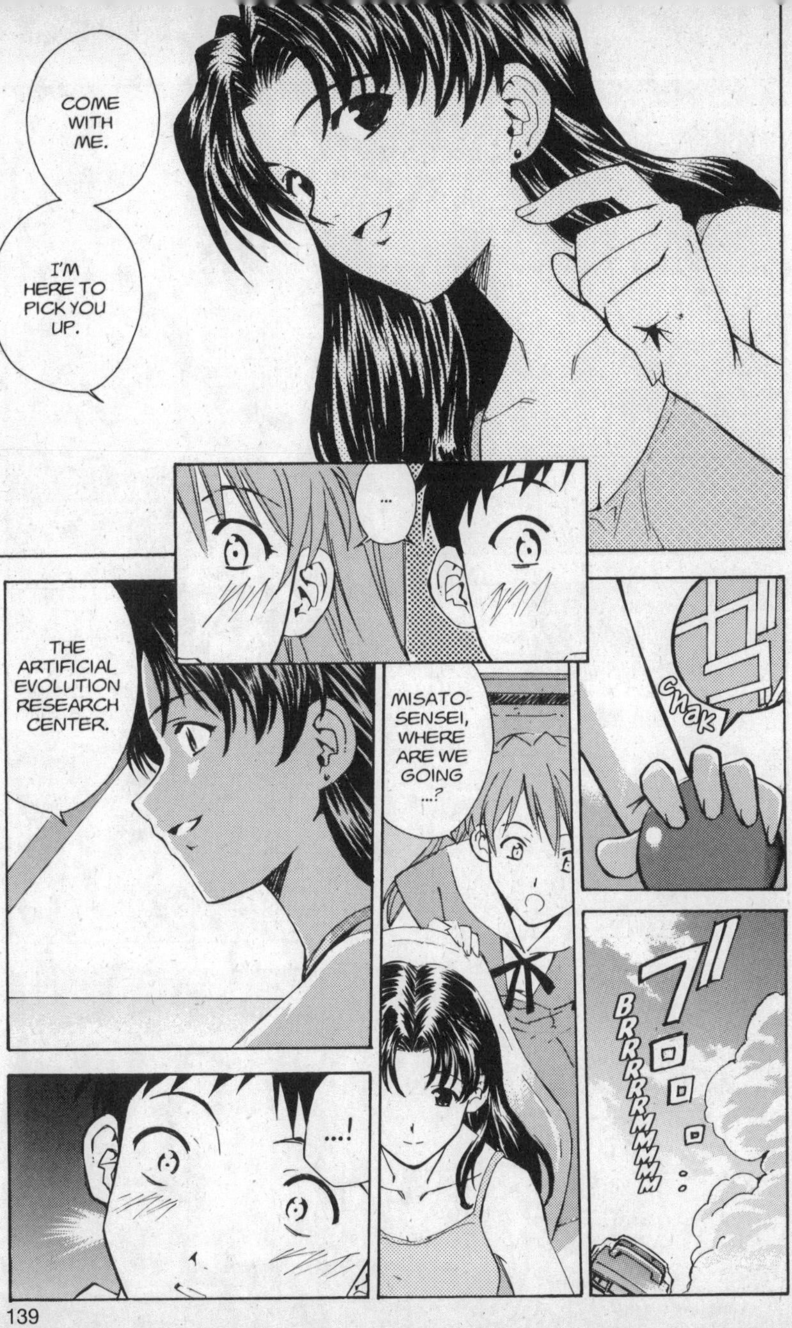
COME WITH ME.
I'M HERE TO PICK YOU UP.
...
CHAK
BRRRRRMMMMM
MISATO-SENSEI, WHERE ARE WE GOING ...?
THE ARTIFICIAL EVOLUTION RESEARCH CENTER.
...!

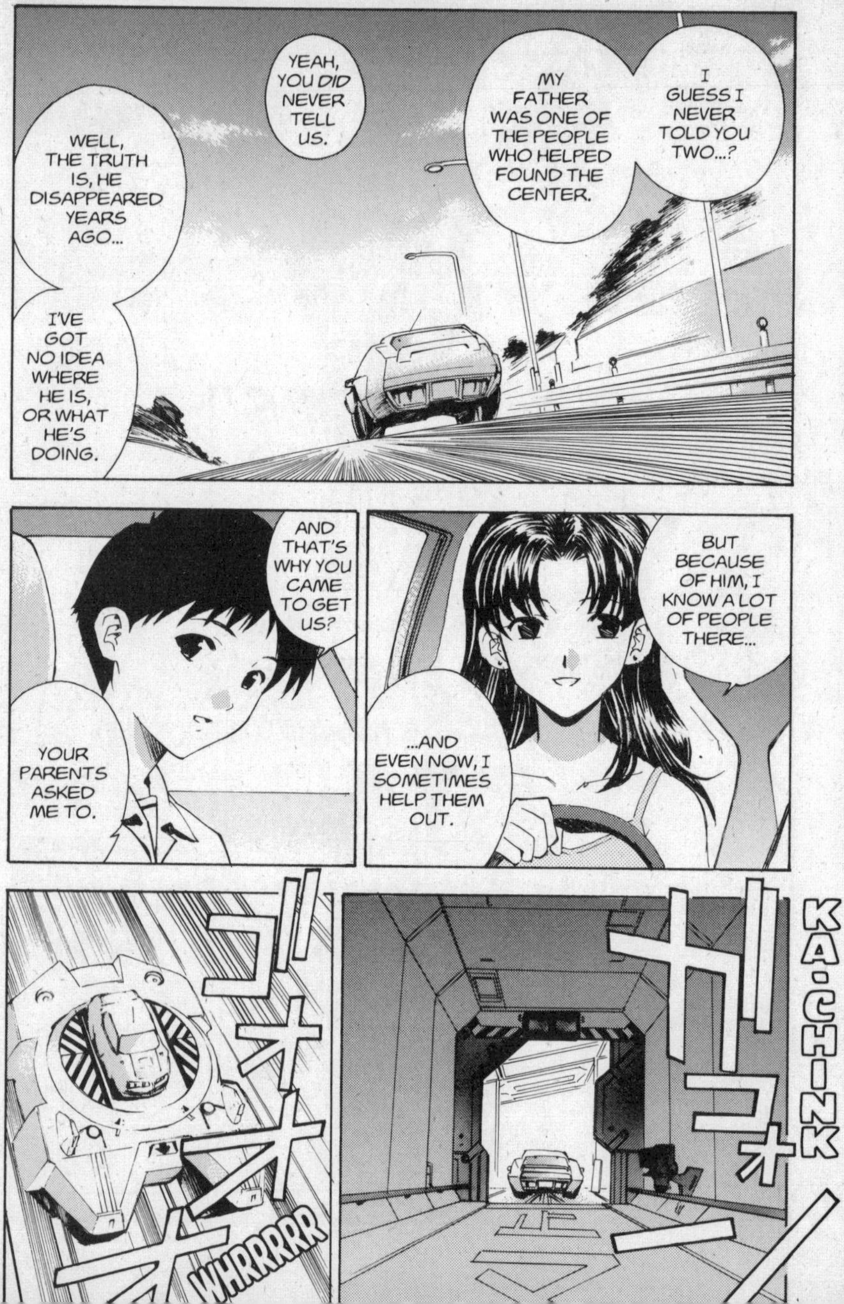
I GUESS I NEVER TOLD YOU TWO...?
MY FATHER WAS ONE OF THE PEOPLE WHO HELPED FOUND THE CENTER.
YEAH, YOU *DID* NEVER TELL US.
WELL, THE TRUTH IS, HE DISAPPEARED YEARS AGO...
I'VE GOT NO IDEA WHERE HE IS, OR WHAT HE'S DOING.
BUT BECAUSE OF HIM, I KNOW A LOT OF PEOPLE THERE...
...AND EVEN NOW, I SOMETIMES HELP THEM OUT.
AND THAT'S WHY YOU CAME TO GET US?
YOUR PARENTS ASKED ME TO.
KA-CHINK
WHRRRRR

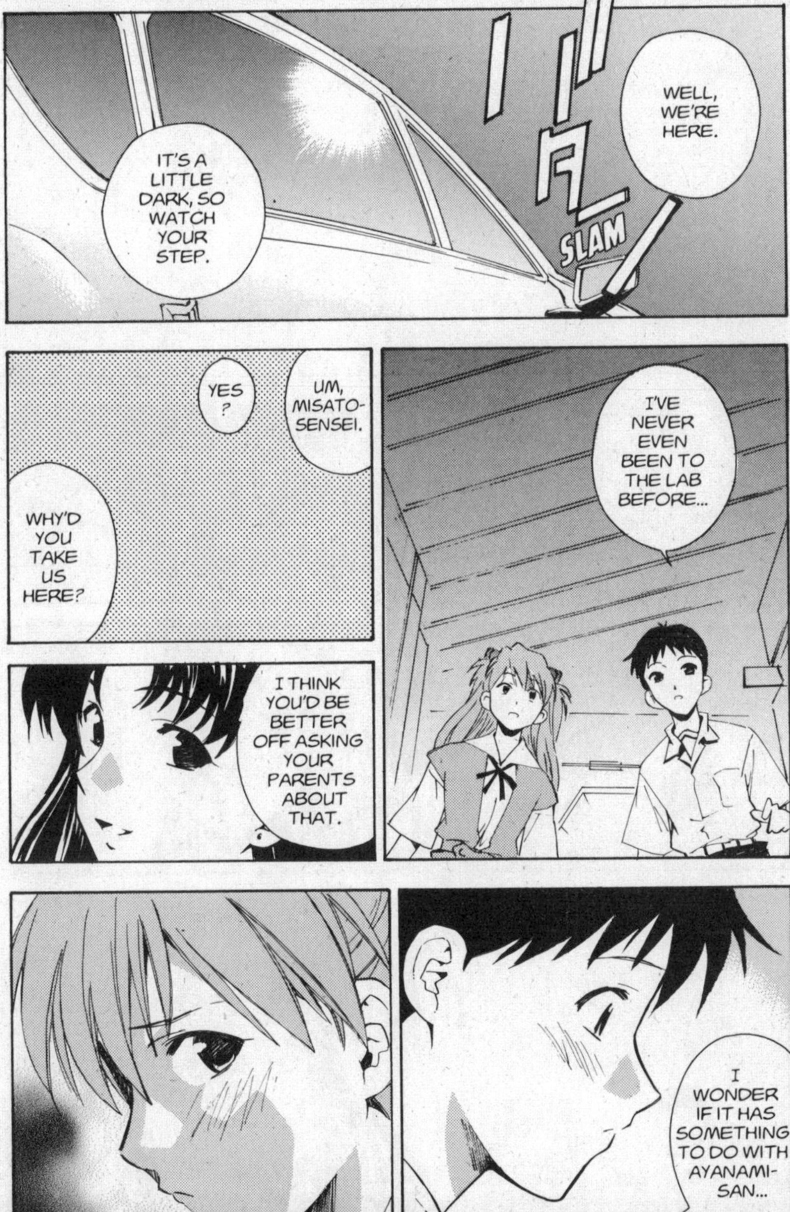
WELL, WE'RE HERE.
SLAM
IT'S A LITTLE DARK, SO WATCH YOUR STEP.
I'VE NEVER EVEN BEEN TO THE LAB BEFORE...
UM, MISATO-SENSEI.
YES?
WHY'D YOU TAKE US HERE?
I THINK YOU'D BE BETTER OFF ASKING YOUR PARENTS ABOUT THAT.
I WONDER IF IT HAS SOMETHING TO DO WITH AYANAMI-SAN...

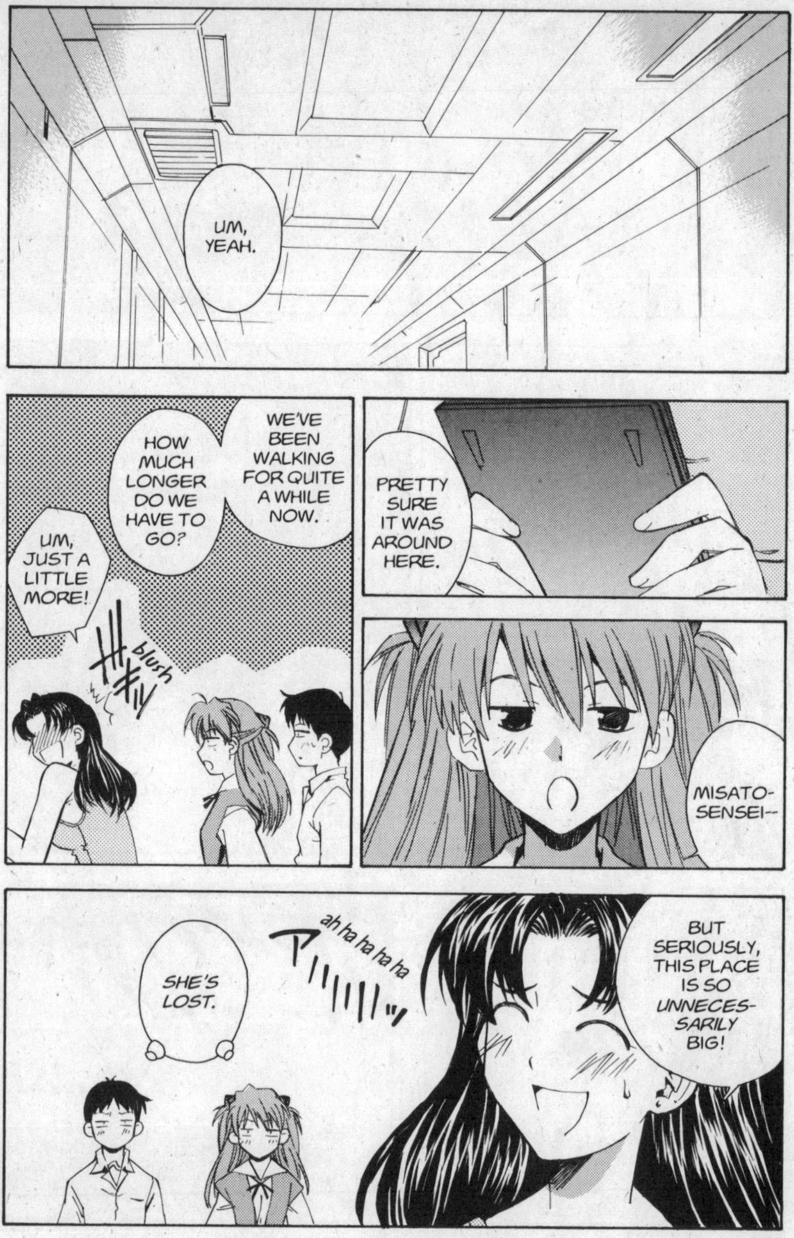
UM, YEAH.
PRETTY SURE IT WAS AROUND HERE.
MISATO-SENSEI--
WE'VE BEEN WALKING FOR QUITE A WHILE NOW.
HOW MUCH LONGER DO WE HAVE TO GO?
UM, JUST A LITTLE MORE!
blush
BUT SERIOUSLY, THIS PLACE IS SO UNNECES-SARILY BIG!
ah ha ha ha ha
SHE'S LOST.

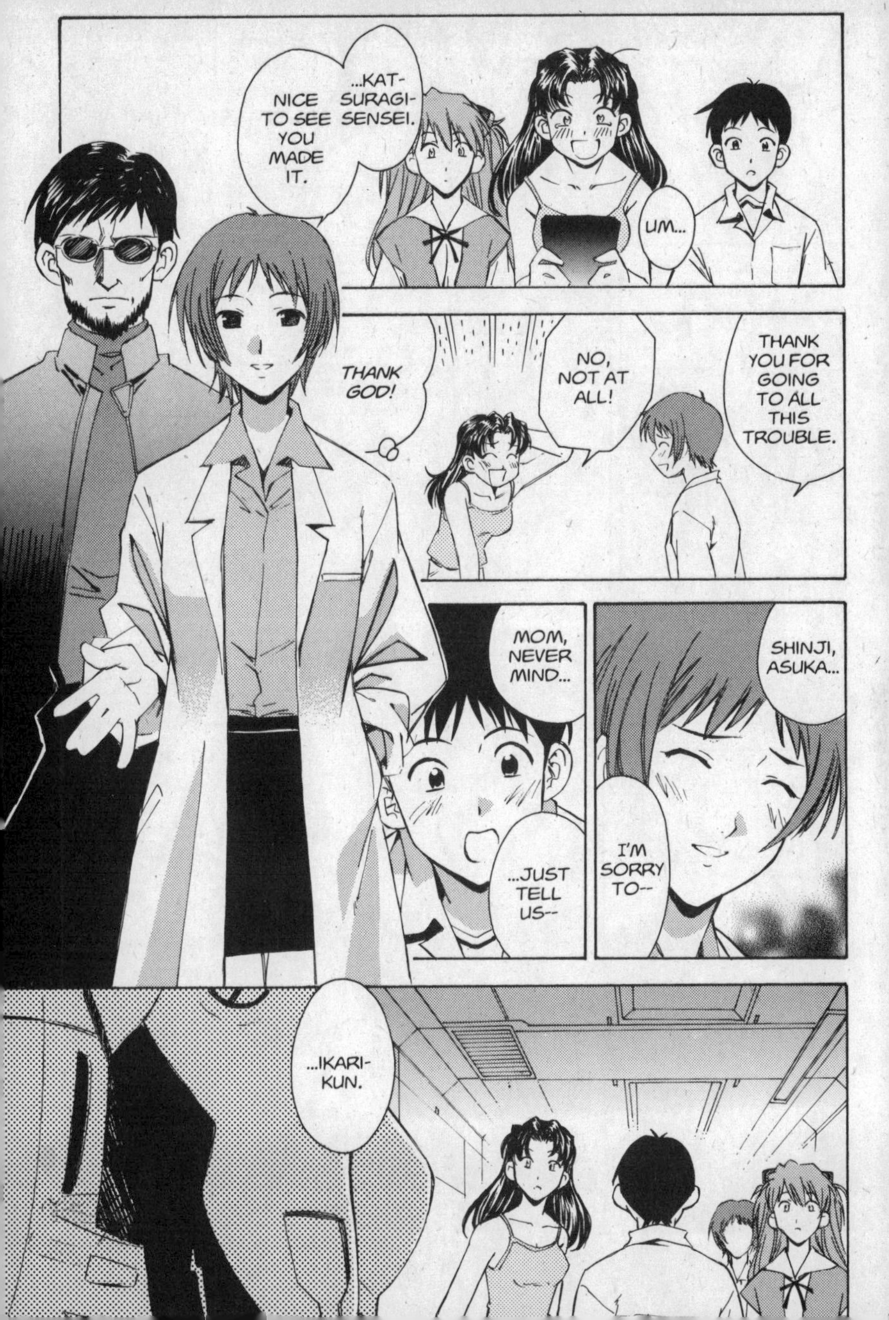
NICE TO SEE YOU MADE IT. ...KAT-SURAGI-SENSEI.
UM...
THANK YOU FOR GOING TO ALL THIS TROUBLE.
NO, NOT AT ALL!
THANK GOD!
SHINJI, ASUKA...
I'M SORRY TO--
MOM, NEVER MIND...
...JUST TELL US--
...IKARI-KUN.

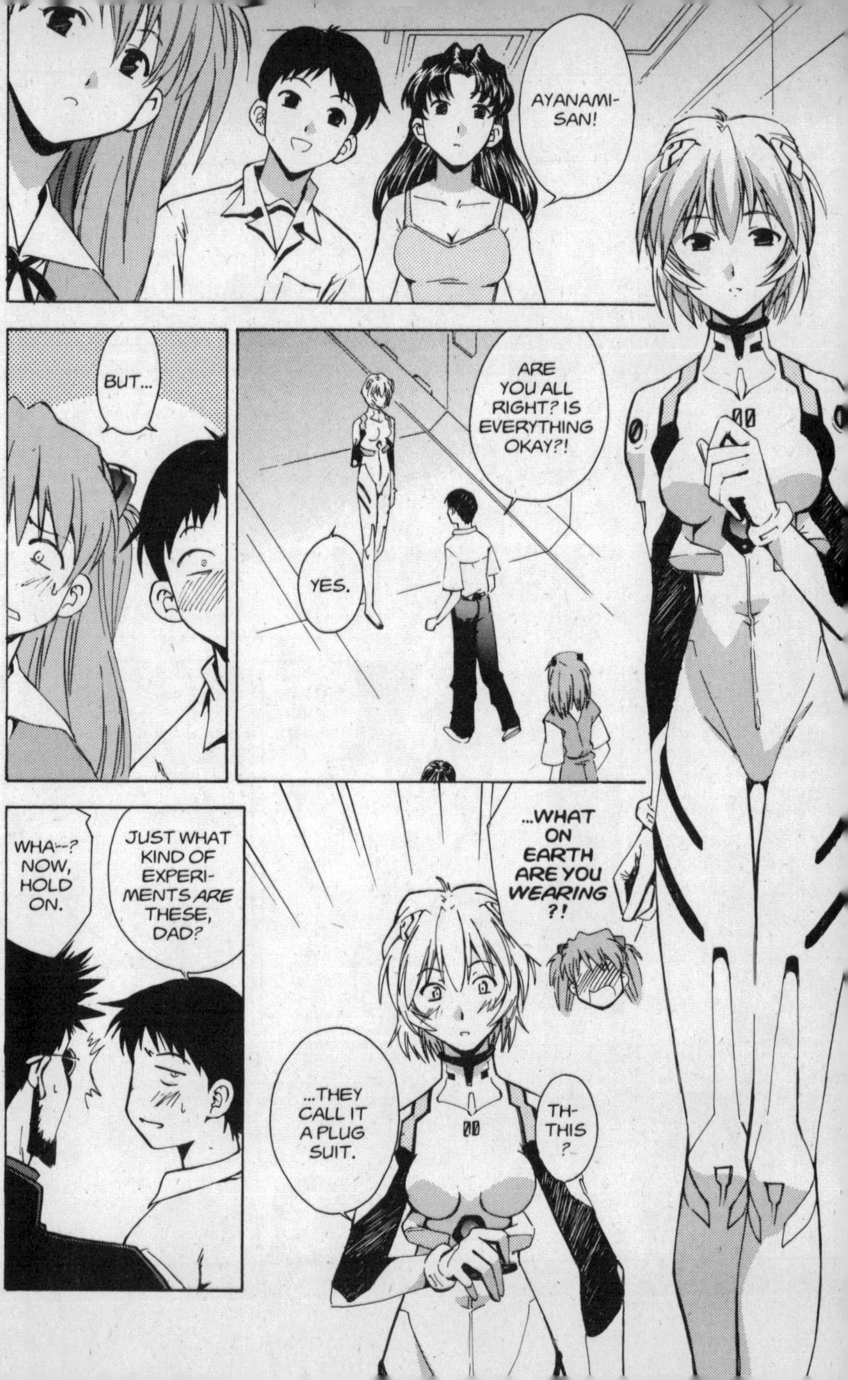
AYANAMI-SAN!
ARE YOU ALL RIGHT? IS EVERYTHING OKAY?!
YES.
BUT...
...WHAT ON EARTH ARE YOU WEARING?!
TH-THIS?
...THEY CALL IT A PLUG SUIT.
JUST WHAT KIND OF EXPERIMENTS ARE THESE, DAD?
WHA--? NOW, HOLD ON.

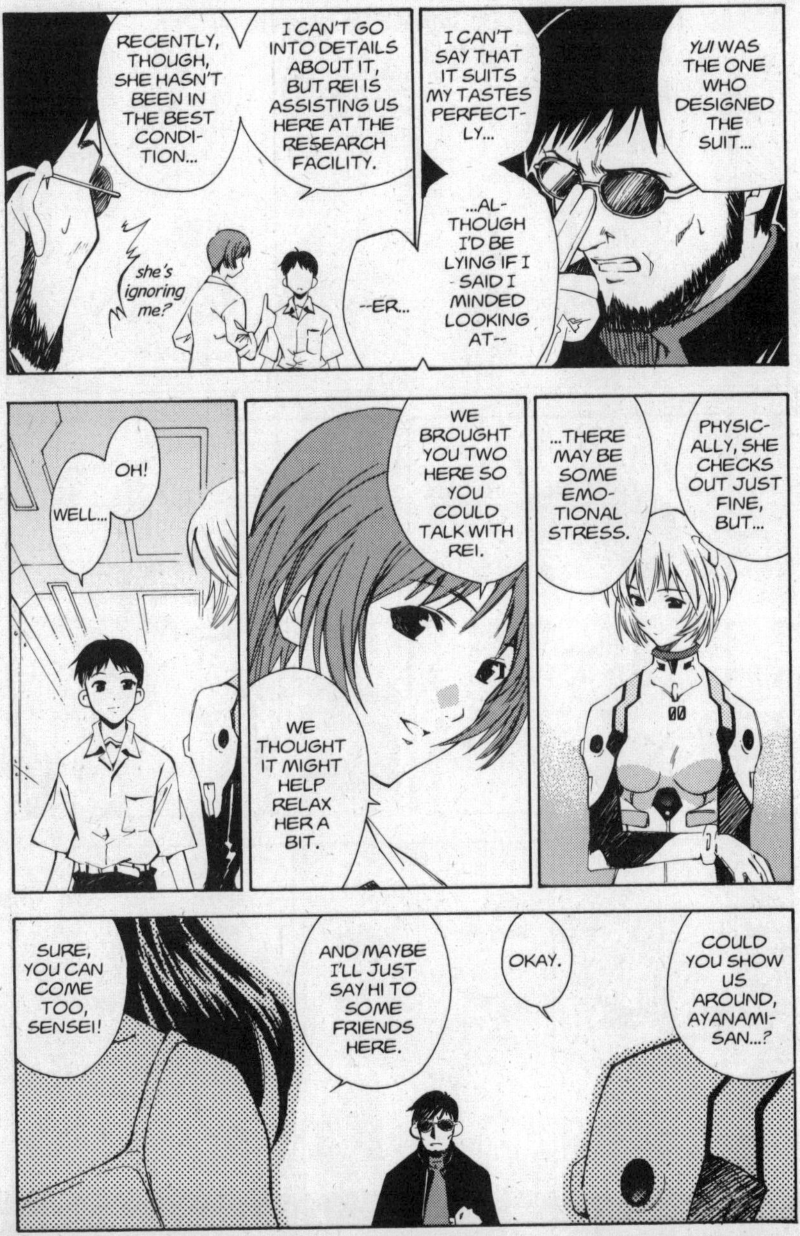
YUI WAS THE ONE WHO DESIGNED THE SUIT...
I CAN'T SAY THAT IT SUITS MY TASTES PERFECT-LY...
...AL-THOUGH I'D BE LYING IF I SAID I MINDED LOOKING AT--
--ER...
I CAN'T GO INTO DETAILS ABOUT IT, BUT REI IS ASSISTING US HERE AT THE RESEARCH FACILITY.
RECENTLY, THOUGH, SHE HASN'T BEEN IN THE BEST CONDI-TION...
she's ignoring me?
PHYSIC-ALLY, SHE CHECKS OUT JUST FINE, BUT...
...THERE MAY BE SOME EMO-TIONAL STRESS.
WE BROUGHT YOU TWO HERE SO YOU COULD TALK WITH REI.
WE THOUGHT IT MIGHT HELP RELAX HER A BIT.
OH!
WELL...
COULD YOU SHOW US AROUND, AYANAMI-SAN...?
OKAY.
AND MAYBE I'LL JUST SAY HI TO SOME FRIENDS HERE.
SURE, YOU CAN COME TOO, SENSEI!

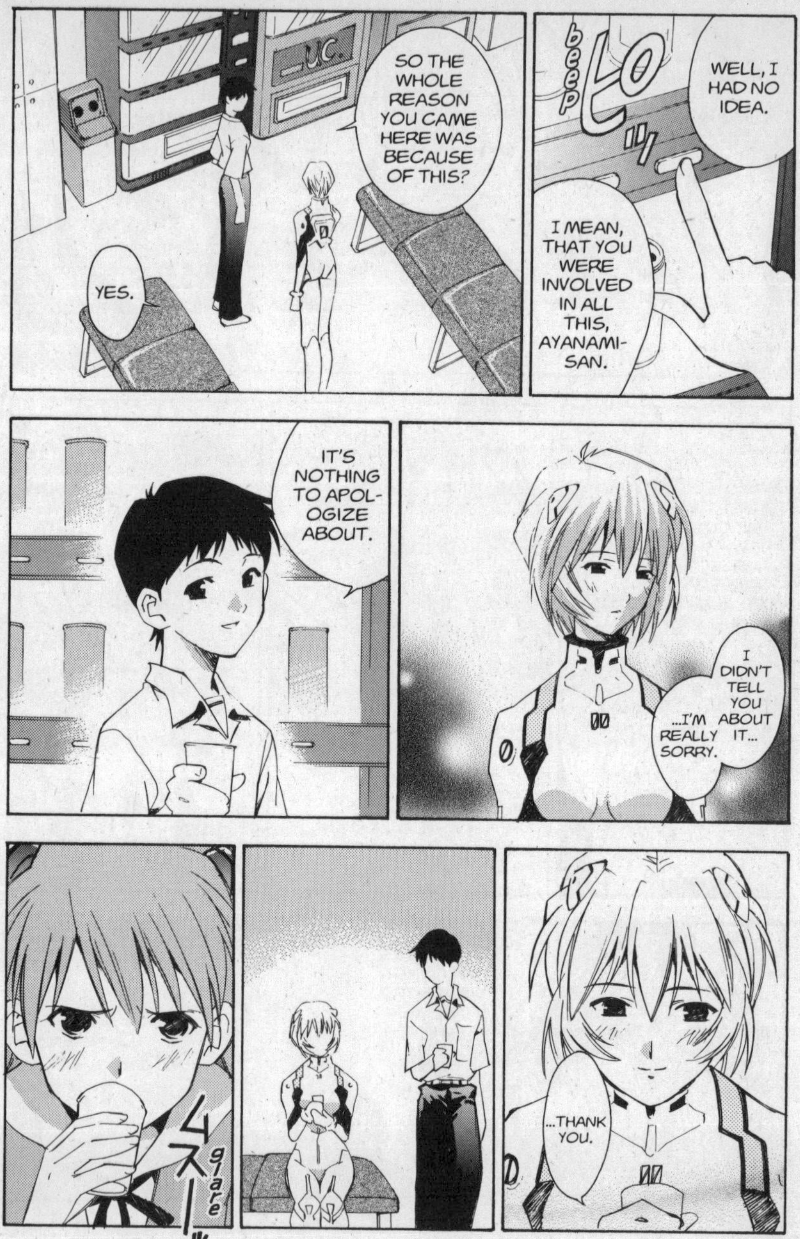
beep
WELL, I HAD NO IDEA.
I MEAN, THAT YOU WERE INVOLVED IN ALL THIS, AYANAMI-SAN.
SO THE WHOLE REASON YOU CAME HERE WAS BECAUSE OF THIS?
YES.
I DIDN'T TELL YOU ABOUT IT...
...I'M REALLY SORRY.
IT'S NOTHING TO APOLOGIZE ABOUT.
...THANK YOU.
glare

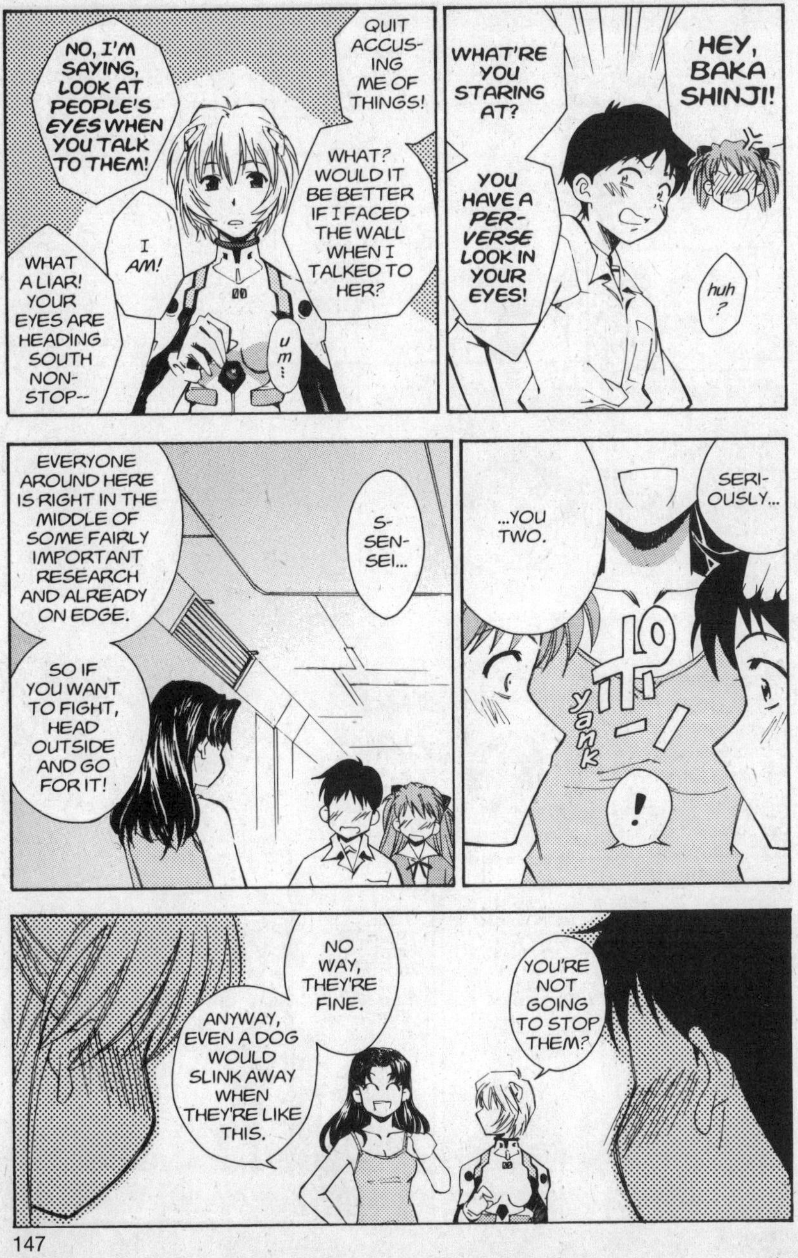
HEY, BAKA SHINJI!
WHAT'RE YOU STARING AT?
YOU HAVE A PERVERSE LOOK IN YOUR EYES!
huh?
QUIT ACCUSING ME OF THINGS!
NO, I'M SAYING, LOOK AT PEOPLE'S EYES WHEN YOU TALK TO THEM!
WHAT? WOULD IT BE BETTER IF I FACED THE WALL WHEN I TALKED TO HER?
I AM!
um...
WHAT A LIAR! YOUR EYES ARE HEADING SOUTH NON-STOP--
SERIOUSLY...
...YOU TWO.
yank
!
S-SENSEI...
EVERYONE AROUND HERE IS RIGHT IN THE MIDDLE OF SOME FAIRLY IMPORTANT RESEARCH AND ALREADY ON EDGE.
SO IF YOU WANT TO FIGHT, HEAD OUTSIDE AND GO FOR IT!
YOU'RE NOT GOING TO STOP THEM?
NO WAY, THEY'RE FINE.
ANYWAY, EVEN A DOG WOULD SLINK AWAY WHEN THEY'RE LIKE THIS.

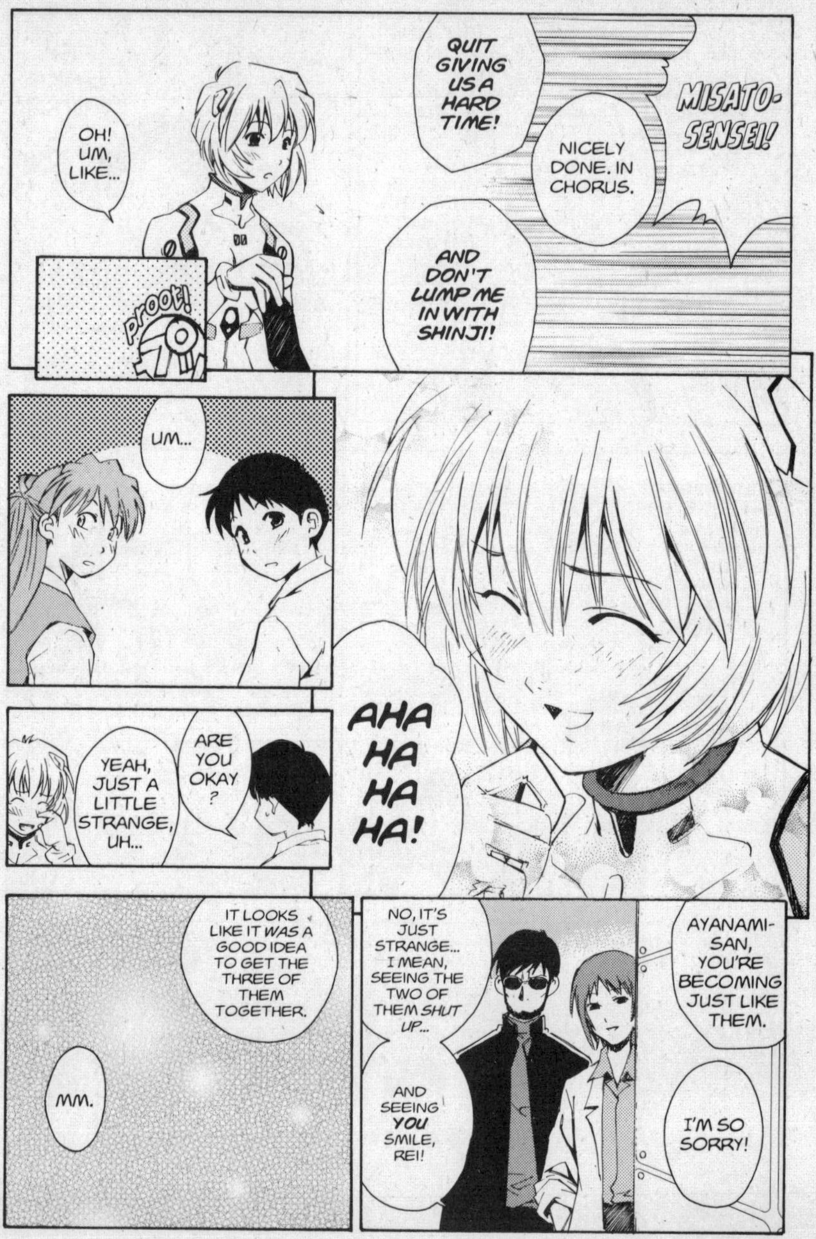
MISATO-SENSEI!
QUIT GIVING US A HARD TIME!
NICELY DONE. IN CHORUS.
AND DON'T LUMP ME IN WITH SHINJI!
OH! UM, LIKE...
proot!
AHA HA HA HA!
UM...
ARE YOU OKAY?
YEAH, JUST A LITTLE STRANGE, UH...
AYANAMI-SAN, YOU'RE BECOMING JUST LIKE THEM.
NO, IT'S JUST STRANGE... I MEAN, SEEING THE TWO OF THEM SHUT UP...
I'M SO SORRY!
AND SEEING YOU SMILE, REI!
IT LOOKS LIKE IT WAS A GOOD IDEA TO GET THE THREE OF THEM TOGETHER.
MM.

WELL...

...WE'RE ABOUT TO START, REI.

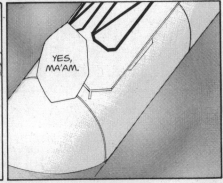

YES, MA'AM.

TE

ON MY MARK...

...PROCEED WITH SYNCHRO TEST.

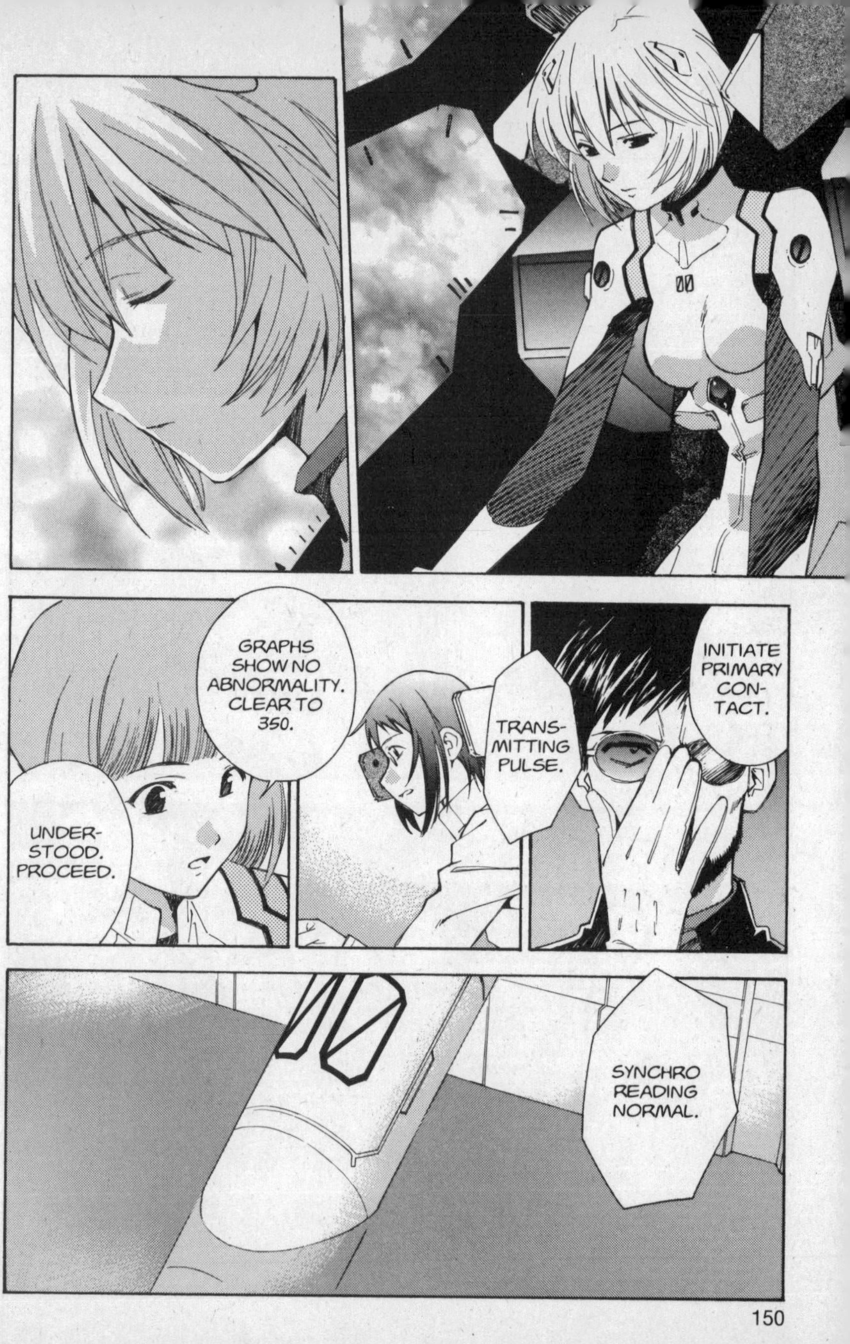

INITIATE PRIMARY CON-TACT.
TRANS-MITTING PULSE.
GRAPHS SHOW NO ABNORMALITY. CLEAR TO 350.
UNDER-STOOD. PROCEED.
SYNCHRO READING NORMAL.

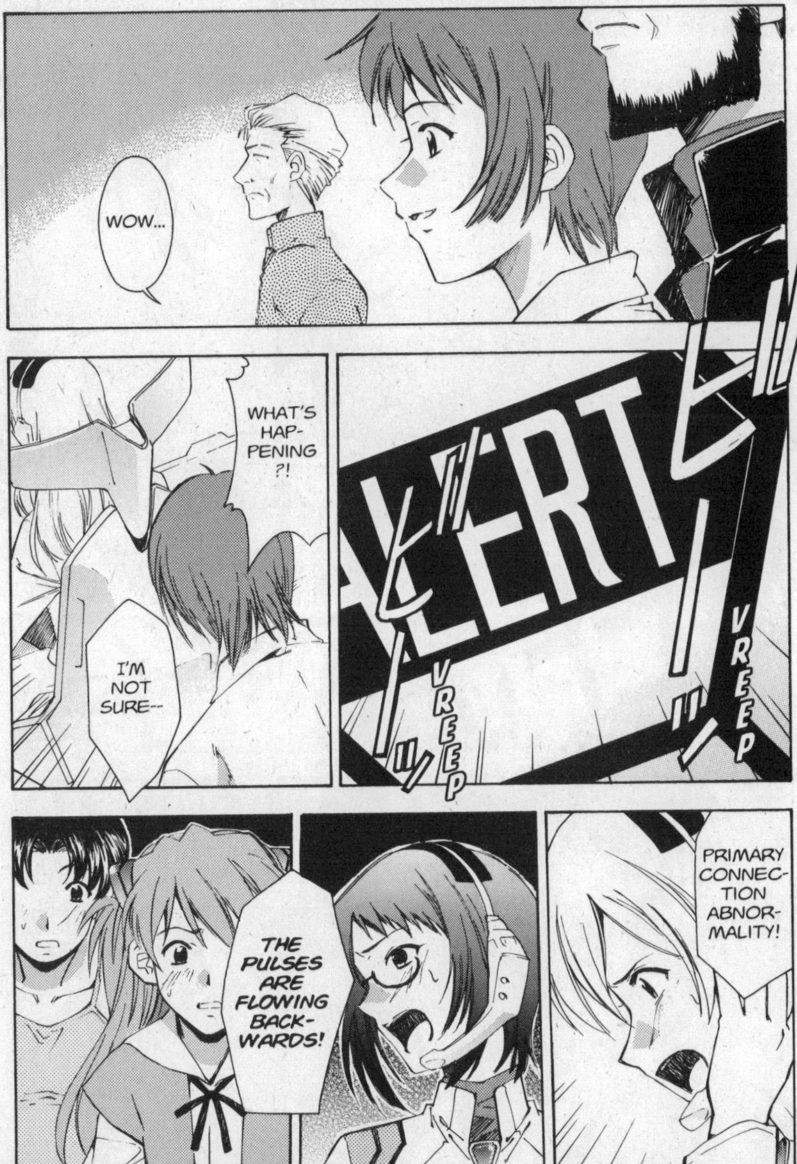
WOW...
ALERT
VREEP
VREEP
WHAT'S HAP-PENING?!
I'M NOT SURE--
PRIMARY CONNEC-TION ABNOR-MALITY!
THE PULSES ARE FLOWING BACK-WARDS!

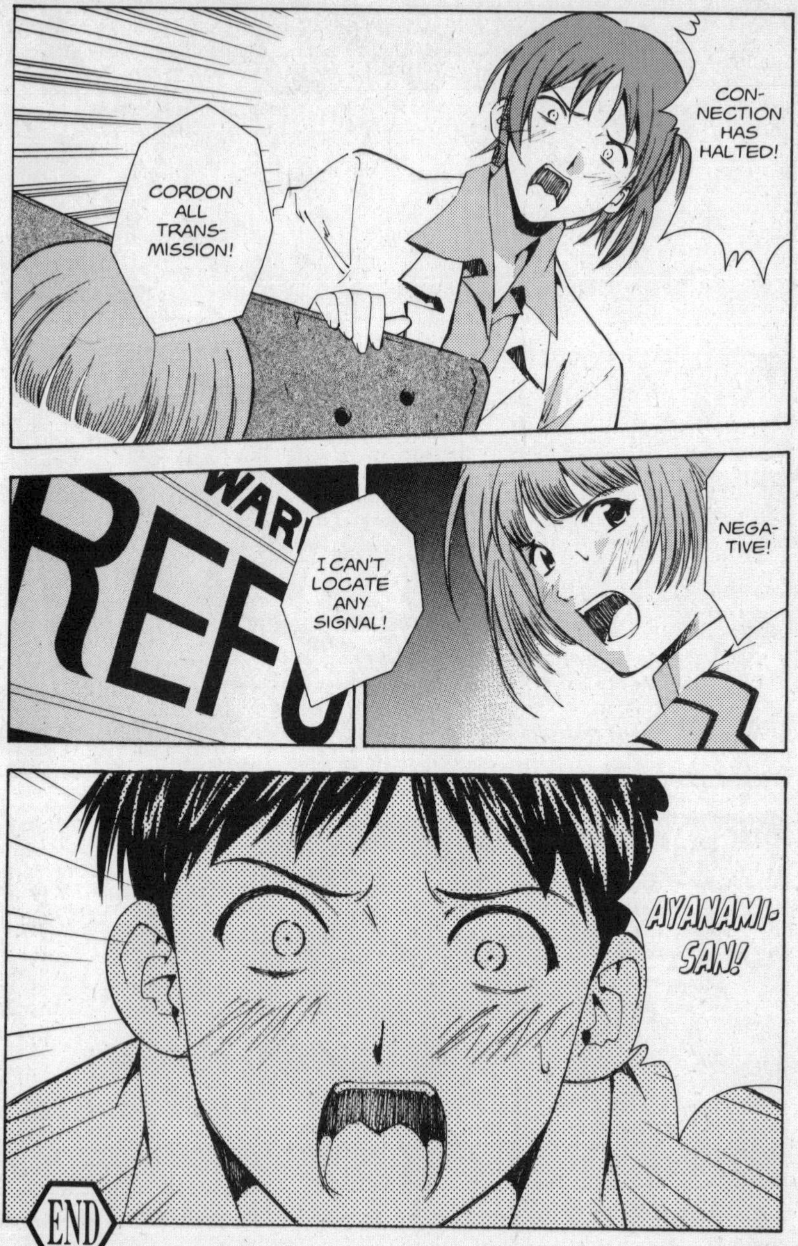
CON-
NECTION
HAS
HALTED!
CORDON
ALL
TRANS-
MISSION!
NEGA-
TIVE!
I CAN'T
LOCATE
ANY
SIGNAL!
AYANAMI-
SAN!
END

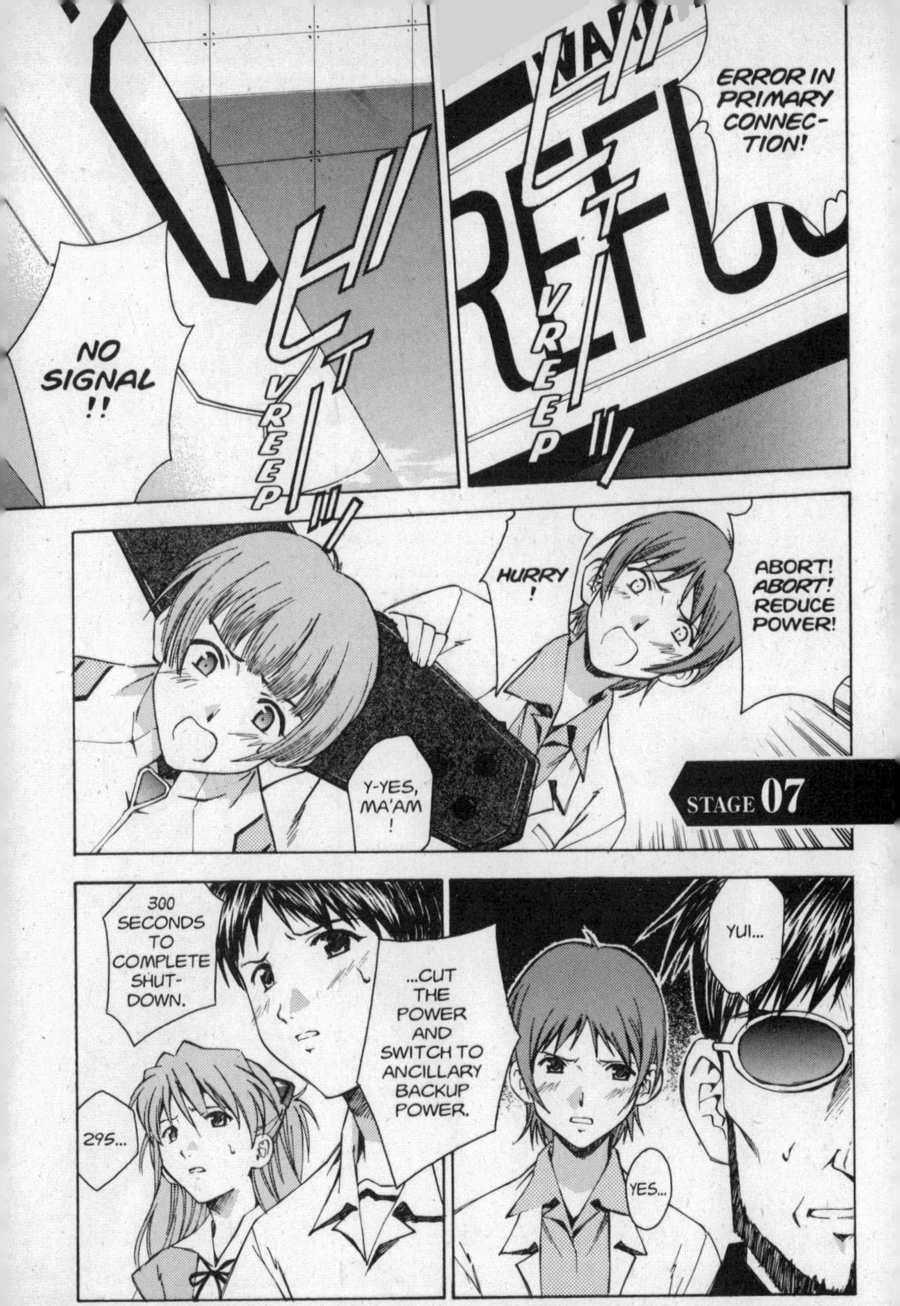
ERROR IN PRIMARY CONNECTION!
VREEP
VREEP
NO SIGNAL!!
ABORT! ABORT! REDUCE POWER!
HURRY!
Y-YES, MA'AM!
STAGE 07
YUI...
YES...
300 SECONDS TO COMPLETE SHUT-DOWN.
...CUT THE POWER AND SWITCH TO ANCILLARY BACKUP POWER.
295...

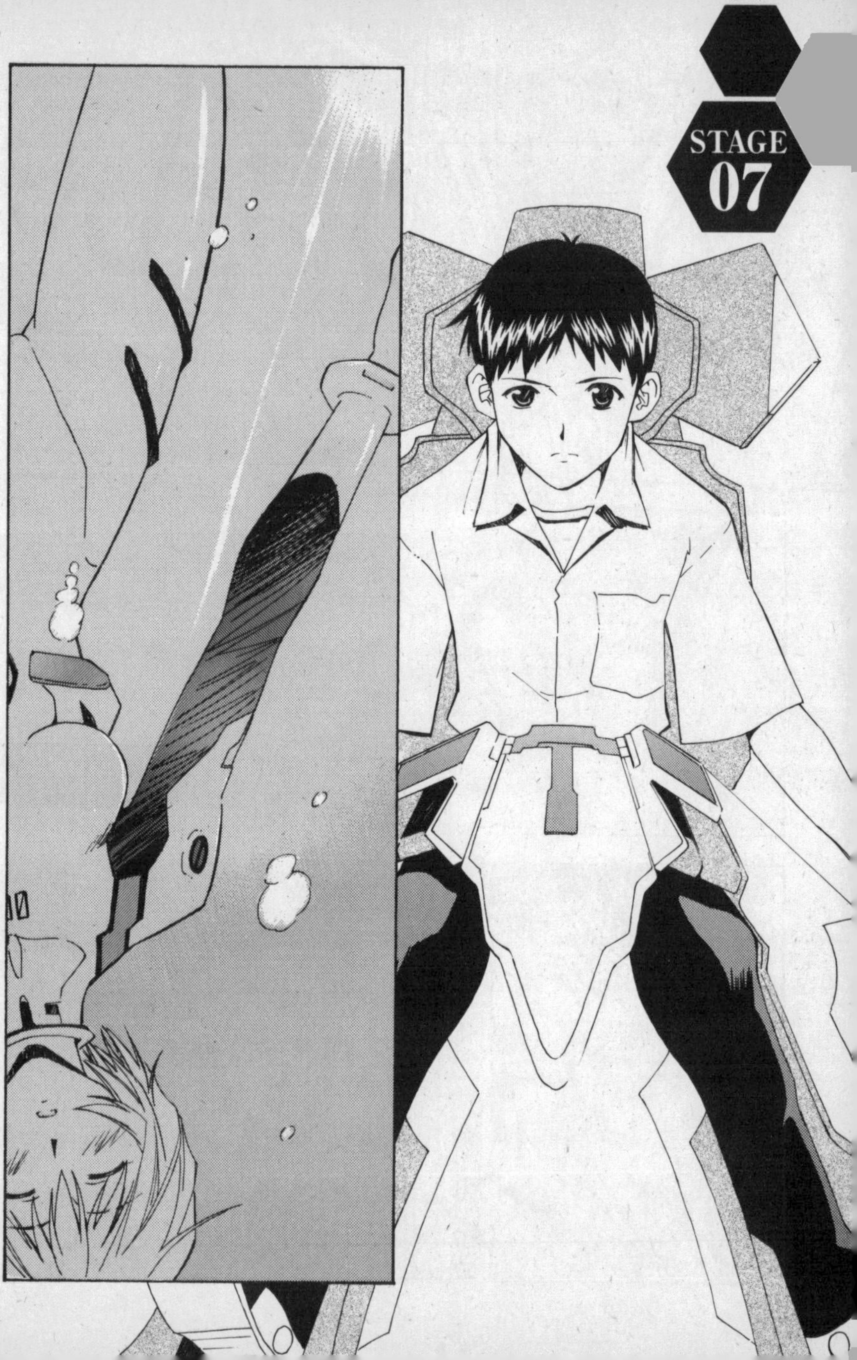
STAGE
07

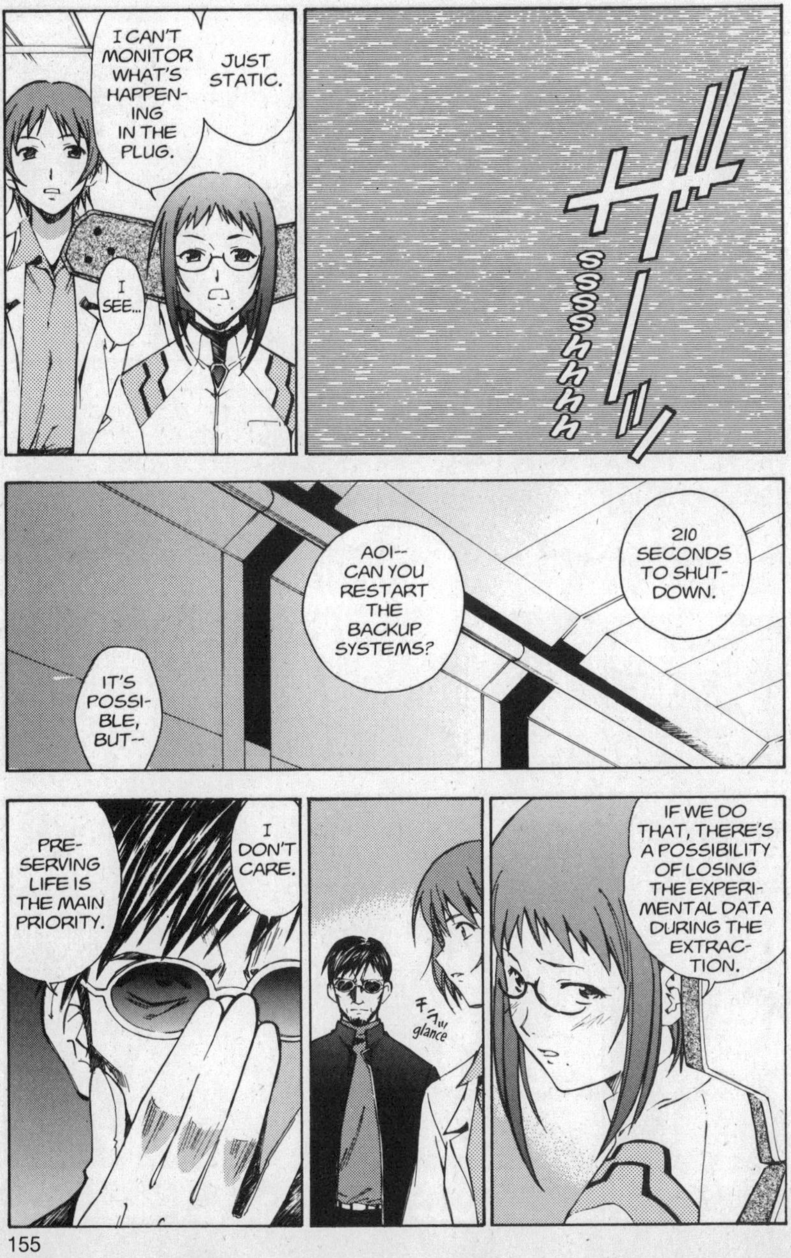
SSSHHHHH
JUST STATIC.
I CAN'T MONITOR WHAT'S HAPPEN-ING IN THE PLUG.
I SEE...
210 SECONDS TO SHUT-DOWN.
AOI-- CAN YOU RESTART THE BACKUP SYSTEMS?
IT'S POSSI-BLE, BUT--
IF WE DO THAT, THERE'S A POSSIBILITY OF LOSING THE EXPERI-MENTAL DATA DURING THE EXTRAC-TION.
glance
I DON'T CARE.
PRE-SERVING LIFE IS THE MAIN PRIORITY.

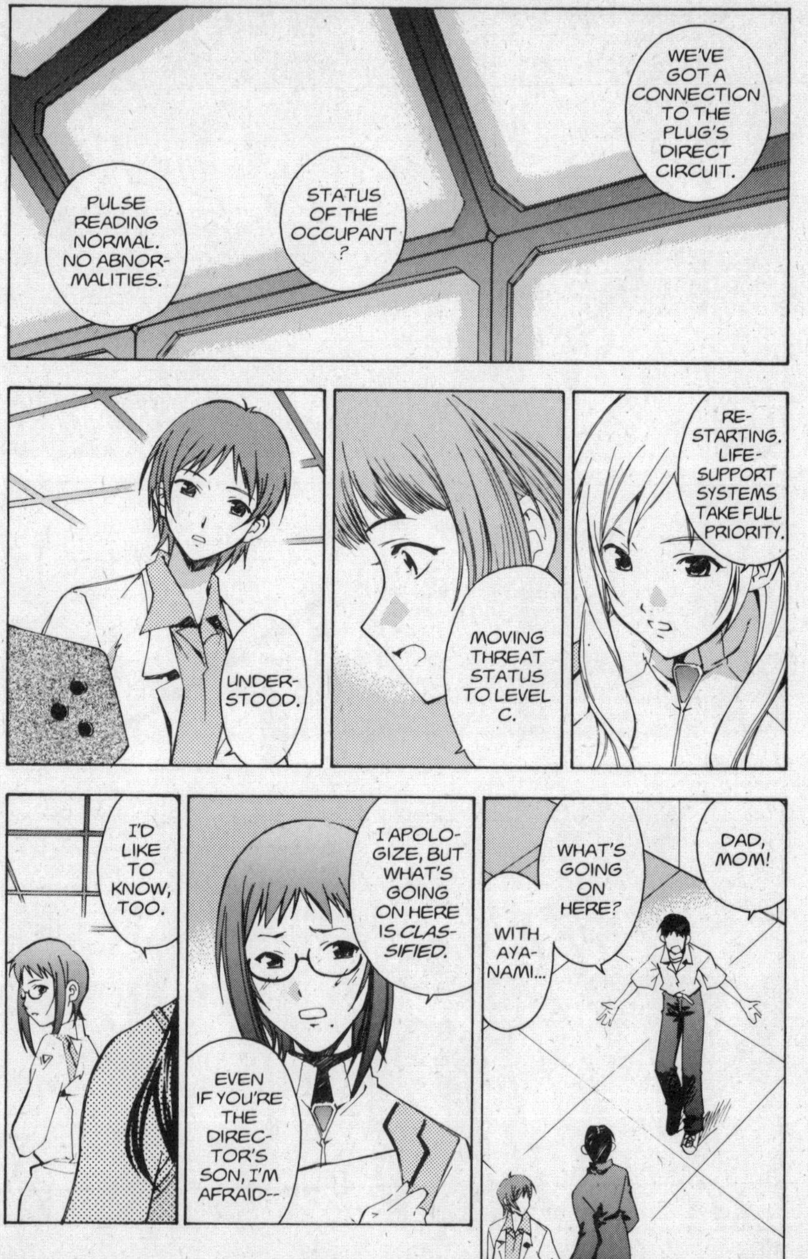

WE'VE GOT A CONNECTION TO THE PLUG'S DIRECT CIRCUIT.
STATUS OF THE OCCUPANT?
PULSE READING NORMAL. NO ABNORMALITIES.
RESTARTING. LIFE-SUPPORT SYSTEMS TAKE FULL PRIORITY.
MOVING THREAT STATUS TO LEVEL C.
UNDERSTOOD.
DAD, MOM!
WHAT'S GOING ON HERE?
WITH AYANAMI...
I APOLOGIZE, BUT WHAT'S GOING ON HERE IS *CLASSIFIED.*
EVEN IF YOU'RE THE DIRECTOR'S SON, I'M AFRAID--
I'D LIKE TO KNOW, TOO.

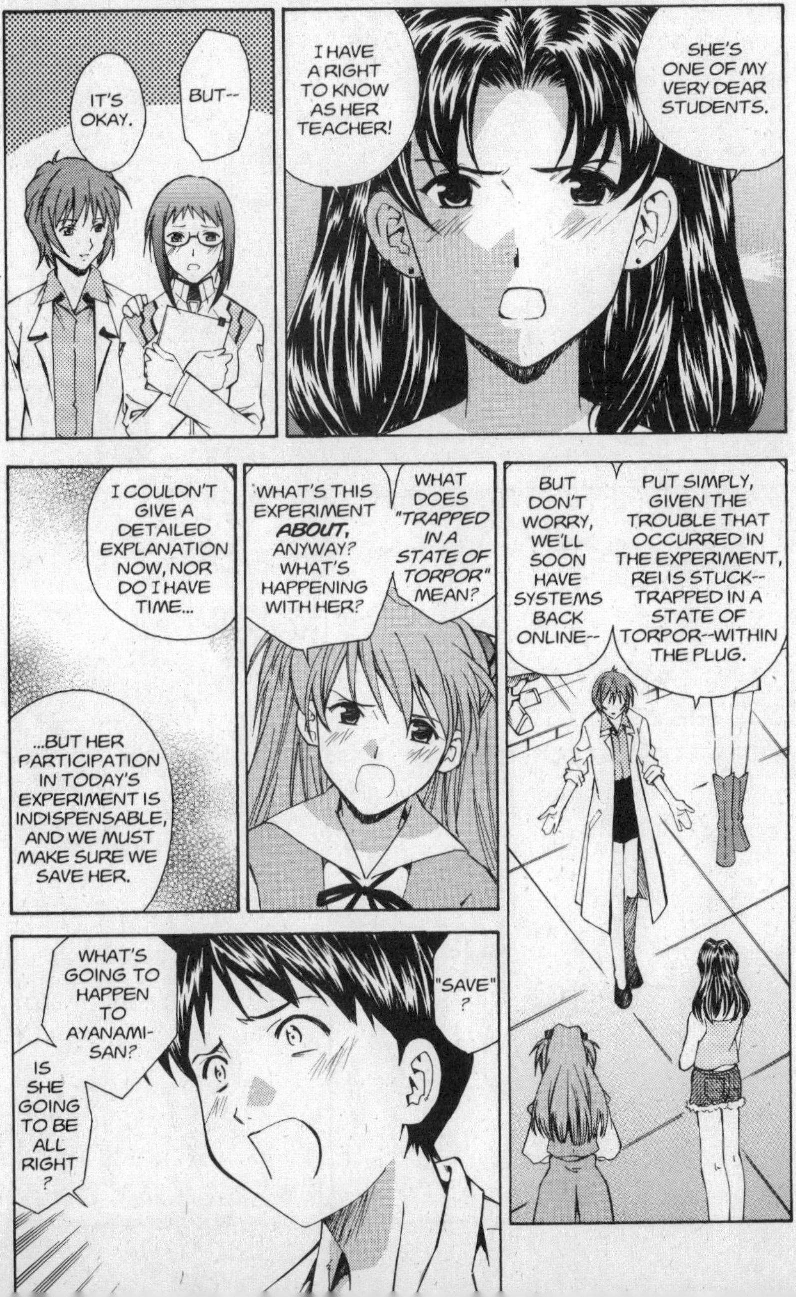
SHE'S ONE OF MY VERY DEAR STUDENTS.
I HAVE A RIGHT TO KNOW AS HER TEACHER!
BUT--
IT'S OKAY.
PUT SIMPLY, GIVEN THE TROUBLE THAT OCCURRED IN THE EXPERIMENT, REI IS STUCK--TRAPPED IN A STATE OF TORPOR--WITHIN THE PLUG.
BUT DON'T WORRY, WE'LL SOON HAVE SYSTEMS BACK ONLINE--
WHAT DOES *"TRAPPED IN A STATE OF TORPOR"* MEAN?
WHAT'S THIS EXPERIMENT ***ABOUT,*** ANYWAY? WHAT'S HAPPENING WITH HER?
I COULDN'T GIVE A DETAILED EXPLANATION NOW, NOR DO I HAVE TIME...
...BUT HER PARTICIPATION IN TODAY'S EXPERIMENT IS INDISPENSABLE, AND WE MUST MAKE SURE WE SAVE HER.
"SAVE"?
WHAT'S GOING TO HAPPEN TO AYANAMI-SAN?
IS SHE GOING TO BE ALL RIGHT?

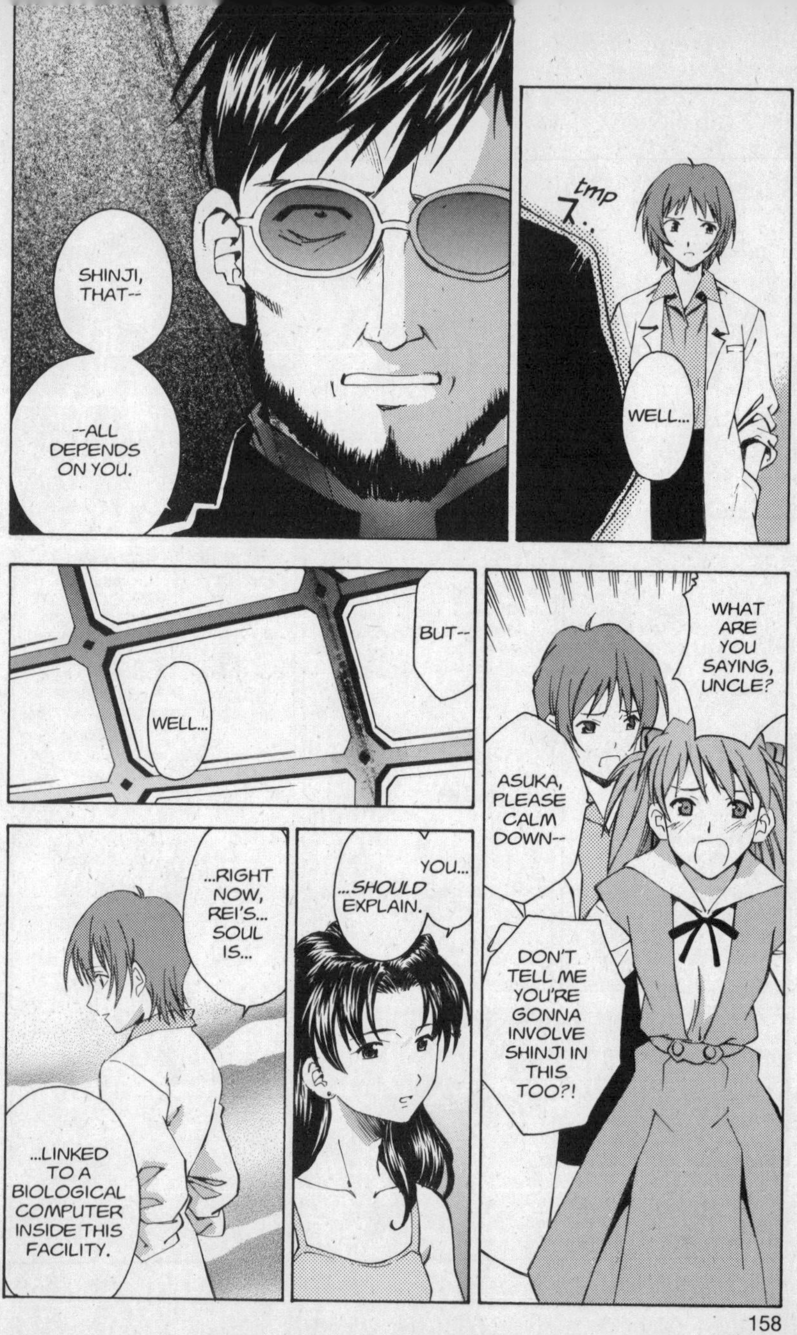
tmp
ス..
WELL...
SHINJI, THAT--
--ALL DEPENDS ON YOU.
WHAT ARE YOU SAYING, UNCLE?
ASUKA, PLEASE CALM DOWN--
DON'T TELL ME YOU'RE GONNA INVOLVE SHINJI IN THIS TOO?!
BUT--
WELL...
YOU...
...SHOULD EXPLAIN.
...RIGHT NOW, REI'S... SOUL IS...
...LINKED TO A BIOLOGICAL COMPUTER INSIDE THIS FACILITY.

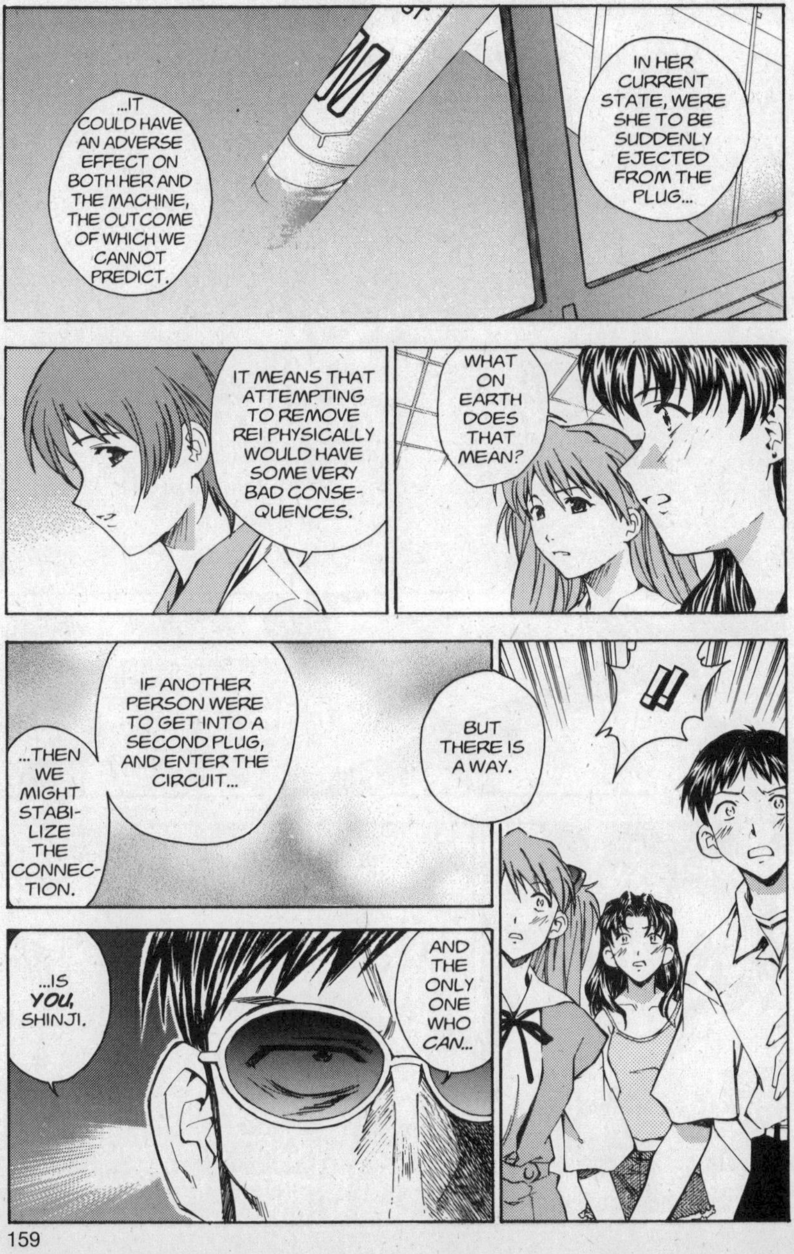
IN HER CURRENT STATE, WERE SHE TO BE SUDDENLY EJECTED FROM THE PLUG...
...IT COULD HAVE AN ADVERSE EFFECT ON BOTH HER AND THE MACHINE, THE OUTCOME OF WHICH WE CANNOT PREDICT.
WHAT ON EARTH DOES THAT MEAN?
IT MEANS THAT ATTEMPTING TO REMOVE REI PHYSICALLY WOULD HAVE SOME VERY BAD CONSE-QUENCES.
!!
BUT THERE IS A WAY.
IF ANOTHER PERSON WERE TO GET INTO A SECOND PLUG, AND ENTER THE CIRCUIT...
...THEN WE MIGHT STABI-LIZE THE CONNEC-TION.
AND THE ONLY ONE WHO *CAN*...
...IS ***YOU,*** SHINJI.

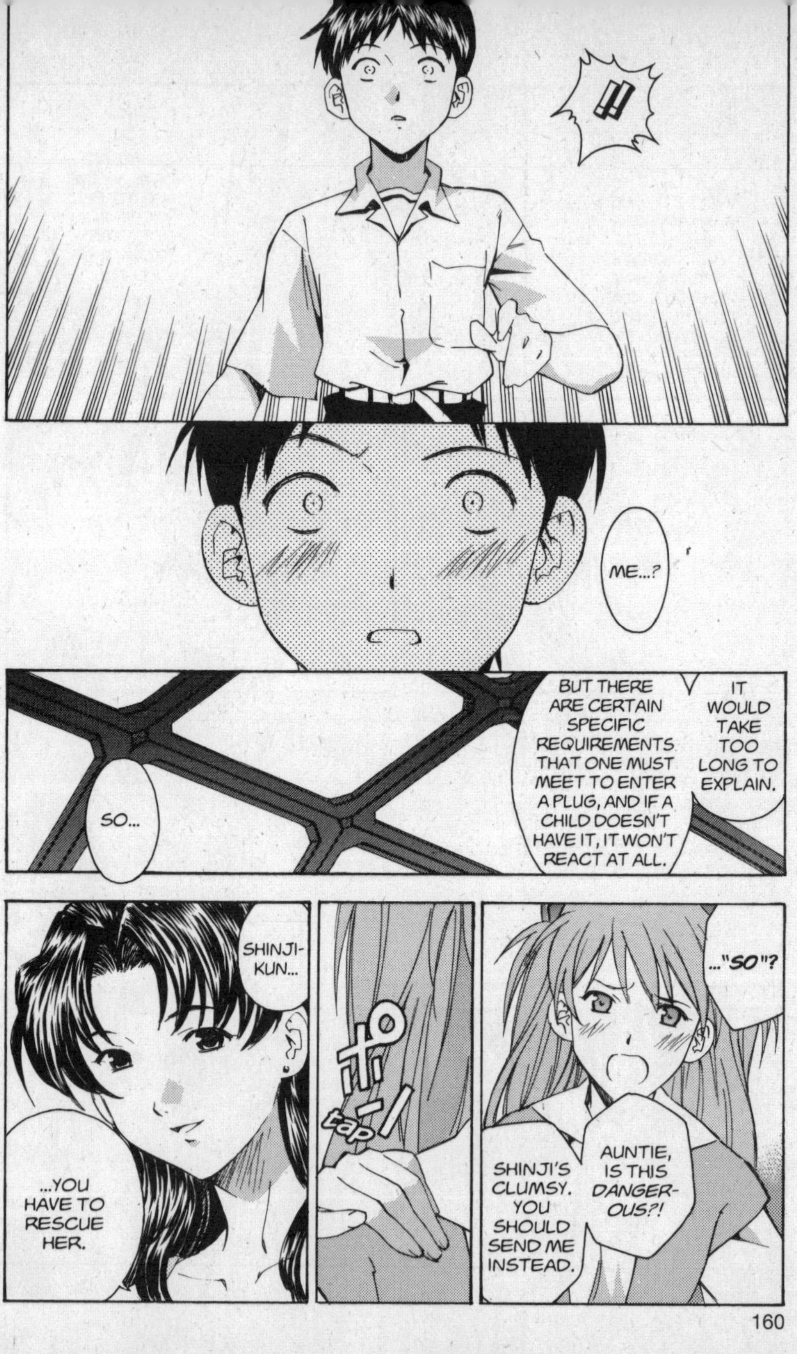
!!
ME...?
IT WOULD TAKE TOO LONG TO EXPLAIN.
BUT THERE ARE CERTAIN SPECIFIC REQUIREMENTS THAT ONE MUST MEET TO ENTER A PLUG, AND IF A CHILD DOESN'T HAVE IT, IT WON'T REACT AT ALL.
SO...
..."SO"?
AUNTIE, IS THIS DANGEROUS?!
SHINJI'S CLUMSY. YOU SHOULD SEND ME INSTEAD.
tap
SHINJI-KUN...
...YOU HAVE TO RESCUE HER.

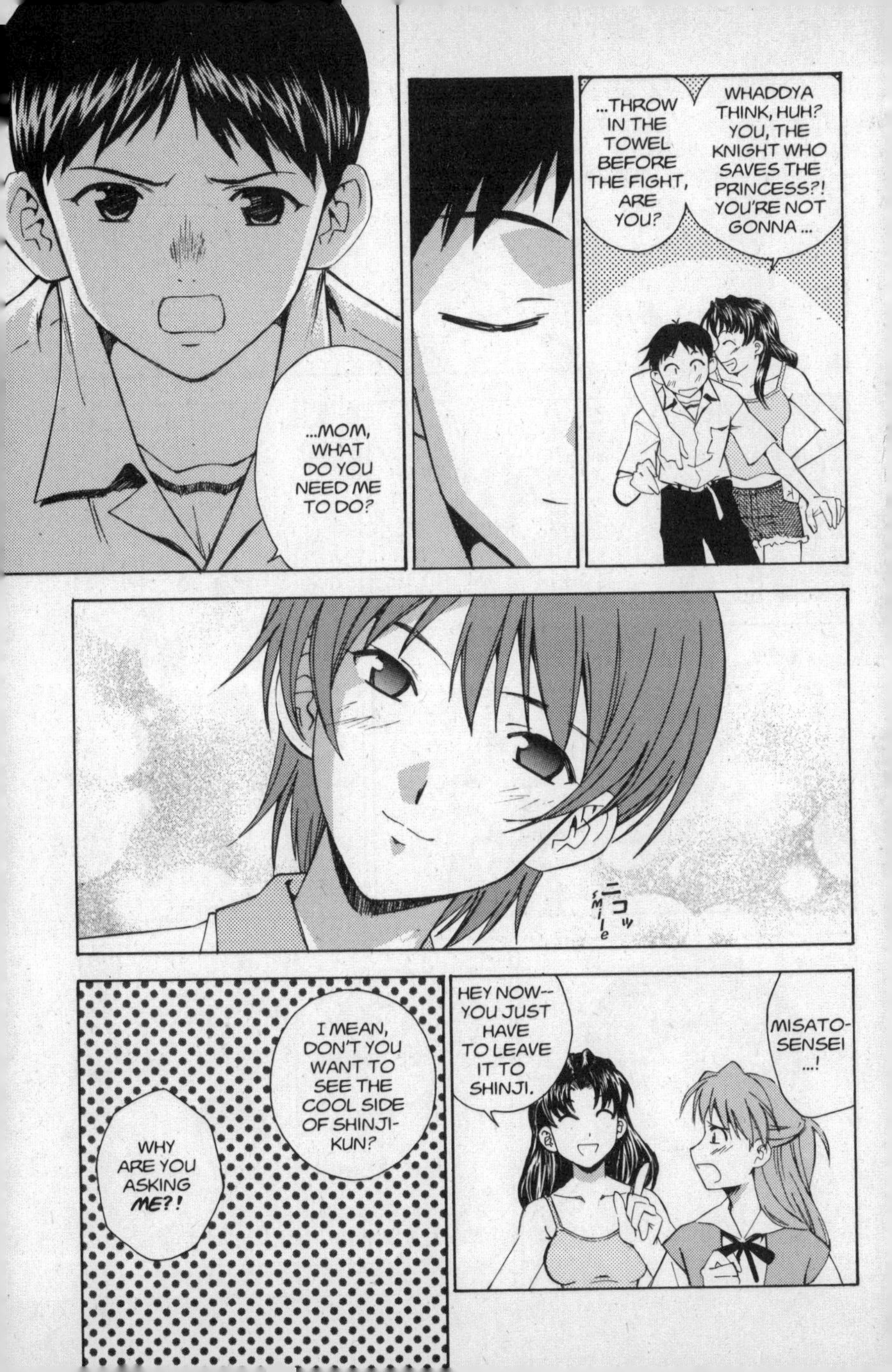
WHADDYA THINK, HUH? YOU, THE KNIGHT WHO SAVES THE PRINCESS?! YOU'RE NOT GONNA ...
...THROW IN THE TOWEL BEFORE THE FIGHT, ARE YOU?
...MOM, WHAT DO YOU NEED ME TO DO?
ニコッ
smile
MISATO-SENSEI ...!
HEY NOW-- YOU JUST HAVE TO LEAVE IT TO SHINJI.
I MEAN, DON'T YOU WANT TO SEE THE COOL SIDE OF SHINJI-KUN?
WHY ARE YOU ASKING **ME?!**

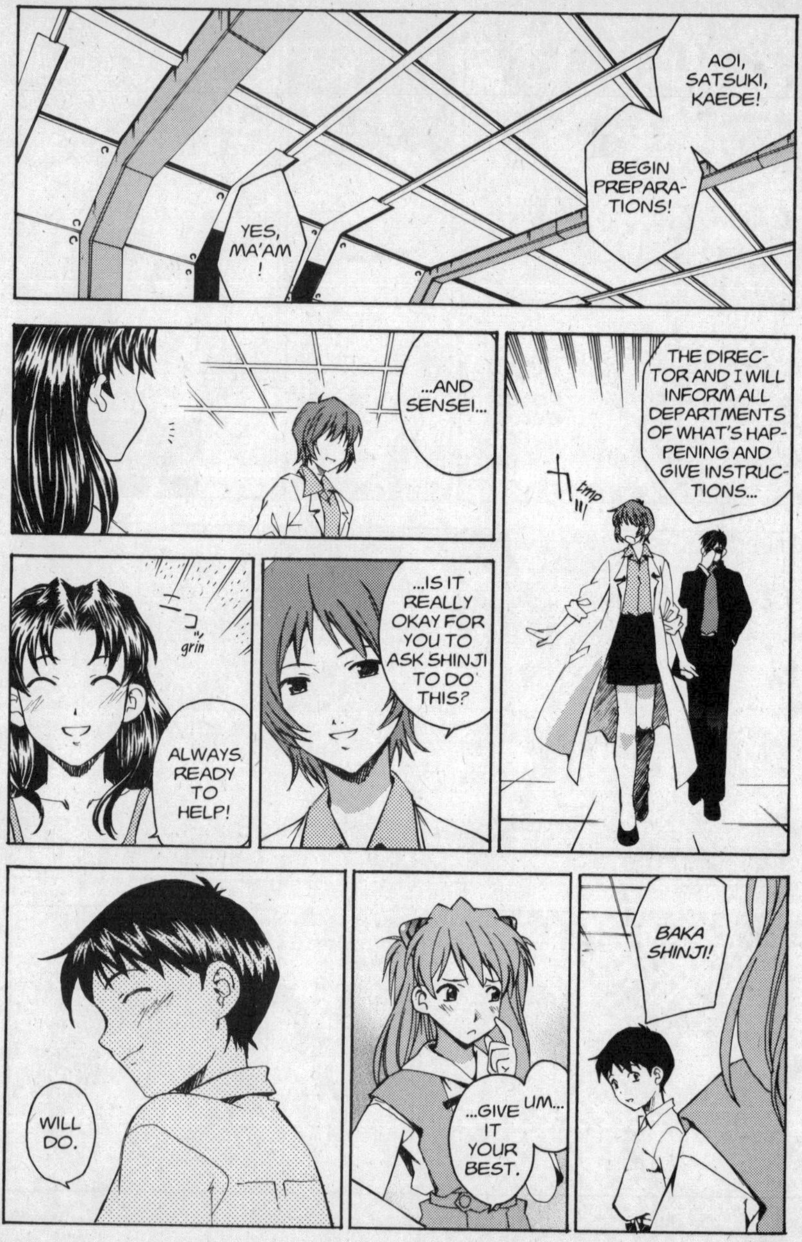
AOI, SATSUKI, KAEDE!
BEGIN PREPARA-TIONS!
YES, MA'AM!
THE DIREC-TOR AND I WILL INFORM ALL DEPARTMENTS OF WHAT'S HAP-PENING AND GIVE INSTRUC-TIONS...
tmp
...AND SENSEI...
...IS IT REALLY OKAY FOR YOU TO ASK SHINJI TO DO THIS?
grin
ALWAYS READY TO HELP!
BAKA SHINJI!
UM...
...GIVE IT YOUR BEST.
WILL DO.

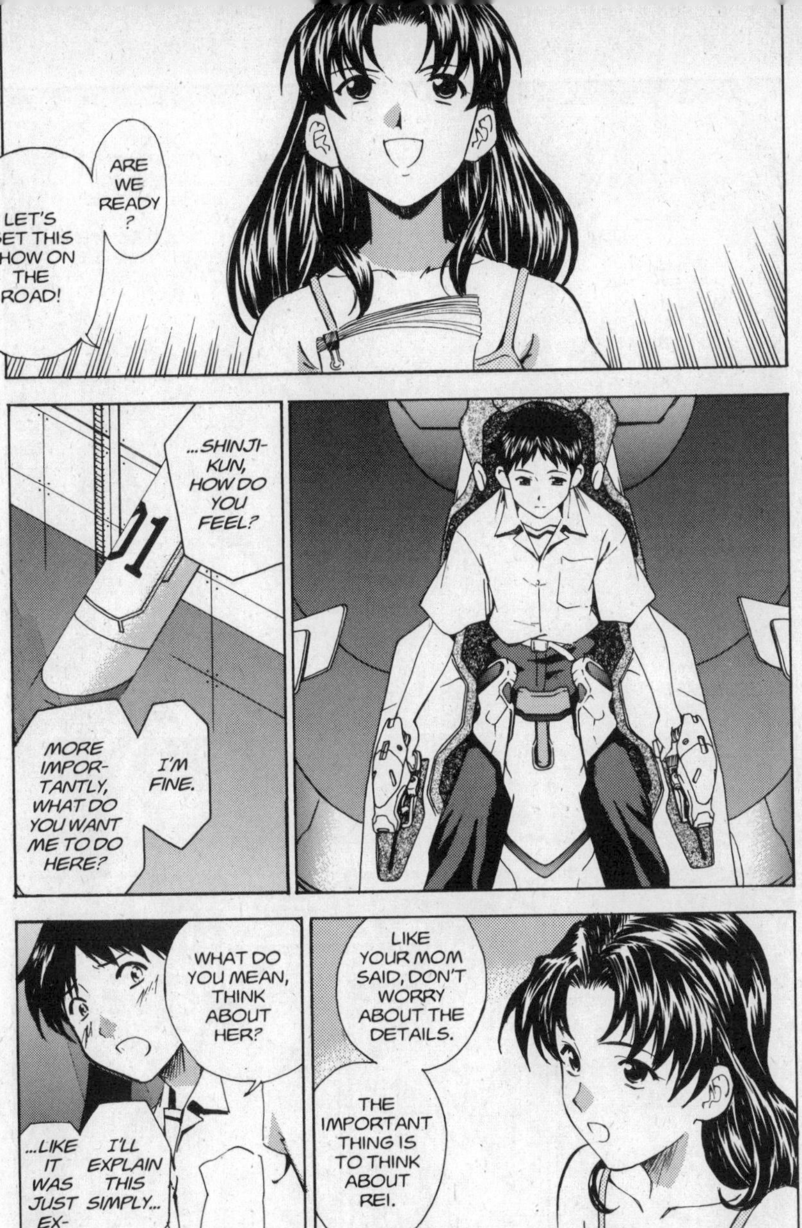
ARE WE READY?
LET'S GET THIS SHOW ON THE ROAD!
...SHINJI-KUN, HOW DO YOU FEEL?
I'M FINE.
MORE IMPORTANTLY, WHAT DO YOU WANT ME TO DO HERE?
LIKE YOUR MOM SAID, DON'T WORRY ABOUT THE DETAILS.
THE IMPORTANT THING IS TO THINK ABOUT REI.
WHAT DO YOU MEAN, THINK ABOUT HER?
I'LL EXPLAIN THIS SIMPLY...
...LIKE IT WAS JUST EXPLAINED TO ME.

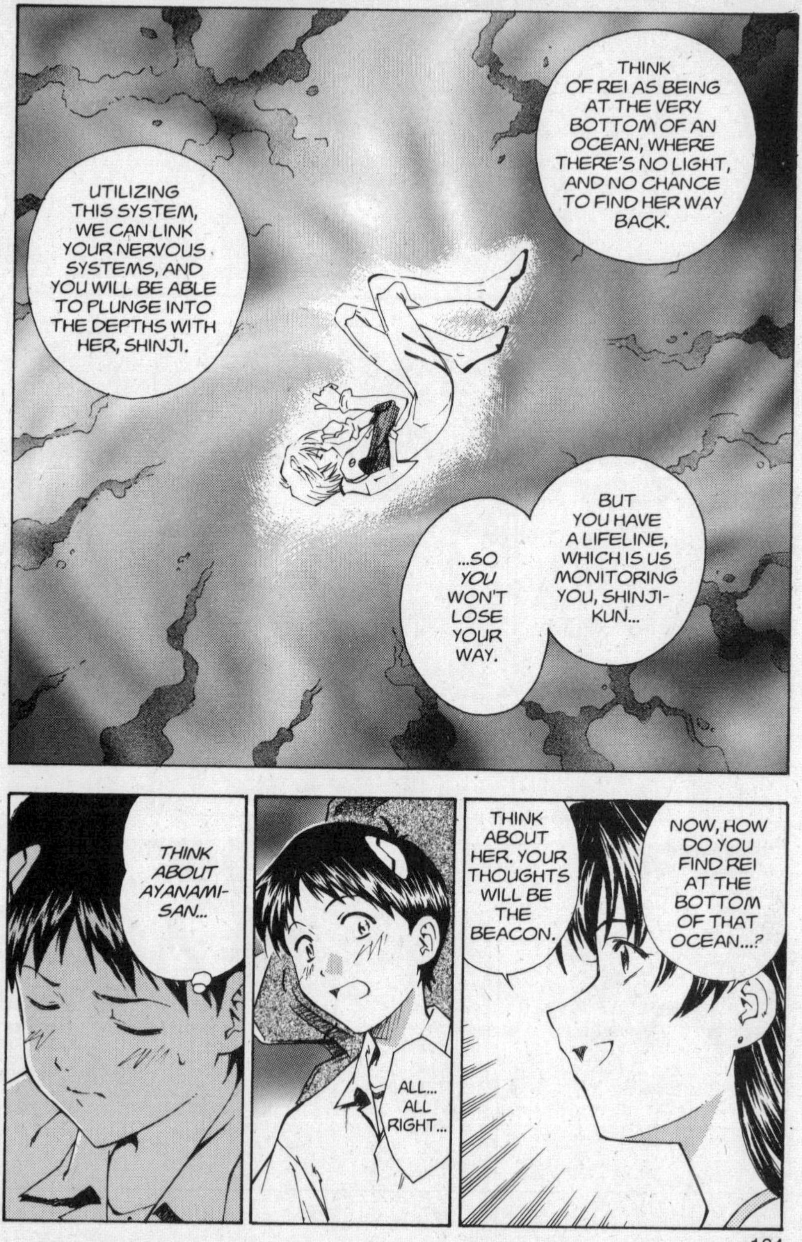
THINK OF REI AS BEING AT THE VERY BOTTOM OF AN OCEAN, WHERE THERE'S NO LIGHT, AND NO CHANCE TO FIND HER WAY BACK.
UTILIZING THIS SYSTEM, WE CAN LINK YOUR NERVOUS SYSTEMS, AND YOU WILL BE ABLE TO PLUNGE INTO THE DEPTHS WITH HER, SHINJI.
BUT YOU HAVE A LIFELINE, WHICH IS US MONITORING YOU, SHINJI-KUN...
...SO *YOU* WON'T LOSE YOUR WAY.
NOW, HOW DO YOU FIND REI AT THE BOTTOM OF THAT OCEAN...?
THINK ABOUT HER. YOUR THOUGHTS WILL BE THE BEACON.
ALL... ALL RIGHT...
THINK ABOUT AYANAMI-SAN...

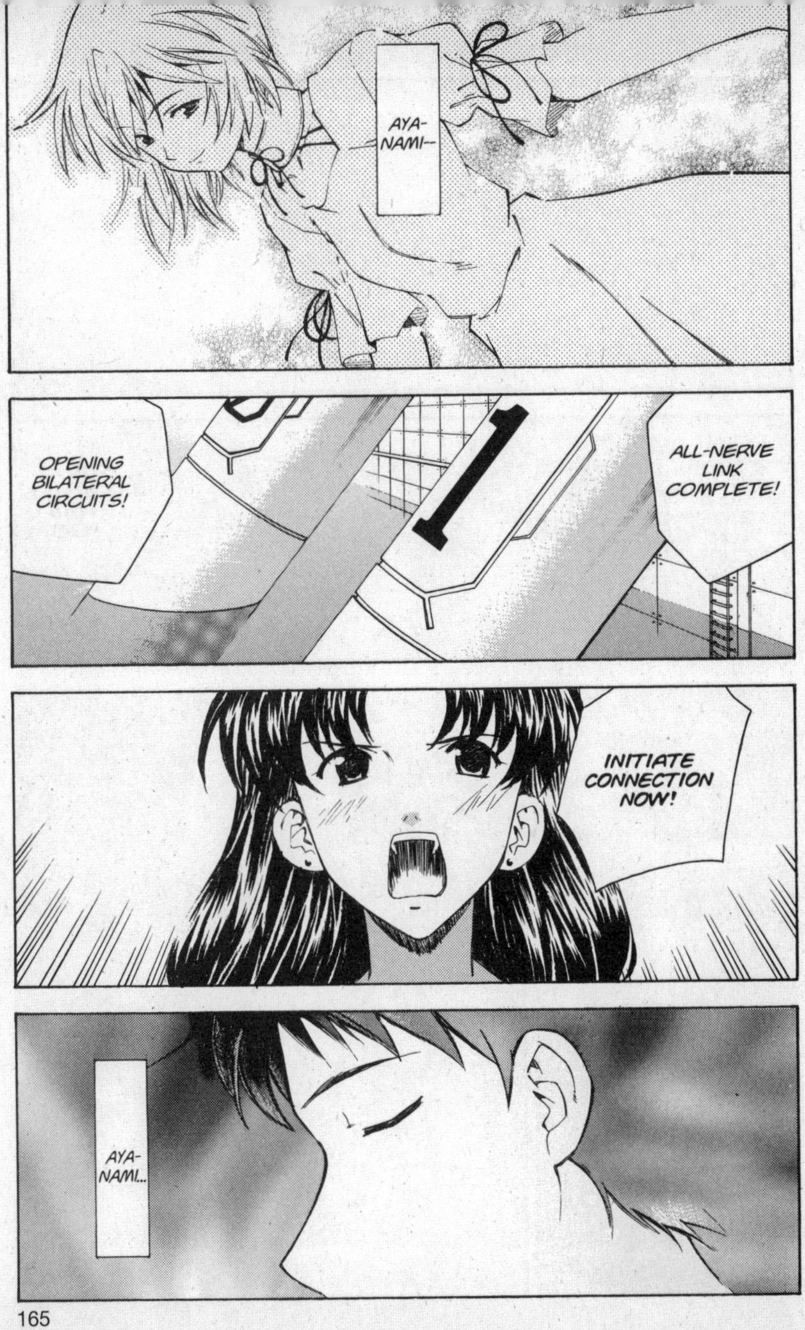
AYA-
NAMI--
ALL-NERVE LINK COMPLETE!
OPENING BILATERAL CIRCUITS!
INITIATE CONNECTION NOW!
AYA-
NAMI...

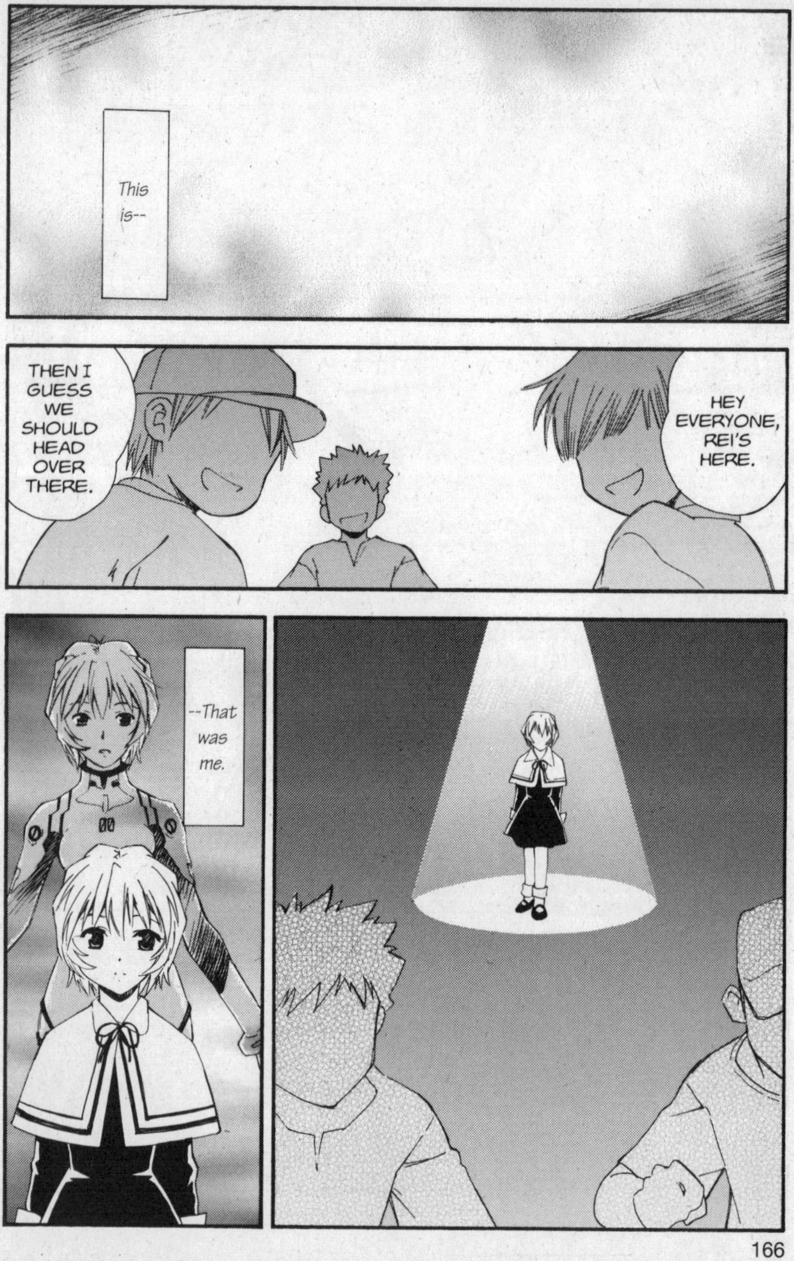
This is--
HEY EVERYONE, REI'S HERE.
THEN I GUESS WE SHOULD HEAD OVER THERE.
--That was me.

Ever since I could remember, I didn't fit in.

That's why I was always alone.

And just when I thought I could get past all of it--

HERE I AM-- AGAIN.

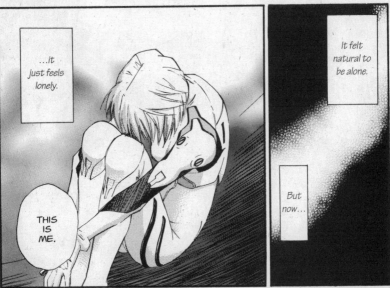

It felt natural to be alone.

…it just feels lonely.

But now…

THIS IS ME.

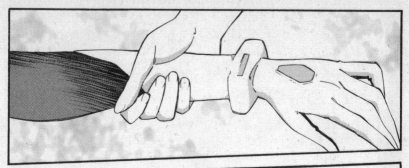

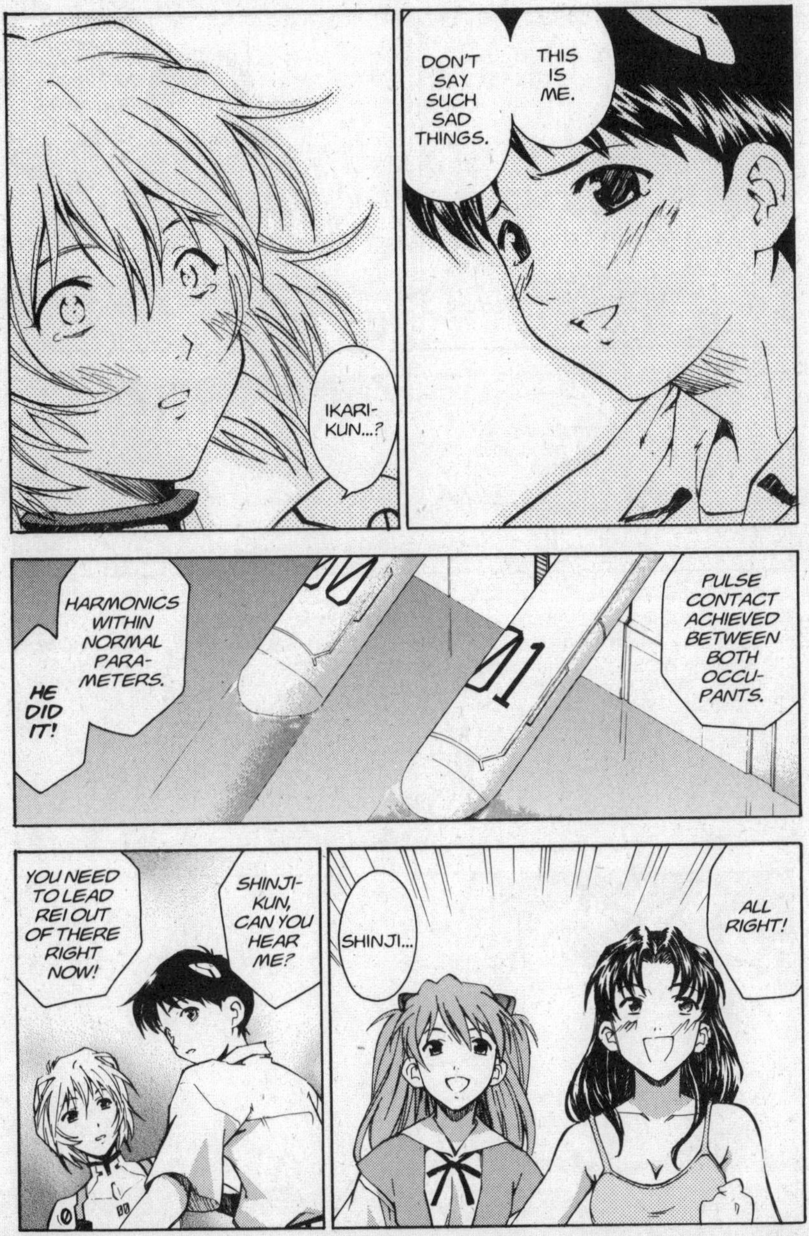
THIS IS ME.
DON'T SAY SUCH SAD THINGS.
IKARI-KUN...?
PULSE CONTACT ACHIEVED BETWEEN BOTH OCCUPANTS.
HARMONICS WITHIN NORMAL PARAMETERS.
HE DID IT!
ALL RIGHT!
SHINJI...
SHINJI-KUN, CAN YOU HEAR ME?
YOU NEED TO LEAD REI OUT OF THERE RIGHT NOW!

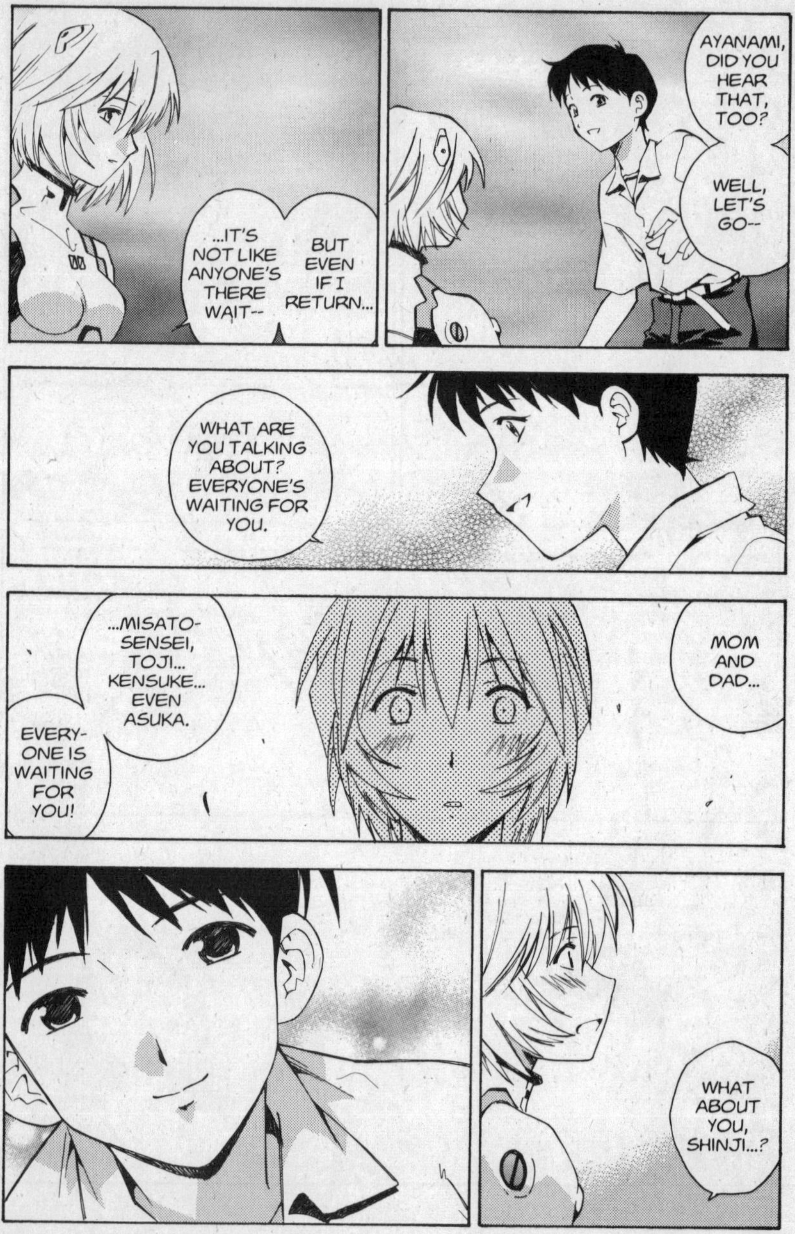
AYANAMI, DID YOU HEAR THAT, TOO?
WELL, LET'S GO--
BUT EVEN IF I RETURN...
...IT'S NOT LIKE ANYONE'S THERE WAIT--
WHAT ARE YOU TALKING ABOUT? EVERYONE'S WAITING FOR YOU.
MOM AND DAD...
...MISATO-SENSEI, TOJI... KENSUKE... EVEN ASUKA.
EVERYONE IS WAITING FOR YOU!
WHAT ABOUT YOU, SHINJI...?

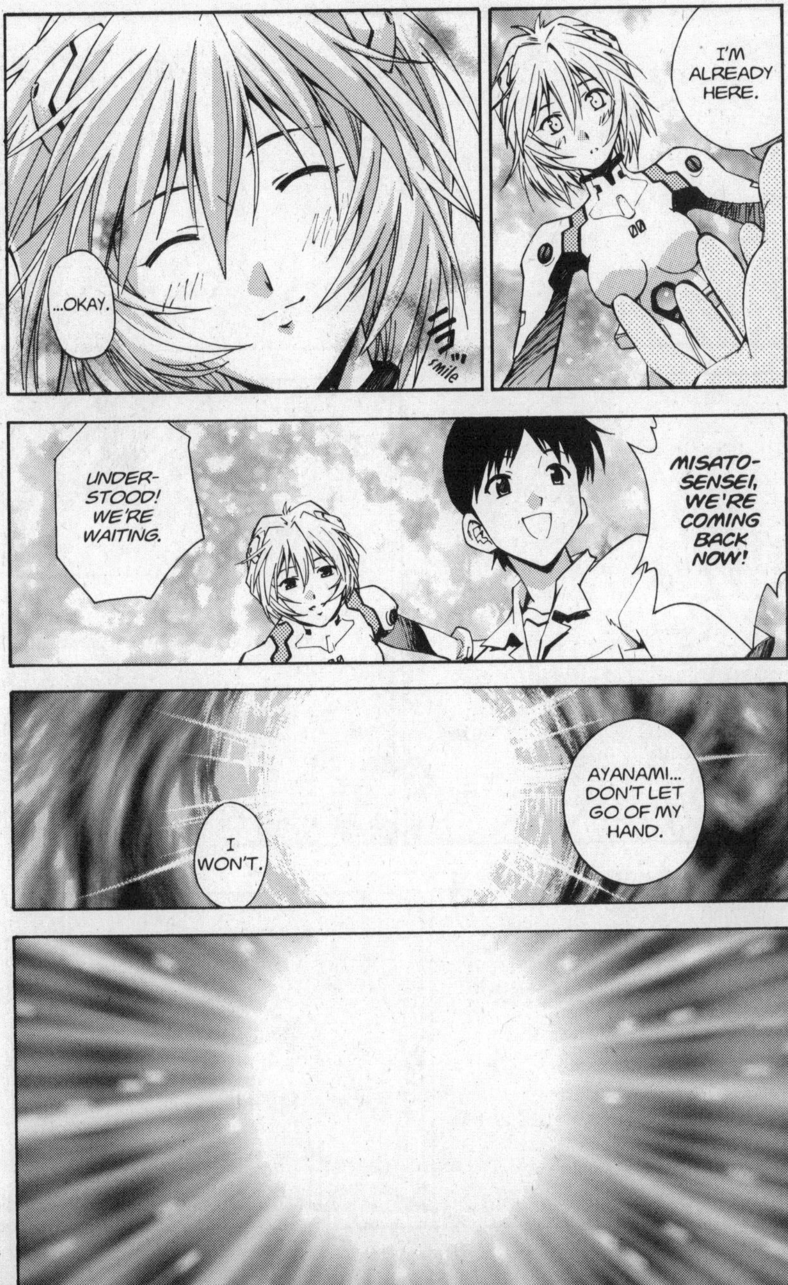
I'M ALREADY HERE.
...OKAY.
smile
MISATO-SENSEI, WE'RE COMING BACK NOW!
UNDER-STOOD! WE'RE WAITING.
AYANAMI... DON'T LET GO OF MY HAND.
I WON'T.

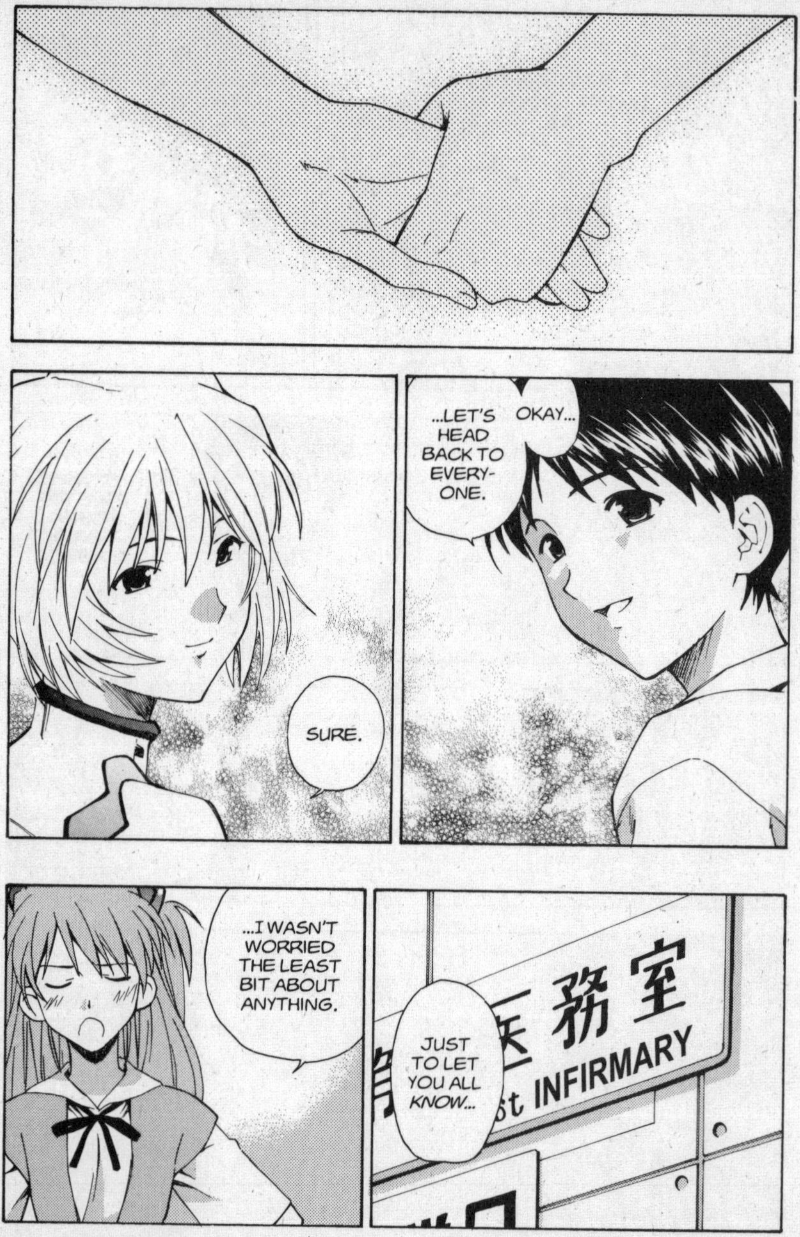
OKAY...
...LET'S HEAD BACK TO EVERY-ONE.
SURE.
JUST TO LET YOU ALL KNOW...
務室
INFIRMARY
...I WASN'T WORRIED THE LEAST BIT ABOUT ANYTHING.

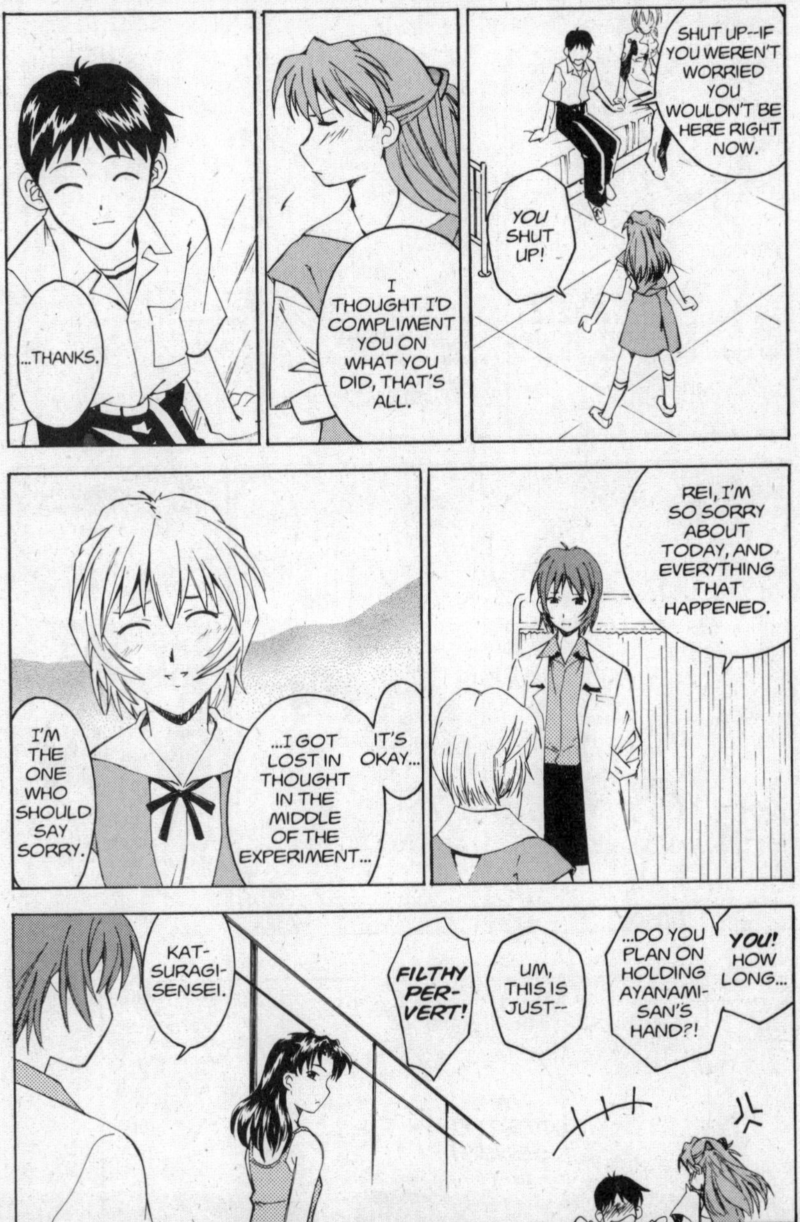
SHUT UP--IF YOU WEREN'T WORRIED YOU WOULDN'T BE HERE RIGHT NOW.
YOU SHUT UP!
I THOUGHT I'D COMPLIMENT YOU ON WHAT YOU DID, THAT'S ALL.
...THANKS.
REI, I'M SO SORRY ABOUT TODAY, AND EVERYTHING THAT HAPPENED.
IT'S OKAY...
...I GOT LOST IN THOUGHT IN THE MIDDLE OF THE EXPERIMENT...
I'M THE ONE WHO SHOULD SAY SORRY.
YOU! HOW LONG...
...DO YOU PLAN ON HOLDING AYANAMI-SAN'S HAND?!
UM, THIS IS JUST--
FILTHY PERVERT!
KAT-SURAGI-SENSEI.

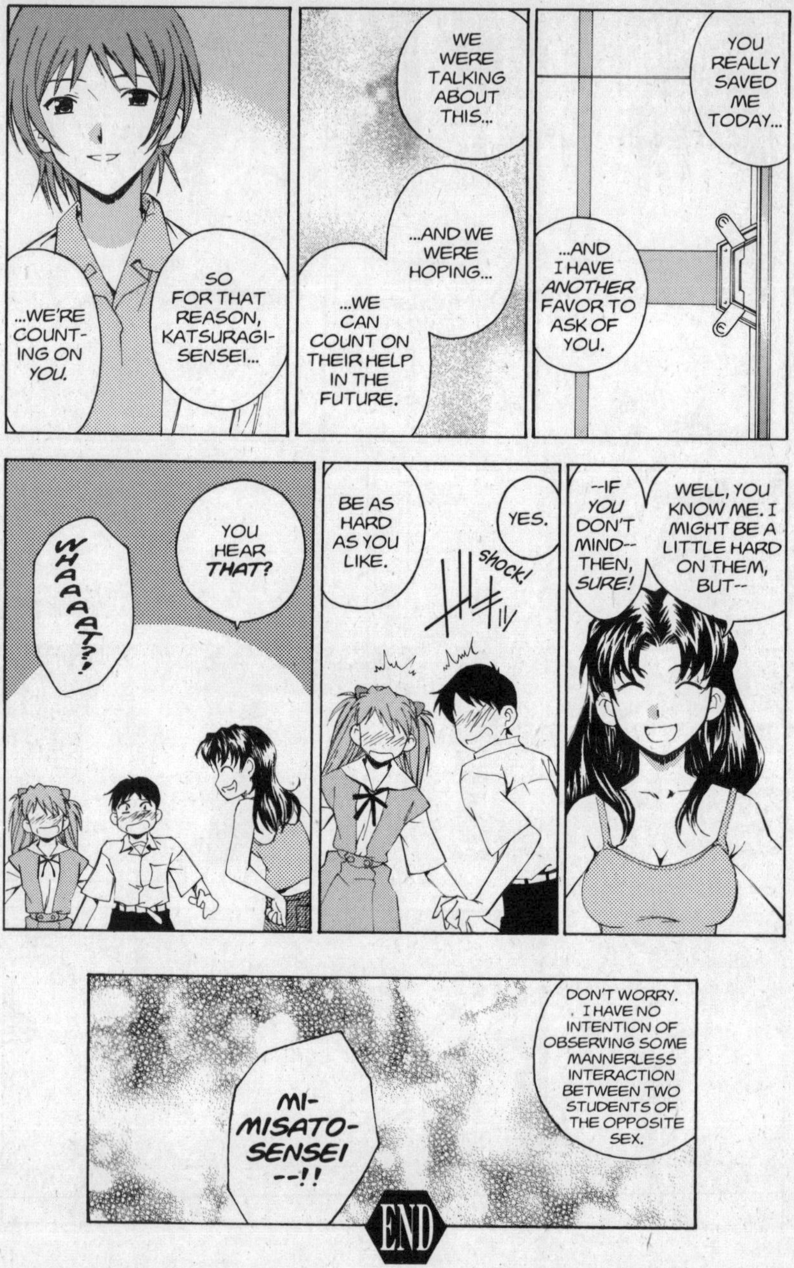
YOU REALLY SAVED ME TODAY...
...AND I HAVE *ANOTHER* FAVOR TO ASK OF YOU.
WE WERE TALKING ABOUT THIS...
...AND WE WERE HOPING...
...WE CAN COUNT ON THEIR HELP IN THE FUTURE.
SO FOR THAT REASON, KATSURAGI-SENSEI...
...WE'RE COUNTING ON *YOU*.
WELL, YOU KNOW ME. I MIGHT BE A LITTLE HARD ON THEM, BUT--
--IF *YOU* DON'T MIND--THEN, *SURE!*
YES.
SHOCK!
BE AS HARD AS YOU LIKE.
YOU HEAR *THAT?*
WHAAAAAT?!
DON'T WORRY. I HAVE NO INTENTION OF OBSERVING SOME MANNERLESS INTERACTION BETWEEN TWO STUDENTS OF THE OPPOSITE SEX.
MI-MISATO-SENSEI--!!
END

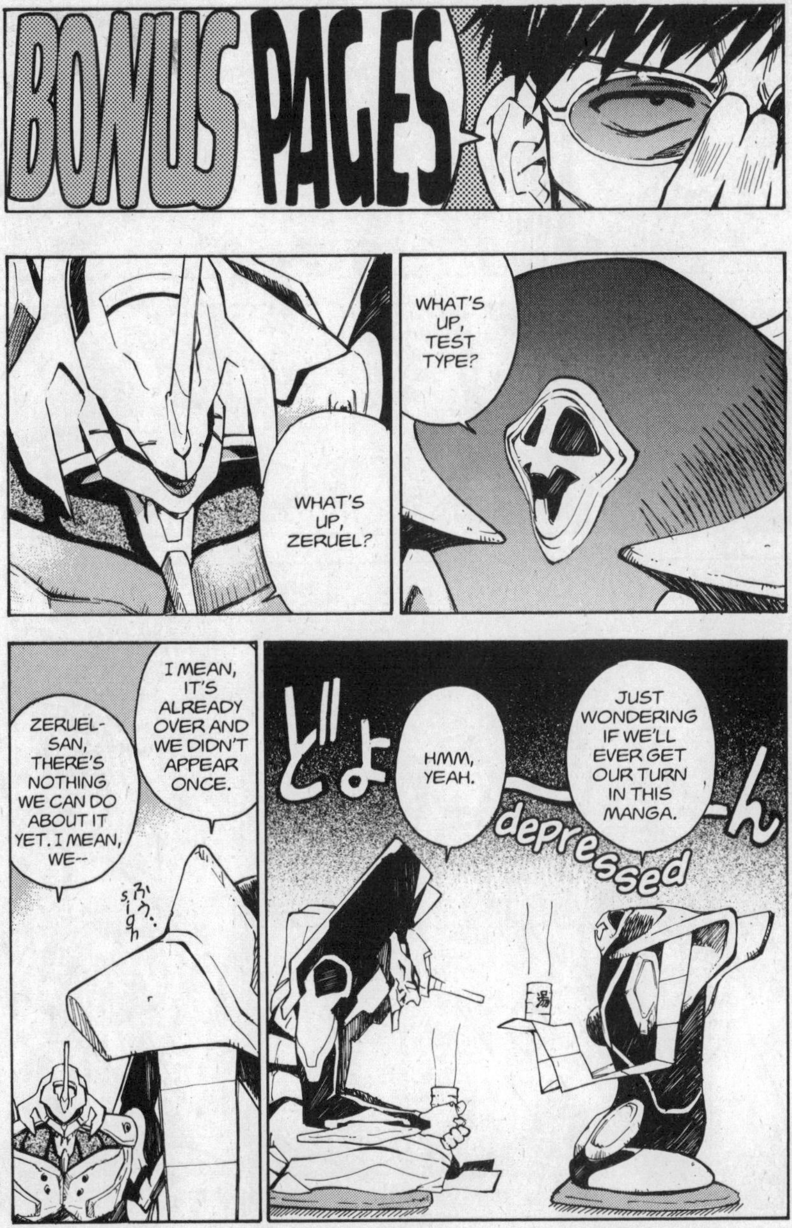
BONUS PAGES
WHAT'S UP, TEST TYPE?
WHAT'S UP, ZERUEL?
JUST WONDERING IF WE'LL EVER GET OUR TURN IN THIS MANGA.
HMM, YEAH.
どよ
depressed
湯
I MEAN, IT'S ALREADY OVER AND WE DIDN'T APPEAR ONCE.
ZERUEL-SAN, THERE'S NOTHING WE CAN DO ABOUT IT YET. I MEAN, WE--
ふう…
sigh

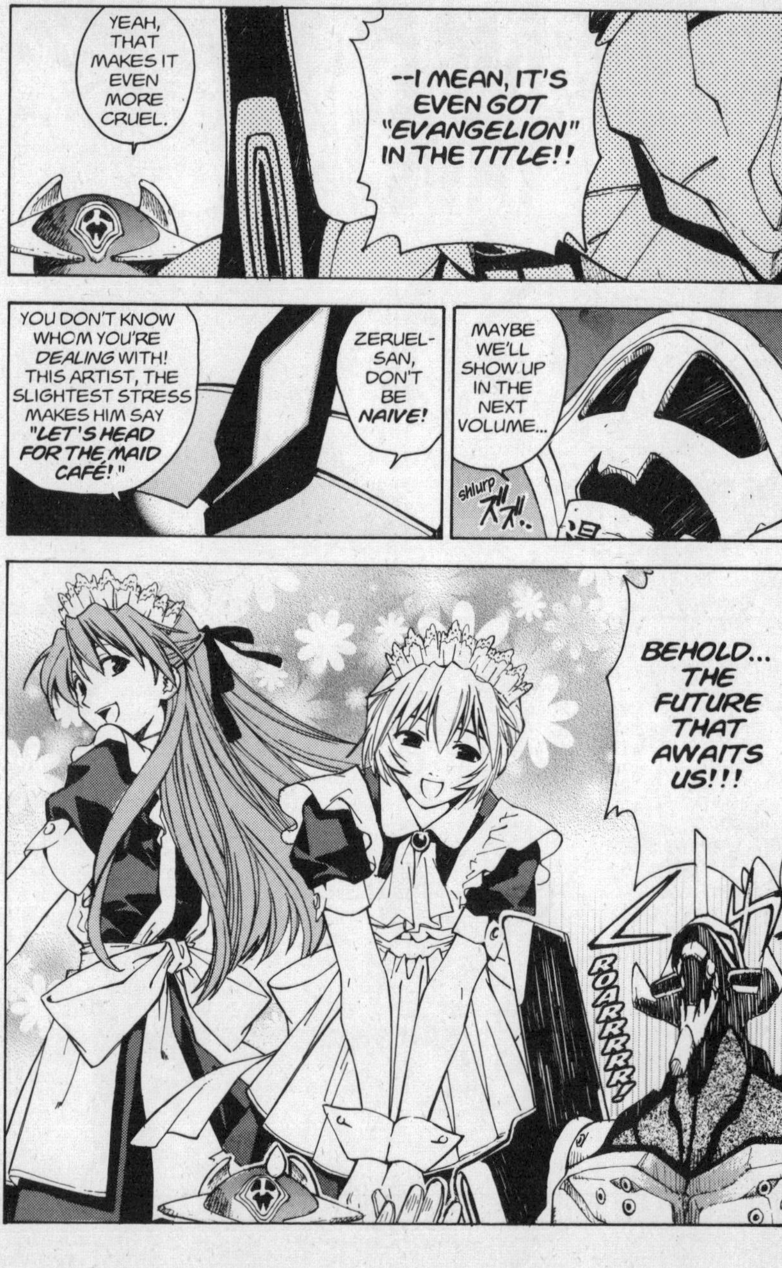
--I MEAN, IT'S EVEN GOT "EVANGELION" IN THE TITLE!!
YEAH, THAT MAKES IT EVEN MORE CRUEL.
MAYBE WE'LL SHOW UP IN THE NEXT VOLUME...
shlurp ズズ..
ZERUEL-SAN, DON'T BE NAIVE!
YOU DON'T KNOW WHOM YOU'RE DEALING WITH! THIS ARTIST, THE SLIGHTEST STRESS MAKES HIM SAY "LET'S HEAD FOR THE MAID CAFÉ!"
BEHOLD... THE FUTURE THAT AWAITS US!!!
ROARRRRR!

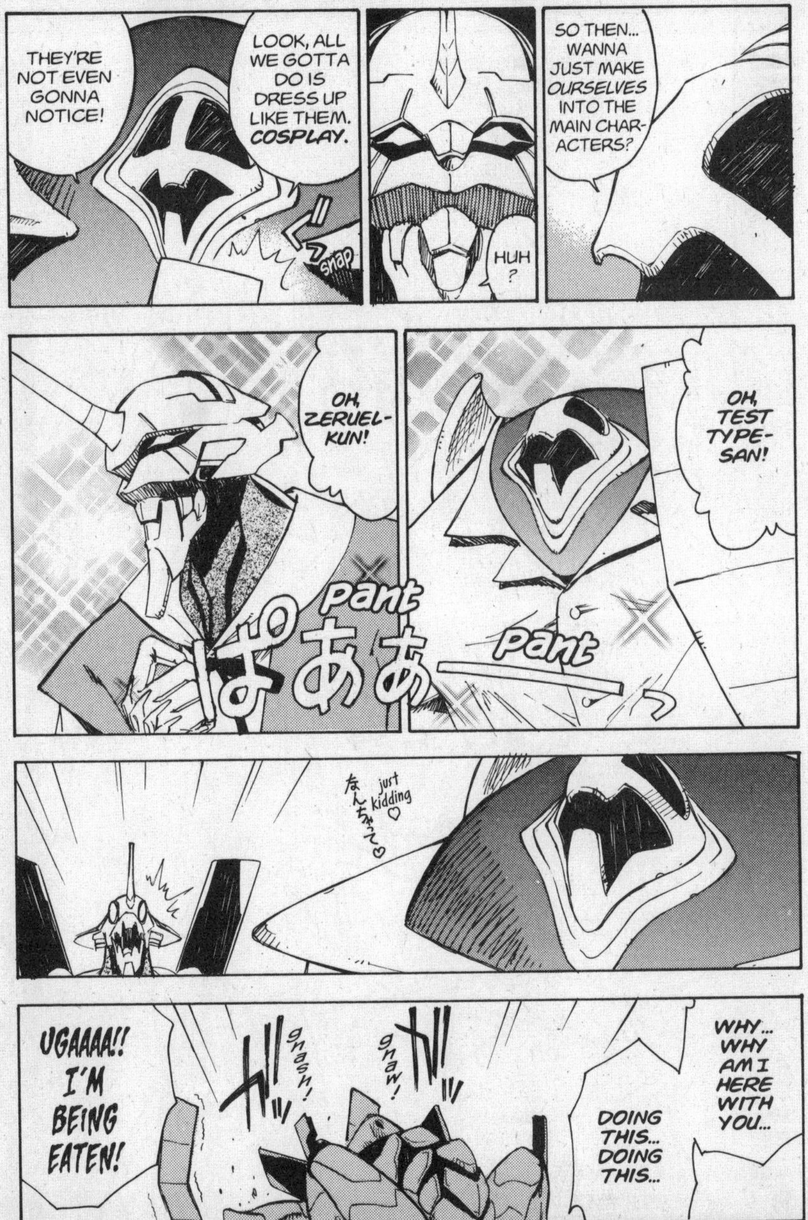
SO THEN... WANNA JUST MAKE OURSELVES INTO THE MAIN CHARACTERS?
HUH ?
LOOK, ALL WE GOTTA DO IS DRESS UP LIKE THEM. **COSPLAY.**
THEY'RE NOT EVEN GONNA NOTICE!
snap
OH, TEST TYPE-SAN!
pant
OH, ZERUEL-KUN!
pant
ぱあぁ—っ
なんちゃって♡
just kidding ♡
WHY... WHY AM I HERE WITH YOU...
DOING THIS... DOING THIS...
gnaw!
gnash!
UGAAAA!! I'M BEING EATEN!

Sorry, I just wanted to do something like this.

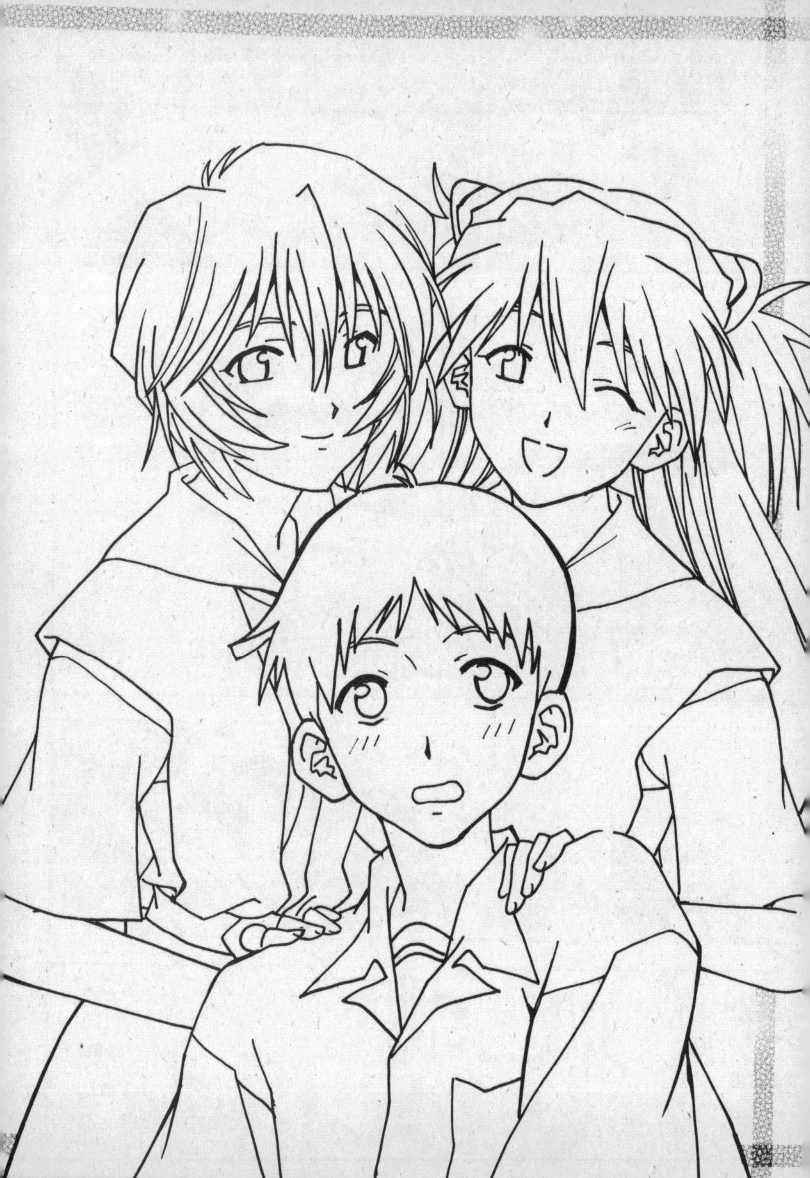

AFTERWORD

Nice to meet you all! This is my first tankobon (graphic novel). A decade ago, I remember being entranced by a certain show that was on TV. I never imagined I'd get the chance to become involved with it this way. We really never know what life has in store for us, do we?

And I never thought my first shot would be at "Evangelion." Ever since they first asked me to do this, I've lost all sense of reality, and my heart's been aflutter. I really want to thank my editor, whom I bothered nonstop; my assistants, who came to help me time and time again; and most importantly, you, who picked up this book! This story's gonna go on a little longer. Hopefully, you'll come along with me for the ride.

-Osamu Takahashi

~STAFF~

Kasumiryo
Tatsuya Kamishima
Kanna
Masanori Suzuki
Seijyuro Mizu
Michio Morikawa
Miki

SPECIAL THANKS
Esuno Sakae-kun

see you in Vol. 2 . . .

EDITOR
CARL GUSTAV HORN

EDITORIAL ASSISTANT
ANNIE GULLION

DESIGNER
STEPHEN REICHERT

PUBLISHER
MIKE RICHARDSON

English-language version produced by Dark Horse Comics

Neon Genesis Evangelion: The Shinji Ikari Raising Project Vol. 1

First published in Japan as NEON GENESIS EVANGELION IKARI-SHINJI IKUSEI KEIKAKU Volume 1. © OSAMU TAKAHASHI 2006 © GAINAX • khara. First published in Japan in 2006 by KADOKAWA SHOTEN Publishing Co., Ltd., Tokyo. English-translation rights arranged with KADOKAWA SHOTEN Publishing Co., Ltd., Tokyo, through TOHAN CORPORATION, Tokyo. This English-language edition © 2009 by Dark Horse Comics, Inc. All other material © 2009 by Dark Horse Comics, Inc. All rights reserved. No portion of this publication may be reproduced or transmitted, in any form or by any means, without the express written permission of the copyright holders. Names, characters, places, and incidents featured in this publication are either the product of the author's imagination or are used fictitiously. Any resemblance to actual persons (living or dead), events, institutions, or locales, without satiric intent, is coincidental. Dark Horse Manga™ is a trademark of Dark Horse Comics, Inc. All rights reserved.

Published by
Dark Horse Manga
A division of Dark Horse Comics, Inc.
10956 SE Main Street
Milwaukie, OR 97222

darkhorse.com

To find a comics shop in your area, call the Comic Shop Locator Service toll-free at 1-888-266-4226

First edition: July 2009
ISBN 978-1-59582-321-2

1 3 5 7 9 10 8 6 4 2
Printed in Canada

publisher Mike Richardson • **executive vice president** Neil Hankerson • **chief financial officer** Tom Weddle • **vice president of publishing** Randy Stradley • **vice president of business development** Michael Martens • **vice president of marketing, sales, and licensing** Anita Nelson • **vice president of product development** David Scroggy • **vice president of information technology** Dale LaFountain • **director of purchasing** Darlene Vogel • **general counsel** Ken Lizzi • **editorial director** Davey Estrada • **senior managing editor** Scott Allie • **senior books editor, dark horse books** Chris Warner • **executive editor** Diana Schutz • **director of design and production** Cary Grazzini • **art director** Lia Ribacchi • **director of scheduling** Cara Niece

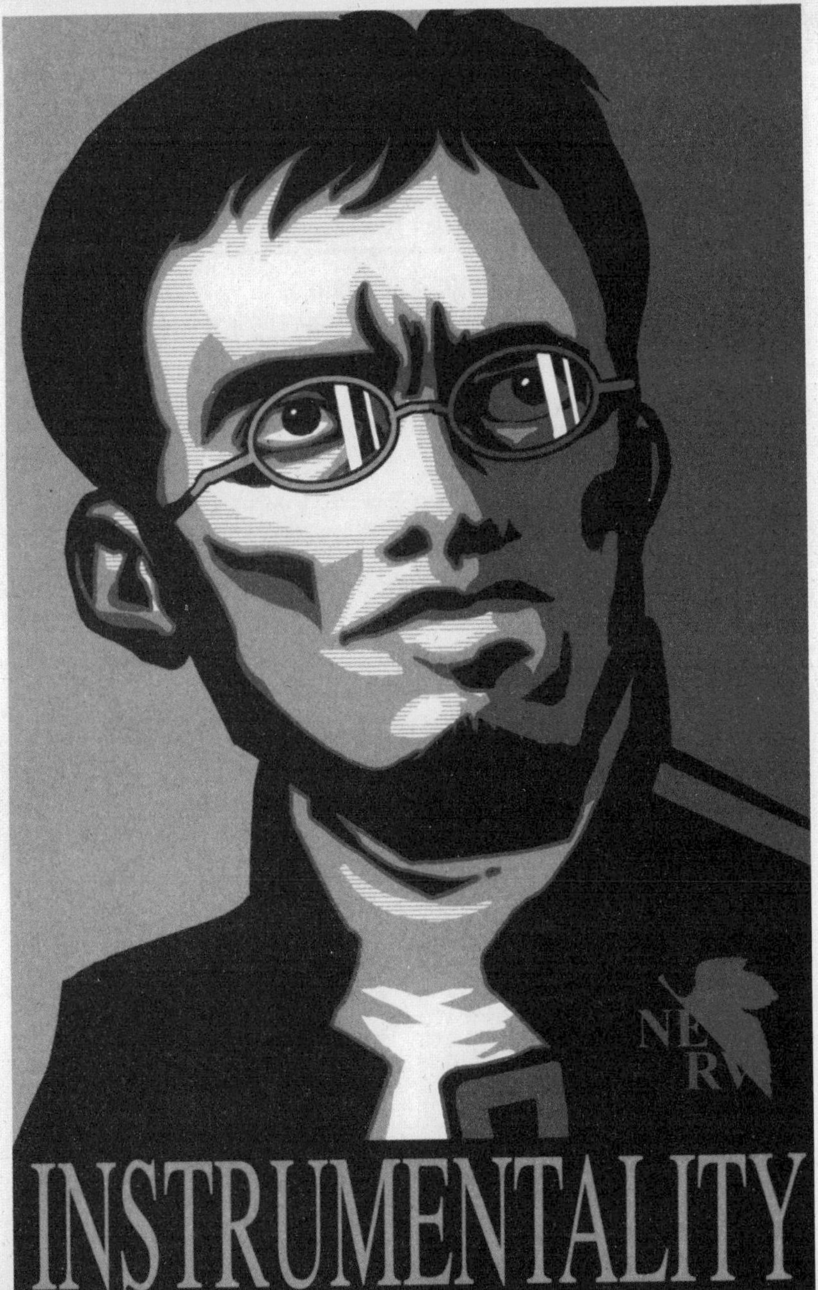
NERV
INSTRUMENTALITY

MISATO'S FAN SERVICE CENTER

c/o Dark Horse Comics • 10956 SE Main Street • Milwaukie, OR 97222 • evangelion@darkhorse.com

Hello, this is the editor of the English-language edition of *Neon Genesis Evangelion: The Shinji Ikari Raising Project*. Welcome to this manga— and welcome also to its fan art and letters column, "Misato's Fan Service Center."

We were lucky enough to get three pieces of fan art even before vol. 1 went to the printer's, so we're showing them off here. On the previous page is Carly Sorge's play on Shepard Fairey's famous Obama campaign poster (itself based on Mannie Garcia's AP photo of the then-candidate).

Carly is a student at Georgia's SCAD (Savannah College of Art and Design), which has a good reputation here at Dark Horse, and I had the chance to meet several other people from the school

at 2008's Anime Weekend Atlanta. In fact Carly had this *Instrumentality* image as a print at her Artists' Alley table; the great thing, by the way, about AWA's Artists' Alley is that they don't put it off to one side somewhere, but instead place it right in front of the main events ballrooms, as if to suggest it's the true spiritual center of the convention. Since AWA was founded by people who did comics and fanzines themselves, that's not surprising.

The next piece of fan art is actually a photo of a decorating project—delicious cake. You must eat it. Inspired by the *Evangelion*-themed food items being offered at Tokyo restaurants (Anime News Network, in their report, described a Sachiel dish at the Cure Maid Café made of squid-ink pasta for